Child Welfare

Policies and Best Practices

SECOND EDITION

Jannah Mather
University of Utah

Patricia B. Lager
Florida State University

Norma J. Harris
University of Utah

BROOKS/COLE
CENGAGE Learning™

Australia • Brazil • Japan • Korea • Mexico • Singapore • Spain • United Kingdom • United States

BROOKS/COLE
CENGAGE Learning™

Child Welfare: Policies and Best Practices, Second Edition
Jannah Mather, Patricia B. Lager, and Norma J. Harris

Editor in Chief: Marcus Boggs

Acquisitions Editor: Dan Alpert

Assistant Editor: Ann Lee Richards

Technology Project Manager: Julie Aguilar

Marketing Manager: Meghan McCullough

Marketing Communications Manager:
  Shemika Britt

Project Manager, Editorial Production:
  Christy Krueger

Creative Director: Rob Hugel

Art Director: Vernon Boes

Print Buyer: Judy Inouye

Permissions Editor: Robert Kauser

Production Service: Buuji, Inc. / Interactive
  Composition Corporation

Copy Editor: Kristina McComas

Cover Designer: Brenda Duke

Cover Image: Group of Young Friends
  Embracing / Corbis

Compositor: Interactive Composition
  Corporation

For product information and technology assistance, contact us at
Cengage Learning Customer & Sales Support, 1-800-354-9706

For permission to use material from this text or product,
submit all requests online **www.cengage.com/permissions**
Further permissions questions can be emailed to
permissionrequest@cengage.com

Library of Congress Control Number: 2006926470

ISBN-13: 978-0-495-00484-4

ISBN-10: 0-495-00484-7

Brooks/Cole
20 Davis Drive
Belmont, CA 94002
USA

Cengage Learning is a leading provider of customized learning solutions with office locations around the globe, including Singapore, the United Kingdom, Australia, Mexico, Brazil, and Japan. Locate your local office at **www.cengage.com/global**

Cengage Learning products are represented in Canada by Nelson Education, Ltd.

To learn more about Brooks/Cole, visit **www.cengage.com/brookscole**

Purchase any of our products at your local college store or at our preferred online store **www.cengagebrain.com**

Printed in the United States of America
3 4 5 6 7   18 17 16 15 14

In memory of Burt Annin; for Tina, Mike, Mikaila and Dylan

Brief Table of Contents

Table of Contents

CHAPTER 4   Cultural Competency in Child Welfare   69

Preface

This text has been developed in response to the learning needs of both social work students and current child welfare workers. The premise of the text is to present a fundamental approach to social work practice that addresses both the issues of residual and universal (preventive) types of intervention. By focusing on an approach that has a multisystemic view, child welfare social workers can move beyond a protective focus and help place an emphasis on prevention. The preventive modes of intervention introduced in this book are reflective of *out-of-the-box thinking*. This term refers to those methods of intervention that do not fit neatly into the framework of the public child welfare system but rather are more innovative and blend both policy changes and practice application into the entire domain of the child welfare practitioner.

Chapter 1 describes the relationship of the profession to the development of the field of child welfare. It also addresses those factors that have affected the welfare of families and children within our society. An overview of current social welfare policies and their impact on families and children is also discussed. Chapter 2 provides a brief review of the foundation of social work practice and the types of service currently provided. Chapter 3 reviews research in relation to policies, while Chapter 4 addresses the use of cultural competency in child welfare.

The second section of the book, Chapters 5 through 11, examines common child welfare situations in which social workers provide aid. The model is introduced in each chapter through a case study of a particular child welfare situation. Neglect, abuse, sexual abuse, delinquencies, divorce/loss, and teenage pregnancies are all addressed in this section through the application of the social work process.

The final chapters of the text discuss the leadership and learning environment needed within child welfare agencies, as well as alternative services that have been tried in child welfare. These chapters discuss the importance of the social worker's involvement in changing policies and implementing interventions that bring equality to all families and provide greater prevention for all children.

REVIEWERS

The editors and publisher would like to thank the reviewers of the manuscript for their helpful comments and suggestions:

Elizabeth Reichert, *Southern Illinois University at Carbondale*

Nancy A. Amos, *Bradley University*

Carla A. Ford-Anderson, *Saint Francis College*

Barbara B. Grissett, *East Tennessee State University*

Barbara Pierce, *Northwestern State University of Louisiana*

About the Authors

Dr. Jannah Mather is the Dean of the College of Social Work at the University of Utah. Previously she was the Dean at Laurier University in Waterloo, Canada. Dr. Mather has written numerous articles and has three books in publication. She also has 15 years practice experience.

Norma Harris, PhD, MSW, launched her child welfare career in Montana as a caseworker in child protective services, foster care, adoption, and service to unmarried parents. She spent many years in the field as a practitioner, supervisor, and director of the child welfare agency. Her national experience includes work for the National Association for Public Child Welfare Administrators, the National Child Welfare Leadership Center, and the Council for Social Work Education. Dr. Harris is currently the Director of the Social Research Institute, where she continues research in child welfare and related programs.

Patricia Lager is on the faculty of the College of Social Work at Florida State University, where she is also Director of International Programs. Ms. Lager teaches in the area of mental health issues in child welfare, both at Florida State and internationally. Her social work practice experiences include mental health, child protection, foster care and adoption, divorce custody, and clinical treatment of children and families.

The Evolution of Child Welfare Services

CHAPTER 1

INTRODUCTION

Child welfare practice can be enhanced by understanding child welfare history, being aware of how society and political forces influence policy and practice, and knowing how agencies have responded to the complex challenges faced by vulnerable families and children in this country. A careful exploration of the evolution of child welfare includes an examination of the traditions, laws, policies, and programs created to address the changing needs in child welfare.

Throughout history, there have been struggles about when, if, and how the government should be involved in the lives of families. The decisions about funding levels for services, health care, cash assistance, and other family supports are directly related to questions about if, how, and when the government should be involved with families (Kamerman, 1983; Moroney, 1986). These philosophical struggles have led to polarization at the federal, state, and local levels of government. Lawmakers have long struggled with family policy and program development decisions centered on what level of societal intervention is needed and appropriate. On one hand, some policymakers believe that selective service provisions with rigid eligibility rules minimize the use of services and thereby reduce family dependency on social programs. The opposing view is that universal services should be available to those when needs arise (Bell, 1983). The current child welfare programs represent the influence of a number of significant historical events and activities. The system that has evolved has been influenced by diverse ideological views, contradicting political forces, volatile economic trends, divergent laws, and widespread changes in child-rearing practices (American Public Human Services Association [APHSA], 1995).

EARLY INFLUENCES AND EVENTS

In the United States, the earliest approach to serving vulnerable families reflected policies and practices from England, including the 17th-century Elizabethan Poor Laws wherein townships had responsibility for individuals and children in need. As was the case in England, almshouses were developed in the United States as institutions for poor and destitute families and their children. The almshouses and workhouses were deplorable environments, especially for children. The Poor Laws raised public consciousness about the problems of poverty and operated in a society where children were regarded as chattel or property of their parents. Consistent with the master and servant relationship, the Poor Laws underscored the rights of parents and guardians to control children without outside interference.

England's *Parens Patriae* Concept was also a major factor governing family life. The doctrine provided authorities with power to intervene into parent–child relationships when parents were not fulfilling their parental responsibilities. The concept is based on the premise that the state is responsible for its citizens and is therefore the ultimate parent. The outcomes of the English Poor Laws and the *Parens Patriae* Concept surpassed the original intention of the laws aimed at protecting children. In England and the United States, interventions were often intrusive, and many children were indentured and permanently placed out of their homes into institutions or foster homes (American Public Welfare Association [APWA], 1995).

In England and the United States, many children were orphaned because their parents had succumbed to illnesses. Because the status of medical practice was somewhat primitive and "nonscientific" (Lindsey, 2004), it was not uncommon for individuals to succumb to what we now consider minor illnesses, and children often lost their parents to illness or disease. Children were often then placed into these almshouses, at times with infirmed, mentally ill, and elderly populations.

As concerns about these inappropriate placements became widespread, orphanages were created in the 1800s as alternatives for the children living in almshouses and for children without parents or whose parents could not care for them. Orphanages remained a primary child welfare institution until the 1940s. These institutions were created for various populations of children, including the deaf and blind, the developmentally disabled, juvenile delinquents, and dependent children (Ashby, 1997). Eventually, deinstitutionalization of children from orphanages and other institutions occurred, and foster care became a preferred placement.

FOSTER CARE

In response to institutional care, the Reverend Charles Brace and the New York Children's Aid Society developed the practice of "placing out" children from orphanages into families who would provide them with a trade in return for employment (Lindsey, 2004). The "orphan trains" became familiar vehicles for children from urban areas to be moved to families in the West and the South; once there, the children would work for the families. From the 1870s and into the 20th century, virtually tens of thousands of children were placed; some were orphans, but many had families (Ashby, 1997). Brace and others believed his practice of rescuing children from unfortunate situations and placing them with families benefited the children, the families, and society.

There were a number of concerns related to the orphan trains. Because the families with whom the children were placed were not evaluated, little was known about them, and this led to mismatching many children. The expectation that the placed child would work for placement was not always realized, and some children were maltreated. Religion was an issue, particularly with the Catholic Church, as children were predominately placed into non-Catholic homes. Widespread concern about the orphan trains and some disastrous outcomes for the children and youths spurred creation of foster homes by many states' Children's Aid Societies.

Concerns about out-of-home placements of children and other family matters were discussed when the first White House Conference on Children was held in 1909. The focus of the conference was the family and the emphasis on rehabilitating the families rather than removing and rescuing children. The conference was the initial thrust for creation of the Children's Bureau in 1912. Greatly assisted by the Children's Bureau vision and support, child welfare systems have continued to evolve and deal with foster care and other programs that serve America's vulnerable children and families.

Early in the 20th century, the vision of foster care was a temporary placement program for children whose safety in their biological homes had been compromised. The original intent was that child welfare agencies would provide services to biological parents to alleviate temporary issues so that children could be reunified with their parents.

Foster care policy and practice were largely influenced by Mass and Engler in 1959. They identified vast numbers of children who were spending long periods of time in foster care, and during the period they were in foster care, many of these children experienced several placements. These authors became prominent because they also reported that, in large part, the children's bonds to their parents had been severed and biological families had received few if any services. At that time, child welfare staff did not consistently pursue reunification of children with their parents nor was permanency for children pursued diligently.

EARLY CHILD PROTECTION

Child protection originated when Mary Ellen, a child abused by her step-mother, was rescued by Henry Bergh. Henry Bergh founded the first chapter of the Society for the Protection of Children in the 1870s in the State of New York, and Societies for the Protection of Children were also established in many other states. These organizations were well intended and provided protection for hundreds of children. However, they focused on child rescue, and this often led to removing children and isolating them from their families. Conflict developed between the practice of rescuing children from families versus supporting families so they could protect their children, and this conflict has lasted for years (APHSA, 1995).

CHILD LABOR LAWS

As the needs in society changed, so too did the roles of children in their families and in society. In the 1900s, economic conditions drove women and children into the workforce. Axin and Stern (2001) reported that almost 2 million children aged 10 to 15 and 5 million women were in the labor force. Children were forced to work long hours and perform many tasks that adults could not. In the 1920s and 1930s, so many children were employed in deplorable working conditions that many reformers sought an end to their exploitation. The Fair Wage and Standards Act brought about better working conditions overall but also addressed protections for children. Around the same time, laws were passed for mandatory school attendance (NAPCWA, 1988).

JUVENILE COURTS

As society became aware of the needs for safety, protection, appropriate work, and schooling, society also recognized that juveniles should be treated differently in the court system. The First Juvenile Court was established in 1899 and represented a major thrust toward justice for youth. The court's creation reflects cooperation between the legal and social work systems as the justice system evolved simultaneously with the child welfare system. Juvenile courts were conceived to protect and rehabilitate children in lieu of the indictment and punishment that occur in adult court. The juvenile court proceedings had the effect of extending the doctrine of *parens patriae* to include juveniles charged with crimes. The philosophy was based on individualized justice, dealing with each child uniquely (Axin & Stern, 2001). The philosophy is a departure from the traditional symbol of justice where a woman holds a balanced scale, meaning the punishment is balanced with the crime. In juvenile courts, juveniles are dealt with on an individual basis because they are viewed as malleable and amenable to rehabilitation. On the other hand, dispositions for adult crimes are more consistent, and rehabilitation is not the primary focus. By 1910, 34 states had created juvenile courts, and by 1945, all states had enacted juvenile court legislation.

The creation of juvenile courts was not without controversy. The original concern about the focus on rehabilitation rather than on punishment continues today particularly because of the seriousness of many juvenile crimes. Most states have passed laws that restrict the jurisdiction of the juvenile court so that youthful offenders who are accused of serious, violent crimes against people can be moved from the juvenile court to adult criminal court.

EARLY WELFARE PROGRAMS

During the early 1900s, the country recognized the need to support families, particularly women with children who were widowed by husbands dying in wars. The forerunner of welfare programs was initiated in the early 1900s with Mother's Pensions. Illinois was the first state to implement pensions throughout the state in 1911, and 35 other states had followed suit within 10 years. The purpose of the pensions was to assist widows or deserted wives and needy children (Kamerman & Kahn, 1989).

MAJOR LEGISLATIVE CHANGES

1935: Social Security Act

One of the most significant and long lasting legislative acts was the Social Security Act of 1935 because it has greatly influenced the lives of individuals and families. The enactment recognized that the Depression, poverty, and loss of work were features of the societal structure and that these external socioeconomic circumstances were responsible for the conditions under which many families had arrived. There was recognition that destitute individuals and families had not arrived at their state through their own doing. The law created a federal responsibility for the welfare of the citizens (Axin & Stern, 2001). Both grants and service programs were created as this act laid the foundation for the present welfare and child welfare systems in this country. Each state was required to make welfare services available to all children and provide for the protection and care of homeless, dependent, neglected, and potentially delinquent children. Aid to Dependent Children (ADC) was established to provide for the care of children who had one or more parent absent from the home, unemployed, deceased, or incapacitated.

Several subsequent amendments to the Social Security Act have both had an effect on families and broadened the scope of child welfare services. In 1939, Survivors Insurance was enacted. The amendment was designed to support widowed mothers whose spouses had contributed to the social security system.

1962 and 1967: Social Security Amendments

In 1962, Congress felt it would be helpful to offer services to families who received cash assistance, and social services were incorporated as part of a broad approach to the ADC program. However, the 1967 amendments separated services from public assistance, and the subsequent cash assistance programs were not combined with other needed service programs. This was unfortunate because many families who entered the child welfare system had severe economic problems that influenced decisions to place children in out-of-home care. Had the programs been combined and these families offered services earlier, the crises that precipitated child placement may have been avoided.

The 1967 amendments also authorized services to recipients of a number of cash assistance programs. These amendments permitted states to contract for services with the private nonprofit sector. Because the services were funded as federal entitlement programs, as long as the private agencies were able to put up the required match, there were no limits to the amount of money agencies had available for services. Consequently, there was a great unanticipated expansion in social service spending. Congress ended the expansion with the passage of Title XX.

1965: Health Care for Vulnerable Individuals and Families

In 1965, one of the more significant amendments related to health care, Title XIX or Medicaid, was passed. Medicaid provides funding for health care to income-eligible individuals and families. A particularly important section for child welfare was the Early Periodic Screening, Diagnosis, and Treatment (EPSDT) program, a health care assessment component for pregnant women and women with young children. The assessment helps identify health issues early on to prevent serious problems later in childhood. In addition to providing funding for physical health services, the EPSDT program also became a funding stream for mental health services for children. In fact, EPSDT led to the funding of wraparound services for children, which is currently considered an effective program (Furman & Jackson, 2002). Wraparound programs are those in which the family identifies the services and supports needed and agencies then provide the services.

1974: Child Abuse and Protection Act

Passage of the Child Abuse Prevention and Treatment Act (CAPTA), Public Law (PL) 104-235, in 1974 brought significant improvement to the protection of children throughout the country. The law clarified and expanded the types of maltreatment that were reported to child protection services (CPS) agencies, including physical abuse, sexual exploitation, and emotional neglect; the law also broadened the group of professionals mandated to report abuse. CAPTA also provided grants to eligible states for child abuse and neglect prevention and treatment programs. The law created the National Center for Child Abuse and Neglect (NCCAN), which serves as a national clearinghouse for disseminating materials about child abuse and neglect, increasing public awareness of child abuse and neglect, and funding demonstration projects.

In 1978, CAPTA was expanded to cover child pornography and adoption law reform. CAPTA was reauthorized in 1996 and included provisions for confidentiality and expunging records. States must establish an appeal process for persons accused of abuse or neglect and establish citizen review panels to evaluate CPS programs.

An amendment to the child maltreatment laws involved cases of medically fragile infants. In 1984, the "Baby Doe" amendment was added as PL 98-457. This act expanded the responsibilities of CPS by requiring them to develop programs and procedures to respond to reports of medical neglect, including reports of withholding medical treatment to disabled infants with life-threatening conditions. The legislative intent was to protect the rights of infants while avoiding unnecessary intrusion into family life.

1975: Title XX

Recognition that the approach to services and supports was fragmented brought about a new section of the Social Security Act when Title XX was passed in 1975. The congressional hope was that this act would provide for a comprehensive approach to services. Title XX replaced Title IV-A as a number of funding programs were absorbed into a single grant. The open-ended entitlement for services that had been authorized in the 1967 Social Security Amendments was eliminated. Several programs were combined under a capped expenditure, and much less money was available to private agencies; thus, they were limited in their ability to provide services.

Title XX required states to conduct planning sessions and provide monitoring and target services to low-income individuals and families. Title XX increased the states' flexibility in how they used funds to achieve five goals in helping families and individuals: (1) achieve economic self-support; (2) achieve self-sufficiency; (3) prevent or remedy neglect, abuse, or exploitation of children and adults; (4) prevent or reduce inappropriate institutional care; and (5) secure referral or admission for institutional care when other forms of care are not appropriate. Funds to states had to be used to support one service in each of the five objective areas (Kamerman & Kahn, 1989). Title XX was funded at a level of $2.5 million in 1976 and increased to only $2.7 million in 1989, clearly limiting the ability of states to create a more comprehensive approach in dealing with vulnerable children and families.

1978: Indian Child Welfare Act

The Indian Child Welfare Act (ICWA) was passed in 1978 (PL 95-608) out of concern about the number of Native American children being placed in non-Native homes and placed out of the geographic area in which they lived. The act protects the cultural heritage of Native Americans by granting tribes authority over Native American children. The law delineates an order of preference for placement of Native American children outside of their homes. The order of placement preference is (1) a child's extended family, (2) a foster home approved by the tribe, and (3) other tribal placement resources.

In spite of the passage of ICWA, studies indicate there has not been much progress in this area. In fact, one study indicated that of 44 state child welfare plans evaluated for compliance, only 34 percent had developed specific measures to identify Native American children, only 27 percent had specific measures for identifying the relevant tribes, and only 41 percent had specific measures related to identification of Native American caretakers (Brown, Limb, Munoz, & Clifford, 2001).

1980: Adoption Assistance and Child Welfare Act

Even though CPS were created to intervene in the lives of families when parents were unable to protect their children, it became evident that states were neglecting children by allowing them to linger in foster care. Out of this concern came one of the landmark pieces of child welfare legislation: PL 96-272. This legislation was focused on foster care and dealing with the thousands of children who were "drifting" in foster care. The intent of the law was to restore the family as the primary caretaker of children. Under this act, agencies became responsible for conducting efforts to prevent placements, accomplish speedy reunification when placement was necessary, or find permanent alternatives when children could not be returned home. The intent of PL 96-272 was to reduce the numbers of children entering care, reduce the time they spent in care, and find permanent placements when necessary.

The act amended Titles IV-A and IV-B and created Title IV-E, which subsequently created improvements in the administration of foster care programs. Child welfare agencies were required to create an inventory of children in foster care and a statewide management system. New legal safeguards were introduced, including 6-month case reviews and a court dispositional hearing within 18 months of placement.

PL 96-272 provided funding for permanency by creating subsidized adoption for eligible children with special needs. In addition to foster care activities, Title IV-E also supported short- and long-term training and provided the thrust for the state child welfare agency university training partnerships. After 1980, many social work programs and public child welfare agencies developed formal arrangements. Using Title IV-E funding, schools and departments of social work developed short- and long-term training programs to professionalize child welfare staff and prepare them to work with the most vulnerable families and children in the child welfare systems.

The original intent of the law was far reaching, particularly with funding for adoption. As required, all 50 states enacted legislation to carry out the mandates of PL 96-272. Initially, there was a substantial decrease in the numbers of children in foster care. However, the intent could not be realized because the Reagan administration brought huge reductions in all social service programs, including child welfare (Kamerman & Kahn, 1987).

1984: Multiethnic Placement Act

Congress passed the Multiethnic Placement Act (MEPA), PL 103-382, in 1984 to address the overrepresentation of ethnically and racially diverse children in foster care and the excessive length of time they spent in such care. In 1994, 60 percent of the children in foster care were from diverse populations, and they waited twice as long as other children for permanent homes. It was customary for most child welfare agencies to match children with parents of the same race or ethnicity. Some agencies were successful; most were not. Congress passed MEPA to eliminate race-related barriers to placement. In 1996, Congress amended MEPA by removing any provisions stating that race could be used in placement decisions. The intent was to enhance the capacity of agencies to provide permanency options for all children regardless of race or ethnicity.

1986: Independent Living

In 1986, the Independent Living Initiative, PL 99-279, was passed with funds to support adolescents preparing for independence from the foster care system. The impetus for this law was the large numbers of youths who exited the foster care system without being adequately prepared for adult living. These programs were aimed at preparing adolescents to manage money, seek employment, dress and groom appropriately, and perform other activities. The 1986 legislation provided for a limited number of programs, but the act was expanded in 1999 and renamed the John E. Chaffee Foster Care Independence Program. The 1999 act took a much more comprehensive approach by requiring states to prepare youths for employment by attending to emotional, financial, personal, housing, and other needs (Barbell & Freundlich, 2001).

1993: Family Preservation and Support

Public Law 96-272 produced short-lived reductions in the numbers of children in foster care. Because of federal funding cuts, child welfare agencies faced many challenges with diminished resources. Consequently, foster care became the main resource for at-risk children. As was the case prior to the passage of PL 96-272, thousands of children entered the foster care system while only a small percentage exited such care. Congress attempted once again to deal with the problems by creating the Family Preservation and Support Program as part of the Omnibus Budget and Reconciliation Act in 1993.

These amendments to the Social Security Act (Title IV-B, Subpart 2) sought to promote family strengths and stability and enhance parental functioning. Federal dollars were provided to states for preventive or family support services and family preservation services for at-risk families. The strengths of the act included suggestions that child welfare agencies partner with other public and private agencies so that resources could be maximized through collaboration (APWA, 1995). This new program was considered a catalyst for interagency collaborations in which prevention, early intervention, and intervention services were available. The intent was to provide an array or continuum of services to meet the individualized needs of families and children.

1996: Personal Responsibility and Work Opportunity Reconciliation Act (PRWORA)

Welfare programs have been controversial for a number of years. Congress made several changes in welfare laws throughout the years in attempts to deal with multiple issues. Before 1962, assistance was provided to single parents or to both parents if one was incapacitated. This policy was disruptive to families as it led to one parent leaving so children could receive benefits. From 1962 to 1990, some states opted to provide benefits to needy two-parent families, and the federal government's policy eventually changed to provide Aid to Families with Dependent Children (AFDC). The Family Assistance Act of 1988 recognized the need to provide financial benefits as well as assistance with child care and work-related support and training.

Ideological and political forces converged in 1996 to bring about the passage of the major welfare reform bill, PRWORA. The thrust of the reform was to move people from welfare to work. This bill replaced AFDC and welfare with work programs by creating Temporary Assistance to Need Families (TANF) as a block grant program to states. One major change was the loss of entitlement status to assistance programs and the devolution of welfare programs from the federal to the state levels. Strict work requirements were included as part of this grant in efforts to move individuals from welfare to work. Benefits are time-limited in that welfare recipients cannot receive benefits for longer than three years at a time and cannot receive lifetime benefits for longer than five years. The law permits states to maintain lower limits in terms of lifetime eligibility. In order to receive benefits, teen parents are required to live with their parents or other qualified adults.

1997: Adoption and Safe Families Act

In spite of passage of the Adoption Assistance and Child Welfare Act of 1980, the Family Preservation and Support Act, and passage of other laws, the number of children in foster care continued to rise. Inadequate funding, worker turnover, and complexities of child and family issues provided insurmountable challenges for child welfare agencies trying to deal with burgeoning foster care caseloads. In 1997, Congress passed the Adoption and Safe Families Act (ASFA). The intent of Congress in passing ASFA was to provide assurances that states would implement the mandates of the Child Welfare Assistance Act of 1980. ASFA requires that alternative plans be made within specific timelines and creates conditions for filing termination of parental rights (Lindsey, 2004). The law represents the most aggressive action taken by Congress to deal with the numbers of children drifting in foster care. States must file termination of parental rights for any child who has been in care for 15 of the most recent 22 months and set the time frame for permanency hearings at 12 months rather than at 18 months. During these hearings, agencies must make determination of whether and when a child will be returned to his or her family. States must also make reasonable efforts to place children for adoption. Long-term foster care is no longer considered an option for permanency.

Clarifications provide that agencies need not make reasonable efforts: if parents have subjected children to "aggravated circumstances," such as committing a felony against the child including bodily harm; if parents have committed murder or voluntary manslaughter; or if parental rights of siblings have been terminated (Pecora, Whittaker, Maluccio, & Barth, 2000).

For the first time, three national goals for children were established: safety, permanence, and well-being. ASFA brought a shift in requiring accountability of agencies based on outcomes such as keeping children safe instead of agencies counting activities such as the number of maltreatment reports investigated. Adoptive placements have increased since the passage of ASFA, and the majority of the adoptive placements have been with the foster parents. There is also an increase in kinship or relative care, as ASFA provided for guardianship as a permanent option used in kinship care.

Establishing timelines for termination of parental rights was appropriate. Children should not languish in foster care. However, this act provided no additional programs or funds to assist biological parents in keeping their children safe. Consequently, parents with substance abuse issues may not get the additional time and resources needed for successful reunification with their children. Language issues for non-English-speaking families may further complicate timely achievement of agency case plans and reunification. Other issues not considered in the legislation include court delays due to excessive caseloads. Child welfare agencies have thus become responsible for implementation of a law that creates incredible challenges.

2003: Adoption Promotion Act

Because so many older children had become available for adoption, Congress passed the Adoption Promotion Act in 2003. This act reauthorizes the incentives of ASFA and provides incentives to states that are able to place additional foster care children into adoptive placements beyond their recognized baseline. However, states have not always received the bonuses available to them and may not receive the full benefits of additional adoptive placements.

EVOLUTION OF CORE CHILD WELFARE PROGRAMS

Evolution of Child Protective Services (CPS)

After 1935, specialized child protective services agencies were created across the country. However, public concern about child abuse and neglect was somewhat dormant until the 1960s, at which time Dr. Henry Kempe identified

Battered Child Syndrome. Dr. Kempe was able to connect multiple bone fractures and subdural hematomas in infants to the actions of caretakers and therefore established that childhood injuries were often a result of physical abuse by the parents. After this discovery, the U.S. Children's Bureau developed the first model child abuse and neglect reporting law in efforts to raise public awareness about child abuse and neglect. This led to a great deal of media attention and national recognition of the plight of abused, neglected, and exploited children. States enacted mandatory reporting laws coinciding with the model child abuse and neglect reporting law (Besharov, 1988). With the advent of mandated reporting laws and education campaigns, the number of maltreatment reports increased dramatically (APWA, 1988). From 1976 to 1986, the increase in reports was 223 percent.

The vast numbers of reports created problems for CPS agencies. The number of reports determined to be substantiated or founded was only between 40 and 43 percent, indicating that agencies did not always find evidence of maltreatment (APWA, 1988). At the same time, research showed that half of the cases of maltreatment where children sustained serious injury or died from parental maltreatment had not been reported to CPS. In addition, many children who had entered the CPS system sustained further injury. These factors fueled controversies about CPS and were responsible in part for changes in the CPS system.

Other catalysts for change occurred in the 1980s when reduced funding for social services created a situation where CPS was one of the only available services, and children were often reported to child abuse and neglect hotlines in attempts to obtain needed services. Consequently, CPS agencies were inappropriately involved in the lives of many families. At that time, community views about the role and scope of CPS were often polarized; some believed CPS to be too intrusive in the lives of children and families while others believed CPS agencies were not sufficiently aggressive in protecting children.

In efforts to deal with this polarization and provide protection for children, national guidelines were produced, and many CPS agencies adopted reforms. In the late 1980s, several national advocacy and trade organizations also responded by developing guidelines to clarify the role and scope of CPS agencies (APWA, 1988; Child Welfare League of America [CWLA], 1989).

However, in spite of guidelines and agency reforms, problems in protecting children continued. Many CPS agencies used a risk assessment protocol to investigate all maltreatment reports, whether the reports indicated low- or high-risk situations. Many agencies adopted a "one-size-fits-all" response in which the focus of investigations was on the alleged report and excluded other safety factors. Consequently, families were provided minimal services, if any, and had their cases closed, only to be re-reported for maltreatment at a later date. Families had to reach a state of crisis before services were provided. It became clear that additional reforms were needed. The American Public Human Services Association (APHSA, 1995) responded with revised CPS guidelines that made a number of recommendations to reform CPS. A number of foundations also contributed to CPS reforms, particularly the Edna McConnell Clark Foundation and the Annie E. Casey Foundation.

Consistent with revised guidelines, child welfare agencies largely view CPS as more of a support than a "police" function, so the purpose of CPS has changed from protecting children from their parents to determining what can be done to assist caretakers in keeping their children safe. Other recommendations that CPS agencies have adopted include providing flexibility in their response to maltreatment reports and replacing a "one-size-fits-all" approach. Responses to maltreatment reports now vary according to the needs of the families and children. Many jurisdictions have developed dual or multiple tracks or differentiated response approaches. These can be generally categorized as the provision of a family assessment or investigatory response based upon the initial referral. If it appears that the child's safety is not compromised but the family needs services, an assessment is conducted.

The assessment may be completed by community partners or the CPS agency. The intent of the assessment is to determine the service needs so the family problem(s) can be alleviated. The intent of providing services to families in these situations is to stop the escalation of problems and prevent future crises. This approach also provides an alternative to intrusive investigations in situations where they are not needed. Individualized assessments require individualized responses. More specifically, families receive the services they need, not necessarily what the agency has traditionally provided. Previously, Weber (1998) found that it had been common for CPS agencies to offer anger management, parenting education, and substance abuse evaluation as "cookie-cutter" approaches.

When maltreatment reports clearly indicate the safety of children has been compromised, the investigatory response is completed by the CPS agency, sometimes in collaboration with law enforcement. Because less-serious reports have been dealt with in an alternative way, CPS staff are better able to focus their resources on those referrals that are the most egregious: when the children are at the highest risk of harm and when immediate responses are warranted.

Currently, national and state CPS policies endorse a family-centered approach. Allen and Petr (1999) describe four core elements of family-centered practice that include (1) recognition of the family as the focus of assessment and treatment; (2) utilization of family's own assessment and decision-making skills; (3) application of a strengths-based perspective; and (4) the application of knowledge and skills that reflect cultural, ethnic, and racial sensitivity. This approach is applied at all times while the family and children are involved with the CPS system. Agency staff work to alleviate any environmental issues that present challenges to the families and threaten the safety of children. These environmental issues may be unemployment or poverty, health or mental health, substance abuse, domestic violence, or others.

A family-centered approach considers protective factors or strengths in addition to the risks to children's safety. The parents' positive adaptive mechanisms can be strengthened while they assume responsibility and are assisted in dealing with issues. If a child is placed, staff continue with a strengths-based approach because placement is generally only intended to be temporary, with a plan for speedy reunification.

It has been generally recognized that CPS should not and cannot be responsible for the safety of all children. Developing partnerships with formal and informal entities enables CPS agencies to create CPS systems. A continuum of services is made available through these systems that includes prevention, early intervention, and intervention programs. Building these partnerships encourages communities to assume their responsibility for the protection of all children and leads to maximization of all community services. Due to the fact that CPS is often the entry into the child welfare system, reforms to establish best practice in this area are pivotal to the entire system.

CPS practitioners often face daunting tasks in their jobs. Therefore, child welfare agencies have recognized that these practitioners need prior child welfare experience. Practitioners must have knowledge of child development and of the ways in which a number of environmental risks in families, such as child maltreatment, substance abuse, poverty, mental health issues, and others, disrupt the normal developmental processes. Furthermore, the ability to accurately assess disrupted development is only the first step. Practitioners must have knowledge of the appropriate intervention strategies and have the skills to implement them. The assessment task becomes more complex in determining when maltreatment began in a child's life, whether the maltreatment has been continuous throughout the child's life, or whether the maltreatment is intermittent. An adolescent's outlook on life is certainly affected more dramatically in a negative way if the adolescent has been maltreated most of his or her life than if maltreatment was limited. A child's own resiliency is a factor, but regardless, maltreatment is a threat to normal development.

Foster Care

Foster care refers to services and programs for children placed in out-of-home care, including foster family care, group care, and residential treatment care. Most of the children in out-of-home placement are in foster family care. Ideally, foster care is a temporary program wherein services are provided to the children, foster parents, and biological parents; attempts are made to alleviate problems within the families; and speedy reunification occurs when the parents can protect their children. Child welfare agencies view foster care placement as part of a continuum; plans are made for reunification and for services to the child's parents or caretakers during the placement in preparation for return of the children.

Children are usually placed in foster care because their parents or caretakers cannot protect them. Many children entering care have physical, developmental, and emotional challenges. Most families have multiple or co-occurring needs. Situations that create the need for placement include child maltreatment, domestic violence, substance abuse, mental health issues, and others (Egami, Ford, Greenfield, & Crum, 1996; Kessler, Gillis-Light, Magee, Kendler, & Eaves, 1997; O'Keefe, 1995; Zlotnick, Ryan, Miller, & Keitner, 1995).

With these factors in mind, child welfare agencies provide a comprehensive approach to practice in foster care. Accurate assessments of children and families are necessary so practitioners can locate foster parents who can meet the physical, emotional, and social needs of children. The assessments include the reasons for placement, that is, if the child was abused or neglected, and the relationship of the child to the parents. Part of assessing the parent–child relationship is determining the attachment status of the child to the parents. If there are attachments issues due to maltreatment, substance abuse, mental health, or other factors, these must be considered in placement selections, so foster parents can attend to them.

When out-of-home placements are contemplated, plans are made for transition of children from their biological homes to foster care to minimize separation trauma. Because of safety issues, some placements occur at the point of CPS investigations. However, most placements can be planned so that transitional services are provided for the children, their parents or caretakers, and the foster parents. Preplacement visits can be accomplished incrementally, with very short visits followed by longer ones. The number of preplacement visits depends on the risks to child safety while the children remain in their home environments. To the degree possible, time should be provided for preplacement activities that attend to the children's needs based on their age, background, attachment to parents, and stage of development. All children should be placed in homelike surroundings, in close proximity to parents, and in homes either matched by ethnic, racial, or cultural representation or supportive of the child's race or ethnicity.

Biological parents also need time to adjust to the anticipated placement. Parents need to understand why the placement is necessary and ideally come to agree with it. Preparation for the family includes visitation plans, so the parents can view the placement as part of the continuum. When parents become partners in placement preparation, it is helpful for the children in their transitions.

Foster parents also need time to prepare. They need information about the children, their eating habits and food preferences; their medical conditions and needs, including medications; their sleeping habits, with any bedwetting issues; the child's interests; behavior problems; and whatever other information is pertinent to a successful transition.

Reunification

Until recently, the criteria for reunifying children with their parents have been problematic and confusing. Reed-Ashcroft, Kirk, and Pecora (2002) developed the North Carolina Family Assessment Scale–Reunification (NCFAS-R), a best-practice initiative for foster care reunification. NCFAS-R is an outgrowth of the North Carolina Family Assessment Scale (NCFAS), a program funded by the North Carolina legislature to evaluate a statewide implementation of intensive family preservation services. The NCFAS-R is an initiative in which intensive family preservation services are provided to biological parents before, during, and after reunification of their children. Ideally, child welfare staff have sufficient time to work with the family prior to their children's return as well as during the reunification efforts and following the placement. Research has shown that risk is increased when children are reunified, so the provision of services is appropriate.

Using an instrument to gather baseline data, child welfare staff gather information about family strengths as well as areas of concern to be addressed prior to and after reunification of the children. NCFAS-R uses an instrument with seven domains of family functioning: environment, parental capabilities, family interactions, family safety, child well-being, caregiver/child ambivalence, and overall readiness for reunification. Several items are measured within each of these domains. The NCFAS-R developers intended that the instruments and program assist child welfare staff and agencies in the foster care reunification process. Many states and localities are using NCFAS-R in their reunification efforts.

Concurrent Planning

Concurrent planning is a process in which child welfare staff work with biological parents to reunify their children in foster care while the staff develop alternative permanent plans. Concurrent planning has been one of the keys to the increase in numbers of adoptions of foster children and in expediting reunification of children with their families. It replaced the sequential, step-by-step process that required much more time to complete case plans. However, concurrent planning often produces confusion for all parties, including the practitioners, foster parents, and biological parents. All parties involved in the concurrent planning process must be made aware of what the process represents, the implications of the process, and the implementation timelines. Full disclosure about the implications of concurrent planning is necessary in dealing with birth parents, resource parents, or relatives, should they be involved, in order for concurrent planning to be effective (Schene, 2001).

Concurrent planning requires careful assessment of strengths and deficits of children and families to determine if reunification is feasible. It requires selection of foster parents who agree to work on reunification of children with their biological parents but are also in agreement to have the children placed permanently with them (Barbell & Freundlich, 2001). Shared decision making among birth parents, child welfare staff, and potential adoptive parents is essential. Family team conferencing may be used to implement a shared decision-making process. Frequent visitation is often necessary to expedite permanency decisions. Therefore, child welfare agencies may find it necessary to make special arrangements for visitation so that practitioners are not overwhelmed.

Because many older and special needs children require out-of-home placements, recruitment of foster parents for these children is a particular challenge for child welfare agencies. Foster families are often referred to as resource families, and the licensing and training materials reflect the dual roles of these families.

Kinship Care

Kinship care or placement with relatives is an option that has become the fastest-growing type of placement. In the past, kinship placement created controversy because of conflicting views. One view was that kinship placement was preferred over placement with strangers because it reduced the trauma associated with placement, and relatives promoted contact between children and their parents. The other view was more pessimistic about the ability of kin to parent children effectively because they (the kin) might have problems similar to the parents. Berrik (1997) found that in California, the kin providers tended to be older and poorer, and they often had mental health and other issues that would preclude provision of adequate child care. Indeed, many states' kinship providers do not receive the same level of training, if any, as nonrelative providers. Child welfare agencies have developed policies that include appropriate training, service supports, financial support, monitoring, and supervision for kinship care providers.

Adoption

Adoption is an alternative permanent placement program in which families are established legally, not biologically. Through the adoption process, the court creates a new family after termination of parental rights of biological parents. Adoption provides the same legal benefits to adoptees that biological children have, such as the right to inherit from parents. Even though all states had enacted adoption laws by 1929, adoption was not valued or realized as a permanent option for children until the 1960s and 1970s (Kadushin & Martin, 1988).

For the most part, adoption proceedings are sealed, and new birth certificates are issued for the children bearing the adoptive parents' names. Adoption records are not public, and one must secure a court order to view any records. In the 1950s and 1960s, adoption became prominent as a permanent placement for children born out of wedlock. Because of societal taboos associated with out-of-wedlock pregnancies, many infants were placed in adoptive homes. Young, unmarried women often traveled away from their home to residential maternity homes where medical care and other services were provided. Private maternity agencies were established, and safeguards were implemented to protect the information about the out-of-wedlock pregnancies. These pregnancies no longer have the stigma attached, and the availability of infants for adoption has decreased substantially.

In the 1970s and 1980s, adoption became an alternative permanent placement for older children and children with special needs. For the first time, PL 96-272 federally mandated adoption as a service, and federal adoption subsidies became available. A variety of program efforts surfaced to attract adoptive families for children with special needs. Adoption exchanges were developed at the regional and national levels.

Agencies ensure that potential adoptive parents are able to meet the social, emotional, cultural, spiritual, and safety needs of children. Agencies should also provide preadoption services for the birth parents regardless of whether the parental termination is voluntary or not. Other services should include counseling, parent recruitment, training, financial, and supportive services. Potential adoptive parents also need transitioning services (CWLA, 1990a).

Child welfare agencies have also developed policy that advocates for siblings to be placed together unless there are compelling reasons for not placing them together. They should be placed in the same home around the same time. Recruitment of a variety of adoptive homes is therefore critical. Black churches have successfully used the One-Church, One-Child approach to recruit parents for black children in need of permanent homes. Other agencies have used "Wednesday's Child," where specific children are presented through the media in attempts to locate appropriate adoptive parents.

Open adoption, now more common, involves situations in which the biological parents may maintain some contact with their children. The level of contact varies with the individual situations and must be mutually established. Open adoptions are viewed positively because these arrangements offer permanency for many children who would otherwise not have permanent homes. Nontraditional adoption by single and gay or lesbian parents has also increased and been successful. Adoptive placements have been strengthened and disruptions reduced through provision of mental health and health services to families when needed and through adoption groups created by adoptive parents as support systems.

Child Care

Child care is needed when either both parents or a single parent enters the workforce. During World War II, many women entered the workforce and worked in a variety of jobs. However, at the end of the war, most women returned to the home. In the 1960s, the number of women entering the workforce began to increase, and by 1990, the number of women in the workplace had increased by 60 percent (Lindsey, 2004). Increases in out-of-wedlock births and divorces have added to the numbers of single mothers in the workforce facing many challenges in addition to child care. In addition to being an employment-related need, child care has been used as a respite service for biological and foster families in some child welfare programs (Downs, Moore, McFadden, Michaud, & Costin, 2004).

Child care is a universally funded service in most of the industrialized countries (Lindsey, 2004). It is not a universal service in this country, although there are federal and state funds available to parents who qualify for the service. Prior to 1988 and passage of the Family Act, there was minimal federal support for child care. Until that time, support for daycare depended upon individual state appropriations. Child-care entitlement programs became available in 1988 and 1990 and were related to moving individuals from welfare to work. The welfare reform legislation changed the landscape of child-care funding because the federal child-care entitlements ceased with transfer of welfare administration to the states. Initially, fewer resources were available to pay for child care, but funding for child care has increased as most states now focus on child-care funding to assist parents in achieving employment. Founded in the 1960s during President Lyndon Johnson's War on Poverty, Head Start is a program intended to provide economically disadvantaged children an education program with the availability of medical care, social services, and nutritional aspects. It is one of many comprehensive programs in limited number found to be effective in this country.

Finding quality child care has been problematic because it is expensive for those who need it. Many low-income mothers seek relative or informal care because it may be more convenient and also cheaper. Such narrow choices may limit the nurturing, stimulation, and child development activities needed for children to grow and thrive.

RECENT INNOVATIONS: FAMILY-CENTERED, STRENGTHS-BASED PROGRAMS

Family Preservation

Over the 1980s and 1990s, many family preservation programs were created to strengthen families whose children were at risk of out-of-home placement. Generally, the goals of these programs are to assure children's safety, improve functioning of the family, and prevent out-of-home placements through the provision of concrete and clinical supportive services.

Homebuilders of Tacoma, Washington, was among the first organizations to provide family preservation services on a large scale. Homebuilders claimed to have prevented out-of-home placements for over 90 percent of participating families (Haapala & Kinney, 1988). Pecora, Fraser, and Haapala (1991) found treatment success in program sites in Utah and Washington State.

Because family preservation programs are individualized responses to families, research shows they have been effective with culturally, ethnically, and racially diverse populations. Recent students of Native American family preservation programs are positive (Red Horse, Martinez, & Day, 2001). In three North Dakota tribes, family preservation services and the Sacred Child Project, which was a wraparound service, were provided. The Sacred Child Project adapted the programs by adding a circle of extended family, clan, and community supports that reflect cultural traditions. The reframing of the wraparound program combined with family preservation provided a continuum of programs that was effective.

Critics of family preservation have claimed that it has been used when not appropriate and that agencies have insisted in using family preservation services at any cost to children's safety. Others have claimed that preservation programs may not be sufficient to detour the effects of multiproblem families. In addition, evaluation studies of family preservation indicate short-term gains of families involved in these services were not sustained over time. In other studies using experimental and control groups, no significant differences were found in the incidences of child maltreatment, out-of-home placements, and other factors.

Reed-Ashcroft, Kirk, and Fraser (2001) reported that negative results from family preservation studies have been due to issues such as the dose-response and deficits in methodological aspects. Kirk (2001) has examined family preservation evaluation studies and found that researchers have encountered a number of problems in conducting the evaluations. These problems have included a lack of model fidelity where the service designs were not consistently applied, programs that served families where children were not at imminent risk of placement, and problems related to random assignment and measurement error. Under these circumstances, Kirk suggested that the controversies surrounding family preservation services have been related more to how programs were implemented and evaluated than whether or not the programs could be effective.

Family Group Conferencing

Family group conferencing is an alternative strategy for dealing with family violence and other issues. The model is based on the assumption that people seek nourishment, security, and a sense of belonging within their families. Families are considered circles within other circles, including relatives, communities, and government. The belief in this intervention model is that families can contribute to their own decision making and that having input in decisions is directly related to achieving positive outcomes. One early demonstration project in Newfoundland, Canada (Pennell & Buford, 2000), adapted the original model from New Zealand. The project objectives were to reduce violence against child and adult family members and enhance their well-being. The project strove to foster partnerships within and around families. There were five stages in this project that are common in most family conferencing programs: (1) receipt of referrals, (2) conferences organized in concert with family group members and service providers, (3) conferences convened; (4) family development of a plan, and (5) referral agency approval of the plan. In this project, there were project and comparison groups. The results were that in the project group, conferences enhanced family unity and increased the safety of children. Opposite findings occurred in the comparison group, where the number of CPS events increased. A Calgary study (Sieppert, Hudson, & Unrau, 2000) had similar results to the Newfoundland study. The program offered better protection of children and more stability for families.

Merkel-Holquin (2000) reported on the increased growth of family group conferences in the United States. The number of conferences has risen to over 100 communities since the early 1990s. These programs have become popular in this country, and many have experienced positive results. However, Merkel-Holquin cautioned that conferencing has experienced many of the same problems that family preservation experienced. These problems included program drift, uneven quality in the family conferencing coordinator's ability, role confusion about the coordinator, insufficient preparation and planning for conferences, physical location of conferencing activities, funding issues, and others. Merkel-Holquin posited that all of these factors, when not adequately addressed, produce variation in results.

Wraparound

Wraparound is another strengths-based program. The term *wraparound* originated in North Carolina, where flexible funding was made available to respond to individualized needs of children and families (Katz-Leavy, Lourie, Stroul, & Ziegler-Dendy, 1992). One unique feature of wraparound is the "wrapping" of formal and/or informal services based on needs. Another is the concept of "no rejection," especially not rejecting children who have multiple risks, such as maltreatment, emotional disturbance, and health and other issues.

Wraparound programs are community based, composed and operated by interdisciplinary teams, and focused on family strengths. Initially, wraparound was used in the area of mental health to provide and prevent placement into institutions. Wraparound is now used in many different arenas, including child welfare and schools.

One of the most recognized wraparound programs is Kaleidoscope, developed by Carl Dennis in Chicago (Kaleidoscope Inc., 1999). Developed as an alternative to burgeoning numbers of children in institutions, Kaleidoscope offered community-based services for all children, including those representing diverse ethnic and racial backgrounds. Their therapeutic treatment foster care, family preservation, and pediatric AIDS treatment foster care programs are viewed as national models. The therapeutic foster care program offers alternatives to institutional care as professional foster parents serve challenging youth. Because the program serves those youths who are considered the most difficult because of mental or behavior issues, it offers resources to the public child welfare system. Children in this program are generally involved in the programs for long periods of time because their chances of returning home are minimal. The family preservation or intensive therapeutic services provide wraparound to intact families so that children who would otherwise be institutionalized can remain in their homes. They also work to reunify children with their families. Consistent with their mission of serving the most vulnerable populations, the families generally experience poverty, are racially and ethnically diverse, and are often single parents with substance abuse and mental health issues.

Many child welfare agencies have found it necessary to place youths with severe behavioral and emotional disturbances in residential programs. The Alaska Youth Initiative provided an alternative model for serving these children. They developed wraparound services for children who were returned to Alaska from out-of-state residential placement and effectively dealt with them in their own homes or in foster homes. As a result, only two of the children were placed in out-of-state programs, and the costs for the program were significantly less than those previously paid for children in residential care.

MULTIPLE ISSUES IN CHILD WELFARE SERVICES

Children with Emotional Disturbances

Children with emotional disturbances have been served in the child welfare system for a number of years. Although progress has been made in the field of child mental health, particularly during the 1980s and 1990s, children with emotional disturbances continue to contribute to the crisis in child welfare programs. Jane Knitzer's *Unclaimed Children* (1982) outlined the poor state of services for children with emotional disturbances and their families. In 1984, Congress authorized the Child and Adolescent Service System Program (CASSP) at the National Institute of Mental Health. This program makes grants to states for the provision of services to children who are seriously emotionally disturbed. The focus of the grants is to provide comprehensive, community-based, coordinated, individualized, and culturally sensitive services to children and their families. Since the inception of CASSP, a number of changes have taken place in the design, delivery, and evaluation of services for children with emotional and mental disorders.

In spite of these changes, many children with emotional disturbances continue to be placed in residential facilities, which are the most restrictive and most expensive settings available. In addition, evidence suggests that placement of children into these facilities is not always appropriate. Congress estimated that 70 to 80 percent of the 7 to 8 million children and adolescents who were emotionally disturbed were not receiving appropriate care (Select Committee on Children, Youth, and Families, 1990).

Children with serious emotional disturbances have become the responsibility of child welfare systems across the country. This is due in large part to deinstitutionalization of adolescents from mental health institutions, creating a big need for placement resources for children with severe emotional disturbances (Baker, Wulczyn, & Dale, 2005). Over time, the responsibility for most of the severely emotionally disturbed population has shifted from mental health to child welfare agencies. This appears to have been an unanticipated consequence for which child welfare agencies were not prepared because child welfare policies and adequate funding levels have not kept pace with the practice of placing emotionally disturbed children into residential group homes, treatment foster homes, and residential treatment centers.

Baker and Dale (2002) suggested that children with severe emotional disturbances need a mental health model of care rather than a child welfare setting because a mental health model is operated under the auspice of a mental health agency and, as such, is better funded, allows for closer supervision, and offers more intense clinical services. To achieve normal development, emotionally disturbed children need to have adequate mental health care with strong linkages to families involved in their aftercare.

Racial/Ethnic Characteristics of the Child Welfare Population

An examination of the racial and ethnic backgrounds of families served by the child welfare system revealed striking disparities in the numbers of children and families of color who were served by the system and the manner in which they were assessed and handled. Previously, Close (1980) had documented that ethnically diverse children were more likely to come into the child welfare system than White children, and the American Humane Association (1986) reported that more children of color than White children are reported to CPS agencies. The overrepresentation had been a common characteristic of reporting since 1976. Stehno (1986) had documented that assessment results of children and families of color were harsher and more pessimistic than assessments of White children and families.

Although most states used some kind of model to assess risk to children in reported maltreatment situations (Harris, 1988), most were not sensitive to diverse cultures but reflected instead the child-rearing values of the dominant culture. Few risk assessment instruments or processes used to assess maltreatment reports made distinctions between parental behaviors that reflected divergent cultural practices not harmful to children and parental behaviors that did indeed compromise the children's physical, emotional, cognitive, social, cultural, and spiritual well being.

There was also overrepresentation of diverse racial groups in the foster care system (Voluntary Cooperative Information System [VCIS], 1988). In a summary of eight years of foster care, Tatara (1992) concluded that children entering the foster care system tended to be of a racial minority. Once in foster care, children of color remained there longer, had fewer adoptive placements, and had fewer permanency plans than did White children. Public agencies had also been criticized for their poor performance in recruiting minority adoptive parents and failing to approve them once they were found.

CWLA (2004) reported that overrepresentation continues to be a factor for children of color in the foster care population, especially for African American children. The following table clearly illustrates the overrepresentation.

Foster Care Population	Race/Ethnicity	Percent of Population	Percent in Foster Care
	White	61 percent	43 percent
	African American	15 percent	40 percent
	Hispanic/Latino	17 percent	15 percent
	Native American/Alaska Native	1 percent	2 percent
	Asian/Pacific Islander	3 percent	1 percent
	Children of two or more races	1 percent	3 percent

According to CWLA (2004), the overrepresentation is linked to social class and economic factors. This is supported by data from the Department of Health and Human Services (DHHS). In 2002, 12.1 million children under the age of 18 lived in families with incomes below the federal poverty level and represented 16.7 percent of all children in the United States. Of the 12.1 million, 32.1 percent were African American (including Hispanic); 28.2 percent were Hispanic and 13.1 percent were White (including Hispanic) (DHHS, 2004).

Substance Abuse and Child Maltreatment

According to national data (National Household Survey on Drug Abuse Report, 2004), over 8 million children are living with substance-abusing parents. Therefore, substance abuse programs that offer services to child welfare populations are particularly important, and many child welfare agency staff have established partnerships with substance abuse agencies so that families involved with substance abuse are better served. Nancy Young, Director of a newly formed consortium (National Center on Substance Abuse and Child Welfare [NCSACW], 2003), suggested that a number of required timelines in various agencies need to be considered when working with families in which substance abuse is a factor.

The ASFA timelines are challenging because permanency decisions about children in placement must be made within 12 months of placement, and termination of parental rights are sought after children are in placement 15 out of 22 months. In addition, timelines for welfare may be a crucial factor. Families receiving welfare benefits have work requirements of 24 months, and families are able to receive welfare benefits for no more than 60 months. These families therefore have limited accessibility to cash assistance. Child development timelines must also be considered. A child's developmental clock never stops, and care must be taken to make timely decisions that will provide the most optimal environments for all children, especially infants and toddlers because they develop at a faster rate than other children. The timeline for recovery is a lifetime. Recovery is one day at a time, and parents may face challenges to sobriety as crises arise. All of these timelines create challenges for child welfare staff and the families; it is therefore critical to establish partnerships among child welfare agencies and all other stakeholders.

CASA Safe Haven is a program for families with substance abuse, maltreatment, domestic violence, mental health issues, and poverty. CASA Safe Haven collaborates with child welfare and other agencies to provide cohesive and comprehensive programs for families. They establish teams of professionals representing a number of agencies and provide innovative services such as family group conferencing, family services, employment, and others (O'Connor, Morgenstem, Gibson, & Nakashian, 2005).

The program builds parental capacity while dealing with the addiction issues. Parents learn about developmental needs of children and substance abuse concerns, such as recovery, relapse, and how to plan to avoid relapses.

Research also indicates that a high number of women who abuse substances, particularly alcohol, have been sexually abused as children. Alcohol and other drugs serve to anesthetize emotional conditions such as anxiety, depression, hypervigilance, PTSD, and flashbacks. Abused children tend to use alcohol earlier in their lives than do nonabused children (Briere, 1992). Substance abuse becomes the coping mechanism for many individuals who have been maltreated as children. These individuals have co-occurring needs and dual diagnoses of addiction and mental health conditions. Consequently, treatment of the sexual abuse is critical to the recovery from substance abuse (The Source, 1998).

Domestic Violence and Child Maltreatment

Because domestic violence occurs in families of all ages, ethnicities, and religions, it is a particular challenge for child welfare agencies. Over 50 percent of all women will experience physical violence in intimate relationships, and between 24 and 30 percent of this number will be ongoing victims of violence. According to the Office of Child Abuse and Neglect (2003), 10 to 20 percent of children are at risk of being exposed to domestic violence. Exposure to domestic violence has adverse consequence for children, as many of them may develop behavior problems, including aggression; develop physical health problems; have more hospitalizations; and perform poorly in school. Because domestic violence is closely related to child abuse and neglect, it is critical that CPS, law enforcement, and domestic violence agencies collaborate to ensure that women and children are safe and the batterers are held accountable. In situations involving children of battered women who have been maltreated, it is appropriate for the assessments and intervention strategies to be coordinated. Cross-training is essential because CPS staff have been trained to work with children and families while domestic violence workers have been trained to work with victims and batterers. It is often useful for domestic violence and CPS staff to be co-located. Collaborating with other agencies, such as shelter facilities and safe homes, has also been effective.

CHILD WELFARE AGENCIES

Child welfare agencies are responsible for providing services to vulnerable children and families and are one of the most important social services. Most child welfare programs were created after the Social Security Act of 1935 and have expanded since then with development of specific programs to meet particular needs that have arisen. By 1979, 20 federal programs had been created for children, including foster care, child abuse and neglect, service programs for runaways and children with developmental disabilities, and adoption assistance services (Yankey, 1987). Mental health, public health, child welfare, and juvenile justice programs were developed to deal with different aspects of familial problems, but in designing these programs, developers established few, if any, linkages, resulting in much fragmentation, duplication, and ineffectiveness.

A number of components must be present in child welfare agencies to ensure best practice at all levels. These components include a supportive internal environment that offers a number of supports for staff, adequate resources so caseloads and workloads are at a reasonable level, salaries that are commensurate with job responsibilities, job qualifications with appropriate levels of educational and experience requirements, preservice and in-service training that builds knowledge and skills of all staff, and accountability standards based on outcomes. Child welfare agencies must also partner with other public and private agencies, so an array or continuum of services can be made available to vulnerable families and children.

Internal Environment

A supportive internal environment is particularly important because of the stress related to child welfare work. Recognition of outstanding performance is valued by staff and is not costly to the agency. A supportive environment can help reduce turnover. Expert consultation should be available to staff when needed. Flex-time offering flexibility in work hours for those staff that would benefit is not costly to implement. When children in the child welfare system sustain injury or death, parents are traumatized. Practitioners are also affected by such incidents, and counseling should be available to them. Additionally, safety measures in the office and in the field should be in place to assist in safeguarding staff in their work. All of these factors are part of a positive internal environment.

Resources

Resources are a key factor necessary for provision of quality programs. Resources must be adequate to assure staff workloads/caseloads are appropriate and manageable. Maximizing all federal, state, and local funds is necessary to assure an adequate funding base. In child welfare, various federal sources include Title IV-B for family preservation, community-based family support services, time-limited family reunification services, and adoption promotion and support services; Title IV-E for foster care and special needs adoption payments for eligible children, some administrative costs, long- and short-term training, independent living funds; and CAPTA funding for protective services.

A number of other federal funds can be used to support child welfare services. Medicaid dollars can be used for targeted case management and EPSDT; TANF funds can be used in prevention services; Title XX funds can be used for social services for all population groups. Developing partnerships with other agencies can also produce funding from the Mental Health Services Block Grant, the Substance Abuse Block Grant, the Office of Juvenile Justice and Delinquency Prevention (OJJDP), the Children's Justice Act, Court Improvement Act, and Title V of the Social Security Act. A number of federal discretionary grants are also available to states. State and local funds are needed to match federal funds but can also be used in other ways. The leadership must make the decisions to maximize all funds, but the practitioners and supervisors play key roles in obtaining funds. Most funds have specific eligibility rules, and establishment of client eligibility is generally completed by practitioners.

Job Qualifications

Social work is the professional arena for child welfare services. Staff at all levels should have degrees in social work or a closely related field. Research findings support the efficacy of social work for public-sector child welfare practice. A Nevada study showed that staff with bachelor degrees in social work (BSWs) and master's degrees in social work (MSWs) were more effective in developing permanency plans for children who had been in foster care for over two years (Albers, Reilly, & Rittner, 1993). In Maryland, the overall job performance of MSWs was significantly higher than non-MSWs; higher education, specifically an MSW, was the best predictor of overall performance in social service work (Booz-Allen & Hamilton, 1987). A study of social workers in Kentucky found that staff with social work degrees were better prepared than workers without social work degrees (Dhooper, Royse, & Wolfe, 1990). Staff turnover was found to be greater in states in which workers did not have academic social work preparation for child welfare work and lower in states that required an MSW (CWLA, 1990; Russel, 1987a, 1987b). In a recent study, Okamura and Jones (2000) found that graduates of a Title IV-E MSW program at San Diego State University who were hired by the Children's Services Bureau showed significant differences between comparison groups. Title IV-E graduates scored higher on child welfare knowledge and tended to remain longer with the agency.

Hiring practice should recruit staff that represent the cultural and ethnic diversity of the families and children served by the child welfare agencies.

Job Performance

Most child welfare agencies measure themselves and are measured by others in terms of outcomes that are achieved for families and children. Child welfare agencies must know whether staff have conducted accurate safety assessments and developed appropriate safety plans to keep children safe. There are also behavioral anchors such as those articulated in the Child and Family Services Review for other services. Job performance must therefore be measured by these behavioral anchors.

Training

Training is needed for all levels of staff, including paraprofessionals, practitioners, supervisors, and leaders. Child welfare agencies that propose strengths-based child welfare practice as part of their vision must train all staff in terms of their responsibilities in its implementation; all have some responsibility related to best practice. The same is true in other areas; there should be a systemic approach to major policies and practices. Newly employed staff must have orientation training. Practitioners need regular in-service training, so they can learn the critical knowledge and skills needed to perform well. Supervisors also need training. Often, outstanding practitioners are promoted to supervisors. Being a supervisor requires a new skills set and supervisory training. Likewise, leaders need training in order to perform the various tasks of planning, budgeting, monitoring, evaluating, and advocating for their programs.

Training should be competency or ability based. Training should provide knowledge and skills; it is useful for training to be provided to child welfare and partner agency staff. Training must encompass diverse cultural and ethnic aspects, so accurate and appropriate decisions are made for all families and children. A number of national organizations have developed excellent training programs that cover a variety of topical areas for all levels of staff.

One area in which training is needed is secondary trauma stress (STS) because of the trauma related to families and children in child welfare services. Child welfare workers are vulnerable to STS because it occurs while professionals work and listen to traumas that occur in families (Nelson-Gardell & Deneen, 2003). Training teaches staff to be empathetic in their work. However, providing empathy in their interactions with traumatized children and families creates vulnerability. Many human service professionals have themselves experienced trauma in their background and are therefore more vulnerable to STS in their child welfare work. Training about STS should be available, explaining what it is and how staff can deal with it.

Outcome Accountability

The Adoption and Safe Families Act mandates three outcomes for children: safety, permanency, and well-being. The federal government evaluates the states in a process called the Child and Family Services Review (CFSR). The review covers all three outcomes, assessing the level to which the state complies with the prescribed performance levels. Most child welfare agencies have automated information systems that provide indications related to activities completed, services that are needed, and information to measure outcomes.

Partnerships

In order to offer more-effective services to vulnerable families and children, it is necessary for child welfare agencies to partner with other public and private agencies. A number of reform initiatives have emerged to provide a more comprehensive approach on behalf of children and families. These initiatives have proposed a fundamental reorientation and reexamination of the premises on which current systems were built, the way resources were organized, and the functions of the systems and the individuals within the systems. Partnerships and collaborations among public and private agencies serving families are necessary so that prevention and early intervention services can be provided. The initiatives have provided a comprehensive array of services and changed relationships to ones of cooperation and collaboration. These initiatives have created best practices in a number of agencies.

Fragmentation and Staffing Issues

Fragmentation in the delivery of services to families and children has been identified as a significant problem since the 1980s. Although the needs of children and families require a broad continuum of prevention, early intervention, and treatment services, studies show most child welfare agencies were not able, either directly, through contractual arrangements, or interagency agreements, to provide a comprehensive approach to meet their needs (APWA, 1990). According to the Select Committee on Children, Youth, and Families (1990), inadequate and inappropriate services were common features of child welfare systems.

Child welfare agencies have been faced with staffing issues, including inadequate educational requirements, lack of career ladders, salaries that are not commensurate with responsibilities, insufficient training opportunities, inadequate supervisor/caseworker ratios, and stressful work environments that lead to high staff turnover.

The problems created by child welfare staff turnover and the need for better recruitment and retention practices have spurred action on the part of public and private organizations at the state and national levels. At the request of Congress, the United States General Accounting Office (GAO) (2003) published a report about how the Department of Health and Human Services (DHHS) can play a role in helping child welfare agencies recruit and retain staff. In 2001, the Alliance for Children and Families, the Child Welfare League of America and the American Public Human Services Association, all strong national organizations for families and children, collaborated on a national survey about current workforce issues related to child welfare practice. Over the past several years, a number of studies have also been conducted in individual states in attempts to discover the causes of child welfare staff turnover and develop strategies for dealing with it.

The GAO interviewed staff and made site visits in four states, analyzed exit interviews of child welfare staff across the country, examined the results of the federal Child and Family Services Reviews in 27 states, and interviewed child welfare experts across the country. The GAO found the causes of turnover to be low salaries, high caseloads, administrative burdens, limited supervision, and inadequate training. They also found that turnover creates additional problems for agencies as remaining staff must cover the caseloads of exiting staff. This also created discontinuity in services provided to families and children. Under these circumstances, it was deemed very difficult for child welfare agencies to achieve the federally mandated outcomes of safety, permanency, and well-being.

The collaborative study conducted by three national organizations surveyed public and private child welfare organizations across the country (Cyphers, 2001). The survey results were discouraging: Workloads and caseloads were too high, paperwork requirements were too burdensome, child welfare workers did not feel valued, salaries were too low, there were supervision problems, and communities had insufficient resources.

Other studies have produced similar results. Pecora and colleagues (2000) state that a number of issues are related to recruitment, selection, and training, including the need for job descriptions to accurately reflect the job responsibilities, diminishing educational requirements to work in child welfare, a lack of clear guidelines for supervision and supervisor/worker ratios, poor working conditions, and poor public image. In an earlier study, Pecora, Briar, and Zlotnik (1989) reported similar challenges: low minimum qualifications, poor work environment, high caseloads, low salaries and lack of promotional opportunities, poor public image, lack of training opportunities, and liability issues.

One study (Graef & Hill, 2000) conducted a comprehensive study of the costs of turnover. The authors calculated the CPS staff turnover cost in a Midwestern state by looking at the tasks related to separation of workers or the administrative functions to process the exit; replacement costs, including the advertising, screening, and interviewing process to fill a position; and training costs, including classroom and field exercises. The salaries and time of the individuals responsible for each of the tasks were then calculated to come up with the total cost. They also included the differential related to turnover, that is, the reduction in performance levels of newly hired staff. The conservative estimate of the cost of one staff turnover was $10,000 in 1995. The national organizations study indicated that the average mandatory training is 136 hours, or 3.5 weeks, for CPS staff and 98 hours, or 2.4 weeks, for the other professional staff. In addition, some counties and states require that newly hired child welfare workers carry a reduced caseload for a specific time. The cost of orienting and training newly hired child welfare workers adds to the overall cost of turnover.

State and county agencies have developed and implemented strategies to deal with the problems of recruitment and retention. The GAO recommends that child welfare agencies reduce caseloads, reduce the ratios of supervisors to staff, and encourage child welfare staff to obtain MSWs; that agencies review improvements made by other states; and that agencies implement leadership and mentoring programs, competency based interviews, and recruitment bonuses. The GAO also recommends the development of university agency partnerships, as studies indicate the Title IV-E programs have produced favorable results. It is too early to study the results of other recommendations because the report was published in 2003.

Gary Cyphers (2001) of APHSA reported that many of the public agencies have implemented strategies to deal with turnover and recruitment. The strategies either required increased resources and funding or required "soft responses," just as policies allowing for flex-time. Even though many states implemented a variety of changes, there is no quick fix for the problem. In fact, many states rated specific strategies as ineffective while other states rated the same strategies as effective. One state that raised salaries at a rate above the cost-of-living increase was not successful in reducing turnover.

SUMMARY

This chapter has included the earliest societal influences on child welfare policies and practices. The chapter has also included a summary of the major laws relating to individual programs and the overall child welfare service systems. Related issues of poverty, emotionally disturbed children, and others were presented to illustrate how child welfare practice is influenced by events outside of its control. The chapter also included the challenges child welfare agencies face, such as staffing and turnover, high caseloads, low salaries, fragmentation, and others, and concluded with strategies for dealing with some of these issues.

There are a number of reasons why the child welfare system has been challenged beyond its capacity. Funding for child welfare has never been adequate. Appropriations were attached to some laws with promises of increases. The funding has therefore not kept pace with inflation and the growth in populations with needs. Some events, such as the decision to create vast media campaigns about child abuse and neglect, resulted in drastic increases in maltreatment reports that overwhelmed the ability of the systems to respond. Laws passed over the years were always well intended but have always dealt with a crisis and not the underlying problems. Prevention and early intervention have not been priorities in Congress or in state legislatures. Child welfare agencies cannot achieve their goals single-handedly. They must interact with court systems that also have tremendous caseloads. Consequently, the activities of child welfare agencies are often delayed unintentionally by the courts. Coordination and collaboration with other public and private agencies are needed to truly meet the needs of vulnerable children and families.

Questions for Discussion

1. What are the positive effects of some of the major child welfare laws?
2. How have the laws created major challenges for child welfare agencies?
3. Describe the evolution of topical areas in child welfare, such as child protective services, foster care, and adoption services.
4. Why are family-centered, strengths-based programs considered to be best practice?
5. What are co-occurring needs, and how can they be addressed?

2 CHAPTER | **Child Welfare Services**
Formal and Informal

INTRODUCTION

A critical part of understanding the types of interventions you can provide is your ability to utilize both the formal and informal services available in the child welfare field. In working from the strengths continuum, you can provide more services that focus on preventive and innovative interventions for families and children within a multisystemic approach. This chapter will examine the different services currently available in child welfare and present several ways to integrate more innovative methods and programs.

CURRENT SERVICE CONTINUUM

The structure of child welfare training and child welfare agencies has focused on approaching problematic family situations from a residual service program continuum and perspective. The emphasis on more formal service programs rather than a flexible practice model is due in large part to public policies defining the services in programs. In an effort to provide aid to children and families in need, programs and services that serve specialized functions in support of or in lieu of the family have become the mainstay of public child welfare.

These programs and services have been commonly categorized as supportive, supplementary, and substitute. They have been explained by many child welfare experts (Kadushin & Martin, 1988) as being on a continuum of least restrictive to most restrictive. The reason for this description has been the shift in public child welfare to a protective focus (Lindsey, 1994). This focus in turn has been influenced over the years by the perception of what is the best course of action for the children. The question becomes whether to leave the children in their homes while receiving services or to remove the children to temporary care until it is determined whether or not to reunite the children with their biological family. This debate has had far-reaching effects on child welfare services and will be discussed in greater detail later in the text; however, as you read through this chapter, you will come to understand how this debate has had much to do with the concepts of permanency planning, family-centered care, family rights, and the best interests of the children.

Despite the effort of the profession to discern the best approach, the fact remains that most child welfare services have been delivered not necessarily based upon what the families and children need but based upon what is available from the agency. This is not to suggest that the services and programs in the formal child welfare system are not valuable; however, they can be limiting and are often implemented through a process that is not concerned with strengths building. To better understand the strengths and limitations of the more formal residual system, we will thoroughly examine the continuum on which these services have been based.

CHILD WELFARE SERVICE CONTINUUM

Highlight 2.1 shows the child welfare service continuum as it encompasses supportive, supplementary, and substitute services. Supportive services are seen primarily as those services provided for children within their home. They include, but are not limited to, homemaker services, Temporary Assistance for Needy Families (TANF) and other types of financial and in-kind aid, social services provided in child and family disruptive situations, parenting skills classes, and self-help groups.

| **Highlight 2.1** | **Child Welfare Service Continuum** |

least restrictive   most restrictive

supplementary services   supportive services   substitute services

These services are family-based in nature and represent the least restrictive environment. The term *supportive services* is based on a belief that the best environment for the development of children is within their own families if the family can be supported in providing a safe and loving home.

Supplementary services are primarily programs provided to the child and family in order to assist the family in the raising of the child. Supplemental services can include, but are not necessarily limited to, respite care; daycare; homemaker services; parenting skills classes; TANF and other financial and in-kind aid; supportive agencies, such as Big Brothers/Big Sisters; and social services provided in disruptive family situations. As you can see from this list, many of the supportive and supplementary services overlap.

Substitute services (the most restrictive service) encompass emergency care, foster care, adoption, community care, and institutional care. These services are at the opposite end of the continuum from least restrictive care. These services involve the children being placed out of the home of the biological family and into the care of others. Generally, the intention of substitute care was for a temporary amount of time in an out-of-home placement while issues within the children's family were worked through or another environment was established for them. Substitute care was the predominate method of handling most child welfare cases before the 1970s and 1980s.

Ivanoff, Blythe, and Tripodi (1994) note that the differences between these types of services are reflective of the aforementioned continuum of least restrictive to most restrictive care on the part of a child welfare agency. They further note that both supportive and supplementary services are offered to support the family remaining intact and tend to be family focused, although the welfare of the children is not neglected. Substitute forms of care, however, are more protective in nature and have more focus on the children. As a child welfare social worker, you will need to assess the family in deciding which types of services are most appropriate in each case. There will often be times in protective child welfare work where you and your supervisor will be the only ones making this decision. This can be one of the most significant decisions a social worker makes. Your understanding of which of these services is the most appropriate to be implemented will determine the children and family's course of intervention. Although risk assessment tools are part of this process, the child welfare social worker still utilizes his or her own decision-making skills in making these assessments.

The established service fields as related to the child welfare service continuum in public child welfare are familiar to most social work students. These include, but are not limited to, daycare, foster care, adoption, child protection, homemaking services, aid to pregnant adolescents, and community and independent living. However, it is important to recognize that these service areas do not necessarily describe how the practice process is to be implemented. Alone on a continuum they are limiting because they do not explain how or in what manner the varying resources and supports available from the community can be utilized in making these services not only effective but also preventive. Although you may be familiar with these fields of service described in terms of policy and history, the actual practice in these service areas in conjunction with preventive approaches, created though the community, has not been emphasized in social work education. Specialized training programs that do respond to the practice and training needs of the social worker in the child welfare field are often implemented by the agency in the community. The practice process related specifically to child welfare is unique in many ways to other forms of social work practice. It frequently begins by nonvoluntary design, with the social worker being viewed as an interloper into the family. This process is then further hampered by the residual focus of the intervention in working with the family.

Another factor related to the manner in which this service model is placed into operation is that the service fields, although conceptualized on a continuum of least restrictive to most restrictive, are not organized on an infrastructure in the child welfare agency based on a continuum of practice. Most child welfare agencies compartmentalize services and divide the social worker's role according to the service provided rather than the case's needs. Often, a family and child who come into the child welfare system may receive a disjointed, unorganized approach to practice. They may become entrapped in a process that worsens because not all of the care available at the least restrictive point of the continuum has been recognized or implemented. This design is very different from a strengths-based practice continuum, which focuses on the strengths of the family and child and moves toward the least restrictive environment through the goal of achieving an independent, healthy family situation. In this approach, each individual case is assessed after investigation, and the same social worker continues to work with that family in their service needs.

As we have noted, many of these formal services overlap in their classification. For example, homemaker services can be seen as both supportive and supplementary, while foster care can be interpreted as both a form of substitute care as well as a supplemental service. What distinguishes these services is their primary purpose as it relates to each individual case situation and how they are utilized to achieve an independent family living situation for each child.

INFORMAL SERVICES

Understanding what services are available and how they are provided within the child welfare system is an important part of your training, but services are not just about what the formal public child welfare system can provide; services can also come from informal systems that may include extended families, friends, neighbors, communities, or nonsocial service organizations, such as schools, hospitals, or even work settings. The use of informal services has not been a focus of public child welfare because these services have generally not been easy to integrate and have not been part of the more formal system; however, in this approach informal services become as important as formal services. Preventive services can be part of formal systems; however, because child welfare policies tend toward residual care, there are limitations to the financial resources used for preventive services within public child welfare agencies.

To better understand how both formal and informal services can be integrated, this chapter will review both types of services in more detail and suggest ways both may exist within social service organizations.

SUPPORTIVE SERVICES

Homemaker Services

Homemaker services in child welfare situations are now used as part of intensive family services. They are generally offered under the auspice of an agency and are part of an overall treatment plan. Homemaker services are utilized to supplement the needs of a family with children when the primary parent is unable to provide the homemaking needs in the family or when a child has special needs and the parents are not able to provide all the services the child requires.

Homemaker services have been replaced to a large degree by volunteers who work with at-risk parents to teach them how to handle basic household skills and raise children. Volunteers may also work with families that have parents who are critically ill or are experiencing mental health difficulties. Although homemaker services still exist in some agencies, the focus on supporting the whole family and not just focusing on the mothering role, as well as utilizing volunteers for cost efficiency, has led to a lessening in the use of these services. Homemaker services are often seen as the positive side of intervention by those families who have protective services involved, while the child welfare social worker plays the negative role (Pecora, Whittaker, Maluccio, Barth, & Plotnick, 1992).

As noted, the more informal types of homemaker services utilize volunteer programs that focus on helping at-risk parents. These tend to be preventive in nature, as parents are not necessarily identified after an incident but rather are identified because of certain factors about them that may make an incident of child neglect or abuse more likely, for example, teenage parents, parents with drug and alcohol addictions, parents with mental illnesses, and so forth. Examples of these types of volunteer programs can be seen throughout the United States. Your goal as a child welfare worker is to ensure that opportunities for such programs are developed in your community. Whether the child welfare agency you are working in has these types of preventive programs will often depend on your willingness to work with individuals and institutions in the community to establish them. The use of these volunteer programs also should extend beyond the limits of professional auspices and become part of the network in a community of neighbors.

TANF and Financial/In-Kind Services

TANF has replaced Aid for Families with Dependent Children (AFDC), Emergency Assistance, and the Job Opportunities and Basic Skills (JOBS) program through the PRWORA. TANF provides temporary financial assistance to needy families. This assistance is allocated to states through block grants/entitlements. The change from AFDC in the PRWORA was to encourage families to move forward in supporting themselves through work programs and opportunities rather than remaining on public welfare; however, the opportunities have not yet been put in place for individuals and families to procure jobs and a financial income capable of supporting a family. The changes to financial aid for the poor through TANF have provided no guarantee that needy families will receive the assistance they need. States have so much discretion in deciding the eligibility of families to receive any services, whether they are financial or in-kind, that there is no consistency in the type of aid that can be provided. Additionally, the limitations placed on certain families, like new immigrants, who tend to be among our poorest, have begun to concentrate more poverty in these areas. Services such as food stamps, housing, health care, and education have now all been limited to such a degree that the prospect of greater poverty in this country for more children and families is inevitable.

While many informal services exist to provide aid to children and their families, they cannot be expected to offset the increasing numbers of families without support. The major informal provider of financial aid and in-kind services to families and children has always been spiritual and religious denominations. Popple and Leighninger (1996) note that according to a 1986 survey by Netting, 14,000 social service agencies were affiliated with national religious groups. Netting notes from this study that this is probably an underestimation, as these numbers represent agencies and not all the programs that may be offered by religious groups through other means. The types of services these organizations offer are as varied as those that are offered by public welfare agencies. In many cases, they are residual in nature and seek to supplement the family with food, clothing, and money. In other situations, preventive programs focus on financial and in-kind aid. An example of this might be a church or temple sponsoring immigrant families into their community. The importance of being involved in the community through informal networks cannot be overstated; however, it will be opportunities in working with spiritual or religious organizations that may provide access to the types of preventive services needed.

Social Services

Social services in formal child welfare are generally defined as, but not limited to, counseling services for families with child protection, juvenile delinquency, special needs, and adolescent pregnancy cases. These services are offered differently according to which state is providing them. As with many other federally funded social service programs, states are given discretion in how they utilize the monies from federal block grants. In some states, the emphasis in child welfare may be on investigation and protective services while the counseling services are contracted out to another state or not-for-profit agency. In another state, the work of investigation, protective services, counseling, foster care, and adoption may be handled by only one agency or even just one child welfare social worker. In other states, investigation work is handled by the legal authorities, such as police, and child welfare social workers only provide social services or counseling to the members of the family. In some situations, for example, specialized programs that work with the spouse of a sexual perpetrator, as well as with the sexually abused child and the perpetrator, have existed for several years in child welfare agencies as part of their ongoing services.

Social services in the form of counseling have been a primary function of social workers since their work in charity organization societies; however, because public welfare agencies began with the Depression and out of a need for more concrete services, the primary function of social workers in these agencies has been to supply concrete needs. Yet the concrete resources that each state provides are seldom enough to help pull a family up to a point where they might be able to concentrate on more of the emotional issues within the family. In cases where the emotional interactions in the family must be dealt with, many child welfare social workers are limited in the amounts of time they can spend in these areas. Contracted services in these situations have come to play an important role. Family Services of America, child guidance clinics, community mental health centers, and HMOs, to name a few, often work under contract with public child welfare agencies.

Informal services provided by religious organizations and programs within other types of institutions, such as schools and hospitals, have been utilized to a large degree to provide counseling or precounseling services to individuals and families. Parent training and premarital classes are a few of the classes that are often offered free-of-charge in a community through hospitals, schools, and religious organizations.

Natural helping networks within neighborhoods and communities are once again being looked to for supportive services as budgetary cutbacks influence what can be obtained through more formal services. Natural helping networks as discussed in this text are those networks available within a community or neighborhood that have always been there but have not been utilized in a more structured manner. The use of natural helping networks is not new. Historically, natural helping networks in neighborhoods and communities were the only ways in which to obtain extra support during difficult times. A neighbor who watches children while parents are at work, a community of families that organizes a cooperative daycare, a church group that organizes a toy and clothing drive for children in need, and a group of concerned neighbors who help develop programs for the teenagers in their neighborhood are a few examples of natural helping networks. As budgetary cuts occur, more development and use of natural helping networks are needed to counter those social forces affecting families and children and to provide social services as well as in-kind services.

Parenting Skills

Training in parenting skills is another form of supportive services in child welfare practice. Parenting skills classes and programs are provided through child welfare services, hospitals, schools, and maternity homes to educate young and at-risk parents. These supportive services can also take on a preventive vision and are offered through more informal means. Parenting skills training is also often part of a protective service contract in which the worker and the family have determined that extra training is needed. These skills are sometimes taught within the family's home or through programs in the community. The difficulties with having programs in the community that a welfare family needs to attend include transportation, child care, and time scheduling. Whenever you are working with a family on a contract, you will find that these issues need to be addressed in order for families and children to take advantage of the services provided.

More informal types of parenting skills classes can be identified as mutual aid or self-help groups. These community groups are often initially organized by a professional; however, the work is done by the individuals or families themselves without the help of a professional. Examples of this are Parents Anonymous, Families with Mentally Ill Members, Families with Children in Foster Care, Alcoholics Anonymous, and Foster Care Families. The value of these informal groups is the lack of stigma attached to membership.

SUPPLEMENTARY SERVICES

Many of the same services available in supportive services also serve as supplementary services. These services will not be discussed again; however, a few provide for special situations and can be viewed as possibilities for broadening their use in other child welfare cases.

Respite Care

Respite care serves to relieve parents of their responsibilities for limited periods when their stress level is overwhelming from dealing with children with special needs or with chaotic family issues. Often, respite care is provided by volunteers who are arranged through agencies to help a parent or family with the special needs child for several hours a week, over a weekend, or through a vacation. In other situations, children can be dropped off at centers for limited periods to give parents a few stress-free hours. Use of these services is set up both through formal arrangements with child welfare agencies setting up the programs and through informal arrangements with religious organizations, volunteer agencies, and special social service agency programs.

Daycare

Daycare is a vital supplementary service that constantly increases in demand. In 1990, a National Academy of Sciences report, by Hayes, Palmer, and Zaslow (1990), estimated that close to 16 million children under the age of 6 and another 18 million between the ages of 6 and 13 had a parent or parents in the labor force. In 2000, close to 80 percent of school-age children and 70 percent of preschool children had a parent or parents in the labor force.

Of these children, less than 10 percent are in regulated daycare in the form of centers and family daycare. This leaves approximately 20 to 30 million children in some form of unregulated daycare that may be unsafe.

Daycare has become such an important component of family life in the United States that families who can afford to will spend enormous amounts of money to procure the best care. The American family can spend anywhere from $100–$1000 a week for two children in child care. Obviously, from these figures it is easy to understand why families below the poverty line or receiving welfare funding must have greater access to reasonable child care if they are to attempt to become a part of the workforce. The increased numbers of single-parent families with children, as well as the number of dual working parents, has made daycare a necessary and critical component of family life in the United States.

The PRWORA has added to these child-care issues. A National Association of Social Workers (NASW) governmental release (1996) notes that this act passed in October of 1996 established that child care would be funded with matching block grant/entitlement to the states. Increased numbers of parents are being required to find child-care space for children under age 6 so that they may follow the state's work requirements under this law. Because the number of spaces needed increased and the amount of funding for these spaces decreased, there is little hope for quality care for the majority of children receiving any type of welfare subsidy. Financial support for child care has been limited in this society, as is seen in the changing economic programs and the lack of financial support to parent children under the age of 6 at home.

The daycare services provided have generally been directed through three main streams: working parents, young child education, and the remediation of family deficits (CWLA, 1988). The last two streams have been the major focus of formal services within the child welfare agencies; however, with the new PRWORA, child welfare social workers have become even more involved in attempting to find regulated care for new working parents. Regulated child-care centers and daycare homes are authorized through most state offices of child welfare. It once again depends upon the state in which you work as to who will oversee these agencies.

Several different programs and services intended to make daycare more accessible are provided through formal governmental sanctions. These include the Dependent Care Tax Credit, which allows a credit against the federal income tax; a guarantee under certain conditions in the PRWORA for child daycare while parents are completing their training and obtaining a job; child-care subsidies to low-income families when the tax credit would not be as helpful; and Head Start, an early childhood education program for disadvantaged preschoolers. Additionally, other formal services might be available within the state child welfare agency, including subsidies for child-care services for families at risk and child-care food programs for needy children (CWLA, 1990c). How these services will be provided is subject to the discretion of the state in which the client lives.

Working with families and agencies to establish more regulated services will be a major activity of the child welfare social worker in the future. With the PRWORA stipulating that families on welfare be trained and assume jobs or not receive funds, many families will be in need of affordable daycare services. Because the jobs of many of these individuals will provide incomes that make their children ineligible for quality daycare, it will be critical for quality care supplemented by the government to be available. Many research studies have suggested that the early childhood environment can create in children the qualities of hope and motivation (Zigler & Styfco, 1994). Studies such as these suggest that while quality daycare can lead to longer-lasting positive results for children, they do not guarantee success as long as factors such as poor living conditions, poor health programs, and substandard schools exist.

Informal services are often available in the child-care field and include family care, in-home daycare, unregulated family daycare, cooperative programs, and neighborhood outreach care services. While these types of informal services exist where there are no formal regulated care spaces available, it is important to recognize that not all care is good care. Helping groups of families in neighborhoods to develop their own resources for daycare is a positive approach, but this must be matched by careful planning in setting up the arrangements and in how the services will be monitored. In most states, self-help groups establishing daycare will need to meet the standards of the state in operating a child-care center. The costs and requirements can be high to bring an informal care center into regulation; however, this is part of your role as a child welfare social worker to aid in the development of the resources to accomplish these goals. In some cases, a cooperative center may be necessary because not all parents need child care from 8:00 a.m. to 5:00 p.m. In fact, the need for late evening and overnight care has greatly increased as parents take employment that requires their presence away from the home in the evening and at night. When this happens, not only is care often needed when the parent is at work but care can also be needed when the parent is at home during the day trying to sleep. In some families, some form of child care is needed 18 hours a day.

SUBSTITUTE SERVICES

Substitute forms of service incorporate the majority of time and financial resources spent in public child welfare. Although family-based service has played a major role in the changing public child welfare system, the residual focus of service still leads to many out-of-home placements.

Foster Care

Foster care has been a major intervention since the beginning of philanthropic endeavors to help children. Often these early endeavors involved the farming out of children from the city. Children abandoned or without parents were often placed on trains from cities and sent to farming areas to become laborers or adopted children of families in rural areas. Foster care took on a more formal aspect with the initiation of public child welfare services. Although out-of-home placement for most children was in institutions during the mid-1900s, realization of the need for children to have a single home environment began to emerge during the 1960s as the concept of childhood began to be acknowledged. The emergence of childhood as an important aspect of our society and its future led professionals to emphasize the use of better services for children. The growth of foster care as a method of out-of-home care became very popular, as it was seen as a better service for children. Although there have more recently been attempts to lower the number of children placed in foster care, there are still an estimated 500,000 children placed in foster care each year (Terpstra, 1992). These high numbers and the increasing focus on leaving a child in the foster care system led to many of the family-centered services now being utilized.

Although foster care initially focused on the care of the child in a stable home for a fee, foster care is now being reexamined as a more structured process by which foster families are carefully selected and trained in their responsibilities. Issues in the past regarding foster care families have strongly brought into question how a strengthening continuum toward independent family care can be achieved. Whether or not the children are able to be returned to their biological family, the foster family plays a major role in decreasing the harm done to children by their removal by establishing a nurturing independent family life in another way. Because of these issues, foster families are being selected more carefully in most states and are receiving training to enable them to aid the child placed with them. Additionally, training has focused on developing a cooperative relationship between the foster parent and the biological parent. The purpose of this cooperative relationship is to aid the child and biological family in maintaining contact and fostering success.

Reunification

The process involved in the reunification of children with their biological family following foster care is a careful process that begins at the same moment the children are removed from the family. If the family is aware from the beginning that the first goal is the return of the children to the home through work with the child welfare social worker, foster family, and the children themselves, then families are much more likely to become involved in the intervention and take an active role in bringing this situation about. According to Pecora, Whittaker, Maluccio, Barth, and colleagues (1992), there are several guiding principles to understand, including seeing the reentry into the family of origin as based on a continuum. This process encourages the biological family in a continuing involvement in the life of the child while in foster care. Secondly, from an ecological perspective, all family members must be involved in the reunification process, with an emphasis on the empowerment of all family members. Third, and finally, there needs to be an interaction and a planning toward this reunification by all those involved in the situation. Carlo (1991), in his study of out-of-home care, found that parental involvement led to a greater degree of family reunification. Bicknell-Hentges (1995) identified several stages in the re-unification process that deal with emotions: (1) defining the family, (2) fear and distrust, (3) idealism, (4) reality, (5) second phase of fear, and (6) return. The social worker, foster parents, family, child, and other systems affected by this process need to understand these stages and recognize the normalcy of them.

Independent Living

Independent living is a term utilized for situations in which adolescents who have been living in foster care are at an age and a stage where they can live on their own. Independent living has been used not only for foster children but also for many adolescents who, for whatever reason, are no longer able to live with their families and are given the opportunity to live on their own. Independent-living services began as a reaction to the results of foster children leaving their homes and going out on their own. Foster children tended to be more developmentally delayed than other adolescents their age, and many did not have the ability to manage on their own. Wood, Herring, and Hunt (1989) found that adolescents discharged from foster care were more likely to have behavioral and emotional problems and difficulty in assimilating into the culture. Many of these adolescents ended up on public welfare or homeless, as they did not have the skills to support themselves (Maluccio, 1990).

In 1989, the Independent Living Initiative was added to the Social Security Act. This initiative provided special services to those adolescents who had begun to live on their own. It specifically provided aid toward socialization, education, and counseling. Although the initiative began to insert funds into the programs for emancipated adolescents, many needs continue to be unaddressed. Needs for housing, medical care, and ongoing support remain limited.

Adoption

Adoption is another form of substitute care and is utilized in situations where children have lost their parents, been given up for adoption, or have become wards of the state because parental rights have been severed. There are approximately 100,000 children available for adoption in the United States each year through public and not-for-profit agencies, private resources, and foreign programs (Cohen, 1992; Pecora, Whittaker, Maluccio, Barth, et al., 1992; CWLA, 1988). Despite these numbers, the number of couples wanting to adopt far outweighs the children available for adoption. Healthy nonminority infants are in great demand, but few are available. The majority of children available for adoption consist of older, ethnic, and special needs children. These children arrive in the child welfare system and, due to their special needs, age, or ethnic/racial background, do not receive the same opportunities for adoption as healthy, White infants.

Many children who arrive in substitute care in the child welfare system are often not available for adoption due to the fact that their parents' rights have not terminated. The Adoption Assistance and Child Welfare Act of 1980 was a significant piece of legislation designed to promote both the prevention of placement of children out-of-home and the adoption of those children who had to be removed from the home and whose families did not follow through on plans to regain their custody. The purpose of permanency planning was to provide children in foster care the opportunity to have a plan for a permanent family placement within a certain time. As noted, permanency planning did initially have a positive effect, but because of rising numbers of children in need of care, there is difficulty in providing this service.

Residential, Community, and Group Care

Many different types of residential and community care have been designed for children and adolescents. Historically, community-based care in group settings tended more toward the use of institutional care during the early part of the 20th century. From the beginning of children being placed in workhouses and orphanages, institutional settings have generally been perceived as negative environmental placements for children. The use of orphanages has not been generally supported since the mid-1900s; however, during the late 1980s there was a movement to reinstate these facilities. The reasoning given focused on the numbers of drug-related births in terms of "crack" babies and the increasing need for out-of-home placement (Pecora, Whittaker, Maluccio, Barth, et al., 1992). The end result, however, was not a movement back in this direction because of the negative outcome results of institutional care for children.

The definition of residential or substitute group care has varied throughout the history of child welfare. Initially, out-of-home care placements in group settings consisted only of institutionalized settings and were more likely to be for the care of homeless or parentless children. Substitute and residential group care, however, has narrowed in its definition of the type of situation by which a child comes to be placed. Most homeless and parentless children are now placed in foster care homes or shelters for limited periods. However, children who have been identified by the state and/or their parents as having behavioral problems, often related to delinquency, substance abuse, or mental health, are the ones more likely to be placed within an institutional or group-home setting. In 1990, Gershenson estimated that 750,000 children would be admitted to juvenile facilities; 200,000 to child welfare residential situations; and 50,000 to psychiatric hospitals or treatment centers.

The following describe different types of residential care.

Group-Home Settings In order to more clearly differentiate between institutional and group home settings, an overview will be presented here. Unlike institutional placements, group-home settings are more limited in numbers of children in residence, generally have a behavioral and/or cognitive approach to therapeutic change, and rely heavily on peer-group influence. The use of smaller group homes or cottage-like settings for adolescents came about as a result of deinstitutionalization in the 1960s. This focus made clear how many individuals in state facilities were often forgotten by family and even the agencies that placed them there. The movement in the 1960s back to community or small-group care led to the establishment of therapeutic situations where the medical model of treatment was not the primary focus. In particular, children and adolescents were encouraged to work with their peers as well as in family therapy to bring about change in their lives. These smaller programs continue today and focus mainly upon psychiatric issues, substance abuse, and/or delinquency as the major criteria for placement. Generally, placements in even these smaller group settings take place as a last resort when outpatient intervention has not worked. Studies related to the placement of children in residential group settings support the continued involvement of the family during the placement and the community-based support following the placement (Curry, 1991; Fanshal, 1982; Whittaker, 1988). Residential placement for rehabilitation is best seen as a continuum, according to Pecora, Whittaker, Maluccio, Barth, and colleagues (1992), as it pertains to positive outcomes. This continuum focuses on the continuation of the child's relationship with the family and community during and following the placement.

Therapeutic Settings   Most residential and group-home settings incorporate a therapeutic approach to intervention with children and youths. Although most remaining training schools for delinquency claim to be rehabilitative, very few are. The therapeutic approach, as mentioned, includes the use of groups, one-on-one counseling, family work, and work within the community to support the child in school and in socialization.

Shelters   Shelters are generally utilized in emergency situations related to short-term care. These shelters can be for the care of children removed from a neglected or abusive home when a foster care placement has not been established, for runaway youth who do not have homes, and for pregnant adolescents awaiting the birth of their child.

State Facilities for Delinquents   The use of institutional care has become more limited to those situations of delinquency and crime. Although there is generally a hierarchal process involved in the types of facilities in which children are placed outside their family because of delinquency, many states have kept prisonlike facilities for youths. The hierarchal process involved for most delinquent adolescents today involves first a family-based approach in which the youth is left in the home and the family and youth are provided intensive services. The next approach is through community-based group homes where youths are given an opportunity to resolve their issues without being removed from their peers and finally, through state-run facilities and institutions when no other resources have been able to affect change. The decision to utilize large state-run facilities for children and adolescents is a very serious one. Because their development at this point is still in progress, the placement of young people within this type of setting tends to have a more negative effect than a positive one. A decision of this kind can be made by the court without input from family members or professionals working with the child.

Wraparound Services   Wraparound services is a strengths-based program. The term *wraparound* originated in North Carolina, where flexible funding was made available to respond to individualized needs of children and families (Katz-Leavy et al., 1992). One unique feature of wraparound is the "wrapping" of formal and/or informal services based on needs. Another is the concept of no rejection, especially not rejecting children who have multiple risks, such as maltreatment, emotional disturbance, health, and other issues.

Wraparound programs are community based, composed and operated by interdisciplinary teams, and focused on family strengths. Initially, wraparound was used in the area of mental health to provide and prevent placement into institutions. Wraparound is now used in many different arenas, including child welfare and schools.

ALTERNATIVE SERVICES AND PROGRAMS

Alternative services and programs within the context of child welfare involve more than techniques and methods; they are about a philosophy that envisions and creates possibilities beyond the current manifestations of the aforementioned services. The use of more macro services and programs that are preventive in nature and that create change in policies is most beneficial to the welfare of the child. The ability to not only envision these types of services but to also implement them is a skill in which social workers are trained and yet is often difficult to implement within the parameters of residual child welfare agencies. A front-line child welfare social worker can begin to create these types of changes through small, alternative steps in his or her work with families. This does not preclude major changes in policies to affect all families, but it does give front-line child welfare social workers an opportunity to make a difference.

We will now begin to look at some of these "out-of-the-box" services and programs that you may be able to create for the families and children with whom you work. It is important in examining these different ideas to understand that they do not need to fall only under the labels of supportive, supplementary, and substitute services. These services and programs can be referred to as *strengthening* because this term describes the strengthening continuum.

Strengthening Services and Programs

Strengthening services and programs are based on the premise that families and children are inherently strong in their abilities and desires to keep their family together; therefore, the services and programs described here will be ones based on that premise. They will be described related to specific needs of families and children rather than to the services provided. Some of the examples may seem like major endeavors; however, use your creative thinking to envision smaller steps to take in arriving at these goals.

Holistic Family Foster Care

Holistic family foster care is a term used to describe a foster care situation in which the entire family might receive care. An example of this would be a program in which foster families were trained in taking in not only the children but also the single mother who is having difficulty providing for and caring for her child or children. In many cases, these types of programs are focused more on young, single mothers with little knowledge or support in caring for their children. Foster families would provide space for the mother and children in terms of providing the family with a shelter and training skills to get started on their own. The foster parents would provide information on parenting skills, aid the mother in learning to care for her children, and provide support and positive reinforcement to the mother in her learning and caring for her family.

Another form of family-like foster care is called *foster care communities*. These communities are neighborhoods or streets where the homes have been purchased by the child welfare agency and are co-owned by the foster parents. This community is linked by a community center specifically focused on the needs of these families and children. The unit operates as a neighborhood network and serves as mutual aid support for the families.

School-Based Agencies

For the most part, schools have not seen themselves as providers of social services; however, schools are the mainstay of the interaction between society, the family, and the child. Programs such as daycare have finally begun to be accepted as part of the public school service to the community. Beyond this is a need to recognize the ability of schools to be providers of a variety of programs. The term *providers* in this sense does not refer to utilizing funding or resources of human capital from the schools but refers to allowing the location of different agencies, programs, and services on the grounds in order to facilitate the needs of families and children. This type of shift to a multifaceted community school provides all families and children with the opportunity not only to obtain services they need but also to work together to bring about focus on families in our society.

Wolf (1991) has indicated that the prevention of emotional and physical abuse of children would be best served through the implementation of general awareness of family roles and responsibilities at an early age. He advocates for educating children at both the elementary and secondary level about their needs and the role and responsibility society and the family have to provide for these needs. The social worker's part in this goal might be the presentation of these issues and the organizing of parents within a school district around issues in their community.

Mediation Programs

While most individuals continue to think of mediation as part of business or legal negotiations, more and more social workers are finding that the skills in mediation can help them immensely in the child welfare field. Kassebaum and Chandler (1992) have noted that negotiation skills in child welfare situations appeared to be the best practical solution in child abuse cases. Both social workers and family members found that a negotiation approach to dealing with different factors in protective cases that brought together the concerned parties had a positive effect for outcome in the cases.

A proposed use of mediation in the child welfare system appears especially appropriate for adolescents, according to Godman (1998). Considering the issues adolescents face when they attempt to remain independent within the child welfare system, the use of mediation seems to give back some of that sense of independence and at the same time provide a safety net for the adolescents. Additionally, because mediation includes learning skills such as listening, communicating, problem solving, and conflict resolution, these skills can be invaluable in the development of the adolescent (Godman, 1998). There are examples of programs that have implemented this mediation process for adolescents, among which Teen Mediation Program in Vancouver is one of the more well known for its work in resolving issues of teens and their families (Godman, 1998).

Outdoor Camp Programs

Outdoor camp programs have provided services to children and their families for many years. Camps for children began during the mid-1900s as a means for children and their families to receive recreational activity either together or separately. Since the 1960s, an increasing number of camps focus more on the therapeutic needs of the child. The philosophy behind most therapeutic camps in the 1990s was on the development of the strengths and self-esteem of the child, as well as requiring the child to learn to work with others in dealing with life on a day-to-day basis. Outward Bound is an example of such a program. Designed to aid adolescents who have behavioral difficulties, this program develops their strengths and skills to create a positive environment where they survive and work with others in a wilderness setting. Most programs such as this are time limited and carefully planned for the individual needs of each child.

Mutual Aid Groups, Self-Help Training, and Advocacy Groups

The utilization of self-help groups has long served as a means for empowering individuals to care for themselves and make their own decisions. Groups such as Alcoholics Anonymous (AA), Parents Anonymous, and single-parent organizations have had a significant impact on many families served by the child welfare agencies. Additionally, advocacy groups that focus on the development of consumer leadership have had an enormous impact on changing policies in society as they affect particular groups. Examples of this include the gay and lesbian coalitions, the Gray Panthers, and welfare rights groups. An example of a group that has benefited children is the Community Action Project for Children (CAPC) (Cook, 1998). This organization of individuals who had received child welfare services came together to produce a community-based coalition of parents and professionals concerned with the well-being of children. Many of the activities of this group have focused on creating a center where young children can receive an early, successful start through socialization activities, education, recreation, a toy-lending library, child care, support groups, parent education groups, and outreach activities. The center developed in partial response to the stigma attached to child welfare agency centers and the need of the community to provide their own neutral facility where families can be seen from a strengths perspective rather than from a problematic perspective. This group is what is known as a mutual aid support group. They are able to support one another and at the same time take actions to better their own families and communities.

Family-Centered Programs

Although we will discuss at some length the family-centered and family preservation programs now being instituted in the United States, it seems important to identify some suggestions for the expansion of these programs on a wider-based scale. Wells and Tracy (1996) suggest that an expansion of services from a family-based perspective in child welfare would provide a type of tertiary prevention for children and families. This expansion would not be limited to short-term care but would involve a long-term plan that would provide an elaborate assessment of the needs of families and children and then the procedures needed to carry out these services. This would require the involvement of many professionals, such as physicians, psychologists, addiction counselors, and educators, as well as social workers. This type of family-centered care would refocus the policies in our society back onto the needs of families and children and provide recognition of the preventive types of services that are needed (Nelson, 1995).

Child Advocacy Programs

Advocacy for children's rights in this country has existed since the early 1900s; however, the real emphasis began in the 1960s. Advocacy in child welfare systems is a major part of bridging the gap between preventive and residual intervention. Litzelfelner and Petr (1997) note that the special program in Seattle begun in 1977 called court-appointed special advocates (CASAs) has served as a model for development throughout the United States. Between 1990 and 1994, the program grew by 78 percent. This program provides trained volunteers sponsored by the court system to advocate for the best interests of the child in child welfare situations. The training of these volunteer child advocates has not included social workers to any great degree. Litzelfelner and Petr argue for more involvement on the part of social work in providing technical assistance and training for these volunteers in order to help them understand the profession's strengths-based form of practice.

Homeless Family Shelters

A type of care that has developed in many cities relates to homeless families and the development of shelters that serve the needs of all family members. These shelters prevent the separation of parents and children and at the same time aid the family in developing resources for themselves. Phillips, DeChillo, Kronenfeld, and Middleton-Jeter (1998) found that the use of shelters for homeless families led to many positive changes in the short term. An extension of this idea has been the development of homeless family apartments that serve the needs of a family for longer periods, with employment counseling and child welfare services.

SUMMARY

This chapter has provided an overview of the present service continuum in the child welfare field in terms of residual services. A brief review of these formal and informal services has been examined in light of the current issues and trends with which child welfare social workers must deal. The final section of this chapter presented some examples of "out-of-the-box" services and programs in which you, as a child welfare social worker, can create innovative ways to bridge prevention with intervention. These services can be developed and applied within the present child welfare system based on a strengths perspective.

Questions for Discussion

1. The child welfare continuum is currently based on services. Discuss the three areas of services and give examples.
2. How can mutual aid groups be utilized in the formal child welfare field?
3. Discuss your view of interracial adoption.
4. Describe why training for foster parents is important for biological parents.
5. Using an adolescent runaway case example, describe how wraparound services might be applied to assist this adolescent.
6. Choose an alternative service program described in the chapter and discuss the steps needed to operationalize this program in your local community.

Policy and Research in Child Welfare

CHAPTER 3

INTRODUCTION

This chapter provides relevant policy and research information about the major child welfare programs. The major policies are outlined, beginning with the Child and Family Services Review (CFSR), then the major federal child welfare policies, followed by a summary of how states fared in the review process. Policies related to specific child welfare services are presented with evaluation and research studies of these services. These programs include child protective services; out-of-home care covering foster family care, congregate or group care, treatment foster care, residential group care, and residential treatment care; adoption, services to unmarried parents, family preservation, and family support. Because research shows strengths and deficits related to policy and practice, the information provides directions for child welfare agencies, their partner agencies, staff, advocates, and policy makers about how to improve services to vulnerable families and children.

FEDERAL POLICY: CHILD AND FAMILY SERVICES REVIEWS

The federal government established requirements for states to follow in child welfare programs in Titles IV-B and IV-E of the Social Security Act. In previous years, federal officials reviewed state child welfare agency activities and the

51

states' compliance with procedural requirements. States that were out of compliance were generally sanctioned and had to return federal dollars received for out-of-compliance programs.

As a result of the Adoption and Safe Families Act (ASFA), the federal government developed and implemented a new process for reviewing states' compliance with federal requirements. The Child and Family Services Review (CFSR) is the review system mandated by the federal government as a comprehensive examination intended to assist states in improving their child welfare programs. There are three stages in the CFSR: Similar to accreditation processes, states first complete thorough self-assessments of their child welfare systems. In the second stage, representatives of the Children's Bureau visit states and conduct extensive on-site reviews. In addition to the state child welfare office, the federal representatives also visit three other sites in each state. For the third stage, the state agency develops a corrective action plan to deal with deficits identified in the review; the plan is called the Program Improvement Plan (PIP).

All states, Puerto Rico, and the District of Columbia had completed the first two stages of the review by 2004, and all were working on their PIPs. In the reviews, the states were measured against activities related to safety, permanency, and well-being outcomes. States are required to reach certain standards related to each of the outcomes. Two outcomes related to safety include having children protected from abuse and neglect and having children maintained in a safe home environment. The outcomes related to permanency require that children have stability in their living environment and have continued family relationships. There are three well-being outcomes: (1) Children's needs are met by families; (2) educational needs of children are met; and (3) children's physical and mental health needs are met.

The CFSR also measures systemic factors related to the state's management information system, their case review system, training of child welfare staff and resource parents, the quality assurance system, continuum of services, relationship to the community, and licensing functions. In order to receive substantial conformity on the CFSR, states must achieve a rating of "substantially achieved" on 90 percent of the cases reviewed.

By 2004, no state had achieved substantial conformity with all outcomes. The Children's Bureau summarized major problems states had in reaching satisfactory compliance. Related to the safety outcomes, states did not have risk and safety assessments that assessed families in a comprehensive way; states were not able to provide adequate levels of services to children in their homes; and states were not able to determine if, over time, harm to children had been reduced in families.

In efforts to comply with permanency options, states were not able to offer the necessary number of appropriate placement options, and some states were not able to implement concurrent planning. Meeting the compliance standards for well-being has been problematic for many states. Some of the issues were related to insufficient face-to-face contact with family members, foster parents, and relative caretakers. Agencies were also out of compliance because of problems over which they have little or no control, such as insufficient mental health services and insufficient numbers of available doctors and dentists.

Because the CFSRs reflect federal policy mandates, states must be committed to dealing with deficits in the plans they have developed and are implementing. The Children's Bureau continues to assess states' programs against the specified outcomes and provides technical assistance to assist them in their efforts.

RESEARCH STUDIES IN CHILD PROTECTIVE SERVICES

The results of child abuse and neglect in this country are devastating to the families and children involved. In addition to the impacts on the victims, the costs to this country are extensive. Prevent Child Abuse America (2001) calculated the direct and indirect costs of child abuse and neglect in this country. The costs associated with the victims, including hospitalizations, mental health care, law enforcement, and the judicial system, along with the costs of child welfare agencies are approximately $24 billion each year. Adding the indirect costs of special education, mental and health care, juvenile delinquency, and lost productivity brings the approximated costs to $70 billion each year. It is therefore critical that research studies identify programs that can prevent and reduce maltreatment and offer effective services to victims.

Child Abuse and Neglect: Previous Studies

Previous studies have attempted to obtain information about what features in CPS systems are necessary to produce effective interventions and the conditions under which these features produce positive outcomes. Previous studies of CPS interventions were not conclusive. Cohn (1979) studied 11 child abuse and neglect demonstration programs over a 40-month period. The intent of the study was to determine what factors produced positive results. Over 1,700 parents were studied, representing families similar to those reported for maltreatment across the country. The results were that families who were involved in treatment programs over six months fared better. Other factors that influenced positive results included same-day contact following the maltreatment report, contact with the referral source, use of multidisciplinary teams, continuous use of expert consultants, weekly contact with families, and follow-up upon completion of treatment.

Cohn and Daro (1987) reported on four major multiyear evaluation studies that were funded to determine the effectiveness of different treatment programs. The studies used a variety of methodological techniques with sufficient similarities to allow for comparisons. The families who were involved represented a broad spectrum, and there was wide variation in the types of maltreatment. Both qualitative and quantitative approaches were used to gather data to assess the most effective organizational and staffing patterns used in working with maltreatment families, to determine the relative costs of providing various services to families, to determine the critical elements of well-functioning community system responses to maltreatment, and to assess what attributes were involved in quality case management.

These researchers found that treatment efforts in general were not very successful. The child abuse and neglect continued despite early and sometimes costly interventions. The treatment programs were relatively ineffective in reducing child maltreatment and in reducing the likelihood of future maltreatment. One-third of the parents maltreated their children while in treatment, and one-half were evaluated by staff as likely to maltreat their children in the future.

Recent Studies

Unfortunately, many CPS agencies continue to be "incident driven," meaning the focus of the investigation into the family situation is based only on the incident reported to officials, not on other factors affecting safety. Information from many studies suggests that CPS agencies serve large numbers of children over and over again. In a New Jersey study (Wolock, Sherman, Feldman, & Metzer, 1998), the two outcomes, repeated reports and substantiated rates, were studied over a period of five years. The average family in this study had been reported to CPS agencies at least four times in the five-year period and had highly vulnerable environmental and emotional stressors. Half of the families were ethnically diverse; the majority were single parents; about one-third were receiving welfare; and several had serious emotional problems.

DePanfilis and Zuravin (1998) reviewed 45 studies of recidivism in CPS agencies. They found repeated reports for children who had been assessed at moderate or high risk of maltreatment. These findings were consistent with other studies that suggested recurrence of maltreatment was more likely with multiple forms of maltreatment, younger children, parents with emotional problems, and the presence of substance abuse.

Inkelas and Halfron (1997) found that prior protective service openings were found in nearly 50 percent of the cases in 1993. They also found that even though the maltreatment had been substantiated for the majority of children, the cases were closed after the intake process, and few services and referrals were made available to these children and families. They concluded that assessments of risk were inadequate, services were not effective, CPS agencies were unable to track the status of children, and there were repeated case openings and closings. The result was that vulnerable children lived in unsafe environments.

National Study of CPS

The Administration of Children, Youth, and Families (ACYF) commissioned a study of child protective services (U.S. DHHS, 2003). The national study dealt with three areas: state CPS policies, a description of how policies are implemented at the local level, and new innovations and improvements in CPS. The three study documents are comprehensive and provide insight into CPS systems in the United States.

Evaluation of Policies

The policy review summarized policies related to the core functions in the front end of CPS, including screening, intake, investigation, and assessment, including alternative responses. States have requirements for mandated reporters, or those individuals who must report maltreatment. It is generally felt that professionals who report maltreatment, such as law enforcement, medical officials, and school personnel, are fairly accurate in their reports, while nonprofessionals, such as neighbors or anonymous reporters, are not. Professionals reporting maltreatment generally provide more specific and comprehensive information about the situations. When accurate information is provided to CPS agencies, their investigative resources can be used more efficiently. The national study found that most states required professionals to report; two-thirds accepted anonymous reports and one-third did not.

The purpose of CPS investigations has evolved over the years. Some states are less focused on whether or not a report is substantiated and more focused on child safety. Over half of the states stated the purpose of an investigation was to determine if maltreatment had occurred, and 20 states said the purpose was to evaluate the safety of children. Once agencies began investigations and collected information, there were variations in the level of evidence needed to legally become involved with the family. Over half of the states reported the standard as preponderance of evidence, which is similar to the level required in criminal procedures, while less than 20 states had lower standards, including reasonable evidence or probable cause. The disposition of cases also varied; most states had two disposition categories, which were "substantiated/not substantiated" or "founded/not founded," but a few states had three or more disposition categories.

The four types of maltreatment reported by DHHS included neglect, physical abuse, sexual abuse, and emotional maltreatment. Even though these four were considered the core types of maltreatment, 25 states had added abandonment; 27 included medical neglect; and other states had added exposure to domestic violence and/or substance abuse. Expanding the core types of maltreatment requires thoughtful consideration because when states expand their CPS responsibilities, they must also expand their resource levels to deal with the expansions.

CPS agencies have timelines governing the response time. The national study indicated that most states required immediate response or responses within 24 hours to reports of high-risk situations. There was variation in the response time to situations of low-priority, including seven days, two to four weeks, and beyond. Although the intent of response time requirements was to offer better protection of children, the ability of staff to respond is often based on the size of their caseloads. When caseloads were extremely high, very tight timelines often resulted in cursory investigations and less protection for children.

The due process accorded to individuals alleged to have committed the maltreatment also varied. Almost all states had central registries, which are lists of perpetrators, and the registries are accessed for background employment checks and for licensing child-care and other facilities. Twenty-three states had regulations that restrict names on central registries to substantiated or founded reports; only 21 states notify the perpetrator when his/her name is entered on the registry.

Over half of the states had policies for alternative or differentiated response wherein assessments were conducted when maltreatment reports were not serious but families may have required services.

Implementation at the Local Level

Once the policies are articulated, the implementation is critical. From a nationally representative sample, the researchers concluded that almost all of the local agencies studied screened reports and conducted investigations. Many also provided alternative responses, which offer flexibility and individualize responses to reports. Alternative responses are conducted to determine the safety of the child rather than to determine if the maltreatment report is substantiated or not.

Screening is generally a function that determines if the report is within the statutory definition of child abuse and neglect. If a report is screened in, an investigation or an assessment is conducted. The study determined that local agencies have responsibility for screening and investigating reports.

National guidelines suggest that CPS staff have social work or related degrees. The study revealed that more than half of CPS staff performed only the specialized functions related to child protection; others performed other child welfare tasks as well. The study did not define specialization in terms of educational or experience levels. Based on national standards, the caseloads reported by local agencies were excessive, with an average of 64 referrals per month completed by screening/intake staff, while investigative staff conducted 43 investigations a month. The number of assessments completed averaged 16.

Many states had centralized hotlines to screen reports. However, most local agencies also screened reports reported directly to them. The researchers reported that not all local agencies were able to accept non-English-speaking reporters; this represented a significant problem given the high numbers of families representing diverse cultures speaking Spanish and other languages in various parts of the country.

Because screening activity determined if the report was accepted, much of the work was administrative; it was not necessary to make personal contact with the child, family, or neighbors. Screening activities generally included searching records for previous reports. However, once a report was screened in, the study indicated that an investigation or an assessment was conducted, and the families, children, neighbors, and other individuals were interviewed in person.

In the past, state and local CPS agencies have spent considerable time and money developing specific risk and safety assessment protocols. This study, however, indicated that only a few agencies used any formal assessment instruments during the investigation or assessment process. Although the staff used general guidelines for investigation or assessment, they did not utilize specific protocols.

Most CPS agencies had access to other professionals, including medical, mental health, substance abuse, and other officials. The study also indicated that using professionals occasionally caused delays for CPS practitioners when the professionals did not respond in a timely fashion. Law enforcement was one of the primary agencies that CPS worked with closely and that often shared the investigatory response with CPS agencies.

Innovations and Change Efforts in CPS

The national study indicated many changes taking place in this country. Many agencies have implemented a family-centered approach that changed the way CPS agencies viewed and approached families. A family-centered approach strengthens the capacity of families to function; engages families in designing all aspects of CPS involvement; and links families with more comprehensive, diverse, and community-based networks of supports and services. Instead of investigations, family assessments were conducted in situations where safety did not appear to be compromised.

Thirteen states were identified as having community-based collaboratives. The community programs varied; some involved co-location of CPS staff with other programs; in some situations, referrals were made to other agencies, such as substance abuse or domestic violence agencies, for assessment. In some situations, informal entities such as churches participated in providing oversight and services to vulnerable families. Another arrangement involved contracting with law enforcement to conduct investigations. At least one county in Florida has contracted with law enforcement to assume CPS responsibilities.

The Missouri Model: Results of Alternative Responses

Missouri implemented a multiple-track or differential response several years ago, and the Institute of Applied Research (1995) provided a comprehensive evaluation. Even though other states had implemented alternative responses, Missouri conducted an extensive evaluation and demonstrated positive outcomes for the families, children, and the agency. The Family Assessment and Response Demonstration provided assessments in response to some reports of child abuse and neglect. Hotline reports were screened for either an investigation or family assessment, depending on the severity of the situation. There was sufficient flexibility in the process that if family situations changed, the families could be switched either to an investigative or to an assessment response, if appropriate.

Baseline information on numbers of reports, responses to reports, identification of safety issues, and many other factors was gathered prior to and after implementation of the initiative. There were pilot and control counties involved in the study. Major findings were that safety of children was maintained during the demonstration. In fact, safety of children was improved in certain types of maltreatment, including neglect, lack of supervision, and less severe cases of physical and verbal abuse. Safety of children was achieved sooner in the pilot areas. In the end, there were fewer reports to the hotline, indicating that families were served prior to reaching crises. Additionally, assistance was provided to families who had problems meeting their basic needs, to families whose physical abuse was not severe, and in situations with parent–child conflict. Staff in CPS and other agencies were asked how they felt about the multiple-response initiative. All of the responses were positive. Likewise, the families involved were contacted, and their response was also positive.

FOSTER CARE

Foster care has frequently been the focus of federal and state policy makers. Much of the legislation has been directed at reducing the numbers of children placed in foster care, reducing the time spent in foster care, and moving children into permanency sooner. The Child Welfare Act of 1980, the Family Preservation and Support Act, and the passage of other laws provided direction to child welfare agencies to prevent placements, reduce time in placements, and find alternative permanent homes for children who could not return to their biological families. Because of administrative problems and complex family issues, child welfare agencies were not able to deal with the problems. In 1997, Congress passed the Adoption and Safe Families Act (ASFA) to provide assurances that states were providing to families and children the outcomes of safety, permanency, and well-being.

One benefit of the ASFA legislation was its responsiveness to research outcomes that supported the need to develop permanency for children as quickly as possible. However, even though policies were well intended and led to better outcomes for foster children, recent studies have demonstrated the need for additional action in a number of areas. Even though federal and state policies required states to take speedy action to achieve permanency, there are not sufficient resources to address many physical and mental health issues of children while they are in care.

Foster care children have generally arrived there because of maltreatment in their biological homes and the inability of their caregivers to protect them. Many studies indicated that children in foster care because of maltreatment are behind other children academically; they have more developmental delays and psychological problems (Zetlin, Weinberg, & Kimm, 2003). Whatever types of maltreatment foster children experience prior to placement, these children have been traumatized, and this impacts their capacity to do well in school. Child welfare agencies must be diligent in dealing with the issues as soon as the children enter placements, so the effects are not cumulative. If a child needs remedial work in school, the child should receive it as soon as possible.

If a child experiences multiple placements, the child is often transferred from one school to another, further compounding the gap in educational achievement and in attendance when compared to children not in care. Altshuler (2000) established that success in school helps stabilize foster care placement but that when children cannot adjust at school and in the home, they often experience breakdowns in placements in homes and in schools. A study conducted by Zetlin and colleagues (2003) found that neither child welfare agencies nor schools attended to the educational challenges of foster children. They pointed out the challenges for child welfare staff of dealing with the educational deficits of foster children in addition to all their other responsibilities. However, the authors also pointed out that policies and practice in child welfare agencies must include efforts to secure positive educational outcomes so that children can become self-sufficient as adults.

Reunification

Research has shown children may be at continued risk when they have been reunified with their parents; therefore, continued services may be needed. One study showed that some children reunified with their families were still at risk because domestic violence continued (Litrownik, Newton, Mitchell, & Richardson, 2003).

A study of over 200 youths in the Midwest looked at educational needs and the experiences of youths in foster care who were participating in independent-living classes. The study examined a number of youth factors, including their educational experiences, suspensions, repeated grades, placement history (present and past), maltreatment history, and behavioral issues such as alcohol and drug use. Many of these youths had experienced failed classes, suspensions, trouble with peers, and other issues. The study authors (McMillen, Auslander, Elze, White, & Thompson, 2003) identified a number of educational and remedial services necessary for these youths to succeed. An innovation they suggested is for child welfare agencies to have informed educational advocates that assist educationally troubled youth, even if placements change. These advocates hired by the child welfare agencies would have expertise in foster care and educational issues and thereby be advocates for the youths and provide them with educational stability.

Exiting Foster Care

Studies on youths who exit foster care are particularly troublesome. Annually, about 20,000 children exit foster care to live independently. Because of poor outcomes for these exiting youths, Reilly (2003) recommended that agencies reduce the number of placements and provide educational opportunities, even beyond high school. Youths who have had multiple placements and less education have much more difficulty when they exit foster care (Freundlich & Avery, 2005).

Pecora and colleagues (2005) have published several documents about the Northwest Foster Care Alumni Study. The study examined two foster care models, the public agency model and the Casey Family Program. The Casey Family Program had offices in a number of states, and their foster care model included one in which most staff were MSWs with caseloads of 16 situations, staff and foster parent turnover was very low, and ancillary services were provided when needed. Mental and physical health, educational, and other issues were dealt with on a timely basis. The intent of the Casey program was to provide long-term care to youths whose plans did not include reunification or adoption (Pecora et al., 2005).

The Northwest Foster Care Alumni Study looked at outcomes of over 650 alumni between the ages of 20 and 33 who had been in foster care as children. These alumni fared fairly well in terms of education, as over four out of five had completed high school, which is much better than that found in other studies of such educational achievements. However, many of the alumni were found to be in precarious economic conditions, and the employment rate was lower than the general population.

The data related to mental health issues was troubling. More than half of the alumni had at least one mental health problem, such as depression, social phobia, panic syndrome, posttraumatic stress disorder (PTSD), or drug dependence. The study did not differentiate between alumni from Casey Family Programs and state agencies, so it is not possible to determine the extent to which services offered by the Casey Family Programs influenced the outcomes. What is known, however, is that post–high school educational programs are needed to assure employment capacity, and mental health issues must be dealt with early on in placement.

The recommendations made by these experts included dealing with mental health issues that may impede educational pursuits; minimizing placement changes; providing concrete resources, such as money, household items, driver's licenses, and other items; and providing opportunities for postsecondary education (Pecora et al., 2005).

Conclusions about Foster Care

Approximately 500,000 children are in foster care, and this number is likely to increase. An expanded definition of reunification has been proposed by Pecora, Whittaker, Maluccio, and Barth (2000) because they believe the definition in the ASFA is very limiting. ASFA requires that parental termination take place if children are not reunified with parents within a prescribed period of time. These child welfare experts propose a new definition in which services and supports would be provided to all parties: the children, biological parents, and foster parents. The intent is to provide supports so that children and their families can achieve their "optimal level of connection." This would include other levels of connection with families besides full reunification because some families are not able to be full-time parents. This alternative proposal maintains the relationship between children and their parents, perhaps even after termination of parental rights. This is not unlike open adoption, where parents may maintain some contact with children. This alternative would continue the strengths-based perspective because it is based on the individual assessments and needs of children and families.

Group/Treatment Foster Care, Residential Group Care, and Residential Treatment Centers

In the United States, about one-fifth of all children in care are in congregate/group care or residential treatment (U.S. DHHS, 2004b). Group care facilities have traditionally been placements for adolescents who were considered inappropriate for foster family care. Group care is different from residential group care, which offers more structured environments than group care and provides more intense mental health services.

A recent study of group care in New York City typifies many facets about group care in general. In a qualitative study of group care, Freundlich and Avery (2005) meticulously implemented a study of youths in congregate care. The researchers sought to identify what factors were needed to ensure permanence for youths in congregate care. Data from their study indicated that congregate care in New York City was not supporting permanency for the youths in care and that the youths were not involved in their own planning activities. A number of factors inhibited the transition of the youths from congregate care into independent living. Among other things, their study confirmed that youths who transition to independent living must have a committed adult who can advocate for them. If an adult is not available, the chances of achieving self-sufficiency and successfully transitioning into adulthood are limited.

The experiences of youth congregate care are very different from the experiences of children in foster or kin care. Many of these congregate facilities are located geographically far from their families, so maintaining family contact is difficult. In spite of the passage of ASFA, the permanent plan for many of the youths in congregate care is permanent foster care (Ansell & Kessler, 2003). ASFA does not recognize long-term foster care as a permanency goal.

The data from the study also indicated that even though some independent-living services were offered to the youths in congregate care, these services were not identified in research as being effective. The authors concluded that many caseworkers were confused about the philosophy of permanency for this population and that neither the caregivers nor the caseworkers were involved in permanency activities with the youths. They recommended that foster and adoptive parents be located as alternatives for these youths and that permanency, more broadly defined, needs to be the goal for youths in any and all placements.

Therapeutic foster care, residential group care, and residential treatment are placement resources intended for children with more serious emotional disturbances. Traditionally, younger children with special needs have been placed in therapeutic foster care and older children have been generally placed in group and residential treatment facilities. Curtis, Alexander, and Lunghofer (2001) provided clear definitions for these programs and stated that all three programs—therapeutic foster care, residential group care, and residential treatment programs—should offer specialized mental health services to children. Treatment foster homes have been generally licensed by child welfare agencies and intended to be family-based alternatives to more restrictive care. The foster parents in these homes are highly trained professionals who generally care for small numbers of children, have intense agency support available to them, and receive much higher rates of payments than regular foster homes.

In this country, two well-known models of residential group care are the Teaching Family Model and Project Re-Ed (Phillips, Fixen, & Wolf, 1973). Both of these programs are highly structured, with well-trained house parents or caregivers who provide academic enrichment and other programs. Even though these programs were established in several locations in the United States, there is little, if any, credible research or evaluations on their impact.

Boys Town is a well-known program that has developed a system of care intended to be more responsive to the needs of children. The Boys Town Residential Treatment Center, a psychoeducational model, was designed with a comprehensive assessment and services approach that includes working with families during and after placement. In this program, youths can also move from more to less restrictive settings. The preliminary outcomes of youths who were studied indicated multiple prior placements and serious emotional problems. Using a multitude of scales, the preliminary evaluation revealed that over three-fourths of the youths had improved outcomes at the time of discharge (Larzelere et al., 2001).

Residential group care facilities are community-based group homes offering structured environments for children with emotional and behavioral disturbances. Youths who are appropriate for these facilities generally cannot tolerate the intimacy found in therapeutic foster care, often because they have significant problems with their own families. Residential treatment centers (RTCs) are generally large facilities for the treatment of children with emotional and behavioral disturbances. RTCs represent the second most restrictive living environments for children and youths. Only inpatient psychiatric units are considered more restrictive than RTCs.

There are no specific diagnostic tools or guidelines for determining when or if children should be placed in residential care facilities. A study in Colorado found that most residential treatment centers offered the same services to all children (Libby, Coen, Price, Silverman, & Orton, 2005). Instead of individualized treatment services, the children largely received the same kind of treatment in the same doses. Because of this study and others, many are questioning the high costs and effectiveness of residential treatment. Much of the research that has been conducted are single studies in which pre- and posttests of children's behavior are compared rather than experimental design studies with treatment and control groups.

More research is needed on the treatment programs discussed in this section, particularly experimental research that has treatment and control groups. More information is needed about what factors lead to positive, sustainable, and long-term outcomes. Information now available suggests that long-term outcomes are related to the environment into which the youths are placed and the extent to which the youths have continued contact with their biological families after leaving care. While data recognizes the positive effects of connecting and working with biological families during and after residential treatment, the data also now suggest that any gains made in residential treatment may be lost or diminished depending on what happens after discharge. Additionally, information on cost-effectiveness is needed.

The children who enter these facilities are a subpopulation of the 500,000 children in out-of-home placement. All of these placements are therefore governed by the same federal and state policies for all children in out-of-home care for whom child welfare agencies are responsible. This is problematic because the directives of ASFA are not sensitive to this subpopulation of children and youths. It is particularly difficult to conform to federal permanency outcomes because these children/youths have generally been in multiple foster homes and have significant levels of emotional and behavioral disturbance that preclude placement into less restrictive environments. Additionally, many of the families are not functioning well and should not be considered as resources. Fanshel and Shinn (1978) have estimated that at least one-third of the children in foster care are so emotionally or behaviorally disturbed that permanency will not be an option for them.

Not only are permanency options limited but also ASFA's timeline is problematic. In one study of a residential treatment center (Baker, Wulczyn, & Dale, 2005), children stayed 1.72 years on average. The study revealed that only about 45 percent were reunified with parents, 40 percent were sent to other facilities, and 14 percent had run away. Therefore, the data suggested that the time frames for permanence need to be extended for these populations.

ADOPTION

Federal policy has changed the face of adoption in this country. The Adoption Assistance and Child Welfare Act of 1980 provided for adoption assistance payments for special needs children. States were also provided with bonuses for increasing the numbers of adoptive placements. The subsequent passage of ASFA significantly increased the number of adoptions. However, another effect of ASFA was that the number of older children in foster care placement freed for adoption has also increased. The Adoption Promotion Act was passed in 2003 as a result. This law provides additional funds and incentives for the adoptive placement of children age 9 and older.

Child welfare agencies responded positively to ASFA and have been successful in their efforts to place children. About three-fourths of the placements have been with relatives or foster parents (Green, 2003). However, more adoptive parents are needed to respond to the increasing numbers of children becoming available for adoption each year.

In addition to the efforts of child welfare agencies, DHHS, the Freddie Mac Foundation, the Dave Thomas Foundation, and other programs have produced significant results in the adoption arena. DHHS initiated the AdoptUSKids program. This program has a national website of children available for adoption. Wednesday's Child, a well-known recruitment activity was established by the Freddie Mac Foundation. This effort presents adoption segments on TV in cities throughout the United States on a regular basis. A study showed that waiting periods were briefer for Wednesday's Child youths than for children not featured on the program. There has also been an increase in the number of available adoptive parents through this effort.

Adoption Disruption

With the growing numbers of adoptive placements, there is concern about adoption disruption. The National Adoption Information Clearinghouse (NAIC, 2004) presented a number of statistics on disruption (Barth, Gibbs, & Siebenaler, 2001; Berry & Barth, 1988). There is a 10 to 16 percent disruption in adoptive placements of children over the age of 3; an Illinois longitudinal study showed a 12 percent disruption rate; and older children (ages 12 to 17 years) disrupt at a higher rate of 24 to 25 percent.

The reasons for disruption were attributed to child, family, and agency factors (NAIC, 2003). Behaviors of children that tended to lead to disruption included sexual acting out, aggression, stealing, and suicide attempts. Data on family factors showed that single parents fared better with children with emotional or behavioral disturbances. Attachment-disordered children achieved more stability in single-parent homes or in situations where there was no competition with other children for parental attention. Mothers over the age of 40 also offered more stability (Barth & Berry, 1988). Kinship care also offered adoption stability.

Service providers also influenced disruption. Factors that were negative influences include multiple caseworker involvement with adoptive families, lack of information provided to families, and insufficient adoption subsidies and services.

Improvements can be made at several levels. The families of special needs children must be able to access services from several sources, including the medical community, schools, mental and behavioral health programs, and agencies providing financial resources. Other supports, such as counseling, support groups, and respite services, are needed. Child welfare agencies should collaborate with formal and informal entities to provide comprehensive resources for the families who need additional services.

Cowan (2004) recommended that Congress deal with issues related to the Interstate Compact on the Placement of Children (ICPC) and the Interstate Compact on Adoption and Medical Assistance (ICAMA). The ICPC has regulations to protect and facilitate placement of children across state boundaries, and the ICAMA deals with the protection of children receiving adoption assistance who are placed with adoptive parents in other states. Not all states are members of the organizations and abide by the standards, producing inconsistencies in how states fulfill their responsibilities. Congress should pass legislation that results in consistency across all states.

Services to Unmarried Parents

Providing services to unmarried parents is critical because most unwed parents are teenagers. The children of these parents are at risk for child abuse, neglect, and other environmental risks. Data also showed that these issues are intergenerational and therefore required comprehensive approaches to deal with them.

The challenges faced by teenage parents are profound. In order to pave the road to self-sufficiency, these parents must continue their education. Affordable, quality child care becomes an issue. To deter the risk of these girls having additional pregnancies, family planning is critical. It would indeed be useful to provide incentives for fewer pregnancies, not incentives for additional babies. The children of these teenage parents had minimal or no prenatal care, their birth rates were lower, and their percentages of having other physical problems were higher (Maynard & Rangarajan, 1994). Regular and routine medical care is not only preferred for these children but is a necessity for life. Parenting infants is at times frustrating for most parents. For parents with limited knowledge of appropriate developmental expectations, parenthood becomes an awesome task. Parenting programs must be offered for the parents and for the children. Comprehensive and coordinated programming must be established for these parents, and it must be provided as soon as possible.

Family Support Programs

In 1993, Congress amended Title IV-B and created Family Preservation and Support Services; thus, funds were made available for both family preservation and family support programs. These two programs have different foci and different target populations. Family preservation programs are generally aimed at vulnerable families and children at risk; the children are often at imminent risk of placement. On the other hand, family support services are community-based programs for all families or for those needing specific services, such as respite care, developmental screening, parent training, and so on. Funds from the Family Preservation and Support Services amendment were appropriated to states in 1993.

In response to desire by the Administration of Children, Youth, and Families to evaluate family support programs, ABT Associates (2001) completed the National Evaluation of Family Support. Essentially, the evaluation sought to identify what factors in family support programs provided positive outcomes for children and families, what the results were for various types of programs and services, and if there were relationships with various family and child characteristics.

The final report was a meta-analysis in which studies from a vast number of family support programs had been statistically analyzed to estimate the effect across all studies. Meta-analysis allows researchers to translate data from several studies into a single study with a statistically effective size. Meta-analysis is conducted in three phases that include specifically stating what the task is, reviewing the literature for completed studies to determine which ones will be included, and developing a coding system in the third stage that describes the various programs, research designs, and study impacts. In the meta-analysis of family support, the first phase defined *family support* as all programs having a purpose of building parental capacity to support child development. The second phase of review resulted in the examination of 900 studies on family support, of which 665 were selected for coding.

There were 10 program variables selected for examination: (1) purpose, (2) what services were delivered, (3) how services were delivered, (4) staff information, (5) location of program, (6) type of program, (7) population targeted, (8) age of service provided, (9) length of service provided, and (10) level of family support provided. The results of the meta-analysis resulted in questions about what kind of programs should be funded.

The data showed that for children, small positive results were found in development of children's cognitive skills and their social and emotional development; small average effects were related to socioemotional outcomes. No meaningful effects were found on children's physical health and development. For outcomes related to parents, there was average effect on parent knowledge, attitude, and behavior; these programs had no meaningful effect on the mental health of parents. Programs that had a focus on community change had no effect; programs providing case management had no effect on parenting behavior. Overall conclusions were that there are small but significant effects on a number of outcomes for both parents and children. This is not surprising because the family resource centers were not well funded. No program model was found to be effective across a range of populations, although some programs targeting specific populations were effective with the population. "Almost two-thirds of the programs studied had very small or no effects on parents' understanding of child development, attitudes about childrearing or behavior with their children, and more than half of the programs had small or no effects on family functioning" (ABT Associates, 2001).

SUMMARY

Laws and policies that govern child welfare services have generally been initiated at the federal level because of laws passed by Congress. New programs and policies evolved when particular needs of families and children surfaced and became widely known. Child welfare agencies became responsible for implementing these programs. Consequently, the responsibilities of child welfare agencies have become quite broad.

Child protective services are the entry point into the child welfare spectrum. CPS has always been a controversial service because investiga-

tions are often intrusive in the lives of vulnerable children and families. The public is generally polarized about what the responsibility of child protection should be. For some, CPS does not intervene enough; others believe CPS should play a much smaller role in the lives of families. Making the decision to intervene in the lives of children and families in situations of confirmed maltreatment represents an awesome responsibility for practitioners and other CPS staff.

The research and evaluations of CPS services indicate that most programs have been ineffective.

There are various reasons for this. The responsibilities of the child protection agencies are broad, and studies are difficult to replicate because of the inconsistencies in laws and a number of other factors. A national study on CPS indicated some promising initiatives, particularly in the areas of multiple tracks or providing flexibility in the response to maltreatment reports.

From CPS, the pathway for children is often to out-of-home care in a number of placement resources, such as foster family care, group care, residential group care, or residential treatment programs. These programs represent the least and most restrictive placements in the child welfare arena. The most restrictive placement is the inpatient psychiatric hospital setting. Foster care studies indicated that many children who had been placed in foster care suffered with physical, emotional, and educational deficits, and many of these deficits were not addressed during the time children spent in foster care.

There are many challenges for youth exiting the foster care system. Because a large percentage have not achieved adequate educational levels, they are often faced with poverty, unemployment, and homelessness at times in their lives. Much more needs to be done in the foster care arena to produce better outcomes.

Major legislation related to foster care occurred in 1980 with the passage of the Adoption Assistance and Child Welfare Act (Public Law 96-272). The passage of this law encompassed three major directions for child welfare agencies. First, preplacement services were required to prevent and detour unnecessary placements into foster care. Second, early reunification of children with their caretakers was the intent, and finally, when reunification was not possible, agencies were to find permanent alternative placements for children. The foster care population dropped temporarily in the 1980s but began to rise in the late 1980s and early 1990s for various reasons.

The Adoption and Safe Families Act was passed and implemented in 1997. The act established strict time frames for permanency and requires child welfare agencies to make permanent plans for children in an expedient fashion. Both PL 96-272 and ASFA established adoption assistance payments for children with special needs. As a result of ASFA, the rates of adoptive placement for children have increased dramatically. However, because of the requirement to terminate parental rights if appropriate parental actions have not been completed within specified time frames, there are more children awaiting adoptive placement than there are homes for them. More needs to be done to find permanent alternatives for these children.

At various points in the legislative process, Congress became involved in attempts to offer services to families so that out-of-home placements of their children could be prevented. Additionally, legislation was passed to offer more support to families before they reached the crisis level. Now entitled Promoting Safe and Stable Families Act, Family Preservation and Support was an effort to strengthen the capacities of families to protect their children and stabilize their environment. Although sometimes controversial, the research on family preservation is positive, and many studies show that placements have been reduced as a result of these programs. The studies on family support programs do not confirm the efficacy of these efforts, and perhaps alternatives resources should be funded.

There are conflicting studies about the efficacy of group care, residential group care, treatment foster care, and residential treatment placements. Even though many children continue to be placed in these costly categories, there is insufficient data to support continued use of these facilities.

In view of the tremendous responsibilities of child welfare agencies, it appears as if the outcomes of safety, permanency, and well-being should be broadened so that the policies and funding levels will be more in line with current practice.

Questions for Discussion

1. Discuss the value of focusing on process and/or outcomes in terms of federal requirements.
2. Should child welfare workers refuse to treat families and children for whom they have no resources?
3. What can be done to deal with families before they reach a state of crisis?
4. Discuss how child welfare agencies can connect better with the biological families?

Cultural Competency in Child Welfare

Jesse, age 15, lives on a reservation with his mother, grandmother, grandfather, and two sisters (ages 12 and 13). His mother works in the child welfare agency on the reservation. She is a case manager. While Jesse's two sisters are doing well in school, he began having problems with his teacher approximately 6 months ago. Recently, he was caught drinking with five friends behind the school and was expelled for two weeks. Since being home from school, he has started to have angry outbursts and to become violent with family members. His grandfather, whom he respects, tried to talk with him but is not able to calm him down. His mother suspects the use of drugs. She recognizes she needs outside help but is embarrassed about the situation, especially because she works with cases like these at the agency.

INTRODUCTION

This chapter examines the issue of cultural competency and sensitivity in child welfare practice. A discussion of power and the empowerment approach is first presented as a lead into understanding the role of cultural competency and practice. The foundation and description of cultural competency are then presented with a discussion of how it is applied in the child welfare field. Additionally, characteristics surrounding different populations will be examined. Because this is the first chapter that contains specific cultural content, it is important to note that the comments made refer to research that has been carried out through many studies related to that particular ethnic group. As in any situation, the characteristics and behaviors mentioned are based on a significant proportion of any research sample, and exceptions for many reasons occur in all groups. For example, the economic, class, religious, geographic, age, and acculturation factors of any individual or family in a society affect their behavior regardless of their cultural background.

The need for cultural competency in child welfare is demonstrated in the high numbers of ethnic children who find themselves within the child welfare system and the disproportionate number of minority children who find themselves in the foster care system. Much research has examined the reasons for this, and although poverty has often been found to be a key factor, many other studies point to the dominant cultural perspective of what a family should be as affecting the decisions made in regard to minority families. This dominant cultural perspective points to the role of power and how it affects the child welfare system.

POWER

The role of power in dealing with culturally different populations is an important issue that affects how your culturally sensitive intervention is received and utilized. What contributes to the confusion of power is the different interpretations of it within a particular setting. Power, according to Balswick and Balswick (1995), is the ability of one person to influence another. On the other hand, "powerlessness is the inability to control self and others, to alter problem situation, or reduce environmental distress" (Leigh, 1984, as cited in Lum, 2000, p. 105). The term *power* should never be used as a simple definition. Power can be held over others, over self, or in association with others. According to Lukes (1976), there are three dimensions of exercising power. One-dimensional power tends to be oppressive and come from the top down. Two-dimensional power, on the other hand, is more democratic in that more than one person is exerting it. It allows for two opinions and the equality of authority. Three-dimensional power, however, asks the individuals involved to suspend values and beliefs and to think beyond their worlds together, coming up with creative approaches to problem solving and opening the door to social justice. This type of power is what leads to "empowerment." Empowerment allows the social worker to be culturally competent in most situations and to aid a client in becoming more culturally competent.

EMPOWERMENT THEORY

When Barbara Solomon coined the word *empowerment* in 1976, "her idea was that workers, service agencies, policies, and educational and training programs must work to meet client needs in ways that are congruent with each individual's cultural background and community setting" (Green, 1999, pp. 5–6). Additionally, she believed "that people and communities should be encouraged to define their own best interests, promote their self-sufficiency, and be free to live out their historic values" (p. 6).

Browne and Mills (2001) write that there are different definitions for empowerment in social work. "Browne's (1995) review of the social work literature on empowerment identified three ways in which the term is generally defined: (1) as an intervention and product, (2) as a process, and (3) as a skill benefiting wide and diverse populations" (Browne & Mills, 2001, p. 23). It is sometimes referred to as a process by which individuals, groups, organizations, and communities can become more powerful in terms of their functioning. It often entails the development of increased skills in influence and of internalized power to bring about change. Pinderhughes (1983) believed that the use of empowerment brought about changes in individuals to take action and accomplish goals in their own environment.

One cannot forget that empowerment is used more often for oppressed individuals and groups. This oppression affects generally every aspect of their lives. Whether we are talking about minority cultures, gender identification, or sexual orientation (to name a few), millions of people in the United States are oppressed. When someone is oppressed, it is often the case that empowerment is more difficult to learn. The following are some general guidelines that Simon (1994, pp. 25–29) proposes for empowerment to work:

1. "Shape programs in response to the expressed preferences and demonstrated needs of clients and community members" (p. 25). It is important to be aware of what exactly is needed by clients and communities, so you are not providing services that match only with your values and beliefs.

2. "Make certain that programs and services are maximally convenient for and accessible to one's clients and their communities" (p. 25). In many oppressed communities, the services needed are not located near the clients, and public transportation may not be available. It is critical that the services created are made convenient for the clients to reach.

3. "Ask as much dedication to problem solving from one's clients as from oneself" (p. 25). To encourage clients to take responsibility for resolving their issues, tell clients that you believe they have strengths that can help resolve the issues.

4. "Call and build upon strengths of clients and communities" (p. 26). Building upon clients and community strengths enables them to utilize these strengths in other situations and encourages them to keep these strengths in the forefront.

5. "Devise and redefine interventions in response to the unique configuration of requests, issues, and needs that a client or client group presents. Resist becoming wedded to a favored interventive method" (p. 27). Interventions need to fit clients. Each person's unique cultural background and individual needs should be considered when choosing an intervention. These may then need to be modified in order to better fit with the client.

6. "Make leadership development a constant priority of practice and policy development" (p. 28). It is critical to ensure that clients build their

strengths into leadership skills. Through these skills, individuals learn to stand up for themselves and others.

7. "Be patient, since empowerment takes substantial amounts of time and continuity of effort" (p. 28). In undertaking an empowerment approach, one must recognize that the changes will not occur overnight. It is important to be patient in your work and allow change to come from the individual. As this occurs it will build a continuous worldview of how clients might shape their lives and the lives of others.

8. "Take ongoing stock of social workers' own powerlessness and power at work" (p. 29). In order to help clients be empowered, we must be empowered ourselves. It is our responsibility to deal with our feelings of powerlessness and power and to be able to demonstrate to our clients what we have succeeded at through our own achievements.

9. "Use local knowledge to contribute to the general good . . ." (p. 29). It is important to be aware of and sensitive to what the local perspective is so that it can be a basis for change.

Using these guidelines allows the social worker to set up situations in which clients have every chance of succeeding at developing self-esteem and power to make changes in their lives. Okazawa-Rey (1998) proposed the following practice guidelines for empowering people of color to change their lives:

1. It is important to look at not only micro but also meso and macro issues that affect people of color. The environments in which individuals live, including groups and communities, have a powerful effect on social, economic, and cultural factors. Without knowing what is going on in these areas, social workers have less ability to work with the client.

2. The cultural backgrounds of clients have many strengths, and these unique factors can add to the empowerment process. An example of this is natural helping networks within particular cultural groups, which can play a significant and strengthening role in moving people of color forward.

3. Recognize the structural inequalities in society that affect people of color and can have a significant impact. Do not allow clients to blame only themselves for all the negative aspects in their lives. Help them understand what effect outside factors can have.

4. Help clients work together collaboratively and collectively. People who work in groups can often accomplish more than those who work alone. The power generated by many people can also take on societal oppression.

These suggestions are all a part of culturally competent approach that will empower individuals, groups, and communities to move forward. The following are some practical steps in using empowerment, according to Gutierrez (1990, pp. 151–152).

1. "Accepting the client's definition of the problem" (p. 151). In accepting clients' definitions of the problem, you are choosing to give power over to the clients and focusing with them on what is important and what strengths they have been using.

2. "Identifying and building on existing strengths" (p. 151). As noted in the earlier point, when social workers help clients identify and build on strengths, they are reinforcing the value of the person. They are empowering the clients to utilize their talents to take on their own situation.

3. "Engaging in a power analysis of the client's situation" (p. 152). In a power analysis, the social worker looks carefully at the power issues that are affecting the client both on a personal level and on a societal level. Then an examination is made of the power the client already has and how these sources of power can offset externalized issues.

4. "Teaching specific skills" (p. 152). In teaching specific skills, such as problem solving, parenting, and stress reduction (to name a few), the social worker is aiding the clients in obtaining more strengths and is giving them methods by which to resolve issues.

5. "Mobilizing resources and advocating for clients" (p. 152). It is important in an empowering situation to be able to mobilize resources from the community and social service organizations. By working from this perspective, we can advocate for clients and teach them to advocate for themselves.

These steps toward empowerment for our clients are a base for competency.

CULTURAL COMPETENCY

Cultural competency can be defined in many different ways. According to Samantrai (2004, p. 32), cultural competency is defined as "ways of thinking and behaving that enable members of one cultural, ethnic, or linguistic group to work effectively with members of another." In order to do this, child welfare workers must have the ability to be (1) self aware, (2) know basic knowledge about the client's culture, and (3) have the ability to adapt practice interventions to cultural context (Samantrai, 2004).

Self-Awareness

Self-awareness is an important first condition of being culturally competent. In a society so dominated by the Euro-American point of view, it is difficult for most individuals to think beyond this perspective. Samantrai (2004) notes that one way to begin self-awareness is "with learning about the history of one's own cultural group, the beliefs, values, customs, practices, legends, myths, music, art, folklore, [and so on]" (pp. 33–34). Through the understanding of one's own experiences, those factors that most affect us in our lives can be seen and read as valuable perspectives. Understanding one's own beliefs, concepts, and even prejudices allows social workers to open their minds more to the cultures of others.

In child welfare, it is critical that those beliefs a social worker has about families and children be examined from a personal perspective. As an individual with your own family experiences, you may have particular ingrained ideas about how a family should operate. These can involve your beliefs about parental roles, discipline, child–parent relationships, family values, religious affiliations, and the role of extended families, to name a few. There are many ways to go about self–assessment, but perhaps the first step is to ask yourself a variety of questions about your beliefs in terms of families. The following are some basic questions that should open your own thinking about yourself and how you perceive families.

1. How do you define a family? This is an important question in that either you will be looking for a specific configuration of a family or you will be open to a more broad concept of the term *family*. In child welfare, the broad concept of family allows for greater understanding in the field.
2. What are your beliefs about roles in the family? This question helps you examine your beliefs about male and female roles and parental roles versus child roles. Perspectives that take into account the uniqueness of the family and the way responsibilities are handled allows the child welfare social worker to better work with the family and children.
3. How should discipline in a family be handled? Your views and experiences with discipline will effect how you view the discipline going on in the families you investigate. Knowing what behavior you are used to can affect the way in which you perceive another culture's handling of a disciplinary situation. While there are guidelines followed by child protection workers, knowing cultural behavior can help you better assess a situation.
4. What role does extended family have? In many cultures, the role of extended families is quite significant. In others it is not. Being aware of your own background and experience with extended family can help you accept other roles of extended families.
5. What level of involvement should parents and children have with outside systems? You may have been raised to have an open exchange with systems other than that of the family's. These systems might include schools, church, and outside organizations. In some situations, children and their families have outside involvement and often outside support. However, there are cultures in which families keep more to themselves and operate only within their cultural system. Knowing your own beliefs about the openness a family should have with outside systems allows you the opportunity to look at things differently and accept cultural differences.

Knowledge about Client's Culture

Critical to the whole issue of cultural competency is the social worker's knowledge of other cultures and the way in which social workers handle their own beliefs and those of the family. To understand the culture of another person, one might seek course work, field work, or research on culturally diverse clients (Lum, 2003). Perhaps the best way to learn about different cultures is through real experiences with those different from us and by seeking information from them about their culture.

There must be a willingness in order to learn about other cultures. Okayama, Furuto, and Edmondson (2001) state that you must have a positive attitude. In order to use a positive attitude, you must be able to do the following:

- Listen and identify that which is different
- Suspend habitual judgments, pay attention to the difference, face it, and engage in dialogue leading to a better understanding of differences
- Explore, try out, and learn effective ways to work through misunderstandings and conflict based on differences
- Sustain positive intentions and an attitude of mutual respect even when misunderstandings and unintended conflicts occur
- Take risks in interaction: ask for clarification, admit ignorance, and reach out with understanding and forgiveness
- Become aware of culturally influenced responses (For example, how do you react when someone says something that hurts at a deep and culturally based place? Anger? Avoidance? Rationalization? Helplessness? Blame? How can you move beyond that initial reaction to form a positive cultural bridge?)
- Share such hurt more directly with an attitude of openness toward cultural learning, forgiveness, resolution, and connection
- Make efforts toward learning about and feeling more comfortable with differences (including differences in race, ethnicity, cultural values, religion, and other cultural differences)
- Know and be open about your limitations in culturally sensitive circumstances. When appropriate, seek consultation with a cultural consultant or language translator or make a referral for services from a member of the client's own culture (Okayama et al., 2001, pp. 90–91)

It is important that the information you gather from sources about different cultures be filtered through an understanding of the individuality of the person and the family. While there may be general themes that run throughout a culture, these need to be tempered by the experience of the family itself. Samantrai (2004, p. 34) notes that the child welfare social worker should have the following knowledge about another culture:

1. Religious/spiritual orientations and views of metaphysical harmony
2. Cultural views of children
3. Cultural style of communication—whether information is transmitted primarily through spoken words or through the context of the situation, the relationship, and physical cues
4. Culturally prescribed and proscribed behaviors in formal and informal relationships
5. Family structure and roles; child-rearing practices, including nurturing, meeting physical and psychosocial needs; methods of discipline (including use of corporal punishment)

6. Norms of interdependency, mutuality, and obligation within families and kinship networks
7. Health and healing practices
8. Views of change and intervention

McPhatter (1997, p. 6) notes the following areas as important for cultural competency in child welfare practice:

1. Knowledge of the history, culture, traditions and customs, preferred language or primary dialect, value orientation, religious and spiritual orientations, art, music, and folk or other healing beliefs of the groups for which the worker carries out professional responsibilities is required.
2. Child welfare workers need intimate familiarity about social problems and issues that have different impacts on minority group members.
3. Because children and families live in and relate to neighborhoods and communities in deeply interlocking ways, workers must include neighborhoods and communities as vital aspects of their practice domain.

These areas of knowledge can help the social worker better understand the behaviors of parents related to the upbringing of the children. Knowledge in these areas can create an environment of mutual respect for the child welfare social worker and the family.

Adapt Practice Interventions to Different Cultures

Being able to adapt practice interventions to different cultures requires the child welfare social worker to be knowledgeable about practice theory and techniques and to understand which interventions are most practical for use. Interventions that support strengths-based approaches and those that take into account the ecological perspective enable the social worker to better facilitate services for culturally different families. Strengths-based interventions support the uniqueness and strength of the family, while ecological interventions fit well with understanding the environment of each family's situation (Fong & Furuto, 2001).

Lum (1999) believes that culturally competent practice has four areas the social worker must be capable of doing. These include cultural awareness, knowledge acquisition, skill development, and inductive learning. It is the latter two points that are important to understanding the actual adaptation of intervention to work with different cultures.

Skill development is the process by which the child welfare social worker develops and acquires methods for working with clients. "Skill is the practical application of cultural awareness and knowledge at the actual helping interface between the social worker and the multicultural client" (Lum, 2003, p. 380). Lum (2003) defines the skills a social worker needs as (1) process skills, (2) conceptualization skills, and (3) personalization skills. Process skills refer to the specific techniques and interventions the social worker possesses and applies to the case situation. Conceptualization skills are the processes by which the social worker conceives the situation and identifies methods for utilizing interventions. Personalization skills relate to the social worker's ability to learn, behave, and grow (Lum, 2003). Through use of these skills, the social worker can intervene with the family from a multicultural perspective.

Inductive learning, according to Lum (2003), involves the process of "continuous discovery" (p. 382) about the nature of multicultural families. By taking what we know and adding to it the data we gather through open-ended techniques, we are able to draw continuous findings as we move along in our practice. Through the use of understanding, we build constantly on our relationships with the family. The basic use of data about other cultures serves as the foundation for the inductive learning process we utilize in experiences with families. Utilizing skill development and inductive learning enables the social worker to adjust and begin to adapt interventions to fit with different cultures.

Fong, Boyd, and Browne (1999) propose a process by which ethnic clients are not forced into Westernized interventions. The following five steps in the process allow the social worker to adapt an intervention to all different cultural groups:

1. Be aware of the values of the ethnic culture that serve as strengths that can work within an intervention.
2. Choose interventions whose values fit with the cultural values of the family.
3. Be aware of cultural interventions that may fit with the intervention you are using, and use techniques from this to empower the intervention you are using.
4. Use an approach that allows cultural values and techniques to be integrated into the intervention you are using.
5. Explain to the family the intervention you are using and how their cultural values and indigenous techniques are part of the approach.

Along with these steps, the child welfare social worker, according to Samantrai (2004), needs to be: (1) accepting and genuine, (2) able to communicate with the client, and (3) skilled at using interviewing techniques that address "level of intrusiveness, directness, social distance, formality, and forms of address" (p. 35).

Samantrai (2004, pp. 35–36) also recommends the following principles:

1. Start with some level of self-awareness and basic knowledge about the client's culture. Be particularly careful about knowing what words, gestures, and body language may be perceived as pejorative or complimentary, and the significance to the client of nonverbal behaviors such as eye contact, proximity, touching, silence. Learn cultural strengths as well as weaknesses.
2. Recognizing the great variety of mixture of races, ethnicities, and cultures, make no assumption from the client's physical appearance about [his or her] racial/ethnic/cultural identity, or the concerns, priorities, and resources. Ask the clients how they identify themselves, how closely or not they follow their traditional cultural beliefs, customs, and practices, and what their

culture means to them. Understand the differences between individual family practices and broader cultural traditions.

3. Assess the level of cultural assimilation, acculturation, and culture conflict of the family with their environment, and between members of the family. Assess the role cultural factors may be playing in the creation of the client's current difficulties and the role they may play in the resolution of those difficulties.

4. Use the authority of professional knowledge and competence to gain the client's trust and cooperation, rather than the power of law to induce fear and coerce compliance. The use of legal authority does become necessary sometimes; use it judiciously when needed.

5. Despite best intentions, mistakes will be made, cultural faux pas will be committed. It's best to acknowledge them and perhaps ask the client what might have been a more appropriate word or action under the circumstances. Respect for the client and worker intent can be conveyed not only in words but also in the worker's intonations and nonverbal behaviors.

These important points allow the child welfare social worker to have greater cultural competency and to work with clients in a manner that respects their own culture. In the child welfare system, the issues between families and the social worker often are tense and difficult. It is the social worker's responsibility to make this as comfortable as possible considering the situation. Highlight 4.1 looks at a case situation in which cultural competency is needed.

| Highlight 4.1 | **Cultural Competency Case** |

The Liang family had immigrated to the United States from China approximately 10 years ago. Mr. Liang worked on the waterfront docks in New York City. Mrs. Liang was a homemaker, and the couple had four children. The oldest son (Junji) had been 2 years old when the family immigrated. They had no difficulties with their children until Junji had become involved in some gang activities in the last year. They had tried within the family to resolve the issue, but the last incident (stealing from a grocery store) had led to an arrest and a referral for services with a local agency that did family and children intervention. The Liangs still had difficulty with the English language and had to depend on their son for some interpretation.

Sarah (the social worker) had graduated from her MSW (master's of social work) program two years ago. She had received cultural competency training in her graduate program and had spent a lot of time working with different cultures in the neighborhood.

The Liang family set their first appointment and arrived on time at the agency. The parents appeared nervous, and Junji appeared reluctant to take part in the intervention. Sarah found it difficult to speak with the Liangs and was unsure of what Junji was telling the parents when she talked. After a difficult session, Sarah set up another appointment for the family. Meanwhile, she contacted the local school to learn how Junji was doing.

Answer the following questions regarding this case:

1. What kind of information should Sarah make sure she has regarding the cultural background of the family?

2. How should Sarah handle the son's reluctance in this situation?

3. What steps does Sarah need to take to ensure that the intervention she chooses is culturally appropriate?

SPECIFIC CULTURAL GROUPS

The following material specifically addresses different cultural groups and their values and beliefs. This material is aimed at aiding the student in general understanding of differing cultures. It is not intended to speak to all individuals in that culture, as everyone has a unique experience of themselves and the environment in which they live.

African American Families

African Americans make up 13 percent of the current population in the United States, with over 80 percent living in urban areas (U.S. Bureau of the Census, 1998). The African American culture is heavily influenced by their history and heritage. The issues surrounding slavery and ethnicity have led to discrimination and prejudice. Despite these negative aspects, African American families have survived with resilience. According to Hill (1972), among the strengths that can be found in African American families are "strong kinship bonds, strong work orientation, flexible family roles, strong achievement orientation, and a religious orientation that helped the black family survive" (as cited in Logan, Freeman, & McRoy, 1990, p. 15).

One important structure within the African American family is that of kinship. Kinship is made up of friends and extended family who provide such things as "child care, financial aid, advice and emotional support" (Crosson-Tower, 2004, p. 42). These kinship ties have remained strong and perhaps grown in strength because of the tremendous stress and pressures placed on African Americans. Kinship bonds for African American families do not necessarily follow only bloodlines. It is common for individuals who are neither related by blood nor marriage to be included in a family. Children will often talk of aunts and uncles unrelated to them. These strong bonds and networks serve as supports for families and communities. Children may often be raised by grandparents or other family members, while the elderly are also cared for on a collective basis. Informal adoption of an African American child is not uncommon as parents often recognize that an extended family member can provide more supervision or guidance than they are able to provide at the time. This type of placement is not seen in the African American community as negative because it demonstrates the parents' love of the child and their desire for the child to have his or her needs provided. Care of the elderly is also an important part of kinship networks. The elderly are often revered and respected and receive care from extended family and informal networks. Often the older African American family member plays a leadership role within the family.

The roles of males and females in the African American family tend to be more flexible than in Caucasian families. African American females have historically worked outside the home, as they were more likely than males to receive employment. Because of this, there is more of a sense of egalitarianism in the parental roles. Although males are still seen as the heads of the household by women and children, the family's definition of this is not necessarily based on who works outside the home (McGoldrick, 1996).

A strong work and achievement orientation allows the African American family to build on the strengths and skills of the individual members. While unemployment rates have placed African Americans in a difficult situation, there is still the desire to work and achieve personal success. One of the great failures of the educational system in the United States is that of its education of African Americans. This has resulted from inner-city schools without the resources to provide good education to African American children. The lack of resources for the African American family has led to increasing unemployment and the severity of poverty within the community.

Another important aspect of the African American family is the religious orientation, where the church plays a major role in the community and in the support of families. The church often goes beyond religious beliefs and can be an influencing factor in community and political situations. This deep connection to church has led to programs that provide preventative services within the community for families and that aid families in crisis situations.

Poverty is a crisis within the African American population. Close to 29 percent of African American families live below the poverty line as compared to 8 percent of White families (Willis, 1998). In 2001, it was determined that a family of three (one parent and two small children) were living in poverty if they made less than $14,269 a year. This crisis for the African American family brings to light the difficulties for families with children. Often, there are not enough resources to provide for children in a way their parents would prefer. Children in poverty situations are often seen as neglected because of a lack of adequate resources and are more likely than their middle-class counterparts to be involved in child welfare services.

Latino Families

The term *Latino* is used as a general term to refer to those individuals who come from Spanish backgrounds. The individuals most often referred to with this term come from the regions of Mexico, Puerto Rico, Latin America, or Cuba. They often have the same common dimensions: "national origin and language, the complexity of racial ascription, the differences between self-ascription and ascription by others, and the role of immigration and citizenship status" (Acevedo & Morales, 2001).

It is important in working with families from a Latino cultural background to recognize that different geographic locations of families affect their culture and behavior. According to Delgado (1992), Latino families in the United States consist of four basic groups: Mexican American, Puerto Rican, Cuban, and other Spanish-speaking people.

Most Latino families are structured on a hierarchical basis, with loyalty being the significant value of the family. Mothers are respected and children are loved, but fathers are the ones who generally receive the highest respect

(Falicov, 1983). There is a high degree of cohesion in the family and, as in African American families, extended families are a major part of the life of the nuclear family. Despite these factors and the primarily Catholic background, Latino families have a rate of divorce of 14 percent, and 18.2 percent of Latino children live in single-parent families (Delgado, 1992). In Latino families, the extended family takes on a special role. Research has shown that while Euro-American families are more likely to turn for help to a friend or neighbor, Latino families turn first to the extended family for support (Keefe, Padilla, & Carlos, 1978).

Additionally, Marin and Marin (1991) state there is a value of collectivism as compared to individualism. There is a sense of the importance of respect or dignity in the presentation of self. There is the role of machismo, which "defines a man as provider, protector, and head of his household" (Green, 1999). These values play an important role in the Latino family.

For the child welfare social worker, these factors affect how you approach the Latino family. It is also important to understand that with this strong extended family cohesion, your involvement with more than the nuclear family will be important. Sadly, child welfare records indicate that these informal supports are not considered first and that Latino families have experienced more outside substitute care through child welfare services (Delgado, 1992).

Language can also be a major barrier, and it is appropriate for the child welfare social worker to be conversant in the Spanish language, as this is denoted as a sign of respect for the culture. As noted, your behavior with a Latino family should be more formal and respectful. It is not until you become more acquainted with the family that informal interactions can occur. Initial focus should be on the individuals in the family rather than on procedures and processes in the agency, if that is at all possible. Once a relationship has been established, the contract agreement may need to be developed through a more informal process, as the Latino focus is generally on people. The process of working through issues should always be culturally sensitive to the different backgrounds and cultural beliefs of the family with whom you are dealing. As with other diverse cultures, acculturation is of key importance in the treatment relationship. How acculturated a Latino family is adds to the diversity you will need to deal with. Acculturation plays a major role in determining just where the family is in relation to society issues and parenting roles. One of your first responsibilities in all families will be to assess their acculturation into the society, as this can often indicate the most appropriate interventions.

Asian Families

The Asian culture contains many different subgroups. The description of those known as Asian American includes "both the Asian continent and the Pacific Islands" (Ross-Sheriff & Husain, 2001, p. 77). These groups are divided by Sue and Sue (1995) as "Asian American (Asian Indians, Chinese, Filipinos, Japanese and Koreans), Southeast Asians (Cambodians, Laotians, and Vietnamese), and Pacific Islanders (Hawaiian, Guamanians, and Samoans)" (Ross-Sheriff & Husain, 2001, p. 77). These groups have enormous differences, and we can only suggest that among the most common cultural traits and values are those of filial piety, self-control in emotional expression, respect for authority, high respect for the elderly, importance of family and relationships, belief in fatalism, and importance of role expectation (Chung, 1992). Respect for these cultural traits and values is critical for the child welfare social worker.

When you are working with an Asian client, be aware of the following factors that can play into your intervention. A major point is that of the value of the collective versus individuality. While Euro-Americans value individuality, the Asian culture tends to value the group and its experience. Working for a company means becoming part of that company, and individual success is reflective of the company's identity. In families, individual academic success reflects on the family and its ability to be successful. In the United States, the primary value of individuality and self-achievement are in direct conflict with the Asian culture. It is important to be aware of your own value system so that you do not put those beliefs onto a culturally different family.

Body language is also an important factor of which to be aware with Asian families. Eye contact is a part of the language of the Asian culture, and it is not unusual for an Asian client to look down submissively if you are seen as an authority figure. Distance between the child welfare social worker and the family is an important communication aspect to respect. Chung (1992) suggests that the social worker sit first and allow Asian clients to set the distance between themselves and the social worker. As trust builds, there will be a willingness on the part of the Asian client to move closer in distance to the social worker.

Communication is an additional problem for the Asian American client. Beyond the difficulty in translation between the Asian family and the social worker is the question of verbal and nonverbal language. Asian families tend to communicate more with nonverbal language than do Euro-Americans (Chung, 1992). They speak more indirectly, and you may need to listen closely for the key points. Another important point for the child welfare social worker to be aware of is the "saving of face." It is often important in some Asian cultures to not be embarrassed by anything. This will often make it difficult for the social worker to learn the whole story before trust has been established.

While we can only hint at these common cultural values, it is important for the social worker to consider the following: "the reason for immigration to the United States, the length of time since arrival in the United States, the degree of involvement of the family in its own ethnic community, the degree to which the family has retained its religious orientation, and, finally, the degree to which American-born children have internalized the values" (Ross-Sheriff & Husain, 2001, p. 79).

Native American Families

The Native American population in the United States has a difficult history in the utilization of social services. Green (1999) describes the following areas as major difficulties for the use of social services for Native Americans:

1. Language is a major issue for Native Americans and social service workers. While a majority of Native Americans speak English, there are those who do not. Without the ability to speak the same language, the social worker is placed in the difficult position of not understanding and not being able to relate to the client in the best way possible.
2. Cultural diversity among the Native American community has a long history. There are many differences among tribes, and these are remembered by many Native Americans. This diversity, while honored by many, adds to the non-Native American confusion over appropriate intervention services.
3. While the majority of Native Americans live in cities, many are geographically isolated. This makes it difficult for them to receive services. Native Americans who live on reservations tend to be poorer and without many resources compared to their urban counterparts. Getting to agencies often proves to be difficult and can keep many people away from services.
4. There are many conflicts between social service agencies, overlapping of services, and the effect of laws on the culture. Social service workers can best serve Native American clients by responding to these issues.

Many of the child welfare programs and services that have affected Native Americans have been destructive in nature. With a high percentage of out-of-home placements (20 times greater than those of children of European descent), the focus of child welfare services for Native Americans has not taken into account the particular cultural needs of the Native American family (Johnson, 1991). Beginning in the 1900s with boarding schools for the socialization of Native American children into the Caucasian culture, there have been direct activities related to taking away the language and religious practices of the Native American family.

The impetuous Indian Child Welfare Act of 1978 was the result of these large numbers of out-of-home placements. The act provided for tribal councils to make decisions regarding Native American youths. This allowed the Native American community to be involved in the adolescent's development and thus furthered greater cultural consideration.

While there are major cultural differences between tribes, a few values are more generalized across Native American groups. Among these values are the following, according to Weaver and White (1997):

1. Respect for others, especially the older person
2. Sharing and collaborating with others besides the family unit
3. A collective vision of self, family, and tribe
4. Working together with others while still valuing independence
5. A worldview that continues to change as experiences affect the self

6. The reluctance to interfere with someone else and that person's own life
7. The importance of religion or spirituality

Through these values, we can see how some might interfere with those of the dominant culture. For example, in a competitive society the values of cooperation and sharing may conflict. The values just mentioned are reflective of strengths in the Native American culture.

The Native American family can constitute a "nuclear" family but more generally includes extended family. In Native American families, even those in urban areas, there is the importance of lineage or a way the family can be traced to common descendants. Lineage plays an important role in the interventions that social workers do with Native American families. Do not assume that the "nuclear" family will be the only part of the family with whom you will work. In a Native American community, there will be many others involved who will aid in the intervention. It will take group skills sensitive to Native American values to help work through a case. Ho (1987) states that "a therapist needs to be attentive, talk less, observe more, and listen actively" (p. 95).

One of the most difficult areas for Native Americans is the intervention of CPS (child protection service) workers, according to Green (1999). Because of the history of children being removed from their families and tribes due to so-called "acculturation issues," there is little trust of the child welfare social worker. It is the responsibility of the child welfare social worker to build this trust through culturally competent practice that takes this history into account.

Euro-American Families

The current majority of families in the United States are made up of those from European descent. These families have many differing cultural patterns, as originating from different countries can affect the values and beliefs of that group. These different Euro-American patterns have an effect on how the families receive and utilize social services.

While these differences can be pronounced, there are some common beliefs accepted by many. One of these is to value the ideas of individualism and competition. This is a common belief in America, which supports the "survival of the fittest." Individuals are valued for what they can accomplish and how they stand out. Independence and striving toward standing out with one's unique talents are all highly valued. Family life is important but can be affected by careers and other outside activities (Green, 1999). The major obligation to the family is the rearing of children, with obligations toward extended family (Green, 1999). The roles of the mother and the father are generally more equal. While men have been seen as the breadwinner, this is changing. There is emphasis on "egalitarianism," and members of a family are encouraged to take part in most discussions.

In terms of religious or faith-based practices, there is little concern by many people about whether others practice or avoid these areas. Personal preference for dealing with the practice of faith is accepted (Green, 1999). While some subcultures differ in the importance of spirituality and the importance of church, there is still some general ambivalence about it. The elderly in Euro-American society are generally not as revered as in other cultures. They tend to live apart from their families and have little power.

These general cultural tendencies are often in conflict with those of other cultures that have strong beliefs in collaboration and the use of extended families. Culturally competent social workers need to deal with their own values and beliefs and be able to set these aside and open their mind to different possibilities. An area that often differs between Euro-American culture and other cultures is the use of outside help. While many families do not wish to utilize outside support, Euro-Americans have a tendency to do so more than other cultures.

The aforementioned groups represent a major number of the citizens in the United States; however, there are many more cultural groups and a multitude of subgroups within the culture. As a social worker, you must be sensitive to all cultures and be aware of the differences in the subculture with which you work.

CASE EXAMPLES

The following section gives you an idea of the different types of situations in which you may find yourself. It is important to place yourself in these situations as the social worker and answer for yourself the questions presented. Be honest in your answers and examine the ways your personal cultural background may have affected the outcomes. For the purposes of this exercise, please assume that the individuals presented do follow some of the general values and beliefs of their culture.

| Highlight 4.2 | **Teenage Pregnancy** |

Sarah (age 17) was the first child of Teresa (age 42) and Nickolas (age 46) Caputo. Teresa and Nickolas are second-generation immigrants from Italy. They have two other children, Len (age 16) and Karen (age 12). The Caputos have lived in Chicago most of their lives, with Nickolas working in the paper factory and Teresa working as a secretary in an attorney's office.

When Sarah was 16, she became pregnant with her first child, who is now three months old. The father of the child did not want to be involved and does not offer child support. He is still a junior in high school. While Teresa and Nickolas do not want to accept aid from the government, they feel their daughter must as they have no money for child care or education. Sarah dropped out of school upon the birth of her child and has not returned. Sarah has not been involved in the welfare system as she is living with her parents and they are the ones who must qualify. Her parents do not want to go on assistance and would probably not meet the minimum standards if they did apply.

Sarah's parents are embarrassed by the situation and feel she will be a negative influence on the other children. While they love her and their grandchild, they want her to move out and live on her own. Sarah is frightened to do this, not knowing how she will support herself. Although they are not forcing her out of the house, they are placing enormous pressure on her. In order for Sarah to receive welfare services, she must be emancipated from the family legally because welfare resources are not available to her unless she is emancipated.

(Continued)

Sarah needs 10 more credits to graduate from high school, and she has been looking into taking a GED test. TANF services will require her to work 30 hours a week or attend high school full time in order to receive resources. Even if she does go to school, she must work at least 20 more hours a week in order to qualify for child care. The resources are time limited after that. In considering this case from a cultural basis, you will need to ask the following questions:

1. What aspects of this cultural background are affecting the situation?
2. How may Sarah's and her parents' cultures be different?
3. How might you work with the parents and Sarah to overcome the issues?
4. In what ways might TANF conflict with cultural situations?
5. What is one thing you have assessed about yourself from reading this case?

Highlight 4.3   **Child Protection and Delinquency**

Jose, age 14, has been gone from his home for four days. The police have been notified. While his mother and father fear for him, they are also familiar with his running away. The day he ran away, he had gotten into trouble for skipping school, and his father had hit him with a belt. Teresa (age 36) and Manuel (age 38) Hortes are fifth-generation Mexican Americans and have lived in Los Angeles all their lives. Manuel works as a car salesman in a nearby dealership while Teresa maintains the home and raises their five children, ages 2, 8, 7, 11, and 14. The Hortes family lives in a middle–class, diverse neighborhood. They take part in school and community activities and attend their Catholic church regularly. Teresa and Manuel appear to love their children very much but have definite ideas about education and importance of attending school. Manuel does not generally use his belt, but his patience for Jose has run out, and he sees no other way to cope with the situation.

On the fifth day of his disappearance, the police find Jose on a street corner smoking marijuana. He is arrested and brought to the detention center. Because his father hit him, he will not be released to his parents until an investigation has taken place into the safety of the home. The family is assigned a child welfare social worker as well as a court-appointed social worker, who will be working together to determine the best course of action for the family.

1. What cultural aspects will it be important to assess?
2. If one of the social workers were Latino, would this affect the work between the two workers?
3. What role might extended family play?
4. If the situation in the home is found safe for the children, what would then be the responsibilities of the child welfare social worker?
5. How do you think the church might play a role?

Highlight 4.4   **Adoption**

Mary (age 30) and Edward (age 32) Raymond have been on the state adoption waiting list for three months. The Raymonds live in an upscale neighborhood in Philadelphia. Mary and Edward are both physicians in private practice. They are an African American couple who cannot have children.

They are patiently waiting for their assessment papers to be finished when Mary is contacted by her mother that her cousin wants to give her children up for adoption. Connie (age 22) has two children (Letia, age 2, and Derrick, age 3) and has no seeming interest in keeping in them. Connie had Derrick

(Continued)

at the age of 19 by one man and had Letia at the age of 20 by another man. Neither father stayed around to help with the children. Connie has been addicted to cocaine for about two years and has left the children with her mother, who is not well. When her mother told Connie that she could not keep the children any longer, Connie said she would give them up for adoption if Mary and Edward wanted them.

The Raymonds are at first ecstatic about the possibility and then begin to worry over the issues that would go along with this kind of adoption. They fear the children are older and may have already developed some problems because of the situation in which they have been living. They are also worried that Connie might change her mind someday and want them back. The Raymonds call their adoption worker and ask her to help them with this situation. For any adoption to take place, they would need the final approval of the public agency and the support of the child welfare worker who is currently working with Connie and her mother.

1. How does cultural background play into this case situation?
2. What is your role as the adoption worker, and how do you feel about kinship adoption?
3. What concerns might Connie's social worker have about the proposal?
4. Considering your cultural background, would you as the adoption worker have any conflicts with this situation?
5. What role does extended family have in making this decision?

| **Highlight 4.5** | **Violence in the Family** |

Maria Strongheart, age 38, is a Native American. She is a member of the Navajo nation and currently lives in an inner-city area in Albuquerque, New Mexico. She has three children: a daughter Mary, age 8; and two sons (Nick, age 7, and David, age 5). She currently is working in a school cafeteria as part of TANF. Her husband and the father of her children left her about a year ago. He sends a little child support now and then but does not see the children. Maria began living with another man soon after her husband left. He, at first, seemed wonderful, but as his drinking continued, she began to feel less happy with the situation. Approximately two months ago, he hit her in the face, giving her a black eye and breaking her jaw. While he was sorry immediately afterward, his abuse of her continued whenever he drank. He has not hit the children, and she keeps telling herself that he will quit.

David, the youngest, has begun to wet his pants at school. His kindergarten teacher spoke with his mother about it, but his mother said she was not worried because she was sure he would stop. However, two days later, David confided to the teacher that his "uncle" had hit his mother and that he was afraid to go home. The teacher contacted the Child Protection Hotline, and they set up a meeting with David and his mother at the school the same day.

1. What aspects of culture must the child welfare social worker be sensitive to?
2. How will an authoritative social worker be seen if the mother adheres to her Native American culture?
3. How might spirituality be used to affect the outcome of this situation?
4. What cultural history barrier is affecting this case?
5. What cultural beliefs could help in this situation?

Highlight 4.6	Child Abuse

The Yims immigrated to the United States from Korea two years ago and are now working to obtain their citizenship. Young, age 52 and his wife Kim, age 50, live in a poor Asian community in New York City. Mr. Yim works at a local grocery store and his wife stays at home. Their daughter Noreen, age 27, and her two children live with them. Noreen immigrated to the United States after meeting her American-born husband in Korea. Her husband is a sergeant in the Army and is currently stationed overseas in Iraq. The Yims know very little English and depend on their daughter for help.

Recently, the children had been showing up at school with bruises on their arms and legs. When asked, they reported their grandfather had hit them for not doing their chores and homework on time. The school administrator notified the local child protection office, and a social worker was sent to meet with the family at their home. When she arrived, she found the grandmother and mother there but not the grandfather. In speaking with the mother, the social worker soon discovered that the children had angered the grandfather, and he had hit them with a stick. The mother assured the social worker that it would not happen again. After talking with the children, she learned that their grandfather had hit them on two occasions and that he had told their mother that he would not do this again.

1. How does the mother and children living with the grandparents affect how the handling of this situation?
2. What cultural issues may be affecting the mother and the grandfather in their interactions?
3. What role might their culture be playing in the grandfather not being at home when the social worker came?
4. Does the father need to be involved in the situation at this point?
5. Discuss how you would handle your interactions with the grandfather.

SUMMARY

This chapter has looked at cultural competency and the factors that lead to child welfare social workers being well trained. In particular, the stages of gaining cultural competency were examined, and the methods for doing so were presented. Knowledge of self, other cultural information acquisition, skill development, and inductive learning are all part of the achievement of cultural competency. It is also important to examine different cultures in order to gain a better understanding of values and beliefs. In those presented, we saw these differing patterns. It is hoped that the case studies at the end brought you a new awareness of your own personal reactions to different cultures.

Questions for Discussion

1. Describe one cultural value you have and examine why this might affect your work in child welfare practice.
2. Describe Lum's process of "inductive learning."
3. How does empowerment affect cultural competency?
4. What is the process of empowerment?
5. Name some of the knowledge you need to know about other cultures.
6. Compare the values and beliefs of Native Americans with those of African Americans.

Neglect

Samuel, a 3-year-old Black American, had been seen in the emergency room approximately six times in the last year. The emergency room social worker, R. J. Hull, had begun a list of those children and their families most frequently seen, in order to better identify those cases that may be the result of abuse and/or neglect. Samuel's case did not appear to be one of direct physical abuse. The injuries and illnesses for which Samuel had been seen had been appropriate to the circumstances explained by his mother, aunt, and sometimes grandmother, who had all brought him in on different occasions. What was beginning to concern Mr. Hull was the number of situations and the circumstances surrounding the accidents or illnesses. None of the doctors had reported the case for referral for social services. As so often happened in the emergency room, many different doctors had seen Samuel, and although there were some questions as to how the accidents and illnesses might have been prevented, none believed that Samuel was purposely being abused. This was much more likely to be a case of neglect as well as a result of the activity level of Samuel himself. Mr. Hull recognized that not all children are alike, that some are more likely to be more active and take more risks than others. Samuel was definitely a risk taker. At the age of 2 1/2, he had attempted to climb to the top of some monkey bars in the park in which he was playing with his six other siblings. The result of that adventure was 12 stitches. Two months later, Samuel had almost drowned at the public pool in July while being supervised by his 10-year-old sister. Samuel had developed bronchitis some three months before and had not been seen at the emergency room until he had such a high fever and so much fluid in his lungs that the doctors had to admit him for pneumonia. The physicians in the emergency room were reluctant to call in social services under conditions like this as it was clear that his family cared about him and that the illnesses and injuries were not purposeful. They believed calling

89

in social services would provide more problems for his family and themselves. They especially did not want to see Samuel taken away from his family, but it is more than likely that they believed child welfare services would or could do nothing to change the situation. Mr. Hull had urged the doctors and nurses to let him know about cases like this, but in a busy emergency room, no one seemed to have the time. He had even held a workshop on the services that could be provided in a case like this; however, until the doctors and nurses could see the results of how social services could be helpful in a situation like this, it was doubtful that they would call upon them.

INTRODUCTION

The issues surrounding the neglect of children are numerous, and physical neglect is the predominant form of child maltreatment in the United States (Downs et al., 2004). Child protective service agencies found over 500,000 children to have been neglected in 2000 (U.S. DHHS, 2002). Child neglect is more prevalent than physical abuse and causes more child fatalities. Professionals and policy makers have tended to ignore child neglect for many years; however, it is finally beginning to receive the level of attention that reflects the seriousness of the problem. One reason it has been minimized as a problem is the fact that it often does not cause observable harm but, rather, causes damage that accrues over a period of time. It is the cumulative effect of the lack of medical care, adequate education, emotional deprivation, malnutrition, and so on (Downs et al., 2004).

While child welfare has generally considered neglectful situations to be of less immediate concern than incidents of physical or sexual abuse, recent research (Ontario Children's Aid Society, 1998) indicates that it is in neglectful family situations that the child is more likely to suffer severe injury while under the supervision of child welfare authorities as compared to an abusive situation. There are many reasons why findings such as these may have begun to emerge in relation to neglect. In many states, the time frame for an investigative report in a case of neglect is approximately 21 days, compared to an abusive situation, which must be investigated within 24 hours. Additionally, many child welfare agencies have not seen neglect as a serious issue compared to physical or sexual abuse; therefore, children are more often left in their home without the provision of intensive support services. Due to the fact that neglect is often seen as an act of omission rather then commission and due to rising caseloads combined with diminishing resources, child welfare social workers and their agencies often do not place intensive support services in these homes. However, new findings are raising serious questions about the current interventions used and efforts that are needed in working with neglectful family situations. For those reasons, the authors have decided to discuss the issues of abuse and neglect separately, as they are separate issues that must be dealt with in different contexts.

DEFINING NEGLECT

Differences in definitions of neglect in state laws and community standards reflect the significant variations in the judgments of professionals and nonprofessionals concerning what constitutes child neglect. Some state statutes emphasize the condition of the child without any mention of parental fault, while others stress the condition of the child resulting from parental actions. Some communities have determined that no child under the age of 10 should be left alone, while others permit working parents to leave their children at home unsupervised after school (Gaudin, 1993). Some states define child abuse and neglect together as child maltreatment. Neglect is generally defined as deprivation of adequate food, clothing, shelter, or medical care. Some states make the distinction between parents who cannot financially provide for their children and those who fail to do so for reasons other than poverty, with the latter group subject to investigation (U.S. DHHS, 1999).

Part of the difficulty in understanding how dangerous a situation might be for a child rests on these complex and diverse definitions of neglect. As mentioned previously, neglect generally is seen as an act of omission rather than commission. Therefore, understanding whether or not neglect is occurring is often dependent upon a child coming into contact with a child welfare agency through identification of neglect by other institutions, such as hospitals or schools. To better understand the definition of neglect, the following terms are offered as a base in formulating an operational definition:

1. *Physical Neglect:* Physical neglect involves the neglect of the child to the point that there is a risk to the child's physical well-being. This may include a lack of healthy hygiene, poor housing conditions that are not physically safe, and so on.
2. *Health or Medical Neglect:* Health or medical neglect includes the lack of appropriate health care or the delay of health care, the lack of dental care, or lack of treating illnesses as instructed by medical personnel.
3. *Environmental Neglect:* Environmental neglect includes factors related not only to hygiene within the home situation but also to the safety of the areas in which the child plays or receives care.
4. *Emotional Neglect:* Emotional neglect may be the lack of love and nurturing given to the child. One type of neglect in infants and young children is sometimes described as "failure to thrive." Failure to thrive involves emotional, physical, and developmental signs of neglect or abuse. Generally, factors related to failure to thrive include a child not being sufficiently fed, held, or stimulated by the parent or caretaker. This lack of child nurturing is sometimes brought on by factors affecting the parent or caretaker and/or factors that create an interactional problem between the child and parent (English, 1978).
5. *Educational Neglect:* Educational neglect includes truancy of the child from school, failure to enroll a child in an educational program, or failure to provide for a child who has special needs in this area.

6. *Neglect of Supervision:* Neglect of supervision refers to the parent not supervising the child appropriately. This may include the child being left unsupervised, locked out of the home, or allowed to be absent from the home for long lengths of time or at inappropriate hours, without attention being paid to the child's whereabouts.
7. *Neglect of Child Care:* Neglect of child care includes leaving an underage child alone or in the care of someone who is not qualified to care for the child, or the abandonment of a child by a primary caregiver.

Polansky's (1992) conceptual definition of neglect is widely accepted:

> A condition in which a caretaker responsible for the child, either deliberately or by extraordinary inattentiveness, permits the child to experience avoidable present suffering and/or fails to provide one or more of the ingredients deemed essential for developing a person's physical, intellectual, and emotional capacities. (p. 19)

This definition meets the demand of inclusion of parental actions that result in some negative consequences for the child, but fails to specify the required degree of harm to the child. The problem is in defining what is generally deemed essential for a child's physical, intellectual, and emotional development. The definition is basically dependent upon the social worker's level of knowledge about what is physically and psychologically essential for a child's healthy growth and development.

Definitions of neglect are often difficult to discern unless they are blatant, such as a child being abandoned or noticed by a professional, for example, a nurse or doctor who has a child under his or her care. Many other factors also play into the relativity of a child being seen as neglected. In the United States, where there are many deteriorating neighborhoods in which children live in impoverished situations, families feel little hope of moving beyond their current circumstances.

When we define neglect, it is also critical to be aware of the role society plays in allowing these situations to continue. The view of financial efficiency in the United States affects the funding of social services for families by viewing issues from a narrow and immediate perspective. What might save us $50 in taxes this year can often become more important than the fact that $50 could pay for a program that might save a community $2000 in the future. For example, a young child with a learning disability participates in a special program that will enable that child to do better in school and eventually enter a productive profession. Compare this to eliminating the program and causing said child to become an unemployed adult as the result of never having learned to cope with the disability.

ETIOLOGY: FACTORS CAUSING NEGLECT

Many factors can be related to neglect in children. Among these, as we have noted, poverty is highly correlated with neglect (Lindsey, 1994). This is not simply because of a lack of material goods or resources. According to Lindsey, if we consider that some 5 million children are living below the poverty line, then in fact they are being neglected. The question emerges, "By whom are they being neglected: society, the family, or both?"

Individual and Family Factors

Although no single factor causes neglect, many of the outcomes of poverty in a family can lead to neglected children. This does not mean, however, that all children living below the poverty line are being neglected by their families. However, in many families the lack of resources creates an environment of stress, a sense of demoralization, and often depression and a lack of hope. When these conditions occur, the child's opportunities for a positive living environment decrease. The term often used in talking about poverty is *the feminization of poverty*. By this, researchers are referring to the fact that the largest proportion of families living below the poverty line are headed by single mothers. It is also the single-mother family that receives the most notice from child welfare agencies, primarily due to the fact that these families are the predominant users of their services.

Additional individual factors of child neglect include psychological issues that may not be related to the family's economic circumstances. Depression in parents, a lack of knowledge or understanding of what a child needs, a history of a neglected childhood for the parent, as well as alcoholism and drug abuse, are merely a few of the factors associated with neglect (Polansky, Chalmers, Buttenwieser, & Williams, 1981). Parental characteristics may also include a lack of empathy, difficulty relating to others, impulsivity, and ineffective communication skills. Often these parents tend to be unable to demonstrate nurturing behaviors to their children, and their interactions with them lack sufficient warmth. Their lives are generally characterized by chaos, and domestic violence is often a trait that reflects a number of conflictual relationships (Berrick, 1997). They often have extremely low self-esteem and view themselves as being highly incapable of providing adequately for their children. These characteristics can often present a false image of the parent to the child welfare worker, one that reflects that of a noncaring parent who has little regard for the best interests of the child. However, this is generally not the case as most parents who appear to be neglectful are, in fact, very caring but often lack the knowledge and skills to overcome the circumstances of their situation.

Community and Societal Factors

A variety of community and societal factors contribute to neglect, many of which create extreme barriers for families making efforts to change their lives. The lack of affordable, safe housing can create an extreme hardship on a family in a community that also lacks community support from friendly neighbors, family members, churches, community groups, and other informal networks. This can create feelings of isolation for parents who lack sufficient social skills to develop networks of support on their own.

Many communities also lack adequate social services and resources for families in crisis and in need of counseling, emotional support and guidance, and parenting education, as well as emergency financial assistance. The stress created by these factors can lead to insurmountable obstacles for parents in communities that provide no outlets by way of support and recreational activities for their inhabitants.

PRACTICE

Assessment and Process

The processes and procedures involved in a child being identified by a child welfare agency as neglected or at risk of being neglected are, as mentioned, generally the result of the family's involvement in another institutional system, such as a school, hospital, or welfare system. Because the family may be receiving services due to a lack of financial resources, it is not surprising that many of the cases related to neglect or child maltreatment may consist of low-income families. As discussed previously, the significance of poverty in relation to a family being involved with the child welfare system is reflective of these issues. A family in poverty is already within the system for financial reasons and is more visible for situations of neglect and abuse.

The process involved in a case of neglect includes the referral, the investigation, the finding, and the dissolution of the case. Although neglect cases have not received the same intensive evaluation as maltreatment cases, the decision factors involved in a neglect case are similar to those involved in an abuse situation. The safety of the child, whether in a case of neglect or abuse, is the most important factor for assessment.

In child welfare situations involving poverty and neglect, it is often initially difficult for the new social worker to understand or relate to the living conditions of the family. However, a nondeficit, strengths-based approach to viewing the case is extremely important during the assessment process. This approach to assessing a situation requires the social worker to focus not only on strengths within the family but also on viewing the family system from a diverse frame of reference. Although families living in impoverished conditions may be different from the social worker with regard to income level, it is necessary to recognize that the low level of income does not necessarily reduce the family's ability or capacity to provide a loving environment for their children. Highlight 5.1 looks at the environmental situation relating to Samuel's family for the purpose of assessing where the strengths lie.

Assessment of the Child   Assessment of the child in a neglect case is as critical as assessment of a child in an abuse situation. The risk to the child is the primary focus of the assessment. One particular form of neglect that must be assessed immediately in cases involving infants is the aforementioned failure to thrive. This condition first diagnosed in the 1970s is a condition characterized

Highlight 5.1 | **Strengths Assessment**

In reading through the opening example of this chapter, what do you see as the strengths and resources that are positive in Samuel's family situation? How might they be used to work with the family regarding Samuel's frequent accidents? The major strengths that you have probably already picked up on are the strong family bonds, the major responsibilities carried by the adults in the family, and the caring environment surrounding Samuel. Whether or not Samuel displays overexcitability or is hyperactive is yet to be determined.

by poor physical growth, retarded motor and social development, and malnutrition (Pecora et al., 1992). Many of the studies in this area emphasize the importance of the interactions between the mother and the child (English, 1978). Further, Evans, Reinhart, and Succop (1983) describe the issues of neglect as playing an important role in the occurrence of this condition. With regard to the case of Samuel, he will need to be interviewed individually in order to fully assess the safety of the home situation. Has he experienced these types of accidents for a long period or are they of more recent origin? Has he ever been tested for hyperactivity by a professional? What has Samuel's growth pattern been? Has he been on target with his developmental milestones or has he been ahead or behind?

The manner in which these questions are asked is extremely important in order for a level of trust to be developed between the social worker and child. Spending time with the child in his/her own environment is necessary in order to gain an in-depth understanding of how a child functions when in a secure, familiar setting. How does the child handle himself/herself with other children and the adults within the family? This is where the knowledge of child development becomes critical. Knowing how a 3-year-old child typically behaves allows the social worker to assess the situation free of any personal biases relating to child development. It is also critical in this assessment to understand that in different cultures or backgrounds, typical behaviors might occur that may not be consistent with what might be expected, given the social worker's background. For example, Samuel might demonstrate his ability to read by looking at cereal boxes rather than books because the price of books may be beyond the family's means.

Assessment of the Nuclear Family   When a family is reported to a child welfare authority for neglect of their children, the case is generally assessed by a social worker within a specific period of time, based on the level of neglect reported and statutory requirements. Assessment of the nuclear family in a poverty and/or neglect situation, as noted, also requires a nondeficit perspective of intervention. A nondeficit perspective requires the social worker to assess the strengths of the family situation from both an economic and a cultural dimension. Thus, the child welfare social worker needs to recognize that a family, such as the Williams, has many positive attributes. For example, the

Williams's extended family system provides additional support for Samuel while his mother is working. The availability of Samuel's grandmother and aunt are resources the child welfare social worker can call upon to help in Samuel's family situation. Another strength is the family's demonstrated concern over Samuel's upbringing and their appearing to be taking steps to ensure his safety.

Significant information to gather in this phase is not only the family dynamics and developmental processes but also the view of the child within his or her own family. How is the child referred to by the family and in what context? Does the family compare the child to other children? How do family members describe the child's relationship to others in the family? Do they ever focus on positive aspects of the child's personality, or is all of their communication about the child within a negative framework?

As the social worker gathers more information about Samuel's family, it will be important to ask questions about his relationship with his father and his behavior before moving into the apartment to interview other members of his family. What is important in this phase of the intervention is to listen, identify strengths, and reinforce those positive aspects of the family through empowering statements. For example, the social worker might want to express to Ms. Williams and her mother-in-law a sense of respect for their strength and the manner in which they are attempting to raise eight children. An example might be: "I am really impressed by the care and concern you have for your children and grandchildren. You have an enormous amount of strength and love to provide the kind of home environment you are trying to do." The social worker will also want to demonstrate empathy and concern over the loss of Ms. Williams' husband and the grandmother's son. Letting them talk about this loss may be one of the appropriate focuses of this initial meeting once it has been determined that Samuel's safety is not in jeopardy from ongoing maltreatment or neglect in the family. Although Samuel's safety remains the first concern, the decision in how to intervene in this family would initially be from a family-based intervention perspective. Therefore, the first step is to establish a relationship with his mother and grandmother and let them share those issues that may be impacting on Samuel's neglect. Is Samuel experiencing neglect because his mother and grandmother are still grieving their loss? If so, why are the other children not experiencing similar difficulties? What are the issues surrounding Samuel that cause him to have more accidents than the other children? Highlight 5.2 is an example of how focusing on the loss of the husband and son may lead to issues regarding the care of Samuel, as well as establish a positive relationship with the family.

Assessment of Extended Family Systems   The extended family system in a poverty and/or neglect situation can be a significant resource for the child welfare social worker. Many African American families have extended families that play a significant role in the child rearing and care giving. This kind of support may not be available in all families and, as a result, the lack of human resources affects the family's stability. Understanding the differences in various

| **Highlight 5.2** | **Relationship Building with Samuel's Family** |

SOCIAL WORKER (SW): [Concerned facial expression] The loss of your husband must have had a great impact on you and your family, Ms. Williams.

MS. WILLIAMS: [With tears in her eyes] Yes, we had our problems like everyone else, but we were really devoted to each other. He was especially fond of Samuel. You know, that was his father's name and grandfather's name. It was really hard for all of us when he died. I couldn't believe it, and I didn't know how we were going to manage. If it hadn't been for my daughter and my mother and sister-in-law, I don't know what I would have done.

SW: You seem to have a very supportive family in your mother and sister-in-law.

MS. WILLIAMS: I do, but sometimes I'm not sure who is in charge. We all have our good days and bad—and whoever feels the best watches Samuel.

SW: Do you have rules for Samuel and the other children?

MS. WILLIAMS: Yes, but his father was really the only one who could make Samuel mind. Samuel doesn't necessarily follow the rules. And my mother-in-law sometimes lets Samuel do more than the other kids because he reminds her of his dad.

SW: Might that be confusing for Samuel?

MS. WILLIAMS: I know it is.

cultural settings, and the role the extended family plays, is critical for the child welfare social worker. Knowing what resources may be available to help the family stay out of the child welfare system by achieving their individual goals is accomplished through recognizing the strengths within the family system.

The primary reasons that families become involved in the child welfare system are often related to the fact that they have no extended family or friends support system and must utilize the services provided by their community. There are, at times, difficulties that can accompany a strong extended family that takes an active part in the child's life. Often this can result in a blurring of the roles with regard to who is responsible for setting the limits in the child's life. As in Samuel's situation, there are many adults taking charge of the family but with different rules and ideas. The result is that sometimes the whereabouts of Samuel are unknown because each adult believes the other is watching him. Additionally, Samuel does not yet understand his boundaries because they change depending on who is watching him at what point in time. With so many people coming and going in the apartment, it is difficult to keep up with a 3-year-old, as Samuel's family will attest.

Assessment of Social Systems   Many of the families we find in low-income situations do not have access to social systems for support. Social systems such as churches, social groups, family organizations, and friends are often luxuries these families are not able to acquire due to transportation issues and other limitations. Depending on the individual family situation, and often the cultural background of the family, many will have closed family systems. Closed systems reflect the fact that the family has very little to do with others outside the boundaries of their nuclear family. Although closed families are frequently seen in cases of physical or sexual abuse, families living in poverty and/or whose children are suffering from neglect seldom have social resources to which they can refer when needed.

In the Williams family, the system is closed in the sense that the two female adult mothers have little time to seek outside support or activities because of their work schedules and child-raising responsibilities. The grandmother, however, does remain involved with her church and group of friends there. Although the children attend church, their mothers do not. In some ways, this family system is open to outside social supports in that the family allows the children to take part in outside activities, as much as can be allowed with their time limitations. This is a positive sign in the family, in that they are open to their children participating in outside activities, but the adults are so time limited that they are not able to seek this support for themselves.

Assessment of Resource Systems   The resource systems available to low-income and/or neglectful families are often limited to income transfers and protective service resources. Depending upon the state, and the credibility of the resources needed to support families with children within that state, the systems can range from financial supplements to child-care benefits and work/training programs. Which programs are provided and how they are provided can make a significant impact on the intervention to be used in working with a family below the poverty line or experiencing neglectful situations. The major resources needed in a child poverty or neglect situation tend to be those that are the most concrete.

Increased child-care subsidies, food stamps, low-cost housing, school meal programs, Medicaid, and SSI are all programs that may fit with the needs of the Williams family. If there are additional needs to aid Samuel because of hyperactivity or grief reactions, then social services and special counseling programs to aid children in their development are available in many communities.

Assessment of Relevant Programs and Services   The programs and services to be assessed include those that have previously been used by the family, as well as those with which the family has not had contact. Although many low-income families find themselves in the public system of aid, they often do not receive consistent information. One family may be informed of the WIC Program, while another may not. Being very clear and having extensive knowledge of all the resources and services that can be provided for families and children is one of the major responsibilities of the child welfare social worker. Being able to inform the family on not only the availability of the services but also the means of accessing them is critical to the social work process and allowing the family to take advantage of all that is available. For example, a service that requires the parents to go to a particular building and apply for the services means the social worker needs to be able to aid the parents in obtaining transportation to the office and in filling out the forms without diminishing their view of themselves as competent individuals. Very often the families served through the child welfare system are demoralized by the circumstances and regulations they must overcome and so give up on the process before they begin. Additionally, the cultural background of each family will affect how reluctant they may be to access services. Knowledge of and sensitivity to the issues in this regard as they relate to differing cultural standards are a requisite to being able to help clients obtain their needs.

As in the case of Samuel, the social worker and mother decided that some of Samuel's needs related to his opportunity to be more stimulated outside the home. Neither Ms. Williams nor her sister had ever utilized the Head Start program in the community but now believed that this might be a positive outlet for their younger children still at home. This would additionally enable them and the grandmother to complete other responsibilities while the children are attending the program. Samuel's mother decided to return to computer school two hours a day while the children attended Head Start. This was funded through a special training program that Ms. Sheridan had found in the community and that was designed for single mothers like her.

Planning and Contracting

Interventions in Cases Involving Neglect   The selection of an intervention in cases involving neglect can be a challenging process for a social worker in view of the predominant lack of resources for families in which the primary causal factors relate to poverty or lack of knowledge about basic child care. When neglect is primarily a result of individual and family factors, intervention is different from when it is a matter of environment or community conditions. It is important for the social worker to tailor the intervention to the type of neglect and the outcome of the assessment process. Intervention with a failure-to-thrive child usually requires immediate hospitalization of the infant, with intensive nutritional and emotional nurturing for the baby as well as intensive coaching and instruction for the parents. This form of neglect can be the result of high stress related to recent life crises, in which case a crisis intervention model of family preservation may be the most appropriate course of action.

Because neglectful families have a multitude of problems, no one intervention technique or method can be successful. Successful intervention requires the delivery of a broad range of concrete, supportive community services from multiple sources and a combination of individual, family, and group methods. These methods may include individual counseling, behavioral methods, individual and group parenting education, and family therapy (Gaudin, 1993).

Following the assessment process, and prior to initiating an intervention, it is suggested that the child welfare social worker coordinating the case schedule a case review and coordination meeting with representatives from various programs that would serve as referral sources for the family. At this meeting an intervention plan would be developed, which would be presented to the family as a course of action for addressing the identified and prioritized problems.

Case Review and Coordination Meeting   A case review and coordination meeting for a family living below the poverty line or in need of services to help prevent neglectful situations due to financial issues will require the child welfare social worker to spend more time building those networks with agencies and people that can work together to provide well-developed and nonoverlapping services. Although this expenditure of time may seem extensive in the beginning, once these relationships are established they can be utilized repeatedly for cases in shorter and more planned amounts of time. For example, if relationships are established with significant individuals in different agencies in the community and regular meetings are organized between these workers on a regular basis, the social worker will find that many cases can be handled within a few sessions. By providing these regular meetings, different agencies and workers come to know one another and can more readily know what changes in programs are occurring within their community. Although the child welfare social worker is responsible for coordinating the meetings in order to provide the best services for the clients, this type of cooperation also enables other members of the social service community to meet together to inform and work cooperatively on other issues. As a result, the social worker is providing a strengthening process to other social workers in the community by giving them access to more information and a means of employing their strengths together. Partners in the case plan for Samuel might include the director and teacher of the Head Start program.

Family Involvement in Planning Process   The family's involvement in the process of coordination of services is critical to their own feelings of self-worth and empowerment. Their ability to help identify their needs and what services could benefit them the most is an important step in providing the family with skills to bring about change in their environment. As the members of the Williams family became involved in the planning process for the safety of Samuel, they were able to recognize and identify those areas of their lives where they could create change. A unique technique associated with Berg's (1994) solution-focused treatment is referred to as the "Miracle Question." Highlight 5.3 shows how the Miracle Question would be used in the planning process phase with the Williams family.

Highlight 5.3	**Application of the Miracle Question**

SW: Ann, if you could wake up tomorrow morning and all your problems were solved, what would be different?

MS. WILLIAMS: Well, my husband would still be alive. And I guess I want to have a better-paying job, so I could give my children more of what they need. I would also want to get a bigger place to live. I don't really want to leave my sister and mother-in-law, but we do need more space and a yard for the kids to play in.

SW: If these things happened, what do you think would be the first thing you would notice about yourself?

MS. WILLIAMS: Well, I would be less tired, and I would not feel so lonely or helpless.

It is at this point that the social worker can then focus on the change in the family member and how this change might be brought about through the intervention process. In many ways, the change in the client is a way of focusing on the goals and tasks the family member can accomplish.

If Samuel's mother felt less tired and less lonely, this might help prevent neglect to Samuel and his siblings. Although the protection of the child is a priority, it is critical that the child welfare social worker recognize the underlying issues that often are a component of these types of child welfare situations. Furthermore, it is imperative for a social worker to understand these issues and help the family understand them as well, in order for family members to recognize their role and how changing it can have a positive effect on the entire family system.

Contract with Family and Support Services   The actual contract with the family and the support services that will be given is significant in that this may be one of the few times the family has an opportunity to set some objectives and be empowered to accomplish them. Although an example of a contract will be presented in other chapters in this text, it is important to recognize that a family with little power due to their financial status should be involved in the development of a contract that reflects their plan for resolving the identified problems. This contract can represent more than a guide to gaining control over their lives to the family with little power. It can also reflect the strengths they possess and the fact that they are not necessarily the primary cause of the problems. It can help to identify the environmental factors in the society that have inhibited their ability to move forward. This recognition for a family in poverty is crucial to the members beginning to believe in themselves and their ability to bring about change in their lives. For example, in the case of Samuel and his family, the contract clearly identifies the strengths of the family members and the uncontrollable areas that affect them (see Highlight 5.4).

| **Highlight 5.4** | **A Verbal Contract with Samuel's Family** |

SW: I know you want what is best for Samuel, and you and I have discussed the areas that need to be addressed to ensure Samuel does not have so many accidents. Let's just go over those areas we have talked about and then see if we can come up with a way to ensure Samuel's safety.

MS. WILLIAMS: Well, I know we've talked about Samuel needing more stimulation than he gets being in this house all day. He needs to get out and be around different children and learn how to control some of his impulsive behaviors. I also know that we have talked about how sometimes it's confusing in the house because when all the children are around, sometimes we don't let each other know who has an eye on whom.

SW: That's right. It's hard to keep an eye on eight children and even harder when three adults are trying to do it at the same time without knowing who has said what.

MS. WILLIAMS: Well, my mother and sister-in-law have agreed that we will tack on the refrigerator a schedule of who will be watching whom when. We will also make sure that Samuel isn't going around to all of us asking to do something and that only one will be responsible for him at that time. I've also let my daughter know that I want her to help me but that I have to make the major decisions for all of us because I am the mom. I think she was a little hurt by that, but I told her I couldn't have done all I had after her dad died without her help. I hope she isn't feeling too left out now.

Critical to any implementation of any intervention is the continued use of interviewing skills and practice techniques that fit with the model of intervention and that provide the client and social worker with an opportunity to change situations and resolve difficulties. In a case of neglect based on conditions initiated by poverty, the skills of empathy and positive regard for the family are crucial to making any difference. By giving the family positive regard, looking for and identifying strengths the family members have, and assisting them in applying these strengths to their situation, the child welfare worker can bring about positive change quickly. For example, in Samuel's family situation, it was very clear to Sarah Sheridan, the social worker from the Department of Children's Services, that the Williams family members loved and cared about Samuel. There was never any evidence that Samuel was ignored. On the contrary, the difficulty appeared to be that so many adults were involved in the care and raising of Samuel that no one was quite sure of what the other was doing.

Once Sarah and the family had identified the issues and set goals and tasks to be carried out around those issues, it was Sarah's responsibility to continue to encourage and support the Williams family in changing their environment. Although the social worker may try to examine all the issues that will affect the family's plan as the goals are being set, it is impossible to know what precisely will happen as the plan progresses. With a relationship built on warmth, empathy, positive regard, genuineness, and empowerment, the social worker can call on different practice techniques to aid family members in reaching their goals.

Many of the client populations in child welfare settings have inadequate problem-solving skills that have created a series of problems for them in a variety of different areas. One of the most important techniques a child welfare social worker can give to a family living in poverty is the ability to understand and be able to problem solve. Although the process of problem solving can appear simple to most of us because we have been trained in this area, it can be extremely difficult for clients who have experienced poor modeling of problem-solving behaviors throughout their lives. Highlight 5.5 is an example of the steps involved in the problem-solving process that can be learned by many of these families. Highlight 5.6 then looks at how each of these steps can be modeled and learned in the case of Samuel's family.

Highlight 5.5 | **Steps in Learning the Problem-Solving Process**

1. Acknowledge the problem.
2. Analyze the problem and identify the needs of participants.
3. Employ brainstorming to generate possible solutions.
4. Evaluate each option, considering the needs of participants.
5. Implement the option selected.
6. Evaluate the outcome of problem-solving efforts. (Hepworth, Rooney, & Larsen, 2002, p. 416)

Highlight 5.6 | Problem-Solving Child Care in Samuel's Home

SW: Let's talk about what happened the last time Samuel fell down and had to be taken to the hospital.

MS. WILLIAMS: Well, I was at work, and my sister said she left him playing in the bedroom with his toys. My mother-in-law said that she asked him if he wanted to go to the store with her and he shook his head. So my mother-in-law left for the store, and my sister thought he was in the bedroom, but instead he decided to follow his grandma to the store, so he went out behind her and fell down the stairs.

SW: So, it sounds like some of the issue is who is watching Samuel?

MS. WILLIAMS: Yeah, sometimes we get very confused with who has whom.

SW: What sort of things do you think you could try at your house to make this less confusing?

MS. WILLIAMS: I'm not sure what you mean.

SW: Well, the problem seems to be that Samuel has several people watching him, and each one thinks the other knows what he is doing. But that isn't the case.

MS. WILLIAMS: Well, maybe we could have a schedule with who would watch him when, and the scheduled person could always be responsible.

SW: That's a great idea! Can you think of anything else?

Continuing Coordination of Services Continuing the coordination of services is critical for the success of any intervention involving neglect. It is the child welfare worker's responsibility, as well as the client's, to be alert when any member of the contract plan is not fulfilling responsibilities or carrying out assignments. Often clients tell us of their attempts to fulfill some part of their contract, only to find that other individuals involved in this process did not complete their part so the client could accomplish the goal. The process of dealing with a situation like this in an appropriate manner can help clients learn how to problem solve their own situations and increase their level of self-confidence, which will ultimately improve their skills in dealing with future problems.

Empowering clients to continue with services can be accomplished through consistent support. The modeling of good problem-solving skills through the use of role play can make a significant difference in a person's life. If the social worker is able to assist families in learning to stand up for themselves in an appropriate way through the modeling of new skills, by which the client can succeed through small steps, this can often have a positive effect on other areas of the clients' lives.

Support and Empowerment of Child and Family Continued support and empowerment of the child and family not only involves verbalizing their strengths and supporting their steps of accomplishment but also requires that the child welfare social worker encourage the involvement of the family in community and agency issues. The child welfare social worker might identify those individuals in their caseloads who express a desire to bring about change through services and various environmental supports, such as evening child care, transportation, and group support. These supportive services would be provided for the purposes of helping the client accomplish a broader goal, such as attending a welfare rights meeting or a neighborhood support group.

If the environmental supports a family needs are not available or if they need modification, it is the professional responsibility of the social worker to address this situation. Yet, in child welfare, it is known that there is not sufficient time to address all the issues that need to be dealt with and that clients need to learn to help themselves through community action and negotiation. The social worker's role then becomes one of helping clients mobilize and effect change in their communities. For example, if there are no after-school day-care programs in a community, the clients served could be organized and trained in ways to develop needed resources. By training families in community development and assisting them in accomplishing small initial steps, a social worker can facilitate dramatic change in a community and in family members as well.

Identification of Barriers and Resolution   The role of the child welfare social worker is not just to provide support and develop a plan. Rather, the social worker provides assistance in implementing the plan and the goals of the contract by helping the family members identify the barriers impeding progress toward the accomplishment of their goals. In poverty situations, there can be many barriers that, in most cases, require the provision of concrete services. Unlike some other child welfare situations, concrete issues such as child care, transportation, and education are basic barriers to clients accomplishing their goals.

In light of this, many of the obstacles social workers will encounter in their efforts to assist families in overcoming barriers will relate to basic needs. Being able to help provide transportation to an appointment or provide child care so the parent can attend a class or meeting is critical to children and families attempting to achieve their goals. Helping family members identify barriers to their goals early and developing solutions with them to resolve these barriers will ultimately increase the likelihood of success in a case situation.

Monitor Services and Intervention Plan

The importance of continuous monitoring of services and the intervention plan is essential to the successful outcome of a case. This monitoring includes not only the tasks set out by the families and the social worker but also the regular monitoring of external services and programs by having case meetings with other members of the intervention team to ensure that all aspects of the case are progressing smoothly.

Regardless of time limitations, there are numerous ways for the social worker to coordinate these meetings to include reviews of several families at one meeting and, thus, make the best use of time. However, these meetings will be of little value if the child and family are not included in the monitoring of the service and the coordination of any intervention efforts. They must play a significant role in shedding light on the ways in which the plan is or is not working for them.

Evaluate Outcomes and Terminate Services

Evaluating services in a neglectful situation can be both fulfilling and disappointing. It can be fulfilling if the family has been successful in accomplishing its goals, not just for the protection of the child but also for the growth and empowerment of the family. It can also be disappointing because often social workers bond with families, and ending the relationship with a family can be quite difficult. Oftentimes children and families will want to continue the professional relationship despite their need to become independent and self-sufficient. In these situations, it is important for social workers to recognize when their needs are feeding into the process of termination. It is equally important for social workers to recognize that the family may not want to terminate services, and although they are doing well may, as in other social work interventions, relapse or find ways to keep the social worker involved. That is why it is important for it to be clearly communicated at the beginning of the intervention that there will be a completion of the services, at which time the social worker will no longer be involved in the family. Although the family may at first resent the involvement, they may come to see it as a support they would like to keep. Helping them to network with others and work as change agents in their community can also alleviate some termination issues.

Evaluating Outcomes Evaluating outcomes is an important part of any intervention model, and a social worker is able to evaluate outcomes easily if specific goals and objectives are set up appropriately during the initial contract phase. The goals will serve as measures of the outcome in the situation, and objectives will specify how goals are to be accomplished. The use of assessment tools to measure the success of a goal can be an empowering technique when working with families in poverty who believe they have no successes. The use of a self-scoring sheet related to a goal or the use of a standardized questionnaire gives the family a way of visually measuring their success and empowering their efforts to continue working on changing their situation.

Terminating Services Termination of services in any child welfare situation will involve many of the same aspects of any social work treatment situation. Families and children may have a number of different responses to the termination of services. If an intervention has successfully kept the family together and improved the conditions of poverty and neglect, then termination is a much easier process than if the child has to be removed from the family and the parental rights are subsequently terminated. The ongoing relationship with the child in this type of situation will be critical to the child's adaptation to a new environment and family. With the emphasis on adoption becoming more of an issue, many children will find that their families are unable or unwilling to make efforts to provide safe and healthy environments. As a result, they will be placed in new family homes. This type of outcome will not require a termination of services for the child but may be the beginning of an intervention plan for the child's adaptation into a new family.

Follow-Up

The family will need to be contacted following termination to determine if the services they received were satisfactory. Have any changes occurred in the community or agencies with whom they have been working that have hampered their continued growth? Has the family maintained the same level of functioning? Has it increased or decreased? What are the factors that have affected their level of functioning? How might they be helped to regain their higher level of functioning if it has not been maintained?

It is hoped that the skills the families learn will enable them to provide healthy, safe environments for their children, yet we all know that without intensive supports or with the loss of particular resources, it is easy for forward progress to discontinue. Therefore, it is the responsibility of the child welfare social worker to follow-up on all cases within a certain period of time (approximately six weeks) to ensure the continued safety of the child and development of the family.

SUMMARY

This chapter has provided an overview of the role of poverty in creating child welfare situations, especially as it affects situations involving neglect. The role of poverty expands beyond neglect and affects most issues in child welfare practice. More systematic approaches to practice with families in which neglect has occurred, such as the one described in this chapter, will have a significant impact on how child welfare services will be provided in the future. The chapter provides an overview of how child welfare social workers can utilize their skills to make changes in families suffering from poverty and empower them to provide the best care possible for their children.

Questions for Discussion

1. Discuss the causes of neglect.
2. Describe how the adults in Samuel's family were inconsistent in their interactions with the children.
3. Explain how the cultural backgrounds of Samuel and his family create strengths in terms of his care.
4. Describe how poverty can affect a neglectful situation or a view of one.
5. Give your view on whether neglect can be more serious than abuse.
6. Discuss barriers in resolving neglect cases and ways in which barriers may be diminished.
7. Explain how a family like Samuel's might be empowered to create change in their community and in what types of programs.

Abuse and Emotional Maltreatment

Shelly, a 7-year-old second-grader from a Hispanic family background, pulled her sock further over her knee. She hoped Ms. Shanks didn't see the bruise on her leg. Her Mom didn't mean to hit her, but when she drank she just got mad and didn't know what she was doing. It was homeroom period, and Ms. Shanks asked Shelly to speak to her in the hallway for a few minutes. Ms. Shanks asked Shelly how she had gotten the bruises on her legs and if they hurt. Shelly didn't want to tell what had really happened, so she said she fell down the stairs. Ms. Shanks asked how she had fallen, and Shelly replied that she had tripped. When Ms. Shanks put her arm around Shelly's shoulder, Shelly began to cry. "If you tell me what really happened, maybe I can help," Ms. Shanks said.

INTRODUCTION

The overwhelming statistics regarding child abuse can be discouraging to the social work student as well as the child welfare social worker, yet remember it will be your work in the child welfare field that will make a difference. It is estimated that every second of every hour of every day there is a child being abused. Estimates of severe physical abuse of children in the United States are approximately 10 percent, while hitting and spanking are estimated at close to 100 percent (Knudsen & Miller, 1991). Some of the latest statistics regarding child abuse and neglect estimate 1,800,000 suspected cases of child abuse and neglect in the United States in 2002. Of these reported cases, 896,000 were substantiated. This amounts to approximately 41 percent of all reported cases being substantiated by child welfare agencies (National Clearinghouse on Child Abuse and Neglect, 2004). This figure represents only those children reported to child protective agencies and not those children being abused and/or neglected without reports.

DEFINING ABUSE AND EMOTIONAL MALTREATMENT

Substantiation of abuse is dependent on the definition given to abuse. As an individual raised in a family context, you have probably formed your own ideas of what defines abuse or emotional maltreatment. These definitions have been a source of contention for many years, and the debate continues today. Many individuals do not consider hitting or spanking to be abuse. They would argue that only situations that leave visible signs of abuse need be noted. Others argue that any type of physical or emotional punishment administered by an adult to a child is abuse and should not be allowed. Definitions also differ between cultures and societies. The authors take the approach that abuse in any form (physical, neglectful, or psychological) can affect not only the present well-being of children but also their development and future as functioning adults. As a child welfare social worker, you will be asked to establish clearly in your mind the definitions of abuse and emotional maltreatment. Highlight 6.1 gives definitions of abuse and emotional maltreatment.

Abuse, neglect, and emotional maltreatment, as mentioned, are difficult to define, yet these definitions clearly impact the services, programs, and practices that can be provided for the child. Abuse and emotional maltreatment may also be a one-time incident (although rarely), an episodic occurrence, or an ongoing daily event in a child's life. Abuse, neglect, and emotional maltreatment, however, do not occur only in families but may also be the result of treatment from another child or adult outside the family or in the context of an institution or community setting. For example, a child who has misbehaved in a classroom is struck hard across the face by a teacher, causing a nose bleed; a teenager in a group home is abused by several other teenagers after lights are turned out; or a child who is being cared for by a daycare agency is left in a crib all day with no diaper changes or feedings.

| Highlight 6.1 | Defining Abuse and Emotional Maltreatment |

1. *Physical abuse:* Physical acts by parents or caretakers that caused physical injury to the child or might have created this scenario

2. *Emotional maltreatment:* Acts such as berating, ignoring, abandoning, or isolating a child that create a situation of impairment for the child (modified in part from CWLA, 1990b)

The society in which the child is raised has a responsibility to protect all of its members. Children, who are among the most vulnerable, are in need of definitions that clearly articulate when the protective branch of the society needs to step in. The state or government has come to serve as a parent (*parens patriae*) to all children in situations of physical abuse, sexual abuse, psychological abuse, and/or neglect. This term implies that the government has a responsibility to take on the role of parent to all children in need of protection. Through this conceptualization, a third party becomes involved in the child and parent relationship in order to protect the child (Kadushin, 1987). The child welfare social worker will often play this role. How the government becomes involved and, in particular, how you as a social worker intervene is crucial to the future of any society's welfare.

It is important to acknowledge once again that despite a society's definition of abuse/emotional maltreatment, sensitivity must be given to the role of ethnic, cultural, and religious diversity. Within the society, differing subcultures and perspectives must be recognized in implementing any child welfare policy. The government, for example, can set guidelines for the definitions of abuse and emotional maltreatment and then find that they conflict or contradict a cultural norm or religious belief. For example, the concept "spare the rod, spoil the child" is not one taken lightly by several religious groups. Understanding these differences is not the same as condoning them. We as child welfare social workers do not agree with these definitions, but we must take our definition of why they are occurring into account. Many child welfare social workers find themselves battling religious beliefs as well as parental rights when attempting to uphold the policies of the child protection system.

CONSEQUENCES OF MALTREATMENT

The extent of the damage to children who have been maltreated depends on many things, including the type of maltreatment, the age and developmental levels of the children, the length of time maltreatment was perpetrated, and the severity of the maltreatment. It also depends on the individual resilience of the children involved.

In child welfare field guides, Rycus and Hughes (1998a) reported the effects of maltreatment on children depending on their development level, including effects related to five domains: physical, cognitive, social, and emotional, and suggested treatment strategies for caretakers specific to each area.

For infants and toddlers, the impact of maltreatment can be particularly damaging. Physically, these children can sustain long-term growth retardation, brain damage, delays in motor skills, and other problems. Emotionally, they can experience severe emotional trauma, particularly damaging at this age because of the need to develop trust between caretakers and children. These results interrupt attachment and bonding, which does not portend well for continued emotional and psychological development.

Effects of maltreatment on preschool children can also be devastating. Physically, these children may have delayed growth, may be sickly and prone to upper respiratory problems, and may have poor motor skills and muscle strength. Their speech may also be delayed; their attention span may be short for their age level. Attachment issues are evident as children may indiscriminately attach or be emotionally detached; they may exhibit excessive fear, have low self-esteem, and show signs of other emotional disturbance.

School-age children may not be able to tolerate the structure of a school setting and may have difficulty with problem-solving skills; they lack confidence and sufficient perseverance to function well in the classroom. They may begin to exhibit signs of anxiety and low self-esteem and be unable to relate to peers. Because of a chaotic home environment and lack of predictable outcomes, they may be unable to develop and implement coping strategies, show little impulse control, and show signs of antisocial behavior.

For adolescents, it is important to assess the point of onset for maltreatment. If an adolescent has endured long periods of maltreatment, he or she is likely to have severe and pervasive developmental problems. Additionally, it is critical to assess whether the maltreatment occurred at an early age and with what frequency it occurred. If maltreatment occurred early and frequently, the adolescent's developmental level will mostly likely appear to be that of a much younger child. Of course, some children are quite resilient, but long-standing maltreatment will mean the adolescent views the world as hostile and unsafe, and preemptive strikes may be necessary; these youths are often provocative and aggressive in their behavior.

If children and families do not receive adequate and timely intervention, the long-term effects of maltreatment can be devastating. In addition to long-term physical problems or disabilities, mental and behavioral health problems may result in children and youths entering the juvenile and criminal justice systems. The impact of maltreatment goes beyond the children who have sustained the neglect and/or abuse. Many systems are affected, including law enforcement; medical facilities; mental health and other social programs; law enforcement and judicial systems; and many not-for-profit, private, and informal organizations. It has also been shown that maltreatment is an intergenerational problem; children who are maltreated are more likely to abuse and/or neglect their own children.

PROCESSES AND PROCEDURES

Before describing the types of services and programs available in child abuse and emotional maltreatment situations, it is important to explain the general system of processes and procedures that have been put in place to handle abusive and/or emotional maltreatment situations. These processes and procedures are clearly reflective of residual approaches to intervention. They are residual in that they occur only after a difficulty has developed. Family-based care programs were designed for both residual and universal situations in that they are for reported cases of child abuse and families that might be at risk.

The sequence of events that occur in an alleged child abuse and emotional maltreatment situation is (1) the report, (2) the investigation, (3) the decision, and (4) the intervention. The report is the initial awareness that the child protection agency has of an incident of alleged child abuse, neglect, and/or emotional maltreatment. Certain professions are required by law to report suspected child maltreatment or face fines and punishment. Among these professions are social workers, teachers, doctors, nurses, therapists, psychologists, and counselors.

Most states have a 24-hour hotline available for individuals to call to report suspected abuse and emotional maltreatment. The reporting of a case may be anonymous. This has raised issues among the public when the agency is used by a parent in a divorce or custody case to cause problems for the other parent; however, with the increased public awareness of child abuse, reports have increased by 68 percent since 1987 (CWLA, 1995). Reporting of cases varies by ethnicity. Lindholm (1983) suggests that African American children are more likely than Caucasian and Hispanic children to be physically abused and yet are less likely to be sexually abused. Differing findings in this reporting pattern may be related to cultural differences in child rearing and/or prejudice toward a particular culture that leads to overreporting in particular regions of the country.

By law in most states, the investigation into a suspected case must be handled within 24 hours of the report. This requires the child protective worker or investigator to meet with the family within 24 hours of a report. This is a difficult time limitation in that it may be too long due to the possible danger to the child and may also be too short, depending on the number of cases the worker is assigned. It can also become more difficult due to accessibility to the family (if they are at home, if they answer their door, if they respond to the agency trying to contact them). It is also critical at this point of entrance into the family that social workers recognize diverse family situations. This does not mean that an investigation outcome will be affected because a family has a different set of cultural rules; however, it does mean that if you, as the social worker, are required to do the investigation, you can recognize and respect differences related to culture, ethnicity, and religion. These factors allow the social worker to enter the child abuse, neglect, and emotional maltreatment situation from a knowledgeable perspective.

Most decisions in child abuse/emotional maltreatment cases are made as (1) substantiated, (2) unsubstantiated, and/or (3) indicated. Thirty-seven states use only substantiated and unsubstantiated, while 13 others include the decision of indicated. Indicated implies that while the case cannot be substantiated, there is a high risk of abuse or neglect present (CWLA, 1995). The consequences of this decision weigh heavily with the child welfare social worker or investigative officer doing the investigation. This is a decision that requires the social worker to have extensive interviewing skills and an ability to get at facts from the perspective of many different people.

Many factors must be taken into account when making this decision. Foremost in these cases is an understanding of diversity as it relates to child rearing and homemaking practices, and your own attitude as a social worker toward these areas. While there are many cultures for whom "sparing the rod spoils the child" is a belief, there are additional circumstances under which the society must protect the safety of the child. Teram (1988) suggests it is at this point in child protection, when child welfare social workers must make a decision about a family situation and a plan for remedying it, that the worker begins to experience the most difficulty. Your training and understanding of a model of child welfare practice that considers this diversity is necessary for your success. The decision at this point in the process will also be dependent on a valid and reliable risk assessment instrument in which you have been trained.

Once a decision has been made as to the findings of the report, the child welfare social worker or investigative officer must decide on the best course of intervention for the child. As noted, there is a growing tendency in many states to leave the child with the biological family and provide intensive supports. Sensitivity to the cultural diversity of the family is also important in the decision related to the intervention. Does the family allow others to enter into the family or can an extended family system help provide support during this crisis period? What cultural and/or religious factors play into the situation and may affect or be used to aid the intervention? How might the strengths of these factors be part of the healing process?

In many cases, intensive supports and/or extended family systems are not available, and the risk to the child in the home becomes too great. It is at this point where the removal of the child from the home begins to involve substitute types of services. Working with a family after having removed a child places the child welfare social worker at much more of a disadvantage in attempting to provide a treatment environment that will empower and reunite the family. It becomes difficult for the family to be empowered and utilize their strengths when they believe their control and power have been taken away by the loss of their child. However, the safety of the child is primary, and without the resources to ensure this, no other decision can be made.

It is also important for the worker to be aware that it is at this point where feelings of failure and burnout can greatly increase. Especially as more and more agencies embrace family-based care and the goal of working with the maltreated child within the family, child welfare social workers will begin to see their efforts as failures when children are removed from the home (Teram, 1988). The social worker's ability to understand that not all situations are conducive to family-based care but that the appropriate model of intervention may be to bring the child into a loving, outside-family context, will guide the worker through these dilemmas.

SERVICES AND PROGRAMS

In child abuse, neglect, and emotional maltreatment cases, all states are required to serve an investigative function and then provide services for the child and family. The services in these cases, as noted, have primarily been defined as supportive, supplementary, and/or substitute forms of care. The history of which services are most often used in child maltreatment situations has changed throughout the years. As mentioned earlier, there was a period in child protection when substitute care was the core response. Very little thought was given to changing the environment in which the child lived. Instead, there was heavy use of foster care, orphanages, and institutional placement. Programs were developed around the placement of children in these substitute situations.

Initially, as concern grew over the numbers of children in foster care and permanency planning (the planning of long-term care for a child in the foster care system) became so important, special training for foster parents was developed. Early emphasis in child maltreatment situations still focused on removing children from their homes and reconstituting families through work with the foster family and/or an adoptive family. Although biological families were part of the consideration in the permanency planning for the child, they generally did not receive enough services to change their environmental situations during the period in which their children were removed. Normally, they were given an opportunity to complete a contract of behavioral change over a period of time in which their children might be returned to them. Often families gave up hope of getting their children back because the lack of resources within the child welfare system disempowered them from completing their contracts. Even when children were placed back in their biological homes after being removed, very few families had received enough counseling or supports to help in decreasing the possibility of an abusive situation.

This approach has changed during the last two decades. Now the predominant belief is that the biological family is the least restrictive environment and the best place for a child to develop if safety and nurturing can be assured. This belief is reflective of changes that have occurred not only within our society but also within the service delivery systems. In the 1970s, a growing understanding about the healthy development of children, as well as recognition that longer-term foster and institutional care of children could be just as damaging as the biological home, led to these changes. At the turn of the century, there is a new emphasis on securing safe, healthy homes for all children. Governmental pressure is currently pushing toward the reunification of a family within 12 months or the adoption of the child into a new family will take place.

Although the original concept of permanency planning did not focus on the biological family, it eventually supported the concept of focusing on the rehabilitation of the biological family as a priority in intervention (Maluccio, Fein, & Olmstead, 1986). The recognition that the biological families were not affected solely by their individual personalities, but also by the ecological environment and factors surrounding them, has caused most child welfare programs to begin reaching back out to the biological family in a more focused, systemic manner. It was out of this that the reemphasis on strengthening the biological family reemerged and the interventions in family-based care took a priority in the child welfare field.

As noted, intensive family-centered care programs and services have become a mainstay in this society. The beginning of intensive family-centered care appeared simultaneously throughout the country. The focus of these types of programs was primarily on the policies emerging from the Adoption Assistance and Child Welfare Act of 1980; however, the Family Preservation and

Support Provisions of the Omnibus Budget Reconciliation Act of 1993 (pp. 103–166) provided significant financial incentives in child welfare funding to lead many states into the area of intensive family-centered care.

Interestingly, these services have not been used just in abuse, neglect, and emotional maltreatment cases but have also been implemented in other areas of welfare, including poverty, substance abuse, the elderly, and disabilities. Features of these programs include (1) intensive work over a shorter period of time, (2) coordinated services and full involvement of the family in the process, and (3) a multisystemic approach to intervention.

In intensive family-centered care, the model of practice focuses on preserving the family for the sake of the child through the provision of intensive services that deal with the ecological and environmental factors affecting the family, as well as with the issues of individual family members. The early models of intensive family-centered care generally included a caseload of two to four families, a primary worker who nurtured and maintained a supportive relationship with the family, case-managed intervention with a wide range of services involving a number of different workers, and the availability of assistance for the family on a 24-hour basis. Treatment and intervention were based in the home, with the family at the center of the intervention process. In this brief intervention model (two to four months), the family was empowered to make changes and supported in their decision making (Pecora, Fraser, Haapala, & Bartholomew, 1987).

A large majority of these programs were supported by additional funds through Title IV-A and Title IV-E of the Social Security Act. Significant in these programs were the strengths-based perspective and the respect of cultural diversity from a multisystemic perspective. Currently, many forms of these programs are funded through the Family Preservation and Support Act of 1993.

The difficulty, as noted, is that the research consensus about what is most effective in intensive family-centered care programs has yet to be developed. Planners and researchers are working on validating much of their own work but have not necessarily joined together with others to make a consistent difference in the child welfare field. Steps toward this goal have begun with national workshops on intensive family-centered care, as well as a new journal (*Journal of Family Preservation,* edited by Sallee) dealing specifically with articles utilizing this approach. Taken further, the real value of the family preservation movement will be in its development as a preventive rather than a residual program for many different areas of social problems. Studies have noted the successful diversion rates of open child protection caseloads when intensive family-centered care programs are initiated in preventive forms (Hooper-Briar, 1994).

Yet prevention has not been established as a priority in many of the programs. Many states do little to collaborate or replicate other programs in these areas because of resource allocations. Each state is once again directed from its political, economic, and societal ideologies on just how intensive family-centered care should be done, and these directions are often reflective of the lack of funding for child and family programs.

Despite these differences, these programs have helped define the most recent standards set by the Child Welfare League of America (CWLA). Included in the CWLA standards of child welfare practice are descriptions and goals of both FRSE (family resource, support, and education) and FC (family-centered services). These two areas have much in common in that one (FRSE) represents a service that is community based and assists adults in their roles as parents, and the other (FC) represents a belief that families staying together is a critical priority for the betterment of society. FC also states that services provided toward the goal of this belief will be for the betterment of the child, family, and community. Both these service areas are used extensively in providing intensive family-centered services to families dealing with child abuse, neglect, and emotional maltreatment. CWLA has gone further than many of its counterparts in correlating and reporting the best possible standards and protocols for child maltreatment situations.

Although the child welfare practice model presented in this text is based on many facets of intensive family-based care, the authors are not without concerns regarding these programs as they intervene in situations of child abuse, neglect, and emotional maltreatment. Arguments abound as to whether keeping abused or neglected children in a home under an intense intervention situation is a risk worth taking. A few researchers argue that the risks to the child are too great. They speak of case examples from these programs where children have suffered further abuse or died. Highlight 6.2 gives an example of family preservation failure.

The opponents of intensive family-centered care would state that the second abusive situation could have been avoided if Sarah had been removed immediately. Richard Gelles, director of the University of Rhode Island Family Violence Research Program, believes that some families will be unable to change their behavior. Gelles's book, *The Book of David: How Preserving Families Can Cost Children's Lives* (1996), illustrates his growing concern over residual types of family preservation programs that risk the child over preserving the family.

| Highlight 6.2 | **Family Preservation Failure** |

Sarah, age 4, was found to be abused by her stepfather after being seen by a doctor who found burns on her hands and arms caused by cigarettes. In an effort to keep Sarah with her mother and brother, an intensive family preservation program was put into place to create change in the environment. The stepfather, who was arrested following the report by the doctor, showed no indication that he wanted to be a part of the family and moved into another home. Intensive work began involving the mother and children receiving support and resources to prevent an abuse situation from occurring again. However, after three weeks in the program, the social worker arrived on a Monday to find that the stepfather had moved back in with the mother's permission, and Sarah had several bruises on her back and legs. Without the willingness of the mother to keep the stepfather away from the home or for the stepfather to want to change and get help for his actions, there was no recourse but to remove the child.

The responses to these criticisms reflect that most families selected for intensive family-centered care programs have been screened for risks to children and that in the research done in these programs, some 5 percent to 50 percent of cases do end in the child eventually being placed in out-of-home care (Nelson, 1995). Once again, you as the child welfare social worker will face the difficulty in maintaining a balance between protecting the child and keeping the family together; however, the right decision is always to err on the side of protection of the child in dangerous family situations.

The positive clinical processes and perceptions of these family-centered programs appear to support the continued implementation of the Child Welfare Act of 1980 and the Family Preservation and Support Act of 1993 through more preventive types of programs. Studies that thoroughly evaluate family-centered programs might explain many of the difficulties recently seen. Specific training models highlighting the important facets of these programs of practice, whether dealing with a child abuse situation or a delinquency situation, would go far in the prevention and provision of child welfare services. A model that can be implemented in child welfare situations and that will protect the child while still maintaining the overall integrity of providing a functional family unit (either biological or surrogate) is key to the well-being of children and our society.

Another argument that has emerged against family-centered care programs is the high cost compared to what has been considered the "normal" cost in child protection. Yet when the cost of foster care is taken into account, as well as the effects the placement may have on the child, the differences in costs can dramatically shift. The cost of a child placed in foster care for approximately six months may seem nominal compared to the cost of a family being in family-based care for two to six months with intensive interventions and the involvement of numerous resources; however, when the long-term results and costs are calculated in terms of the family treatment and the overall outcome for the child, the picture is quite different. Children who have been maintained in their biological family environment with intensive change taking place and eventually leading to a long-term stable home can be less costly than children placed in and out of foster care and not provided with a stable environment to help them develop as healthy, functioning adults.

Tied to intensive family-centered care are the interviewing and practice techniques related to brief treatment, family therapy, and solution-focused therapy. These three therapeutic interventions are used frequently with family-centered care because they provide an intensive approach to positive change. While the techniques in these approaches are appropriate for all families, it is important to recognize that not all child welfare situations (for example, sexual abuse) can be handled so quickly.

Just as changes are occurring in the child welfare field that might produce better programs and services for children, political ideologies have begun to shift once again. One well-known term in the 1990s is *welfare reform*. Although new welfare reform legislation has just been integrated into the public welfare system, social workers in the field of child welfare who work with with abusers, neglected, and emotionally maltreated children are just beginning

| Highlight 6.3 | Making a Critical Decision |

Amy Lyons has just arrived at the child welfare agency as a child welfare social worker. She has been in the position for approximately two weeks. She assumed the 62-family caseload of her predecessor and has opened 3 new cases herself. Although many of the cases involve neglect, several have been "founded for abuse." Amy must make regular visits to all the homes on her caseload in order to help the families fulfill the contracts both she and her predecessor developed regarding issues around the abuse, neglect, and emotional maltreatment. She has a BSW degree and has had training in her internship in child welfare, but this did not prepare her for the heavy caseload and the concerns she often carries with her regarding particular family situations. Most recently, Amy was called to the school regarding a teacher's report of suspected child abuse.

The young girl, Shelly, had received several bruises on her legs and had shared with Amy, after initial denials, that her Mom had accidentally hit her with a broom. Amy recognized that she needed to meet with Shelly's mother that day in order to make a decision regarding the risks to Shelly and the steps that needed to be taken. Yet she also knew that with 62 open cases, many of the families also needed to see her this day. She made the decision to see this new case immediately. In only two weeks, she was already performing what she called "triage," which involved seeing the cases most at risk first.

to experience the consequences of this reform. Even though child protective services in the field have been spared, there is a significant impact on family-centered care services as changes have occurred to financial aid programs such as AFDC, child-care services, health care, and education. States may consider supporting programs that cut expenses at the front end rather than at the back end (for example, cutting funding in intensive family-centered care programs to save monies and then using these funds to supplement the use of foster care).

As social welfare reform continues to be implemented, it is most likely that social workers will increase their caseloads, thus not having the time to spend in intensive intervention with a family. The amount of time spent with a family will become limited due to the number of cases. A small number of caseworkers overseeing all of these cases without the benefit of supplemental support and services will most likely be forced to turn to foster care unless a different means of empowering and changing families and children can be found. Use of intensive family-centered care can continue, however, if we as a profession can validate its success and politically support those individuals who can see from a long-range and broader view. As a child welfare social worker, you will need to empower the families and children in your communities to advocate for support and change. Highlight 6.3 is an example of a case situation in which you may find yourself as a result of heavy caseloads.

ETIOLOGY OF ABUSE AND EMOTIONAL MALTREATMENT

Understanding why families abuse is perhaps one of the most difficult processes for social workers. There is no clear-cut research that identifies reasons for violence against children; however, it is also difficult to present a practice model unless the social worker understands the underlying causes of abuse. Gil (1971) has stated that the profile of an abusive family is more likely to include one or more of the following: (1) a history of childhood abuse, (2) an environment of poverty, (3) no social support, (4) alcoholism or drug use, and (5) a child with a special need. It is not surprising that these characteristics imply more about the environmental situation than about the abuser or victim. Therefore, it is necessary that the model of child welfare practice you employ has methods for dealing with these issues.

Specially Challenged Children

As noted, there are situations in which the characteristics of the child may increase the likelihood of abuse (Gil, 1971). This study found that children with special challenges (physical, mental, learning, etc.) tend to be the children who are more likely to be abused. Statistics suggest that over 25 percent of children reportedly abused suffer some type of special challenge (CWLA, 1995). Family situations in which this is part of the issue can be more easily identified before abuse occurs, and families can be helped from a preventive perspective.

Children with special challenges (both physical and mental) are often a forgotten and overlooked population in our society. While the term *special challenges* may be more common to those with physical differences, we are not limiting our discussion to this. We are also including illness as a difference, which is not so identifiable. Due in part to the discomfort many people feel around differences, services and programs for this population have not received widespread attention. Morris (1997) suggests this is due in part to the isolation of some of these groups from the rest of the population. The prevalence of these needs varies but is estimated to be between 2 and 4 percent of the child population. The importance of bringing these children more into the activities of the rest of society rests on the belief that it is by this method that children become more adjusted and society assumes a greater comfort around those with special challenges. It is also important so that we as a society will recognize their needs as individuals to self-actualize and will support their growth.

The families of these children are also in need of support and counseling to deal with their special issues. Parental stress and a lack of resources can lead to situations where these children are abused within their own families (Baladerian, 1994). In fact, it is estimated that children with special challenges, whether physical or mental, face greater risk of being maltreated. The identification of abuse in children with special challenges is at times difficult, due in part to the denial of the abuse and the attributing of the abuse signs to the child's disability.

Child welfare social workers are often notified of a possible child-at-risk case by a hospital, health care worker, or therapist. Once identified, the services to these families can often bring quick and positive results. In situations where the child is in immediate danger, such as a drug-addicted infant with a mother who refuses to seek treatment, foster care may be the only alternative until a different plan is worked out. What becomes crucial is the timing of the intervention to prevent further difficulties.

The child's situation must be thoroughly assessed on a full biopsychosocial level. In the case of children with special needs, the physical and mental challenges these children face are at times overwhelming. It is important to clearly assess what strengths and limitations the child and their family are experiencing.

Another part of this assessment is to look at how the nuclear family and the extended family are handling the situation. One of the most common reactions of parents to the birth of a child with special challenges is feelings of guilt and responsibility for the situation. Close attention should be paid toward the parents' desires and those fears they may not be discussing. Other assessment areas include the social systems that support or burden the family, the resource systems that can supply support, and the programs and services available to the family.

The implementation of the plan of action for specially challenged children involves several different steps. First, you will be continuing to work with the family and the child through the skills and intervention the family needs. It is important to remember that often in special-challenge situations, there is a sense of grieving for the child and the possible loss of that child. Grief signifies the pain many parents continue to suffer when they think of their own child's chronic special needs. Helping parents to understand that these feelings are normal enables them to move past more difficult issues.

The second step is the continuing coordination of services. Because special-challenge families and children tend to utilize services for longer periods of time due to the chronic conditions in the family, your role will be to maintain the level of support and coordination needed to achieve their goals. The establishment of groups of concerned parents is also a practical way to aid the continuing coordination of services. As parents are empowered, they move beyond the needs of their children and can focus with other families to monitor and create changes to affect their situation in a positive way.

The continued support and empowerment of the child and family are critical. As the family succeeds in each step, they will feel empowered to move beyond any issues that emerge and to work toward issues that are more preventive in nature. Each step they make becomes a gain to the overall goals of the family and their overall confidence in handling the situation.

To continue your work in these situations, you and the family will need to identify barriers and find resolutions for them. In cases of special challenges, many factors can serve as barriers to a family and child succeeding in the implementation of their contract. Aside from individual interpersonal factors, there are those issues that are most likely to affect the ongoing support that a family and child need to access over time. These tend to be the policies and resources that can be given to the child and family. In special-challenge cases, as we have mentioned, there are extended periods of time in which outside services and resources are needed. Ensuring that policies not only offer the best resources for the families with special challenged children but also offer them for extended periods is an important consideration for them.

The Alcoholic Family

In Shelly's family (see opening case study), the visible difference appears to be in the economic level of the family. As a single parent, Shelly's mother has opportunities likely limited by her educational background and economic status. While we do not know the specific cultural background of the family, it is very possible that the family's cultural traditions affect the parenting within the family.

Of particular significance in this case is the role the mother's alcoholism may play now or in the future for the children. The role of economic factors affecting the use of alcohol by children is noted by Lindsey (1994). He noted that opportunities are limited for many children in oppressed groups, and as a result of this situation, there is an "increased need for residual services for such problems as drug and alcohol abuse, delinquency, and teenage pregnancy" (pp. 193–194). Although studies differ as to the percentage of substance abuse in children, Windle, Windle, and Scheidt (1995) note the significantly high levels of childhood physical and sexual abuse in their study of 802 alcohol treatment patients.

Substance abuse is a significant problem for child welfare agencies. Many children in foster care come from families where substance abuse is an issue. The co-occurring conditions of child maltreatment and substance abuse have dramatic negative effects on children. There is a trauma cycle (Kaplan-Sanoff, 1996) wherein children whose mothers abuse substances are more likely to become addicted adults, and daughters of substance abusers are three times more likely to marry an alcohol-abusing male. These are therefore intergenerational cycles with substantial influence on the lives of families. Effective interventions for women must be organized around their economic and emotional needs. Some residential facilities that house women and their children have been found to be effective. Incorporating parent groups as a component of treatment appears to maintain a commitment to sobriety and provides necessary parenting skills (Plasse, 1995).

Dore, Doris, and Wright (1995), in examining their research statistics related to substance abuse and child welfare, note the crucial need for child welfare workers to be prepared to utilize skills and knowledge to intervene appropriately in substance-abuse cases. Mitchell and Savage (1991) note that there are as many as 675,000 children each year seriously mistreated by a substance-abusive adult. The intervention into the family will be affected by the circumstances surrounding the income level, the substance abuse, and the parental history in the family.

The best training for social workers includes knowledge about programs such as AA (Alcoholics Anonymous), Hazelden (Intensive Interventions), and even programs that do not focus on abstinence and treatment but focus on harm reduction. Harm-reduction programs are controversial in that individuals are encouraged to cut back drinking rather than stop. While the authors believe that AA and other abstinence/treatment programs are best, in child welfare the consideration of harm reduction initially with intensive supervision may be the best alternative until the parent begins an abstinence program.

At-Risk Situations

Other issues in a family's life can also indicate a potential at-risk situation, including poverty, mental illness, age of the parent, substance abuse, history of family violence, and cultural and/or religious beliefs about the use of physical discipline in rearing children. Whether or not the family you are dealing with has one or more of these characteristics, it is important to understand that there will be enormous differences between how these families will respond to intervention from outside sources. Equally important is how you as a child welfare social worker may be able to respond to these family situations from a preventive focus for not only a particular family but for many families in a community. Although protecting children in child welfare still takes precedence over any other issues, recent movement by social workers has been to reach out to all families, stabilize their environment, and strengthen them to create change for themselves and others through networking and empowerment.

PRACTICE

A good model in child maltreatment is based in part on family-based care and the principles necessary to intervene in a difficult family situation with intensity and immediate impact. Implicit in utilizing this approach within a child maltreatment situation is the use of one worker to focus on the family in a supportive and protective manner. It has been clearly established through research that the most successful approach (especially when dealing with a child abuse or emotional maltreatment case) is that the social worker who investigates the case not be the worker who follows through on the intervention with the family.

Many state agencies have begun to utilize this approach to intervention in child maltreatment cases by providing a separate intake or investigative worker to assess the abusive situation. The child welfare social worker who then intervenes with the family to monitor protection of the child and provide services to the family serves as a support for the family. The child welfare social worker will have fewer obstacles to face from the family having not been the social worker who made the decisions regarding whether or not maltreatment occurred and how disposition of the case is to be handled.

A child maltreatment situation requires well-developed skills. The approach taken is often difficult to introduce into a physical abuse, neglect, or emotional maltreatment situation unless you have a full understanding of the issues in each family situation and the practice skills necessary to utilize this model. Regardless of the debate between the importance of child protection versus family-centered care, most trained child welfare social workers recognize the difficulty in intervention from either perspective. The following phases of intervention have been selected from brief and solution-focused treatment to allow the social worker to best provide for the family and child. Examples of different techniques in each chapter of this text will provide you with an extensive range of methods for dealing with differing child welfare situations.

Establishing a Relationship

In a child maltreatment situation, it is not difficult to understand how being the investigator of a case interferes with this initial phase. As an outsider entering into the family with the power to remove a child from that family, you are not seen as genuinely possessing the characteristics of warmth, genuiness, and understanding. The role of authority in the protection of the child clearly is not a comfortable role for the family. You may be viewed initially as an enemy out to destroy their family. While there are cases where families do not care about the removal of their child, the vast majority of families love their children and desire, for all the reasons any of us would, to keep their family together. So it is with fear and often anger that they encounter you, the social worker from child welfare, who is there to investigate issues of child abuse or emotional maltreatment. It is for just such a reason that it has been recommended that the person who investigates not be the same person who intervenes with the family; however, this may not always be the case in all child welfare agencies. Part of your advocate role as a social worker will be to work toward implementing a program that allows for the separation of investigation from treatment.

Regardless of the initial contact with the family, social workers must be prepared to present themselves in a manner that is conducive to the well-being of the child and family. In part, the skills in a child abuse situation will generally be in dealing with what is termed an *involuntary client*. Although this may initially be the case, it is important to remember that if you can provide the type of services needed in a manner that is strengthening and empowering to the family members, they may quickly become a *voluntary case*. Highlight 6.4

Highlight 6.4	Practice Methods

1. Use your authority in a warm, personal, supportive manner and show an understanding of the parents' feelings about the problem.
2. Demonstrate authority in a nonthreatening and noncoercive way as a family may feel less fearful of such an attitude.
3. Help your client to see that you represent a reasonable authority so that he or she can learn that other authority figures can also be reasonable.
4. Demonstrate your authority in a manner that indicates that there are no hidden agendas; that is, be honest.
5. Clarify your protective service role and function. Do not retreat from your responsibility; make the family aware of the expectations for change and the consequences of no change in their behavior. Make them aware that you will develop a plan for your work together and that there are consequences should the changes in their behavior not occur and their child be considered at risk.

6. Make the family aware of your knowledge that child protective service intervention can be traumatic and that you will do your best to minimize that trauma. Remember, the experience may be traumatic for both children and parents.
7. Avoid insensitivity to parental feelings because insensitivity may create anger, hostility, and resistance and will make it difficult for you to establish a helping relationship.
8. Do not allow your behavior to convey to the parents that they are the enemy and that you are working against them.
9. Avoid excessive reliance on your legal authority. (Filip, McDaniel, & Schene, 1992, p. 45)

Highlight 6.5 | **Methods for Engaging in a Child Welfare Intervention**

1. Listen carefully to the family members' feelings, trying to understand how the situation may have reached this point. This is not condoning the behavior but rather accepting that there are factors that play into all abusive situations and that can be improved.
2. Know yourself, what your personal reactions are to the situation, and what your professional responsibilities are. It is your responsibility to ensure the safety of the child, but this can be accomplished through nonjudgmental communication and by reaching out to the family.
3. Allow the family to make decisions about the intervention within the context of your protective function. Remember, the family will be more likely to follow through on a plan and/or contract if they have had some part in making it. Empower the child and family as much as possible to deal with environmental issues and make changes themselves.
4. Be very clear about professional issues of confidentiality and the limits of your decision making. Helping the client to understand the limits of your role allows the client to assume some of the responsibility.

gives several methods to remember when approaching a family regarding a child maltreatment situation. Whether or not you are within a system that requires this dual role, Highlight 6.5 gives additional methods to use when engaging the family in the child welfare intervention.

Foremost in the application of these skills is the social worker's ability to implement professional "use of self." Use of self is a key technique in any practice a social worker undertakes with individuals, families, groups, and/or communities. Use of self implies a conscious use and understanding of your personal reactions to a situation, but from an empathetic and supporting framework. It also implies an understanding and working through of your own personal reactions to and feelings about difficult family situations. It does not mean that you tell stories about yourself but that you can give an indication to the family of how you understand components of the situation. Through an application of this skill, the social worker in the child maltreatment situation has a greater opportunity to affect positive change in the lives of the family and child. Highlight 6.6 is an example of an initial contact situation, followed by a sample phone conversation in Highlight 6.7, and a sample home interview in Highlight 6.8.

Notice how much easier it is now for you as the social worker in a child abuse situation to connect with the parent. You are not entering to make a judgment of the situation. That has already been done and you are there to provide support and guidance to help the family create a new situation for themselves as well as protect the child. Do not think this role is easy. The family will still be suspicious of you, and you will have to engage them in an ongoing working relationship in order to gain their trust and enlist their willingness to change. Research supports this approach as the most productive in the sense that as parents begin to trust you, changes are more likely to occur (McCallum, 1995).

Highlight 6.6	Initial Contact with Child

Amy met Shelly at the school with her teacher in the counseling office. Amy had found Shelly very frightened and shy when she was initially introduced.

AMY: Hello, Shelly. My name is Amy, and I am here from Children's Services. I would like to talk with you about your bruises.

TEACHER: Shelly, Amy can help you if you can tell her how you got those bruises.

SHELLY: It was an accident.

AMY: How did the accident happen, Shelly?

SHELLY: Mom was cleaning up some things last night, and I broke a glass off the table. When she went to sweep it up, the broom hit me.

AMY: Have you had these kinds of accidents before, Shelly?

SHELLY: Sometimes Mom has a bad day and I get in the way. She loves me and is always sorry after it happens, and it usually only happens after she has a bad day and has to lay down with a headache.

AMY: Well, maybe I can help you and your Mom with her bad days, Shelly. I need to call her and talk with her about these accidents.

Highlight 6.7	Phone Conversation with Parent

MOTHER: Hello?

AMY: Ms. Lopez, this is Amy Lyons calling from Family and Children's Services. I'm calling with regard to your daughter Shelly.

MOTHER: Is she all right?

AMY: Yes, Ms. Lopez, I am at the school with her now and she is fine. I would like to come over to your home this afternoon if I could to speak with you about Shelly.

MOTHER: What do you want to talk about?

AMY: I think it would be best if I could speak with you in person. I know Shelly will be home about 3:30, and I would like to talk with you alone and then with both of you if I could. I can come now, it's 2:00, and then see Shelly when she arrives home.

MOTHER: I don't know, I am supposed to go out this afternoon. I guess you can come over now, but I don't know what you want, and I am not sure I want you in my house.

AMY: I understand you're feeling anxious about the visit. Let me explain that I am a social worker for Family and Children's Services, and in that capacity I need to meet with you. However, my role will be to help you with your family situation. I would like to talk with you now so we can get started on that.

MOTHER: I don't need any help.

AMY: I recognize that as a single mother supporting yourself and your child, it may not seem like someone outside the family should be involved in any way; however, sometimes we all need help, and in this case I am required to speak with you before we can make that decision together.

MOTHER: All right, come over.

Assessment

The child is our first priority in the assessment of any child maltreatment case. This will mean a risk assessment must be done for the child. If you serve as the investigator, this will be your main initial assessment, but if you serve as the supportive social worker, you will review the initial risk assessment done by

Highlight 6.8	Home Interview

AMY: Ms. Lopez, the situation I am here about concerns the bruises on Shelly's legs. The school is required to notify Family and Children's Services if they believe a child might need some help in their family situation. Can you tell me how Shelly received those bruises?

MOTHER: That school is always interfering. I didn't know she had any bruises. She's always falling down. What did Shelly tell you?

AMY: She was very reluctant to say, but she shared with me that it had been an accident with a broom last night.

MOTHER: I didn't know she had an accident. She's very accident prone, and she doesn't tell me when she does something silly.

AMY: The bruises on her legs would be very hard to get from an accident with a broom. In fact they were quite large and numerous.

MOTHER: Well, I don't know how she got them—probably out playing at recess. They never watch the kids at school and then try to blame us parents for all the issues.

AMY: Shelly didn't go out for recess today. She came to school with the bruises, and I understand she has had similar bruises before.

MOTHER: [Screaming] I don't hurt my daughter . . . I love her. I don't need you people interfering. Shelly and I do fine.

AMY: [Calmly] Ms. Lopez, I am not here to create problems. I want to help you solve them.

MOTHER: I don't need any interference from outsiders, including that school. I don't need any help. We get along fine.

AMY: At this point, Ms. Lopez, I believe there are grounds for a substantiated case of abuse with your daughter. I really want to work with you, but if you aren't able to tell me what is happening, there is little I can do.

MOTHER: [Starting to cry] I don't want to lose my daughter. I am a good mother. I didn't mean to hit her. She broke several glasses when she was washing dishes, and I got too angry. I won't do it again. I really love my daughter.

AMY: I know this is a very frightening process, having someone from Family and Children's Services come to your door. I am not here to break up your family, Ms. Lopez, but I am here to ensure the safety of Shelly and to work with you so that these situations do not continue. Let's you and I talk together now about what's been going on and in what way I can help. I need to let you know that I will be filing a report with Protective Services regarding my findings. I want to work together to resolve this situation; however, I must ensure Shelly's safety, so we will need to discuss the situation you have at home right now and make some decisions.

MOTHER: I was just angry at her. I just swatted her with the broom. I never intended to hurt her.

the investigator and do an ongoing risk assessment throughout the length of the case.

Of initial concern in this assessment process is the evaluation of the risk situation in which the child is placed. Many tools can be used for risk assessment in a child abuse situation. Holder and Corey (1986) note four areas of critical decision making in risk assessment: (1) Is the child in immediate risk of danger? (2) What services or actions are necessary to protect the child during the investigation? (3) Should the child be removed from the home? and (4) Is there a case plan that can be developed to address the child being at risk? (Pecora, Whittaker, Maluccio, Barth, & Plotnick, 1992). These are the questions you as the social worker will have to answer before making any decisions regarding what services can be used.

Highlight 6.9 | Child-at-Risk Field (CARF)

1. How is the child viewed by the parents?
2. How does the child present self, specifically as related to behavior/emotion?
3. What is the child's current status and vulnerability?
4. What are the pervasive behaviors, feelings, or levels of adaptation apparent in the parents?
5. What is the history of the adults (parents) in the family (recent and past)?
6. What are the parenting practices in this family?
7. How do parents relate to others outside the home (nonrelatives)?
8. What are the demographics of the family?
9. How does the family function, interact, and communicate?
10. How does the environment, which includes extended family, support the family?
11. What surrounding circumstances accompany the maltreatment?
12. What form of maltreatment is apparent?
13. How does the family perceive or respond to the intervention?
14. What influences external to the family will reduce intervention effectiveness? (Holder & Corey, 1986, as cited in Pecora Whittaker, Maluccio, Barth, & Plotnick, 1992, pp. 243–244)

Pecora, Whittaker, Maluccio, Barth, and Plotnick (1992) further suggest that three different types of risk assessments have been developed: (1) matrix approaches, (2) the empirical predictors method, and (3) family assessment scales, such as the Child Well-Being or Family Risk scales developed by the CWLA and the Child-at-Risk Field (CARF) developed by Holder and Corey (1986). They further note how difficult a risk assessment becomes because the child protection worker may not know exactly which areas or issues to focus on. The 14 open-ended questions and anchored rating skills developed by Holder and Corey are shown in Highlight 6.9 and can aid you in identifying what risks exist.

Possibly the most difficult area in assessing risk is the fact that despite all the scales and matrixes, none are perfect. Many do not take into account the multicultural, gender, or age issues as they relate to the child and family. Among these are several points to be considered in the child welfare social worker's mind as he or she processes each case. These points are shown in Highlight 6.10.

Nuclear family assessment of the systems within and surrounding the child and family is an essential component to planning any intervention strategy. Having established a relationship with the family will enable you as the worker to intervene in a positive way. Methods of doing assessments abound in the social work child welfare practice field. What makes the assessment different in

Highlight 6.10 | Points to Consider

1. Know your own limitations.
2. Do not make the decision without the use of a reliable instrument.
3. In making the decision, utilize your own experience in assessing all factors.
4. The safety of the child is the first priority.

a child abuse situation is the immediacy of the situation. The importance of accurate and thorough information based not only on the issues related to the child and family situation but also on the strengths and supports that are visible within the situation will help determine the immediacy of risk to the child.

Two major assessments are done in child maltreatment cases. The first is the risk assessment of the child, while the second is a more extensive assessment for intervention in the family. Most assessments in social work are done on the basis of biological, psychological, and sociological components of the child and family situation.

Inherent in a good assessment is the ability of the worker to integrate these areas as they relate not only to the child and his/her development but also to the family and its development. The family itself follows a developmental cycle that can be short-circuited by environmental factors. Understanding these environmental factors and their effects is important in intervening in a violent family situation.

A written assessment of family members, the situation, and the dynamics taking place in the situation is critical to beginning to coordinate a treatment plan. Many different forms have been developed in child welfare agencies to facilitate this assessment. It is important before examining one of these example forms to reiterate the importance of the methods shown in Highlight 6.11 when doing any assessment, be it for risk or for treatment.

The preceding assessment does not include all the areas that the social worker may have covered before making a decision about an intervention plan. The social worker may have spoken with family members, neighbors, and other systems (such as the family's church) in making this decision. Additionally, a thorough review of records, as well as an assessment of the environmental situation of the family, is extremely important. Family-of-origin material is especially relevant in abuse situations as it may be a repetitive pattern; however, the initial written assessment may not be as detailed as an intervention plan may be.

| Highlight 6.11 | **Additional Assessment Principles** |

1. Be sensitive to cultural values, multicultural differences, and to the family strengths as well as limitations (Pecora, Whittaker, Maluccio, Barth, & Plotnick, 1992).
2. Include the family in understanding the importance of the assessment and how it will aid them in resolving the situation through solution-focused tasks.
3. Although there are many different pieces of information to gather, keep the initial assessment as simple but thorough as possible.
4. Assessments need input from many different sources, so do not just assess a situation based on one system's perspective (such as the school, the family, or the extended family). All perspectives are critical. Also, remember that information can be found in records—the family doctor's records, a hospital's records, as well as previous difficulties at the school—not just in talking with someone.
5. When gathering the assessment, empower the family and child as much as possible, allowing them to talk about what they believe are the issues. Do not, however, lose track of your focus of the assessment, which is first for the protection of the child and second for the stabilization of the family.

| Highlight 6.12 | A Nonstructured Interview |

AMY: I will need to gather some information about you and your family situation before I can provide you with services I believe will help. Let's start by talking about your family now. I know you have Shelly, who is 7, and Kevin, who is 4. Do you have any other children?

MOTHER: No, I had a miscarriage once. I was about 4 months pregnant and fell down some stairs. I was only 17 and was not married yet.

AMY: [Leaning slightly forward toward Shelly's mother] That must have been a difficult time for you.

MOTHER: It wasn't easy, because I didn't really slip. Shelly's dad pushed me down the stairs after we got into a fight. He was always doing something like that. I stayed with him anyway, and we got married but it didn't last long. He left when I was still pregnant with Kevin. I hadn't heard from him until about 9 months ago, when he came and said he wanted a divorce so he could marry someone else. Like he'll be any better with anyone else!

AMY: It must have been hard seeing him again.

MOTHER: It wasn't easy, especially after I had just lost my grandmother. I've been feeling real low—like no one wants to be with me. I know my grandmother loved me, but I still feel real alone now. More than I ever have.

An intervention plan will include details that theoretically lead to the decision to be made. It is important for you to understand that this assessment needs to be done as thoroughly and as quickly as possible in order to protect the well-being of the child and family.

Gathering such an assessment is difficult when there is limited time and the situation may be very tense. Remember to gather the information not simply by moving through the questions on the form but also by discussing with the family and child all aspects that they desire to share. It is significant that some of the best assessment information is gained through simple communication rather than through a structured form. Highlight 6.12 illustrates how the social worker can gain information without following a structured interview.

Visual assessment methods are also very helpful in gathering data quickly and in a manner that provides an overview of more than the problematic situation. In visual assessments, you can also pick up more quickly on the strengths within the family. A common visual tool for assessing family dynamics and the developmental cycle of the family is known as the Kinetic Action Drawing and is shown in Highlight 6.13 (Schachter, 1978). In this technique, the social worker has different family members draw a picture of something the family does together. Through these drawings, the social worker can assess how communication occurs, what level of interaction the family has, and how individual family members feel right now.

Always remember when assessing any family situation to look for the strengths of the family, even in the drawings. Clearly, from Shelly's drawing, the issues of drinking begin to emerge, but there are signs of strength in the family from how the family appears to be together. The person at the end of the table is the father whom Shelly continues to hope will come home.

The purpose of an assessment is not simply to focus on the family and child but also to provide an overview of the external systems that impact the

Highlight 6.13 | **Kinetic Action Drawing**

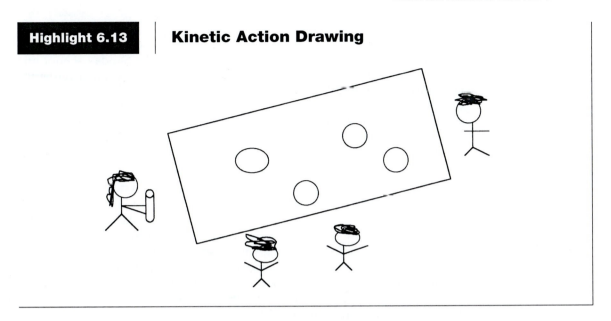

family. A common tool for analyzing external systems and their relationship to the family and child is the ecomap. The ecomap was devised as a method of obtaining information related to the openness or isolation of a family. It provides information about how the family and its members handle issues both internally and externally. The ecomap can be used quickly to gather information about linkages the family and individual members have with outside systems. In doing an ecomap, it is important to share with the family the importance of outside resources and linkages and to explain that a visual presentation of these resources can often be helpful, not only to the social worker but also to the family. An example of an ecomap can be seen in Highlight 6.14.

Highlight 6.14 | **Ecomap**

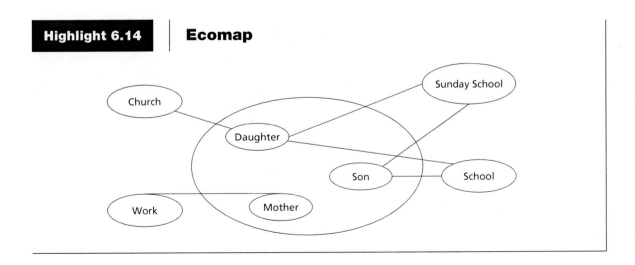

You can note from this ecomap the lack of support this family has on the outside; however, it is also important to notice where there are some supports that may be called on in future situations, such as the Sunday school and church, as well as the school system and Shelly's teacher. By empowering the family with this information and training them in how to seek out additional supports, you are aiding them in reaching more resources through prevention tactics. The more external supports available, the less possibility of child maltreatment.

The resource systems available to a family are defined as those systems within the community that can help provide services, programs, or resources to aid in the intervention with the family. Most resource systems overlap with social systems and/or programs and services. Examples of resource systems in a community might include the school, church, women's shelter, public aid office, juvenile probation office, legal services, family shelter, and family court program, to name a few. Assessing what resource systems a family may have available to them means understanding what needs the family has and what resource systems can meet those needs. This is also the point at which the child welfare social worker and family can begin to make some decisions about who it will be important to include in working on a collaborative treatment program.

It is necessary in the assessment of all child welfare situations to evaluate programs and services provided by the resource systems in the community in relation to each case situation. It is important to begin this process long before your work with cases. In part, understanding the resources of the community in which your families live is critical to providing the services needed. The social worker's understanding and connection with these services provides a significant resource not only to the child and family but also to the community and agency the worker serves. Understanding program and service resources involves more than just knowledge; it also involves the worker's ability to utilize those programs and services in the most productive manner for the families and children. This involves the child welfare social worker knowing not only all the services and programs that can be provided but also the workers involved in these areas and the eligibility requirements of particular programs and services. Having collaborative relationships and networking among social services agencies and workers is valuable to the child welfare social worker. It allows you to readily assess which services and programs may be the most helpful for the child and family.

Once a complete assessment has been done, a written assessment is necessary to help provide the social worker, the family, and other members of the intervention plan with collaborative guidelines and an understanding of the situation. Highlight 6.15 is an example of a written assessment.

Planning and Contracting

The child and family system is not the only system involved in child abuse situations. The resources of the extended family, child-care system, health care

Personal Information: Identifying Information

Name: Shelly Lopez

Address: 214 Wilton Rd., Sugan, California 32317

Phone Number: (532) 675-8923 **Referral:** Ms. Shanks, Sugan Grade School, Sugan, CA.

Physical Condition: Shelly is a 7-year-old Hispanic girl of medium build and height. She is cleanly dressed, and her hair is combed into a ponytail. Shelly's physical appearance appears normal except for three bruises on the back calf of her left leg and two bruises on the back of her right thigh and calf. The size of the bruises range from 2 inches to 6 inches. There do not appear to be any additional physical injuries on Shelly. The bruises appear new as they are purple in color. The school nurse reports there are no fractures or breaks to the legs.

Education: Shelly is in the second grade at Sugan Grade School and generally is an A and B student. Ms. Shanks, her teacher, reports that over the last month, Shelly's grades have been dropping, and she has seen bruises on Shelly's legs at least three other times. Ms. Shanks notes that this has been a recent change, and she had not noted difficulties before. Records indicate that Shelly has been a good student, and there have been no concerns over her until this last month.

Presenting Problem: The presenting problem is suspected physical child abuse. Shelly reports being "accidentally hit with the broom." Ms. Lopez stated after some initial denial that she had "swatted Shelly with the broom" after the child had broken some dishes.

Family Information: Shelly lives with her mother, Racine Lopez, age 32, and her brother, Kevin, age 4. Ms. Lopez states she has been divorced for 3 months and works as a tollbooth operator three blocks from their house. Ms. Lopez states she has worked for the state for 3 years. The whereabouts of Shelly's father are unknown, and Shelly has not seen her father for 5 years, according to Ms. Lopez. The family receives no government assistance, and there is no financial support from the father. Ms. Lopez states that her family lives in Arizona and that the father's family has never been involved with the children. They also live in Arizona. Ms. Lopez does not believe she has much outside support as she has no family in the area and very few friends. Ms. Lopez noted that she has been more depressed in the last few months and that her reactions with the kids are affected by this.

When asked about recent stresses in the family situation, Ms. Lopez reported that her grandmother had recently died and that she had been quite close to her. She also stated that she had felt quite lonely since that loss, as she had talked with her grandmother at least once a week for the past 10 years.

Ms. Lopez noted that generally she disciplined the children by making them stay in their rooms but that lately she seemed to lose control and swatted at them, although she knew this was wrong. Ms. Lopez denied any alcohol, drug, or mental health problems in the family, although she stated that her father had a drinking problem at one time.

Family of Origin: Ms. Lopez notes that she was raised by her maternal grandmother, following the death of her mother from cancer. She states she was the youngest of three children. She has two older brothers whom she has not seen or heard from for over 10 years. Her grandmother recently died, and she expresses that she has experienced depression and stress from this situation. Reasons for lack of contact with her brothers could not be explained by Ms. Lopez. She states that she never knew her father because he left the family before she was born. She describes her upbringing as positive from the love of her grandmother but very lonely.

Social Worker's Assessment of Situation: It appears that the case of physical abuse can be substantiated by the own admission of Ms. Lopez. The abuse appears to be of recent origin and not an ongoing practice in the family. This change in behavior on Ms. Lopez's part appears to be related to some depression and stress she is experiencing from the loss of her grandmother. Although Ms. Lopez denies a substance-abuse problem, it should be noted that there is a family history of substance abuse. Ms. Lopez appears genuinely remorseful about the abusive situation and is willing to work with the agency in any way to correct the abusive situation and stabilize the family.

Recommendation: Due to a lack of prior history of abuse, the rating on the Child Well-Being Scale, and the motivation of Ms. Lopez, I am recommending an intensive in-home support program for the family, with the child remaining in the home. Ms. Lopez and the family are strongly in need of social support, treatment for emotional issues, and further support for single parenting.

| **Highlight 6.16** | **Case Management Practice** |

Social work case management practice:

- Is a process based on a trusting and enabling client–social worker relationship
- Utilizes the social work dual focus of understanding the person in the environment in working with populations at risk
- Aims to ensure a continuum of care to clients with complex, multiple problems and disabilities
- Attempts to intervene clinically to ameliorate the emotional problems accompanying illness or loss of function
- Utilizes the social work skills of brokering and advocacy as a boundary-spanning approach to service delivery

- Targets clients who require a range of community-based or long-term care services, encompassing economic, health/medical, social, and personal care needs
- Aims to provide services in the least restrictive environment
- Requires the use of assessment of the client's functional capacity and support network in determining the level of care
- Affirms the traditional social work values of self-determination and the worth and dignity of the individual and the concept of mutual responsibility in decision making

| **Highlight 6.17** | **Case Management Process** |

1. Engage all systems and individuals to be involved in a mutual and positive manner.
2. Establish quickly the roles of the differing systems within the case management.
3. Work together toward a mutual treatment plan.
4. Contract for responsibilities in the process and case.

5. Meet on a regular basis to review goals and outcomes.
6. Agree with all systems involved on time for termination.
7. Always evaluate the case management process as well as the outcome.

system, educational system, and community resource systems are all vital to implementing any plan with a child and family in an abuse and/or emotional maltreatment environment. These systems are all involved in the interaction of the child and family. Coordination of these systems is necessary in order to prevent inconsistent messages and interventions.

Case review and coordination in child maltreatment situations require the social worker to be skilled in case management as well as interactional relationships. Case management in all child welfare situations is a core intervention skill that will be used throughout all areas of child welfare. Highlight 6.16 notes features of the case management process (Vourlekis & Greene, 1992). Case management services have phases in their process. Most case managers understand that to accomplish their goals, they must follow the process shown in Highlight 6.17. Highlight 6.18 gives an example of the case management process. Critical to good intervention in a child abuse situation is the involvement of family members not only in the planning of the intervention but also in the coordination of the services. Once a determination is made on how the

Highlight 6.18 | **Example of a Case Management Process**

Amy contacted the school with the knowledge of Ms. Lopez and Shelly following the investigation. In contacting Ms. Shanks, she learned that Ms. Shanks had met with Ms. Lopez during the parent–teacher conference and had found her interested in Shelly's progress. Ms. Shanks agreed to stay in contact with Amy over the course of the rest of the school year to report on Shelly's progress. She also offered to help in any way she could. Amy recognized following this conversation that she had found an initial support for the Lopez family in Ms. Shanks. Amy then contacted the support system for respite care for parents, recognizing that Ms. Lopez would need some times of relief in order to attend parenting classes and other support groups that might help her with her depression.

As Amy began to bring these different systems together, she prearranged several planning meetings for all involved, including Ms. Lopez. The initial purpose of these planning meetings was to clearly lay out the intervention plan and agree on the services and focus of treatment to be provided. Later meetings were designed to review the progress of all involved and to reinforce all positive outcomes.

child maltreatment situation will be handled, the family needs to be involved in every step that follows. Ms. Lopez was encouraged by Amy to initiate and clarify between individuals in the planning meetings their responsibilities, services, and time schedule for providing service. After the meeting, Amy empowered Ms. Lopez by applauding and supporting her participation in the intervention and asking her to plan the agenda for the next meeting. This was Amy's beginning step in encouraging Ms. Lopez to take control of her own environment and bring about change.

It is critical at this point of intervention with the family to set up a written contract regarding the expectations and understandings that you as the social worker have with the child and family. In the case we have been discussing, this contract will involve intensive service provisions from the child welfare agency worker and the family. The contract will include time lines and meeting dates, goals and tasks, and ideas of how solutions to difficulties can be accomplished. A contract, as noted, is important in giving specific information to the family and child about the expectations of the plan and as a method for giving the family and child an opportunity to be part of the plan. Highlight 6.19 gives an example of this type of contract.

Implementation of Plan

Key in the implementation phase is the continuation of the interviewing skills and practice techniques that focus on the strengths of the family and child and direct them to solutions for their problems. For example, you suspect from what you know that Ms. Lopez drinks, and you want to deal with this situation immediately. Start with a comment on her strength in being a single mother. For example, "I know it must be difficult for you to support and raise your children on your own. You have to have a lot of strength and energy to do that." Then move into a more direct question related to the alcohol. For

| Highlight 6.19 | Contract with a Family Referred for Child Maltreatment |

The following agreement has been constructed mutually with Ms. Lyons of the Children and Family Agency of California, Ms. Lopez, Shelly, Ms. Shanks, Mr. Williams (of respite care), Ms. Carol (of Parents without Partners), and Mr. Sills (of AA).

A. Strengths
   1. Openness to change
   2. Strong single mother
   3. Cares about children
B. Goals
   1. Learn appropriate parenting skills through group training
   2. Stop drinking and attend AA
   3. Deal with depressing issues in relationship to grief
   4. Receive respite services
C. Responsibilities and Tasks for Resolution
   1. Attend parenting group meetings
   2. Attend AA
   3. Receive assistance from social worker with transportation and child care
D. Outcomes and Evaluation
   1. Improved parenting-skills progress notes
   2. No use of alcohol in conjunction with regular attendance at AA—Goal Attainment Scale
   3. Less depression and more relaxed—Depression and Anxiety Scales

example, "Sometimes when a person has to be as strong as you do all the time, you want to escape from the situation once in a while. And for some people, the way to do this is to drink." When you are dealing with a case that may involve substance abuse, it is best to be direct in your questioning. For example, "I'm wondering if this is the way you escape and how often you need to do it each week to relieve the stress." The reason this issue needs to be raised directly is to avoid denials and shorten the time it takes to begin to deal with the problem. Although the parent may continue to deny the use, you have broken the ice and can call out incongruencies in her statement with your own observations (beer bottles in an open trash bag, Shelly's drawing, etc.).

Part of the work you will do in this phase will be dealing with the adult's parenting skills and helping her develop different ways of parenting. The parent might be involved in parenting classes, or you might help the mother role-play a situation in which she would tend to get upset and have her try different ways of handling these issues. Along with parenting skills are techniques you will use to help the parent deal with her anger and frustration. Some of these may be relaxation techniques, cognitive restructuring, or assertiveness training. Along with these techniques, it is important to continue to focus on the parent's strengths, her previous coping mechanisms, and her ability to change her situation and behaviors.

When implementing the plan, the coordination of services (a case management function) can be given priority in the process. If resources and systems are not coordinated around the contract and treatment plan for the family, little will be accomplished. An established time line with set meeting dates and clarity of roles and responsibilities is critical, as noted in the contract and planning phase. The issue of drinking must continue to be addressed, and the parent will need to take action around the alcohol issue using any number of services available.

Possibly one of the most difficult skills needed will be that of supporting and strengthening the family throughout the process. With so many systems involved and possibly numerous judgmental issues at play, keeping the family empowered is often a challenge. This is in part why it is so important that one child welfare social worker have responsibility for case management and treatment. Also, this process clearly establishes the importance of the Community Network Book and the social worker's ties or connections with outside members of the systems being utilized. If the social worker does not know and feel comfortable with the individuals who will be working with the family and child, all empowerment can be lost. Not using a system or agency may be preferable to utilizing a resource that may not support or empower the family.

As in any process, it is best not to be surprised. When you are working with the family and integrative support systems in developing the contract and treatment plan, it is important to cover what difficulties could emerge at this point. However, it is often the case that difficulties will not be encountered until the plan begins to be implemented. For example, transportation may be an area that could prove to be a barrier. The family may believe they will not have a problem and yet their car could break down, not allowing them to attend required meetings, such as parenting classes. Ensuring that the family has covered these concerns and has alternatives to these barriers in case they happen can save not only time but the potential outcome of the entire treatment.

Monitoring the plan and services being provided to the family requires organizational skills that are inherent in case management practice; however, as the social worker is the primary provider of the treatment, as well as the coordinator, this monitoring process is much more easily supplied. Monitoring within this approach is more than monitoring the family and child. It is equally important that the other systems be monitored and that the family be empowered to monitor their services also. Organizational skills are crucial to this process because the model calls for a multisystemic approach, and this can only be accomplished through the ongoing interaction between systems, services, and the child and family.

As the family becomes more comfortable and trustful about their role in implementation, they can be encouraged to reach out into their environment to facilitate others who may need similar resources. What you are doing in this phase is setting up a preventive outreach program within a community of people through the families themselves. The design in Highlight 6.20 demonstrates how the child welfare social worker fits into this role between the family, systems, and environment.

Evaluate Outcomes and Terminate Services

Evaluation of services is generally an ongoing process that occurs within the context of the intervention. Although evaluation is a process, it is also an outcome. As an outcome, it has the significance of justifying your practice and services. Knowing how to provide outcome information to your clients, funding

Highlight 6.20	Environmental Design

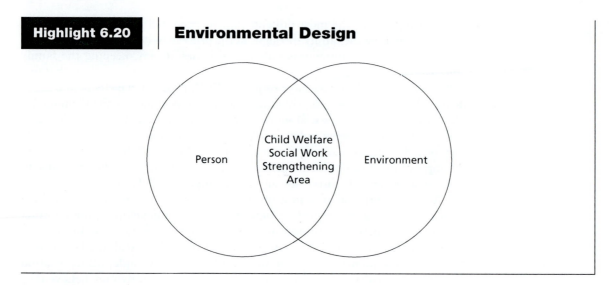

Highlight 6.21	Evaluation Model

Goal Attainment Scale for Weekly Score

Goal 1: Attend AA meeting

−2	Does not attend or talk to sponsor
−1	Tries to talk to sponsor
0	Talks to sponsor
1	Tries to go to meetings
2	Attends meetings and talks to sponsor

Goal 2: Attend parenting group

−2	Does not attend
0	Talks with parenting trainer
2	Attends

Goal 3: Deal with depression issue

−2	Does nothing
0	Works in depression workbook
2	Attends counseling

---

sources, and other systems will help secure your intervention and treatment focus. Highlight 6.21 is an example of how an evaluation model for a case may be established and developed.

It may be surprising for students to learn that the termination of services in child welfare should begin as the service starts. Your goal as the child welfare social worker is to provide the child protection and stabilize the family; therefore, the beginning is only one step toward the termination of practice.

Follow-Up from a Multisystemic Perspective

The follow-up phase in a child abuse and/or emotional maltreatment case is an area that has not been dealt with extensively. Basic services are terminated at that point; however, it is important to remember that the relationship you will have established with this family is a significant one, preferably not as an

| **Follow-Up Situation**

Six weeks following the termination of the intensive services offered to Ms. Lopez and Shelly, Amy contacted the family and set up an appointment at the home.

AMY: It's good to see you and Shelly again. How are things going?

MOTHER: Well, we haven't had too many problems, but the state is cutting back on employees and I am worried about what that means in terms of a job for me.

AMY: When will you hear something?

MOTHER: In about three weeks. I have a lot of seniority, but you never know for sure.

AMY: It's important for you to be prepared for what you might do if that happens.

---

intruder in their lives but as a facilitator for the betterment of their family, especially in terms of their parenting skills and the well-being of the child. Highlight 6.22 gives an example of a follow-up situation.

Follow-up in the community includes assessment of the resources within the community, as well as gathering community support for the education and prevention of child abuse, neglect, and/or emotional maltreatment. Working through the families to help organize and advocate for resources needed to reduce stress in families is part of the follow-up process. This follow-up is based on your work and assessment with many families—more than just the case you have been working with.

Like community follow-up, you will be assessing the programs and services available as well as the quality of what was provided in each case situation. You are quality control for the children and families you serve; therefore, it is essential to follow up on the services provided in each child welfare case situation. One way of accomplishing this is to assess from your clients their thoughts on the programs they were involved in and the services they received. By processing data from each family, you will be able to identity what needs to be modified and what needs enhancement in the programs and services you recommend.

This approach has demonstrated a few of the techniques and tools that can be used in abuse and emotional maltreatment situations. It is critical for the social worker to understand that it is the risk assessment that allows the model to be utilized in this manner. There may be many occasions when the risk assessment dictates that the child is not safe in the home and must be removed. This does not change the phases or steps that the social worker will move through with the clients and, in particular, the family, but it will certainly change the manner and approach taken in dealing with the case. More work will need to be done in working out the trust issues with both the family and child. The removal of children from their home is a serious event, and the manner and accommodations made in this decision will affect the ability of the worker to reunite the family in a stabilized environment.

SUMMARY

This chapter has provided an overview of issues related to abuse and emotional maltreatment. The definitions of these issues and their impact on the policies related to children and families have been examined in light of the impact of the new family-based services being utilized by child protection agencies.

The approach has been implemented in a manner that provides the student with an understanding of how family-based practice or substitute services can be utilized not only within specialized programs in child welfare but also within established child welfare fields. Preventive work in creating change in economic conditions so families have access to equal resources is a major objective in eliminating child neglect and maltreatment. Understanding how the economic conditions of your community affect these issues will enable you to bring about preventive measures against abuse and maltreatment.

Questions for Discussion

1. Describe the meaning of *parens patriae*.
2. Describe the four steps in an intervention of child abuse.
3. Draw your own family's ecomap.
4. What role does case management play in child maltreatment?
5. Discuss permanency planning and its role in family prevention.
6. Do a kinetic drawing of your own.

Child Sexual Abuse

Mandy, a White American 15-year-old in the tenth grade, appeared at her friend's house one evening very depressed and preoccupied. After much coaxing, she tells her friend what is bothering her. She mentioned that her father is strict and will not allow her to do many of the things her friends are allowed to do, particularly dating. She said her father seemed jealous of the attention she received from boys and wanted her to spend all her time at home, where she had assumed many of the household responsibilities. She began to cry uncontrollably upon telling her friend that her father had done "bad" things to her for many years. She confided that he had fondled her on a regular basis from the time she was 10 years old and started having sexual intercourse with her at age 13. Mandy's friend, although sworn to secrecy, is extremely upset and decided to tell her own mother, who then reported the abuse to the authorities. The Department of Social Services began an investigation of the report and the findings were substantiated. Mandy was removed from the home and placed in protective custody.

INTRODUCTION

Sexual abuse has emerged as one of the major forms of child abuse, not only in this country but universally as well. Reports of childhood sexual abuse are becoming increasingly common in both the popular and professional press. One national survey reported that 27 percent of women and 16 percent of men had a history of childhood sexual abuse (Finkelhor, Hotaling, Lewis, & Smith, 1990).

A similar study of the general population revealed that 38 percent of women had experienced some form of sexual abuse by age 18, whereas 28 percent had been sexually abused by age 14 (Russell, 1986).

Recent studies of the prevalence of child sexual abuse in the general population suggest that sexual abuse continues to be an underreported and undercounted situation, by official standards. In the past 25 years, studies have revealed that sexual abuse is much more common than originally thought, and reports of sexual abuse have increased dramatically since mandatory reporting began in the 1970s (Downs et al., 2004). The issue of disclosure is one that has been given considerable attention by various professional groups and organizations concerned with child sexual abuse. Numerous studies on this topic support the fact that the large majority of sexual abuse survivors, both male and female, never disclosed to anyone that they had been or were being abused (Russell, 1984; Salter, 1992). In fact, the research is quite consistent in that not disclosing appears to be the normative response to child sexual abuse. Very often, victims have chosen to remain silent because they feared retribution from the perpetrators, because they were ashamed and they blamed themselves for the abuse, or because they felt that they would not be believed (Downs et al., 2004). Methodologically sound studies have found that as many as 38 percent of female victims of child sexual abuse, with estimates of as many as 38 million sexually abused Americans (Crewdson, 1988), do not disclose the abuse as children. This is a relevant fact that the child welfare social worker will need to be aware of, as there may be cases where sexual abuse is the "secret" in the family's difficulties.

Aside from the obvious moral problem of sexual abuse, social workers cannot ignore the enormous social problems that develop when individuals experience such trauma during childhood or adolescence. Sexual abuse can leave substantial psychological scars on its victims in the form of disturbed self-esteem and an inability to develop trust in intimate relationships. As a result, a large majority of survivors experience difficulty in maintaining long-term, intimate relationships. Numerous studies of adults with substantial psychological problems have indicated a plausible connection with a history of child sexual abuse (Fleming, Mullen, & Bammer, 1997). Studies of various troubled populations such as drug abusers, juvenile offenders, adolescent runaways, prostitutes, and adults with sexual dysfunctions show that high proportions of these individuals were sexually victimized as children (Finkelhor, 1984). The case seems easily made that some fraction of those who are sexually victimized in childhood are affected quite badly by these experiences.

DEFINITION OF SEXUAL ABUSE

Definitions of sexual abuse vary. For the purposes of this text, the authors are employing the definition that is oriented toward mental health issues in child sexual abuse (see Highlight 7.1). This is chosen in light of the severe psychological consequences that occur to the victim. The impact of the abuse on the family system will also be addressed at another point in the chapter.

Highlight 7.1 | Definition of Sexual Abuse

Sexual abuse is any act occurring between people who are at different developmental stages, that is for the sexual gratification of the person at the more advanced developmental stage. This definition assumes a dyadic relationship. However, it is possible to have more than two people involved in a sexually abusive encounter, both victims and perpetrators. Ordinarily, the participants in sexual abuse are adults and children, but occasionally both victims and perpetrators are children. The perpetrator may be an adolescent and the victim a latency-aged or younger child. Alternatively, the victim may be the same age as the perpetrator but at an earlier developmental stage because of mental retardation (Faller, 1988).

A more important distinction to understand is the one between incest and stranger sexual abuse.

Incest

Incest is the predominant form of sexual abuse seen by social workers in a variety of settings. It can be defined as any form of sexual contact between individuals where the perpetrator has a familial relationship with the victim (i.e., parent or stepparent, sibling, aunt or uncle, grandparent, etc.). In the more classical case of incest, the interaction between father (or stepfather) and daughter begins as appropriate displays of physical affection and then gradually progresses to sexual behavior. The psychological trauma may arise in large part from the fact that the child's trust in the father, the primary protector, has been violated. The problem can become much more advanced if the abuse occurs over an extended period of time and if, upon disclosure, the child fails to receive the necessary support from the mother or other significant adults.

Stranger Sexual Abuse

With regard to stranger rape, another form of sexual abuse frequently brought to the attention of social workers, there can be a significant contrast in the resulting psychological trauma to the child. Generally, she or he receives support from parents and the adults involved, thus lessening the depth of long-term emotional consequences. The degree of trauma can also be affected by the use of force on the part of the perpetrator. Use of significant force and resulting injuries may contribute to emotional problems on the part of the victim and will require an appropriate therapeutic intervention.

To sufficiently understand the dynamics of the problems associated with child sexual abuse, social workers must be aware that the interactions in the abuse situation may not necessarily involve physical contact between the perpetrators and the victims. In Highlight 7.2, Faller defines three types of sexual abuse in which there is no physical touching.

| Highlight 7.2 | **Sexual Abuse with No Physical Touching** |

1. *"Sexy talk"* includes statements the perpetrator makes to the child regarding the child's sexual attributes, what he or she would like to do to the child of a sexual nature, and other sexual comments.
2. *Exposure* includes the perpetrator's showing the victim his/her intimate parts (breasts, penis, vagina, anus) and/or masturbating in front of the victim.
3. *Voyeurism* includes instances when the perpetrator either covertly or overtly observes the victim in a state of undress or in activities that provide the perpetrator with sexual gratification. (Faller, 1988, p. 12)

| Highlight 7.3 | **Sexual Abuse with Physical Touching** |

1. *Sexual contact* includes any touching of the intimate body parts. These include the breasts, vagina, penis, buttocks, anus, and perineal area. The perpetrator may fondle the victim, he/she may induce the victim to touch him/her, or the victim and perpetrator may engage in mutual fondling or masturbation. Frottage is sexual contact in which the perpetrator gains sexual gratification from rubbing his intimate parts against the victim's body or clothing.
3. *Interfemoral intercourse* is intercourse in which the perpetrator's penis is placed between the child victim's thighs, a technique that is generally employed with young victims. The terms *dry* and *vulvar* intercourse are also used for this act, as there may be rubbing of the penis against the child's vulva but there is no penetration.
4. *Sexual penetration* is characterized by some intrusion into an orifice. Four types have been noted in sexual abuse:
   a. *Digital penetration* involves placing fingers in the vagina or the anus or both. Usually the victim is penetrated by the perpetrator, but sometimes the perpetrator induces the victim to engage in penetration. Digital penetration is a form of sexual abuse found frequently with young victims and is sometimes a prelude to genital or anal intercourse.
   b. *Penetration with objects* is a less frequent type of sexual abuse in which the perpetrator puts an instrument in one of the victim's orifices—vagina, anus, or occasionally the mouth. The most frequent type is vaginal penetration.
   c. *Genital intercourse* involves the penis entering the vagina; however, occasionally the penetration is partial due to the smallness of the victim. There is usually a male perpetrator and female victim, but occasionally a female perpetrator may be involved in genital intercourse with a male victim. The victim in the latter type of situation is likely to be somewhat older, frequently an adolescent.
   d. *Anal intercourse* occurs when the perpetrator's penis is inserted into the victim's anus. This technique often occurs with male victims but it is also sometimes employed with female victims. (Faller, 1988, pp. 13–14)

Interactions that do involve physical contact between the perpetrator and victim are defined in Highlight 7.3.

PSYCHOSOCIAL DYNAMICS OF SEXUAL ABUSE

The problem of sexual abuse is surfacing as a major underlying issue in a number of dysfunctional behaviors brought to the attention of mental health professionals today. The inability of marital partners to establish a satisfactory level of intimacy in their relationship has often been attributed to a history of sexual abuse of one partner. As indicated, childhood sexual abuse can have a profound affect on the entire worldview of an individual throughout a lifetime. Without appropriate intervention, the damage associated with sexual abuse can be devastating.

Social workers are becoming increasingly more involved in cases involving sexual abuse through not only child welfare agencies but other settings as well. Child protection workers are receiving growing numbers of referrals of cases where children are at risk of ongoing sexual abuse (Berliner & Elliott, 1996). Mental health professionals of all kinds are seeing adults who were victims of sexual abuse as children and, as a result, are seeking treatment. When social workers encounter sexual abuse, it is often manifested under the guise of another problem that is brought to the attention of a professional. An adolescent who might be exhibiting antisocial behavior, alcohol or drug abuse, and/or running away behavior could be dealing with an abusive home situation. Children who might be having problems concentrating in school, consistently withdrawing from peers, exhibiting sexual behavior incongruent with their developmental level, or regressing to childlike behavior of an earlier developmental stage could be expressing symptoms of sexual abuse. Additionally, children who are brought to a physician for treatment of enuresis, encopresis, or sleep problems may also be experiencing the trauma of abuse. Hospitals and other medical facilities treating children who have been physically abused or neglected often discover the likelihood of sexual abuse as well.

Social workers frequently uncover a history of sexual abuse in a variety of treatment settings where adults seek assistance in dealing with problems such as those described in Highlight 7.4.

Likewise, social workers employed in child welfare settings are challenged by the psychosocial problems manifested in children who have been victims of sexual abuse, and they must deal with them from a "nontreatment" approach. Oftentimes these children exhibit sexual acting-out behavior in foster care and occasionally victimize other children residing in the home. They also experience difficulty in peer relationships or in controlling their own aggressive behavior. As a result, they frequently engage in predelinquent and delinquent behavior involving some form of aggressiveness or violence. Social workers

---

| **Highlight 7.4** | **Situations Associated with a History of Sexual Abuse** |

1. Marital discord or unsatisfying sexual relationship on the part of a couple seeking therapy
2. Substance abuse
3. Domestic violence where a woman has entered a shelter for protection

4. Suicidal tendencies or ideation
5. Criminal behavior involving incarceration or other criminal court activity, and so on

Highlight 7.5	Factors in Determining Relationship between Child and Perpetrator

1. The biological relationship between perpetrator and victim
2. The legal relationship that exists
3. The relationship between the perpetrator's and victim's families
4. The frequency of contact between the perpetrator and victim (Faller, 1988)

employed in school systems, juvenile justice settings, or residential facilities are often assigned the task of coordinating services for them.

In order to structure an appropriate plan for services, social workers must have a significant level of knowledge of the deep psychological consequences resulting from child sexual abuse. The closeness or intimacy of the relationship between perpetrator and victim affects the level of intensity and long-term consequences to the child. The factors listed in Highlight 7.5 largely determine the degree of closeness in the relationship.

In light of the complexity of circumstances surrounding the issue of child sexual abuse, the so-called resolutions to the problem are often fragmented, highly simplistic, or superficial and not actually remedies at all. This, to some extent, is due to the societal taboos concerning human sexuality and sexual behavior. It is also a reflection of a general reluctance to invade family privacy, or to interfere with the sanctity of parental autonomy over children (Laird & Hartman, 1985).

As in cases of physical abuse and neglect, the responsibility of child welfare agencies to protect sexually abused children is generally accepted by society and by the law. For this reason, their intervention in such cases is deemed essential by most experts. However, there is continuing debate about what the scope of agency intervention should be (Chapman & Smith, 1987).

PROCESSES AND PROCEDURES

Competing mandates within child welfare agencies compound the complexity of providing effective programs for families and children who have experienced sexual abuse. Child welfare workers must carry out interventions that focus on preserving the family unit while, at the same time, protecting the child. The legal authority given to child welfare workers to remove children who are in imminent danger of abuse creates a serious barrier in efforts to preserve the family unit.

In the majority of communities, linkages exist among agencies that provide services to abused children. These agencies include schools, hospitals, public and private mental health facilities, criminal justice agencies, child protection teams, and a variety of other social service programs. The effectiveness of these linkages is largely dependent upon coordination and communication among social workers to prevent the duplication or breakdown of critical services. To prevent this from occurring, interdisciplinary case review teams are common in many communities. Through the teams, various professionals who might be involved in a specific case involving sexual abuse are able to coordinate services and work toward common goals that support the best interest of the child(ren). The team establishes a case plan in which the role of each professional is clearly defined in terms of the service(s) they are able to provide in meeting a specified goal or service objective.

Child welfare agencies may undertake a range of actions on behalf of the victim, either through juvenile court actions or through service agreements between the agency and the family. When juvenile court actions occur, the child may be removed from the home and placed in protective supervision. This could be either a foster home, a temporary emergency shelter home, or with family members or close friends for a limited period of time as stipulated by state law. Under certain circumstances, the perpetrator is often mandated by the court to leave the home and have no further contact with the child until the completion of an investigation so as to provide immediate protection for the child while the child welfare agency and law enforcement authorities conduct separate (or joint) investigations into the abuse allegations. In most states, child welfare agencies are mandated by state law to conduct these investigations and recommend appropriate dispositions to the court based on the best interests of the child(ren). Concurrently, law enforcement authorities conduct a separate investigation of the case to determine if the perpetrator should be prosecuted for criminal charges. However, more recently some states have instituted a protocol for protective investigators and law enforcement officers to conduct joint investigations in which both entities interview the child(ren) together. This can present a myriad of problems with regard to disclosure, especially in cases of sexual abuse when no prior relationship has been established with the child victim.

Following a child's placement in protective custody, a social worker representing a child protection team conducts an evaluation. Child protection teams exist in many states and function in a capacity separate from the public child welfare agency responsible for protecting the child and the law enforcement agency involved in the investigation. The role of the child protection team social worker is to interview the child to determine (1) if the sexual abuse actually occurred and (2) the circumstances surrounding the situation. The court generally receives the results of this evaluation for consideration in making a disposition in the case.

During the period of time that the child is under the jurisdiction of the child welfare agency (child protective services) and is removed from the home, social workers often develop with the family a contract in which specific objectives are outlined and must be met before reunification can occur. In cases where children remain in the home under formal agreement or court-ordered supervision, a service agreement outlines the services the agency is able to provide in order for the family to remain intact. In either situation, the child welfare agency has legal responsibility for the welfare of sexually abused children and carries out the necessary interventions.

SERVICES AND PROGRAMS

As mentioned previously, a great deal of controversy continues to surround the use of family preservation/family-based programs, especially in cases involving sexual abuse. Although these family-based programs might be highly effective in many situations in which physical abuse or neglect has occurred, the dynamics surrounding sexual abuse raise concern about their appropriateness. In some cases, it is clearly not in the best interest of a child to attempt to preserve the family, particularly if it is extremely dysfunctional and the lives of the children are at risk. Nevertheless, the provision of mental health services to children and families in their homes is a new initiative in the mental health field and is a growing trend across the country (Combrinck-Graham, 1995; Archacki-Stone, 1995). The general purpose is to strengthen the family unit in an effort to prevent the out-of-home placement of sexually abused children. This is done through the provision of intensive support and therapeutic interventions to families in crisis and may only be appropriate in cases where the perpetrator is not residing in the home. In most cases, other more traditional services have not been effective and the child continues to experience persistent emotional and behavioral difficulties.

A number of exemplary programs that provide services for abused adolescents have emerged in recent years. The primary purpose of these programs is serving adolescents and their families through many different services. The programs provide emergency services, such as 24-hour housing shelter for adolescents, in addition to 24-hour telephone hotlines and counseling services. The programs also provide general information, referral services, and ongoing counseling for youth and their families. Adolescent peer counselors and abused youth meet on a daily basis to provide support, share feelings, and explain agency and community resources. The programs might also provide short-term foster homes for adolescents who are awaiting placement, who need longer-term crisis resolution services, or who are preparing to leave home but have not fully developed skills for independent living. The programs reflect a general philosophy that includes a respect for and incorporation of the ideas and self-help abilities of adolescents (Laird & Hartman, 1985).

Other programs that provide services to families who have experienced sexual abuse include Homebuilders and Family Builders, which provide intensive in-home family crisis counseling and life-skills education. These programs come from a family-based philosophy and are designed to prevent unnecessary dissolutions of troubled families and to reduce placements of children into publicly funded care. Homebuilders is based on the belief that it is usually best for children to grow up in their own homes. It draws upon the ecological perspective and developmental concepts as well as the development of competence. Skills required to implement this orientation include assessing the family's strengths, changing the environment, planning goals, setting the limits, contracting with families, teaching specific life or social skills, intervening during crises, working with families in their homes, and individualizing services to meet the needs of a family (Maluccio, 1990). The effectiveness of these types of programs can be questionable in cases of severe dysfunction in families in which sexual abuse has occurred.

PRACTICE

Assessment and Process

The assessment of sexual abuse is a complicated process that differs significantly from the assessment of physical abuse. As indicated previously, the psychosocial dynamics of sexual abuse require that social workers be knowledgeable of each individual's role in the abuse and how that affects the assessment process. Because children lack the emotional, maturational, and cognitive development necessary for adult sexual interaction, an adult's ability to lure a child into a sexual relationship is based upon the all-powerful and dominant position of the adult or older adolescent perpetrator.

The assessment process includes interviews with the child victim, the perpetrator, family members, and other significant individuals involved in the child's system (e.g., teachers, extended family, physician, etc.) to determine the circumstances surrounding the abuse and the level of trauma to the child. The immediate task of interviewing the child and family can be extremely difficult due to the anger and denial that is typically expressed by family members. The victim is likely to experience the stigma of being identified as a participant in the sexual interactions. He or she may even be rejected by the perpetrator, who may be a person who is highly valued by the child. In addition, the victim may also be ostracized if the family chooses to side with the perpetrator, or he or she may be "punished" by placement in foster care or elsewhere outside the home. The family may be torn apart and the child may feel responsible for its demise. On the other hand, perpetrators are not likely to admit they have engaged in sexual abuse and will likely deny it. The overall pervasiveness of anger throughout the family system directed toward the professionals involved in the case can be difficult to penetrate.

Initial Interview with the Child   The first step in interviewing a child must involve efforts to establish a relationship based on warmth, genuineness, empathy, empowerment, and positive regard. Efforts to assist the child in not taking responsibility for what has occurred depend on these factors. In cases of sexual abuse, the social worker's power over the family cannot be disregarded. Attempts to empower anyone in the family at this stage must be based on honesty and a willingness to work through the situation. The social worker's authoritative power provides a barrier that must be dealt with at the onset and may continue to resurface. Nevertheless, the immediate focus should be on the child and the development of a relationship with him or her. The first attempt to build trust should occur at the first contact and prior to approaching the issue of sexual abuse. Once trust is established, which can be fairly quickly in some children, spontaneity in the relationship is more likely to occur, and children are less frightened to reveal stressful information to someone they know as accepting and warm. In some family situations, other adult members of the family may be able to be supportive of the child. It is important to begin to think in terms of the family's own natural helping network when dealing with these difficult issues, if the family is in agreement and willing to comply.

At the beginning of the initial contact, tension usually exists for the social worker between the need to identify the purpose of the contact and the need to develop a relationship with the child. How this should be handled will vary depending on the case and the age of the child. Often, a good approach is to introduce oneself and assume the child has some idea of the purpose of the interview. With a younger child, the use of a toy or game in some type of play activity is helpful. Toys or games should be selected based on the child's developmental age level and area of interests typical of the child's age range. Interviews should begin with open-ended questions that allow the child to discuss topics freely and do not restrict them to "yes" or "no" answers. Initial questions should relate to general areas such as school activities, friends, family members, extracurricular areas of interest, and so on. When the child appears comfortable and responds in a spontaneous manner, it is appropriate to ask the child about the purpose of the interview. At this point, the relationship should be developed before clarifying the purpose of the contact.

Faller (1988) suggests another strategy, which is to make a brief initial statement about the purpose of the contact and then to move on to more general topics or play. For example, the social worker might describe him- or herself as "a doctor, but not a shot doctor, who helps kids when they have problems or worries." Or one might say, "I help kids when grown-ups do things they shouldn't." After a brief statement about the reason for the contact, the social worker can say, "But first maybe you'd like to play with some of these toys," or "But we don't have to talk about it right away. We can get to know each other a little first." The social worker must remember that the child should not be pushed in a particular direction but should be allowed to direct the pace of the interview process.

If at all possible, contacts with younger children should be held in their home or in the place in which they are temporarily residing, rather than in an office setting. This is far less intimidating for the child and gives him or her the feeling of having more control over what might be happening. The issue of "loss of control" is critical for a child involved in sexual abuse because of the chaotic changes that typically occur following disclosure of the abuse. Therefore, interviewing in a "safe," familiar environment helps to facilitate the development of a relationship. It is always important to speak with the child alone, either in a quiet room or outdoors, and free from the interference of others.

Highlight 7.6 provides guidelines to consider when working with children (Sheafor, Horejsi, & Horejsi, 1998, pp. 366–368).

Ideally, a child victim of sexual abuse can work with a primary social worker throughout his or her involvement with the child welfare system. In most cases, however, this does not occur, and children often find themselves transferred from a protective investigator, who is given the responsibility of

| Highlight 7.6 | Guidelines for Working with Children |

1. When planning the interview with a child, determine the child's age and probable level of development, and anticipate how this will affect the child's capacity to understand and use language. Realize that there will be much variation among the children at a particular age.
2. Be clear about why you are meeting with the child and what you need to accomplish during the meeting. Plan several methods to accomplish your goal. Anticipate what might go wrong (e.g., child will not talk, child cries, child will not leave parent, etc.), and plan how you will handle such situations.
3. Prior to the meeting, assemble the play materials that may be needed. Depending on the child's age, provide "open-ended" art materials (e.g., paints, markers, clay, water toys) as well as materials that can be used to portray themes (e.g., dolls, puppets, blocks or Legos for building, toy cars and trucks, toy animals, doll house). For older children, consider card or board games, puzzles, or simple electronic games. Because play is normal activity for children, it is also a child's natural method of communication.
4. Plan to hold the interview in a space that is familiar and comfortable for the child but that affords privacy. As an alternative, consider an accessible community space that allows some privacy (e.g., a spot in a park, a walk in the schoolyard, a private section of a playground).
5. When first meeting a child, explain who you are and how you want to be addressed (e.g., "My name is Jane Smith. Please call me Jane."). Place yourself at the child's physical level, (e.g., sit or squat so you do not tower over the child). Initiate some friendly interaction by showing an interest in items the child may be wearing or carrying, or ask about school, favorite games, or TV shows. If the child refuses to interact, engage in a parallel activity and gradually initiate conversation about the activity. For example, if the child does not talk but begins playing with a doll, pick up a doll and engage in similar play.
6. If the child appears frightened, attempt to normalize the situation (e.g., "If I were in your place, I would feel scared talking to a new person. You are acting brave by just being here."). It may be necessary to allay the child's fear that he or she is in trouble and the interview is some kind of punishment.
7. If the child is at least 6 or 7 years of age, ask what he or she knows about the purpose of the interview. This will reveal what the child is expecting. Then, in language he or she understands, explain why you want to speak with the child. Ask if he or she had talked to anyone else about this meeting and what others have said about it, or discuss what instructions the child was given.
8. Do not attempt to disguise a professional interview as recreation; this may confuse the child about your identity and your role. Also be cognizant that only very limited confidentiality can be provided to a child. Do not promise that you can keep secrets, but describe what you can do to keep the child protected and safe, as well as what might happen after the child shares information with you.

investigating the abuse, to one or more protective services or foster care workers for months or years to follow. Undoubtedly, this profoundly affects a child's ability to attach to others, which can ultimately be debilitating and, in more severe cases, can lead to attachment disorder. Therefore, it is critical for the child to be able to identify a primary social worker who will be assigned to work with the child for an unspecified period of time. It is also important for the child to understand the involvement of other professionals and what their roles might be. Throughout the process, the social worker should communicate with everyone involved in the case and should consistently give the child opportunities to ask questions about what might be occurring. Children need to understand as much as possible about what is going to be happening to them. They should also be given the opportunity to discuss their feelings about this openly and in a safe, nonthreatening manner. In doing so, it is critical to normalize and validate these feelings as much as possible during contacts with them to help them regain some sense of control in their lives.

With older children, particularly adolescents, social workers must be explicit about the purpose of the contact at the beginning of the interview. In the case of Mandy, the social worker would most likely make initial contact with her at school, perhaps in the office of the school guidance counselor, who should be able to assure privacy. Highlight 7.7 represents a typical initial interview in which the social worker attempts to establish a relationship with Mandy and, in doing so, is able to move right into the stated purpose of the interview.

Highlight 7.7 | Example of Initial Meeting in Sexual Abuse Case

SW: Hello, Mandy, my name is Ellen Bowen, and I work with the Department of Children and Family Services. I apologize for having to take you out of class today, but I was wondering if we could talk for a moment. Would you like to sit down?

MANDY: [Appearing confused and concerned] Okay. What did you want to talk with me about?

SW: Mandy, I am a social worker, and my job is to talk with children who might be experiencing some problems at home. I understand that sometimes it's very difficult to talk about problems with a total stranger, and a little scary as well. Maybe you could begin by telling me a little about yourself. You're a sophomore here at Lake City High, is that right?

MANDY: Yes.

SW: What are some of the activities you're involved in here?

MANDY: I sing in the chorus, and I belong to a service club.

SW: Do you have any sisters or brothers?

MANDY: Yes, I have a 12-year-old sister and an 8-year-old brother.

SW: [Humorously] I'll bet you do your share of babysitting, right?

MANDY: [Smiling nervously] Yeah.

SW: Mandy, I'm going to ask you some questions, and you might feel a little uncomfortable answering them. I just want you to know that I am here to help. My office has received a report that you've been experiencing some difficulties at home with your father. Is that correct?

MANDY: Yeah, I guess.

SW: Could you tell me a little bit about these difficulties?

MANDY: Well, my dad is really strict and he doesn't like me to go out with my friends, especially Daryl, my boyfriend. All my other friends are allowed to date and go out together, and their parents don't give them a hard time. Just mine.

SW: I see. Well, how does your mother feel about this?

MANDY: I can tell that she doesn't agree, but she won't go against Dad.

SW: That must be somewhat frustrating for you. What do you suppose your dad objects to?

MANDY: I don't know. He almost seems jealous of Daryl.

SW: Perhaps he is. Has he always reacted this way?

MANDY: No, only since I've been seeing Daryl.

SW: I see. How would you describe your relationship with your dad up to this point?

MANDY: [Looking down] It's been okay.

SW: I'm sensing that there are some problems there. Could you tell me a little about them?

MANDY: [Becoming tearful] I don't know.

SW: I'm sure this must be painful for you. Perhaps I can help. The report I've received states that your

(Continued)

dad has been doing some things to you that are harmful, is that correct?

MANDY: [Shakes her head "yes"]

SW: Are these things sexual?

MANDY: [Shakes her head "yes" and becomes more tearful]

SW: When did your father start doing these things to you?

MANDY: When I was about 8 years old.

SW: Would you tell me how they began?

MANDY: When my mom wasn't home and Dad was taking care of us, he would come into the bathroom while I was taking a bath to make sure that I was washing with soap. Then he would check me to make sure I was getting myself clean all over. He would even check my vagina.

SW: I see. How did you feel about that? Were you confused at first?

MANDY: Yes, then I started feeling bad afterwards.

SW: Perhaps guilty because it was your father showing affection to you?

MANDY: Yeah, I guess. But later he started coming into my room at night to tuck me in, so he said. Only he wouldn't leave and he'd start rubbing me all over.

SW: On your vagina?

MANDY: Yeah.

SW: [Maintaining eye contact and appropriate body language] Please go on.

MANDY: I didn't know what to do. He kept telling me that he loved me and it was okay because he was my father. But I didn't feel okay about it.

SW: I'm sure you didn't. You probably didn't know how you were supposed to feel, only confused.

MANDY: [Shaking her head]

During the interview, the social worker attempts to engage Mandy in a discussion about what occurred while, at the same time, reflecting her feelings and expressing empathy. As indicated in the dialogue, the social worker briefly states the purpose for being there and immediately begins to establish a safe, trusting environment for Mandy to discuss the problems occurring with her father. The social worker would continue to ask more probing questions about the abuse and, at the same time, reflect the feelings being expressed both verbally and nonverbally by Mandy. Highlight 7.8 is an example of how to terminate the interview, giving the child some idea of what he or she might expect to happen as the result of having disclosed the abuse.

Highlight 7.8 | ## Example of Termination of Initial Session with Child in Sexual Abuse Case

SW: Mandy, it's important for you to know that I am required to report what has occurred to the appropriate authorities. It's equally important that you understand that I am going to be working very closely with you at least until this situation is resolved, and longer if necessary. You will have to talk to a judge, but I want you to know that I will be there with you and help you through that. I also would like for you to talk with a counselor who works with victims of sexual abuse and is able to help you understand a lot of what you will be feeling. I'm also going to arrange for you to stay with a relative for a short period of time while the court proceedings are going on, and then we can decide together where to go from there. I would like you to recognize that what has happened to you is wrong and not your fault. There are many other girls your age who have faced this same type of situation and have been able to enjoy a positive family environment in time.

The social worker must convey that the child will be actively involved in the decision-making process in order to help regain the child's sense of control. In order for the relationship to continue to be based on trust, it is important to not communicate false or inaccurate information. It should also be noted that the social worker in Highlight 7.8 does not communicate information about the father but instead comes across as being nonjudgmental and supportive. This, too, is important in light of the fact that most victims of sexual abuse continue to have loving feelings toward the parent–abuser.

The Child The assessment of a child in a sexual abuse situation is difficult as the child will be frightened and often will feel guilty about speaking against a parent or family member. An example of an assessment that might be done has been covered in Highlight 7.7. Throughout the assessment process, the social worker must focus on the child's immediate needs and safety, as well as the conditions that have created the situation.

According to Faller (1988, p. 119), the data listed in Highlight 7.9 needs to be considered during the assessment process to determine if sexual abuse has occurred.

Although this information is necessary in determining if sexual abuse has occurred, it is also important to obtain other information that reflects a "whole child" perspective. The whole child approach encompasses the physical health of the child, the cognitive development, the emotional well-being, the moral development, and social behavior. According to Zill and Coiro (1992), the

| Highlight 7.9 | Assessment Data for Sexual Abuse |

1. *Physical evidence:* This includes medical findings and evidence collected by law enforcement personnel.
2. *Statements made to significant others:* Examples include statements made by the child to family members, friends, or other professionals. Most often, the case comes to the attention of authorities because the child has revealed the abuse to someone close.
3. *Sexual behavior on the victim's part:* This includes excessive masturbation; sexual interaction with younger children, peers, or adults; seductive behavior; and sexual promiscuity. Sexual acting out takes different forms at different developmental stages and, as a rule, is more likely to be observed in children too young to completely understand its meaning.
4. *Sexual knowledge beyond that expected for the child's developmental stage:* Examples include

explicit knowledge in young children about fellatio, cunnilingus, anilingus, intercourse, that the penis gets big and hard when rubbed, that the penis goes into the vagina during intercourse, and that something white comes out of the penis. Such knowledge could conceivably be gained by observing sexual acts or pornographic movies, which also constitutes sexual abuse.
5. *Nonsexual behavioral indicators of stress:* Children who have been sexually abused may present with a range of problem behaviors of a nonsexual nature (i.e., sleep disturbances, enuresis or incontinence of feces, victim's fear of sleeping in his or her own bed, eating disturbances, school or learning problems, personality and interpersonal difficulties, etc.). Other forms of regressive behavior include demanding a pacifier or bottle again, resuming baby talk, developing clinging behavior, and so on. (Faller, 1988, p. 119)

| **Highlight 7.10** | **Whole-Child Assessment** |

1. *Physical health, nutrition, and safety:* Examples of basic health indicators are whether the child's height is within the normal range for his or her age, whether the child's weight is appropriate for his or her height, whether there are any obvious signs of malnutrition, and whether there have been any significant delays in growth or motor development. Significant medical history would include whether the child has any life threatening or life-shortening diseases, or any chronic illness or impairment that causes discomfort or limits play or learning. Whether the child has a regular source of medical and dental care, when he or she last received a checkup, and whether he or she has received appropriate immunizations would also be important.

2. *Cognitive development and academic achievement:* This area includes the child's attainment of the skills, knowledge, concepts, and strategies that are needed to succeed in school and, eventually, to deal with the challenges of being an adult. If the child is school age, it is important to talk with school personnel to obtain information about the child's progress in school. It is also useful to know parental expectations in this area.

3. *Emotional well-being:* The domain of emotional well-being covers the child's overt behavior and his or her moods and feelings, as they can be inferred from parent or teacher reports, through direct observation of children's facial and vocal expressions and conduct, or through interviews with older children and adolescents. Typical problems children might experience are poor socialization with peers, aggressiveness, hyperactivity, depression or anxiety, phobias, withdrawal from play activities, lying or stealing behavior, and so on.

4. *Moral development and social behavior:* This includes information about whether the child has a strong, secure relationship with at least one parent or parent-substitute. Information about playmates and siblings is also important, as is the child's development of age-appropriate competencies, and his or her development of culturally appropriate values, standards, and attitudes. (Zill & Coiro, 1992)

data indicated in Highlight 7.10 represent information collected in a whole-child assessment.

Because young children are likely to express themselves more readily in activities, it is recommended that they be given an opportunity to communicate material in an indirect way, such as in play. A variety of appropriate activities exist, but the more common activities include puppet play, picture drawing, and the use of anatomical dolls. As a rule, doll or puppet play is employed with very young children, those from ages 2 to about 6 or 7; picture drawing requires some fine motor development and is useful with children about age 5 and older. Also, storytelling requires language skills and vocabulary and, therefore, is most useful with children of school age. The social worker's task is to track the number of times sexual content appears in the play and how it might relate to other information gathered.

In *puppet play* children who have not been sexually abused will focus their play on having the hand puppets engage in normal daily activities (watching television, cooking, parenting, sleeping, going to school, etc.). However, children who have been sexually abused will often spend more time undressing the puppets, making sexual comments about them, or engaging them in various types of sexual activity.

Puppet play can be a valuable tool in assessing sexual abuse as the children are more able to communicate verbally their feelings and circumstances surrounding the abuse without having to take ownership of the information. It feels less threatening to communicate through the puppet as children are able to distance themselves from the process, thus allowing the puppet to take responsibility for what is being said. It is important to select puppets that represent nonthreatening characters to children and are appealing. Interpreting and reflecting feelings and various behaviors (anger, aggressiveness, fear, sultry behavior, etc.) that are commonly associated with sexual abuse can be done effectively through the use of puppets. In addition, children are able to play out content that is preoccupying them at the time and is suggestive of sexual abuse. The information might indicate to the social worker that there is cause for concern and that there is a need to explore the situation further.

When the social worker uses *picture drawing,* generally there are four types of pictures that are most helpful for children to draw: (1) a family portrait; (2) a self-portrait; (3) a picture of anything that immediately comes to mind; or (4) a picture in the form of a video game of anything that might be bothering them.

Some sexually abused children will draw pictures that indicate a heightened awareness of sexuality (i.e., putting penises on animals or humans, drawing breasts on themselves, etc.). Occasionally they will draw persons involved in sexual acts, and other times the sexual content will be more subtle. There may be a focus on the genital or abdominal area (a zipper drawn in detail); or when they are asked to tell about the picture, sexual meaning emerges. Children who have been sexually abused may also make drawings that depict their emotional reaction to the abuse (such as in the video game drawing). Finally, pictures sometime indicate an avoidance of sexuality (i.e., an older child drawing her mother as a stick figure) (Faller, 1988).

Storytelling is an excellent method for eliciting traumatic information from children. Relating the information in the context of a story reduces the trauma of telling what happened by enabling the child to initially discuss the situation through the character and circumstances of a story. Material that is often communicated relates to information that is salient to the child, as well as things that are preoccupying the child and that may be "worked through" in storytelling (Faller, 1988).

In beginning the process of getting a child to tell a story, it is helpful to use pictures that might depict material relating to sexual abuse (i.e., a picture of a girl looking sexy or sad, or a picture of a father hugging his daughter, etc.). Anything that might be construed as the least bit sexual by the child, or might in some way relate to his or her own individual experience, is appropriate to use. The amount of content communicated by a child who relates to sexual abuse is influenced by the frequency of the sexual contact, the length of time since the last incident, and the trauma involved (Faller, 1988).

In the case of Mandy, the scenario in Highlight 7.11 demonstrates the technique of storytelling, which can be used with children of any age level. This

| **Highlight 7.11** | **Example of Storytelling** |

In an effort to help Mandy discuss what has been happening within her family, the social worker shows her a picture of a young girl approximately her age standing apart from a group of teenagers and looking very sad. The social worker then asks her to express what she sees.

MANDY: That's a girl and her name is Donna. Her father has been doing things to her for a long time.

SW: What type of things?

MANDY: He's been having sex with her.

SW: When did he start having sex with her?

MANDY: When she was a young child.

SW: What happened when she was a young child?

MANDY: Her father would come into her room at night to kiss her good night, and things would go on from there.

SW: How did Donna feel about what was happening to her?

MANDY: She felt scared and confused.

SW: And how did she feel after she told someone what was going on?

MANDY: She felt different from her friends, and she didn't think they wanted to be around her. She felt sad and confused.

scenario illustrates that Mandy feels rejected by her friends as a result of the abuse. The emotional impact of the abuse is evident here and must be considered when planning an appropriate intervention.

The use of *anatomically correct dolls* is also an effective tool to use in assessing abuse. The child is better able to communicate the details of the abuse by demonstrating what occurred with the anatomical parts on the dolls. The social worker can evaluate what the child is saying about the abuse and what he or she is demonstrating through the dolls. Videotaping the interview is permissible for court testimony in some states, as it often minimizes the trauma of having the child testify in open court in front of the perpetrator.

The dolls have been challenged, generally by defense attorneys and their expert witnesses, as being "leading" and as such, triggering allegations of sexual abuse because they are "suggestive." However, research indicates that they do not elicit sexual responses from children who do not have prior sexual knowledge, and in the few studies that compare the responses of children believed to have been sexually abused to those of children who have not, the former are more likely than the latter to engage in sexualized behavior with the dolls. However, many children believed to have been sexually abused do not engage in sexualized behavior with the dolls (Berliner et al., 1996).

There is no scientifically demonstrated right or wrong way to use the dolls (Berliner & Elliott, 1996) Everson and Boat (2000) have reviewed the various guidelines for using anatomical dolls and have determined that they may serve five different functions—comforter, icebreaker, anatomical model, demonstration aid, or memory stimulus. The dolls can also be used with children of any age level; however, they are more beneficial with young children, who typically incorporate them into play. Highlight 7.12 illustrates the appropriate use of the dolls while interviewing a young child.

Highlight 7.12   Example of Use of Dolls

After a relationship has been established with the child (Mary), the social worker introduces the dolls to her and observes the nonverbal reactions.

SW: Mary, I want to show you my dolls. They really are very special. Can you tell me why?

MARY: [Looking a little embarrassed and smiling as she takes the dolls and looks them over] They are funny looking.

SW: Why are they funny looking?

MARY: Because the girl doll has boobies and hair down there. And the boy doll has hair too and a "thing."

SW: What do you call his "thing"?

MARY: It's a penis.

SW: And what is her "thing" called?

MARY: It's called a vagina.

The social worker could then ask the child if she had ever seen a penis before and ask her to describe what a real one looked like. To get more relevant information about the abuse, she would begin probing by letting one of the dolls represent the victim and the other the perpetrator.

SW: Let's assume this doll is you. Has anyone ever touched you there? [Pointing to the vaginal area on the doll]

MARY: [Nods her head "yes"]

SW: Can you show me how?

The social worker would then hold the male doll while the child demonstrates the incident with the female doll. The worker could also offer the male doll to the child and ask her to demonstrate what he did to her. During this process it would be important to note the emotional responses of the child and consider this information when formulating an intervention.

The social worker then asks questions relating to when this happened. Who did this? How did it feel? Where did it occur? Did it ever happen again? What was the child told to do? What did she want to do? If the child is reluctant to demonstrate exactly what occurred with the dolls, the social worker could normalize the child's feelings of reluctance and allow her to move at her own pace. The social worker could then ask the child to demonstrate how she was touched while, at the same time, asking open-ended questions about what occurred.

The Nuclear Family   A complete and accurate assessment of the child's environmental system, which includes information surrounding the abuse, must be conducted before an appropriate intervention can be implemented. During the assessment phase, subjective judgments are made about whether certain behaviors or outcomes constitute abuse. They are affected by many factors, including the social class and ethnicity of the children and families, the social worker's frames of reference and personal values, local levels of awareness, and local operational procedures, among others. The social worker must be aware of these factors and how they might impact the assessment and interventions. Of particular importance is the need to have knowledge of a family's ethnic and cultural differences with regard to how they might relate to what occurred. The social worker completing the assessment should be comfortable with his or her own sexuality and should be in touch with underlying feelings regarding sexual abuse as they relate to the assessment process.

An integral part of assessment in cases of sexual abuse is the process of assessing the immediate family system before the goals of the intervention phase can be established by the social worker. Family dynamics play a major role in cases involving sexual abuse. The social worker's insight into these dynamics is critical to the development of a systemic approach to dealing with the problem.

In any family assessment, social workers bear the initial responsibility to define the problem that played a major part in precipitating the abuse. In doing so, the social worker must know that the problem, as it is defined by the client or family system, might differ from the social worker's version of the problem. Because the family system will likely have to make the major changes that are necessary in cases of sexual abuse, it is important to always remain in touch with their definition of the problem while negotiating possible solutions. This will likely stimulate more of a commitment to change on the part of family members.

Asking oneself the question of who is most concerned about what problem helps to organize an initial approach to the case in the early stages and is vital to understanding the dynamics involved. The individual most upset about the situation, or most uncomfortable with it, is the one most likely to take steps to solve the problem (Berg, 1994). The parent who expresses some willingness to do something about the situation and appears to be dealing with the problem, and who expresses a sense of hopefulness and is receptive to getting help is the one most likely to take steps to solve the problem. Highlight 7.13 demonstrates a strengths-based approach in dealing with the family of a sexually abused child.

Much significant information about family strengths can be obtained by completing a thorough family history. During the course of completing a history on the family, it would be important to identify functional patterns of coping and problem solving rather than focusing only on dysfunctional behaviors.

Social workers must also pay attention to the strengths of families from various cultural groups as well. Many of these groups have suffered historic discrimination or, as political refugees, have suffered extreme losses. Highlight 7.14 shows examples of strengths in the backgrounds of families from other cultures.

An excellent tool to use in completing an in-depth family history is the *genogram* (Hartman & Laird, 1983). The genogram is an attempt to map out family coalitions, alliances, historically significant events, life-changing events,

---

Highlight 7.13 | **Strengths Approach**

Let us return to the case of Mandy. Interviews with various individuals concerned about Mandy's welfare indicated that Susan, Mandy's mother, was most invested in making a decision about (1) what to do about helping Mandy, (2) how the other children were reacting to the situation, and (3) what to do about her relationship with her husband. After adding this information to other significant details learned about the case thus far (i.e., the problem as defined by the social worker, the child, and the family system), the social worker then progresses to the next phase of the assessment process: identifying the *strengths* in the family. Focusing on strengths rather than weaknesses allows a social worker to achieve far more success in working with families who are believed to lack the most basic problem-solving skills.

Cultural Strengths

1. Demonstration of an interest in keeping alive the folkways, arts and crafts, language, and values associated with their heritage
2. Evidence of a commitment to take care of their extended family members
3. Communication of a desire to preserve family ties through religious, seasonal, holiday, work, or entertainment rituals

family myths and rules (particularly in the area of sexual norms and values), and other significant issues that may have an impact on the family and the problems they are experiencing. In cases of sexual abuse, it would be helpful to have both parents complete the genogram separately to evaluate their individual perceptions of family patterns. Highlight 7.15 illustrates a genogram.

Another instrument that can be useful in the family assessment process is the Index of Family Relations (IFR), which is part of the Clinical Measurement Package developed by Walter Hudson (1982). It is one of nine separate scales designed to measure a client's attitude toward self, parents, spouse, family, or peers. The IFR measures the degree of stress and conflict within the family, as perceived by a particular family member. Other Hudson scales that focus on the parent–child relationship are the Child's Attitude toward Mother (CAM) and the Child's Attitude toward Father (CAF), both of which are completed by the child (above age 12) and measure the magnitude of problems in the

Genogram

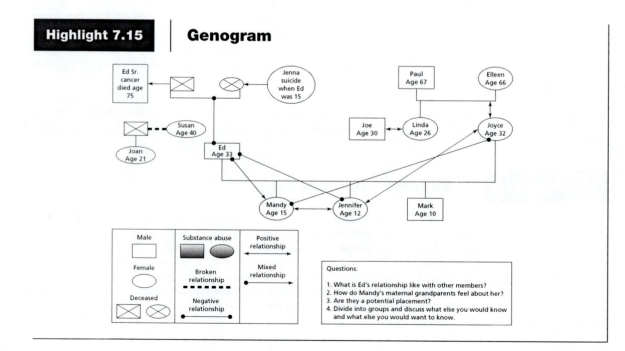

| **Highlight 7.16** | **Example of Family Assessment Questions** |

1. *How does Mandy view her family?* If she views her family as a positive system that meets many of her needs for security, emotional support, and assistance when she needs it, then it would be important to emphasize these positive feelings. However, if her view is negative, the social worker can ask how she has managed to acquire her positive traits and can give her credit for such. It is preferable to accept the child's perceptions and empower her to use them to her advantage.

2. *To whom in the family does she feel she has the closest relationship, and why?* Which family member provides her the greatest amount of support, and has she been able to tell him or her

about the abuse? If not, why? How has she been able to maintain that supportive relationship? How might they be able to help each other make the necessary changes that need to occur?

3. *What is her sense of autonomy within the family, and does she perceive herself as having some control over the changes that will occur in the family system?* The social worker must consider the previous patterns of coping with problems within the family and how much autonomy the child has had in the past with regard to making decisions, setting limits, expressing feelings, and so on, within the family system.

relationship. The IPA, or Index of Parental Attitudes, is completed by the parent and measures the parent's perception of the magnitude of problems in the relationship. Not only are these scales beneficial to use during the assessment process, they are also useful in measuring the outcome of intervention.

Again referring to the case of Mandy, the primary social worker completing the family assessment asks the questions illustrated in Highlight 7.16.

Information gathered from these questions will assist the social worker in constructing a broader picture of the problems within the family system, as well as the potential resources to draw on when planning an intervention. The information is also helpful in providing a sense of direction in which to move.

The characteristics of the child victim's parents are strongly associated with sexual victimization and comprise an important part of any family assessment. The information in Highlight 7.17 should be obtained on both parents individually as well as stepparents, if they are actively involved and assume a major position in the family system.

Extended Family Systems   All families have a power structure that defines the amount of influence each member has upon other members, and who will participate in what way in decision making. Children can also play a significant role in the power structure, particularly if they have been assigned authority over siblings in the absence of parents. As stated earlier in the chapter, this often occurs in cases involving incest in which a child is forced to assume control and decision-making functions beyond his or her developmental level of ability.

Culture also plays a significant role in defining the allocation of power within families. Many cultures are male oriented and clearly define the female's role as subordinate to that of the male (Hepworth, Rooney, & Larsen, 2001).

Highlight 7.17 | Parental Characteristics Assessment

1. Description of current living situation (i.e., who is living in the household, social and economic status of parents, division of responsibilities in home, etc.)
2. Information on family history (i.e., relationship with grandparents, values taught regarding parenting and discipline, communication styles, and use of affection in family of origin, etc.)
3. Education level and employment history (i.e., overall functioning in current and previous employments, ability in combining job and parenting responsibilities, etc.)
4. Relationship with children and attitudes toward parenting (i.e., quality of relationship with victim as compared to other children, overall situation at

time of victim's birth, parental perceptions and feelings about victim, methods of discipline used, etc.)
5. History of substance use and/or abuse, mental illness, and illegal activity (i.e., extent to which these areas related to the abuse, effect of substance abuse or mental illness on child victim, status of recovery, arrest records, etc.)
6. Sexual history (i.e., history of prior victimization of parent(s), sexual practices in the home, sexual patterns of parents, history of promiscuous behavior, etc.)
7. Description of individual roles in sexual abuse (i.e., reactions to the abuse, level of mother's commitment to the child's story, etc.)

Keeping in mind that all families allocate power in some manner, in healthy families the balance of power helps the family system to maintain a state of equilibrium. However, in dysfunctional families, the power differential is much more extreme and causes a great deal of stress for family members. In assessing the power structure, it is important to determine not only how power has been distributed within the family but also whether changing conditions of the family are threatening the power base. Furthermore, the social worker must assess the extent to which the family's rules allow for flexibility in the power structure, and if roles can be adjusted to meet the demands of the family's changing circumstances (Hepworth, Rooney, & Larsen, 2001). In a case of sexual abuse, it is helpful to know how the child victim views the balance of power within the family system.

Family roles are assigned to each member of a family and are integrated into the power structure of the family system. Often they are delegated to members on the basis of gender and societal expectations. Within the past several decades, family roles have become much more equalized with both men and women sharing many of the responsibilities for parenting, and so on. Nevertheless, families continue to experience many difficulties relating to role assignments and performance expectations. In assessing role performance on the part of family members, it is important to consider the following: (1) How are roles assigned in the family? (2) How adequately do members perform their designated roles? (3) To what extent are pressures caused by role overload? (4) To what extent are individuals willing to consider adjusting roles?

Problems experienced by some families arise partially because of inadequate communication in which the open expression of feelings is prohibited. In cases of sexual abuse, it is particularly important to consider the communication patterns between the parents involved. When eliciting details from the parents regarding what has occurred, one is able to pick up on problematic behaviors in interactions that can become targets of change efforts. Incongruent messages might be communicated in which the verbal information that is heard might be inconsistent with the nonverbal information (i.e., a parent communicates affection for a child but pulls away when the child demonstrates affection). The more distressed a family system is, the more incongruence will be apparent in the communication of verbal and nonverbal messages.

Extended family systems in child sexual abuse cases can sometimes create more difficulty than provide assistance. The stigma attached to sexual abuse, and the fact that abuse may be part of an intergenerational pattern, can create further problems for the child if he or she is placed in an extended family setting. As noted, often the pressures on the child to deny the problems will come from extended family members; therefore, the social worker will need to support and empower the child through this process.

Cultural factors must be considered in assessing communication patterns in families. Problems experienced by some families may arise because of cultural prohibitions against openness. Knowledge of cultural norms is essential before determining that change efforts need to be directed toward promoting more open communication among family members.

Social Systems   An adequate assessment includes an analysis of not only the problem, the child and the family, but also the environmental context of the situation. This involves the consideration of the adequacy or inadequacy and the strengths or weaknesses of systems in the client's environment that might have a bearing on the problem. Thus, social assessment aims to identify systems that must be strengthened, mobilized, or developed in response to the client's unmet needs (Hepworth, Rooney, & Larsen, 2001). The systems that might be included in cases involving sexual abuse are not only the family system but also natural support systems (i.e., extended family members, friends, neighbors, etc.), child-care or school systems, health care, law enforcement, religious systems, and the overall physical environment.

Families in which sexual abuse has occurred tend to be closed and have little or no involvement with other family members or friendship groups; therefore, assessments of social supports should include whether the child or family has any contact with extended family or friends and what the quality of those relationships might be. Are there feelings of alienation on the part of family members, and should efforts be made to tighten the social network of these relationships for the purpose of offering support for the client system? In cases where a child's environment is completely void of natural support systems, certain environmental changes may be necessary to effectively match needs with external resources.

In assessing environmental systems, socioeconomic and ethnocultural factors play a major role in the assessment process. Although sexual abuse crosses all socioeconomic lines, reported cases of sexual abuse come predominantly from lower-socioeconomic families, many of whom are socially isolated. The connection between social isolation and both physical and sexual abuse has been frequently noted in the child abuse literature (Finkelhor, 1984). In addition, an awareness of cultural attitudes toward sexual abuse is essential in providing insight into the cultural frame of reference that has helped to shape the client's perceptions of the problem.

Resource Systems   The resource systems available to families and children who are brought into the child welfare system because of sexual abuse are very similar to those who are involved in the child maltreatment cases. Since the 1970s, many child welfare agencies have begun programs for the children and families involved in sexual abuse cases. The resources available to the family differ to some degree as to whether the child's sexual abuse has been an act of incest or abuse by a stranger.

Programs and Services   The types of programs and services available for families in which child sexual abuse has occurred often depend upon the identification of the abuser. If the abuser is a member of the family, specific programs and services are available in most communities to aid both the child and family through this process. If the abuser is a stranger, generally fewer supports are available for the child and/or family, as this type of case warrants criminal proceedings where the focus is centered on the perpetrator rather than on treatment of the child.

Planning and Contracting

As in cases involving physical abuse, the planning and contracting include the involvement of all the client systems in setting goals. Therefore, planning and contracting with these systems requires that the social worker be able to set clear priorities and address one problem area at a time. Involving the client in this process is critical to maintaining cooperation and safeguarding the client's right to self-determination. The client can then feel a sense of accomplishment as he or she achieves goals and masters new skills.

Case Review and Coordination Meeting   Reviewing the case situation and treatment plan with all those involved in the case is a necessary condition for all child welfare cases, especially in a situation involving sexual abuse. Ensuring that all those involved understand the intervention approach and are on board with the process is critical to a successful outcome in the case.

Involve Family in Planning Process   It is important to remember that sexual abuse cases, unlike many other cases in child welfare, often involve multi-problem families experiencing serious, long-term issues that have created a high level of dysfunction within the family system. It is normal for any child welfare social worker to feel somewhat overwhelmed by the numerous problem areas that might need to be addressed. Therefore, it is important to begin by involving the client in prioritizing the changes that need to be accomplished first and what realistic goals should be attached to those changes. After the presenting problem is established, other problems that need to be addressed are identified and listed in order of priority. Again, it is important to elicit the co operation of the client in prioritizing the remaining problems by focusing on each of the environmental systems that should be targeted for change.

With each problem, a corresponding goal is negotiated with the client that reflects the desired outcome of the intervention. For example, if a client is depressed as the result of having been abandoned by a spouse and is lacking adequate social supports, the goal might be to assist the client in establishing a support system that would help him or her to deal with feelings of isolation.

In the case of Mandy, the first problem needing attention would likely be the temporary placement of the child during the investigation of the case and subsequent court proceedings. In most situations involving sexual abuse, the perpetrator is incarcerated or ordered by the court to leave the home so the child can be returned with some assurance of safety. In arranging Mandy's return home, the mother and other family members in the household would need to concur with the plan. In the absence of concurrence, the first priority might be to locate another possible placement for Mandy until reunification is a realistic goal.

The Intervention Plan   In order for an intervention to be effective in achieving desired outcomes, several factors must be taken into consideration. First, the intervention approach must match the corresponding problem area and address the appropriate system targeted for change. The client must be able to understand the relationship of the intervention to the goals and be in agreement with the overall plan. This undoubtedly will enhance the level of investment the client might have in the plan and his or her willingness to follow through with it.

When considering an intervention for a particular client, it is also important to be aware of the skills and strengths that the client has, and to help match the tasks formulated with the client to those skills and strengths. For example, if you as a social worker have referred an adolescent client to participate in a management-training program and he or she is not able to read well, you are obviously setting up your client to fail in accomplishing the goal of the intervention. Additionally, in formulating tasks for clients, it is important to plan with their involvement and immediately address any concerns they might have in performing the tasks. Other factors to consider when selecting tasks for interventions include the age, developmental level, and physical condition of the client, possible transportation barriers, and other resources the client might need to accomplish the tasks.

With regard to developing an intervention for Mandy, the social worker first addresses a plan that corresponds with the problem of locating a temporary placement for her outside the home. If it is learned during the assessment process that Mandy has an aunt and uncle who live in the same city and who have maintained reasonable contact with the family over a period of time, then it is appropriate to evaluate them as a possible placement alternative. The worker first determines if Mandy is receptive to this idea, and then contact is made with the aunt and uncle to determine if they are in agreement as well. The next step is to follow through with the mandates of the agency or court in order to finalize the placement plans.

Setting Goals and Contracting   In tandem with the process of matching interventions with problem areas, goals are set for each of the problem areas. A goal not only relates to a specific problem area but also it is the desired outcome of the corresponding intervention. For example, with Mandy, the intervention is designed to accomplish the ultimate goal of reunification. Goals must be meaningful to her, and she must view the achievement of the goals as having some beneficial and positive results for her.

Goals are designed to facilitate the client's sense of success, not failure. Success in reaching a goal is largely determined by the kind of goal agreed upon and the methods used for accomplishment. "Beginning where the client is" is a fundamental rule of social work practice and is a critical one to follow in setting goals. A client's motivation can be enhanced by the setting of short-term goals that are meaningful to him or her and play on individual strengths. The client will then view the goals as having some beneficial results. It is much more prudent for the social worker to agree with what the client wants to change rather than dictate what to change, which is contrary to the value of client self-determination. In child abuse cases, child welfare social workers may want to give the parents of a client directions for changing their situation, but unless the parents agree with these changes and have a role in deciding how they will come about, the intervention will not be successful. Highlight 7.18 provides guidelines that are useful to follow in setting goals.

After the worker and client have sufficiently established goals, the next step is to negotiate a *contract* with the client, either written or verbal. When establishing verbal contracts, the terms should be recorded in the case record for documentation purposes. Just as goals can change over the course of a social

---

Highlight 7.18 | **Goal Guidelines**

1. Goals should be defined in specific terms rather than general terms. The purpose for setting the goals needs to be explained clearly to the client to encourage maximum participation.
2. Goals should specify changes to be accomplished and should be measurable.
3. Goals must be realistic and achievable. They should reflect the ability and motivation of the client to accomplish them.
4. Setting short-term positive subgoals directed toward the achievement of a larger goal can be useful in situations where goal attainment is not possible for a lengthy period of time.
5. Goals should be ranked and should correspond with the problems that have been prioritized by the client. (Hepworth, Rooney, & Larsen, 2001)

Highlight 7.19	Contract Negotiating

SW: We've discussed the fact that Mandy would like to return home, and you would like to have her home as soon as possible.

MRS. N: Yes, I really feel she needs to be here. We all miss her very much; Mark and Jennifer are always wanting to know when she'll be home.

SW: I know this has been very traumatic for them as well. Before Mandy comes home, I would like for us to put in writing some problems that you have decided you need some help with. How do you feel about that?

MRS. N: That would be OK.

SW: What I am suggesting is that we develop a contract that we would both sign, that outlines exactly what you want to accomplish in terms of resolving some of the problems you've been experiencing, and how you are going to do this, with my assistance.

MRS. N: OK, I'm willing to do that.

SW: So, as we've discussed the various problems, what have been your thoughts regarding this most pressing problem that you would like to address first?

MRS. N: Well, I really need to decide what to do about my marriage. I really believe I want a divorce after what my husband has done to Mandy. Can you help me with that?

SW: Yes, I believe so. I'll refer you to someone who does divorce counseling, and I'll also refer you to an attorney who can inform you of the legalities involved.

MRS. N: Thank you. I really appreciate your help.

SW: We'll make this a part of our contract, along with the other things you want to work on, and try to focus on one or two tasks at a time.

MRS. N: OK, I really have a lot that I'm dealing with right now.

SW: Yes, you do. Would you like to talk about some of the other difficulties you've been having and how they might be resolved?

worker's involvement with a client, contracts can also change. Whenever a contract is initially developed, and when it is renegotiated at any time during the helping process, the social worker and client must be mutually involved in this process and must agree on the terms stipulated.

Highlight 7.19 provides an example of the process of negotiating a contract with Mandy's mother where the goal of reunification has been established.

Implementation of the Plan

Interviewing Skills and Practice Techniques   The use of appropriate interviewing skills that consistently reflect empathy, warmth, genuineness, and positive regard will enable the social worker to be an empowering force for the child and family members. Because the protection of the child and prevention of further abuse is a priority, the empowering will be focused on the child and the non-abusing parent. As noted earlier, in cases of incest, often the non-abusing parent is more passive in nature and needs to be empowered and strengthened to protect the child. The practice techniques can become very complicated if the goal is reunification of the family. Legal as well as intense treatment issues must be addressed with the abusing family member. These may be dealt with by the child welfare social worker or in conjunction with another social

Highlight 7.20	Pink Elephant

SW: Let's talk about those times when you feel afraid or anxious.

MANDY: Well, sometimes I feel that way when I am walking down the hall at school and a large group of boys are walking toward me. I don't know what I think will happen, but I just want to become invisible.

SW: Let's try something the next time this happens. I want you to picture a big pink elephant that floats above these boys' heads, and it drops down on them. Or imagine that they are all bald and how funny they look. Let's try this and let me know if that has caused you to feel any differently when you see them next time.

MANDY: Okay, I'll give it a try.

worker who has responsibility with the court system. The collaboration among all the systems involved in a sexual abuse case is critical to improving the family situation.

Many of the practice skills and techniques used with the child will be based on building self-esteem and empowering the child to protect him- or herself. Depending upon the age of the child, social workers may utilize play therapy techniques or games to help in allowing children to express their anger toward the abuser. The level of anxiety in the child victim may be high, thus necessitating the use of anxiety-reducing methods through the use of age-appropriate toys or games. A number of techniques exist for reducing anxiety in children, one of which is the "Pink Elephant" (Berg, 1994). Highlight 7.20 provides an example of this cognitive thought-stopping process. The purpose of this exercise is to give "the child a secret weapon" (Berg, 1995, p. 186) that helps him or her experience a sense of control over anxiety.

Continuing Coordination of Services   As in cases of physical abuse, a major part of the implementation of the treatment or service plan is to continue to coordinate those services that are being provided to the child and family. As noted earlier, this coordination is critical for the success of the intervention. Because most sexual abuse cases require both short-term and long-term intervention, the ability to work collaboratively with outside service providers over a longer period of time will be essential. If reunification of all family members becomes a goal, the social worker must work in some capacity with both the abuser and the victim through the provision of services to the entire family system.

Support and Empowerment of Child and Family   Supporting and empowering a family embroiled in sexual abuse may seem incongruent with a social worker's role; however, it is important to know that often there are non-abusing members of the family who can ensure the protection of the child if they are empowered to take responsibility. This frequently is true in cases of incest between a daughter and father when the mother is willing to do what is necessary to protect her child.

Because the recidivism rate in child sexual abuse cases tends to be very high, it becomes critical that child welfare social workers expend an inordinate amount of time empowering the child and other members of the family to prevent the abuse from reoccurring. By focusing on empowerment in the beginning of the case, the likelihood of establishing some control in the lives of the family can become a greater reality. In addition, the social worker is often the only support a child has initially, as other family members beside the abuser may be in denial and angry at the child for disclosing the secret of the abuse. Therefore, it is the social worker's responsibility to decide whether the child can best receive the needed support from within the home or elsewhere. Supporting the non-abusing parent in accepting the reality of the situation and making difficult, yet critical, decisions will also be an important part of the social work role.

Identification of Barriers and Resolution   The barriers that can often arise in a child sexual abuse case usually relate to the strong emotional reactions (denial, guilt, anger, blame) that most family members experience. These emotions are best handled by normalizing their existence and by assuring family members that the feelings are all part of the healing process. The focus should be on the healing and strength-building capabilities of the family.

Occasionally, extended family members who refuse to believe the allegations create the barriers in child sexual abuse situations. As a result, the members often pressure the child and non-abusing parent to drop the claims. In these instances, the role of the social worker is to support the child and non-abusing family members and assist them in developing skills to respond to these pressures.

Monitor Services and Intervention Plan   The ongoing monitoring of services as part of the intervention plan is highly important in order to ensure the protection of the child from further abuse. In sexual abuse cases, the child is often removed from the home, or the perpetrator, in cases of incest, is removed for the child's protection. Similar to other child maltreatment cases, the lack of close monitoring or intense follow-through on the part of a social worker can result in the perpetrator returning to the home too soon, or the child being left in substitute care indefinitely.

Evaluation of Outcomes and Termination of Services

Evaluating Outcomes   The evaluation of outcomes in a child sexual abuse case involves more than evaluating the safety of the child. It involves evaluating the impact the intervention has had on all family members (especially in cases of incest) and what interventions need to continue. These cases generally require more extensive, long-term types of interventions for the child, the family, and in many cases the perpetrator as well. Due to the short-term involvement with a sexual abuse case, the child welfare social worker may not be able to provide all the necessary services to a family. Therefore, there will be a need to ensure that these services continue and are coordinated by the appropriate professionals assigned to do so, in order for a successful outcome to occur.

Terminating Services   Termination of services in cases of sexual abuse can be a difficult process for the child, family, and the social worker. Depending upon the outcome of the case and the circumstances in which the sexual abuse occurred, the child may have formed an attachment to the social worker based on feelings of acceptance and support. It is important for this attachment to be recognized and for the social worker to find ways of empowering the non-abusing parent to communicate support and acceptance to the child. In cases where the child may not return to the home, it may be equally difficult for the social worker to let go of his or her involvement as the involvement may be the child's only tie to his or her former family. Careful and planned placement of sexually abused children is important for their success in adapting to a new family. Although the social worker may not be assigned to provide the primary intervention in the case after a period of time, maintaining follow-up contact to ensure the administration of needed services and care is a necessary part of the social work role.

Follow-Up from a Multisystemic Perspective

Family   As has been noted in previous chapters, follow-up is a process by which the social worker can assess the present situation of the family and how they are continuing to be successful from their work with the child welfare system. In cases of child sexual abuse, it is important to assess families on a regular basis to ensure that no further issues exist for a child who is continuing to reside in the home. In such cases, it is not simply a matter of seeing if an intervention has continued to work, but it is also for the ongoing protection of the child.

In situations where reunification of the child with the family has not occurred, ongoing follow-up to assess how the child is progressing and what permanent family plans are being considered is a crucial part of the case plan. If substitute-care placements are going to be maximally set at 12 months, with some states mandated to utilize adoption procedures after this point, then it is important for a primary social worker to have an ongoing relationship with the child and family as this time period nears. If the changes needed to reunite the family have not been successful, the process of terminating parental rights and preparing the child for a new home and family will need to begin.

Community   Social workers must follow up in the community to ensure the provision and access to services that aid children and families with these difficulties. Are there support groups for the sexually abused child and his or her family? Are there provisions for treatment of perpetrators, regardless of the legal consequences that might occur, so as to diminish the likelihood of the abuse reoccurring? Do children have a safe outlet for sharing these types of problems that they know is readily available?

Education is another key element in the community prevention of child sexual abuse. Teaching children to inform responsible adults when something "bad" happens, as well as ensuring that they understand the meaning of "bad," is part of the responsibility of the child welfare worker. Training in schools, churches, and other social institutions on signs of sexual abuse in children is also a step that can be taken to prevent its occurrence.

Programs and Services   As in follow-up related to the community, feedback to the services and programs utilized in these case situations is critical to providing the best care possible for the child and family. Ensuring that these services exist is another task inherent in the social work role. This task is often accomplished by meeting as a network of social service representatives and planning for the development of services that might be needed in a particular community.

SUMMARY

Chapter Eight has provided an overview of cases involving child sexual abuse. This type of child maltreatment differs in many aspects from physical child abuse or neglect. The chapter has pointed out how brief treatment and/or family-based care is often the only intervention chosen for these situations and is the least likely to be effective. Factors related to the relationship of the child to the abuser and the family dynamics that exist are critical aspects of utilizing an appropriate, strengths-based intervention plan. The dynamics that occur in sexually abusing families, regardless of cultural background, often have similarities. Being aware of these similarities, as well as the differences, enables a social worker to assess the situation from a more objective and knowledgeable viewpoint. Working with children and adolescents who have experienced sexual abuse requires a level of skill that assists the child in being able to discuss feelings about the abuse in a safe, trusting environment. Whether through verbal expression, play techniques, or creative arts, treatment of the child needs to focus on the child's emotional expression of pain and how the child might overcome it successfully.

Questions for Discussion

1. Discuss the ways in which sexual abuse is different emotionally from physical abuse.
2. Describe your personal response to child sexual abuse and how this response can affect your intervention.
3. How different is the assessment process in sexual abuse from that of physical abuse?
4. Describe how a community project focusing on the prevention of sexual abuse might be developed.
5. When are children at a higher risk of sexual abuse and why?
6. What role does empowerment play in preventing sexual abuse of children? Give an example of an empowerment program for children.

8 CHAPTER | Behavioral and Delinquency Issues

Derrik Tollefson

Marvin, age 15, is a Native American male who has lived in an urban housing project with his mother and four younger siblings since birth. His mother, Mrs. Simpson, age 30, is employed during the evenings at a local restaurant, and he is often left at home to supervise his brothers and sisters. Marvin has recently begun to hang out with several members of a gang in the area and is becoming increasingly more involved in criminal activities. He has a conflictual relationship with his mother, which is characterized by frequent outbursts of anger, physical fighting, and verbal abuse. He has begun to use drugs and alcohol in addition to participating in other gang-related activities in order to be accepted by his peers. Marvin is quite intelligent and demonstrates a great deal of academic potential; however, he is now skipping school to hang out with his friends, most of whom have dropped out and are unemployed. Recently Marvin was arrested with two of his friends for stealing cellular phones from a local retail store and has been placed under the court-ordered supervision of a social worker with the Department of Juvenile Justice.

INTRODUCTION

The number of children with behavioral and delinquency issues has increased dramatically in the United States. According to the FBI and the Office of Juvenile Justice and Delinquency Prevention (OJJDP), nearly 2.4 million

170

juveniles were arrested in 2000, and approximately 1.6 million juveniles were processed through the courts (Snyder, 2000; Roberts, 2004). The number of children committing delinquent acts is estimated to be much higher, however. Roberts (2004) suggests that approximately 13 to 15 million children commit delinquent acts annually, with the majority of these acts going unreported or undetected.

While the majority of juvenile arrests are made for property offenses, arrests for violent crimes, simple assaults, and weapons violations have increased sharply over the last two decades. Loeber and Farrington (2001) report that arrests for these crimes increased between 1988 and 1997 by 45 percent, 79 percent, and 76 percent respectively. Much of juvenile crime is believed to be directly related to drug and alcohol abuse (Hawkins, Jenkins, Catalano, & Lishner, 1988). According to the U.S. Department of Justice, the number of juvenile court cases involving drug offenses doubled between 1993 and 1998 (Roberts, 2004). Several studies have documented a link between drug use and criminal behavior (see Roberts, 2004, for a list of these studies). One such study conducted by Winters, Slenchfield, and Fulkerson (1993) found that drug usage by juvenile detainees was 34 percent more severe than for other high school students. Moreover, a study by Barone and colleagues (1995) notes that communities with high rates of teenage offenses also appear to have higher rates of substance abuse and other challenges, such as poverty, inadequate housing, and single-parent households. Whether drugs or environmental conditions are more correlated with delinquency is difficult to determine, but both appear to be associated with these behaviors.

The majority of adolescents charged with delinquency offenses are male (84 percent) and White (68 percent). While arrest rates favor males over females, it is important to note that once in the system, females are just as likely to receive similar penalties (U.S. Department of Justice, 1992, 2001). The same cannot be said for minorities, however. As is the case in the adult criminal justice system, minority juveniles are more likely to be arrested and tried for a crime than are White juveniles. In particular, African Americans, Hispanics, and Native Americans share the brunt of this unwanted attention by legal authorities (Mauer, 1990). A number of attempts have been made to address the overrepresentation of minorities in the juvenile court system, but these efforts have been largely unsuccessful. Perhaps the most comprehensive attempt at reform is the Indian Child Welfare Act (ICWA) of 1978. The purpose of this legislation was to protect the rights of Native American children who were being disproportionately placed in foster or adoptive homes because of status offenses and other problems. The act allows delinquent or maltreated Native American children's cases to be handled by the tribal system of authority. While ICWA has certainly brought about positive results for many Native American children, it has fallen short of its goal of significantly addressing the overrepresentation of these children in the nation's juvenile courts.

DEFINING BEHAVIORAL AND DELINQUENCY ISSUES

The differences between behavioral and delinquency issues can be difficult to define, and often these definitions overlap. Acting-out behaviors can escalate as children become older and move into their adolescent years. Stealing, fighting, lying, truancy, and destruction of property are all behaviors that can escalate over time and eventually become defined as delinquent and illegal.

Conduct and/or behavior disorders have been associated with other diagnostic disorders, such as attention deficit hyperactivity disorder (ADHD) (American Psychiatric Association, 1994). The child with ADHD has symptoms of overactive motor response, short attention spans, and impulsivity. Often, these early characteristics set the stage for later acting-out behaviors, which, if not addressed through intervention, can come to be defined as delinquency. The best way to prevent behavioral issues from growing into delinquency issues is through early intervention that targets children who are most at risk for delinquency—namely those from disadvantaged backgrounds. Although it is sometimes questionable to utilize a medical diagnosis (e.g., ADHD) in situations where familial and environmental factors play such a major role, recognizing some common behaviors, such as those attached to a particular diagnosis, can aid the social worker in selecting appropriate interventive methods.

CAUSES OF BEHAVIORAL AND DELINQUENCY ISSUES

The causes of behavioral and delinquency issues have perplexed social work practitioners and researchers for years. Multiple theories of causal factors exist, including inherent predisposition, biological factors, problems during early childhood development, and negative community and family influence, to name a few. With little agreement on causal factors, treatment and prevention have become just as difficult to determine as the etiology; however, the primary focus of research and intervention has more recently been on the family environment and adolescent development (Scherer & Brondino, 1994). Other studies have found family structure, poor parent–child bonding and affection, poor parental monitoring, and family discord to have high correlations with delinquent behavior. Accordingly, this research clearly encourages the development of preventive types of programs that address at-risk children in at-risk families.

PROCESSES AND PROCEDURES

In order to work effectively in behavioral and delinquency cases, the child welfare social worker must understand the processes and procedures of two significant societal institutions, the child welfare system and the court system. The initial processing for all delinquent children usually begins in the juvenile court system. The juvenile court controls entry of juveniles into the justice system because it has been allocated the power and discretion to determine when the state will intervene in the lives of individual youths and their families. It is generally at this point that social workers initially become involved in delinquency cases and are given the responsibility for assisting the client during and immediately following the court disposition. If the juvenile is confined to detention or another residential facility on a temporary basis, the social worker may be involved in assisting the court in developing a long-term plan for the juvenile. This plan may consist of a recommendation for either further incarceration in a secured facility or possibly confinement to a community-based program either in the adolescent's home or in an alternate living situation. This decision would ultimately be made by the court, based upon recommendations provided by juvenile justice professionals.

When working with the confined adolescent, the social worker may be involved in assisting in the development of a plan for the juvenile's release, which would likely include follow-up services and supervision. An assessment of the community resources that the client would need to access for positive support would be an integral component of this plan and would be structured to address specific problems within the adolescent's environmental system. In addition, an assessment of the informal resources (e.g., extended family members, friends, other professionals needed) might also be incorporated into the plan to aid in preventing future problems.

Many children involved with the juvenile justice system are also involved with the child welfare system. Consequently, social workers in the juvenile justice setting work closely with the child welfare system and should be familiar with this system's policies and procedures.

SERVICES AND PROGRAMS

A strong juvenile justice system is one that provides a continuum of services for juveniles who come into the system for a variety of reasons, such as truancy, homelessness, drug abuse, mental illness, or delinquent offenses. Social workers employed within the system will need training that enables them to assess the risk the juvenile offender poses to the community, determine rehabilitative needs, and provide graduated sanctions and treatment commensurate with both conduct and needs.

The primary social worker in the juvenile justice setting coordinates services that target the identified adolescent and family problems within and between the multiple systems in which family members are embedded in ways that meet the treatment or rehabilitative needs of the young offender. These services are best delivered in the natural environment (e.g., home, school, community) to optimize their effectiveness. A good treatment or case plan is designed in collaboration with family members and is, therefore, family driven. Emphasis is best placed on family empowerment and the mobilization of child, family, and community resources by the primary social worker. Interventions based on the strengths within the client's system and other systems involved, as well as the "fit" between these systems and the identified problems, are most likely to succeed.

There are many different kinds of programs for adolescents experiencing delinquent and behavioral problems. Community-focused interventions that involve the whole community, as well as the institutions with which adolescents are the most familiar, are becoming methods of choice for supporting adolescents and families through difficulties. Such programs include house-arrest models of intervention with mentors and caseworkers and have proven valuable in preventing incarceration (Borduin et al., 1995). These types of programs, along with aftercare interventions, have led to lower recidivism rates (Barton & Butts, 1990). The Florida Department of Juvenile Justice (2006) defines some of that state's programs as follows:

Host Home: Provides safe housing, care, and surrogate parental supervision in a neighborhood family dwelling to one or two male or female youths who have committed minor offenses and need alternative living arrangements in order to participate in nonresidential day treatment.

Group Treatment Home: Provides custody, care, and 24-hour awake supervision to a committed population of approximately six to nine all-male or all-female youths in a therapeutic residential environment that offers opportunities for personal growth, social development, and responsible behavior. This program typically serves younger adolescents who have committed minor offenses and is most likely the youths' first residential commitment placement.

Youth Development Center: Provides care and supervision in a structured treatment environment for male or female youths committed for minor offenses. This model provides an array of services, including a residential hub for assessment purposes, alternative home placement, in-home counseling services, and family counseling. Therapeutic services are offered to each youth in order to promote prosocial behavior, personal growth, family reunification, school attendance, mental health and substance abuse counseling services, recreation, and community involvement.

Boot Camp: Provides custody, care, and 24-hour awake supervision to a population of approximately 30 all-male or all-female youths at least 14 years of age but less than 18 years of age at the time of adjudication. This program generally serves youth who have committed third-degree felonies or second-degree felonies that have been mitigated. The program employs a highly structured impact incarceration approach that emphasizes paramilitary training, physical and mental discipline, and prosocial activities.

Halfway House: Provides custody, care, and supervision to a population of approximately 15 to 30 all-male or all-female youths, aged 14 to 18 years, who have typically committed first-degree misdemeanors, felonies, or similar offenses and are classified as moderate risks to public safety. The program provides an intentional therapeutic community based on control theory, structured learning, and behavior management techniques that emphasize social skills, academics, prevocational and/or vocational training, and life skills.

Clinical Psychiatric Program: Provides custody, care, and supervision to a population of approximately 20 to 35 all-male or all-female youths, ranging in age from 14 to 18 years, who have generally committed serious felony offenses and usually have significant offense histories. This program provides traditional services characteristic of a halfway-house model, as well as on-site psychiatric, psychological, and physical health care, and mental health and substance abuse treatment. These services are provided by appropriately licensed and certified professionals through a multidisciplinary approach.

Training School: Provides custody, care, and supervision to 100 or more male felons or violent misdemeanants, typically ranging in age from 14 to 18 years. Provides services through a multidisciplinary approach within an institutional setting, including services in the areas of behavior management, academics, vocational training, mental health, substance abuse, physical fitness, and health care.

These differing programs offer a range of services, and some of them emphasize continued involvement of the adolescent and community in resolving the problems together.

Zigler, Taussig, and Black (1992) note that few programs have been effective in preventing or reducing delinquency issues. They theorize that the causes of the problem are multifaceted and based on a number of social, cultural, and/or familial issues. In a review of four studies that had shown reduction of delinquency in children who received early intervention services, they found an ecological perspective, which considers multiple factors that impact delinquent behavior, to be the most effective (Struck, 1995). Some early childhood intervention programs that have primarily focused on improving educational achievement by building more adequate social skills and helping parents provide for their children's basic physical and emotional needs have shown the unexpected benefit of reducing later delinquency and criminal activity.

The underlying assumptions of early intervention programs are such that if a family is able to provide for itself in a socially acceptable manner and is able to embrace effective social skills and emotional coping, then the family unit as well as its individual members will be able to maximize their function (Mills, Dunham, & Alpert, 1988). Several studies have shown that delinquency is linked directly or indirectly with key characteristics of youths and the family, peer, school, and neighborhood systems in which they are embedded (Borduin et al., 1995). Effective interventions then need to address the multiple causes of delinquent behavior and be delivered within the ecological system. The use of a primary social worker to direct and coordinate interventions has enormous value in addressing three primary concerns: (1) the need for integrated services to overcome the fragmentation of service delivery systems, (2) the need for continuity of care as needs change, and (3) the need for individualized treatment to meet individuals' different constellations of need. The value of addressing these needs will become more evident as we progress through the model and apply its protocols to the juvenile offender.

PRACTICE

Working with children involved with the juvenile justice system requires no small amount of knowledge and skill. In this section, several suggested practice methods are described. These methods, which are presented as practice objectives, offer the beginning practitioner some direction in how to intervene with this population of children.

Establishing a Relationship

A working relationship based on a level of mutual respect and trust needs to be established with the juvenile and his or her family. This can be an extremely difficult task in situations involving delinquency. First, there is usually an enormous amount of anger and dysfunction within the family system, and the social worker often encounters this at the time of the initial contact. In addition, a number of other problems reflecting the adolescent's developmental stage can interfere. These may consist of problems of time distortion, exaggerated sense of peer loyalties, mistrust of adults, periodic suspension of logic, and insufficient motivation for change; and finally, adolescents are often unable to look back and see the need for change. At times they mistakenly believe that their problems will suddenly disappear without effort on their part (Zarb, 1992). Therefore, this type of situation initially calls for a much more directive approach with considerable reliance on structured interview techniques.

In the beginning stage of establishing a relationship with the adolescent, the social worker needs to find out how he or she is perceived by the client. Does the adolescent perceive the social worker as an advocate of the parent, school, or court system, thus embodying qualities that the adolescent may be rebelling against? The juvenile offender is typically viewed as being idealistic, in conflict with parents or other adults over authority issues, fiercely attached to peers, seeking conformity within the peer group, and desperately trying to develop a sense of identity apart from the family. An overt attitude of distrust is often projected immediately onto the social worker, who may represent a position of authority. While these are common characteristics of the nonoffending juvenile as well, they are not usually as heavily masked by a hostile, angry persona. Regardless, in working with the juvenile offender, it is extremely important to be oneself and to be genuine. Adolescents, in particular, are highly sensitive to any hint of phoniness or artificiality in others, even though they themselves often pretend to be someone they are not. It is also important to be alert to the fact that when working with adolescent offenders, social workers' own adolescent struggles can rise to the surface, and they may project them onto their clients. The worker's own unresolved authority issues and parent–child conflicts are especially likely to be reactivated by the juvenile client.

Berg (1994) suggests the following ways to build cooperation and decrease resistance in adolescent clients and their families:

1. Have an open mind about the client and be prepared to give him or her "the benefit of the doubt."
2. Put yourself in the client's shoes and look at everything from that perspective.
3. Figure out what is important to your client at this time, and see this view as a valuable asset that has served him or her well over the years, although this point of view may get him or her into trouble now and then. Maybe as the client begins to develop more insight, he or she will be willing to change.
4. Do not argue or debate with the client. You are not likely to change his or her mind through reasoning.
5. Evaluate how realistic your expectations for the client are, given his or her limitations and circumstances.
6. Look for the client's past successes, however small, ordinary, or insignificant. Ask how they were achieved. This question alone becomes an indirect compliment.
7. Look for any small *current* successes and ask how he or she accomplishes them; what would it take for the client to repeat or expand these to other parts of his or her life? This indicates your confidence in his or her ability to solve problems.
8. Look for positive motivation behind the client's behavior and comment on it. He or she will begin to believe in himself/herself.
9. Be willing to apologize to the client for any mistakes or misunderstandings. It takes strength, self-confidence, and professional integrity to be willing to apologize but, paradoxically, it gives you credibility and power in the relationship.
10. Always frame information in a positive manner and refrain from using negative, threatening communication. (pp. 58–59)

Essential to the establishment of a relationship is a sensitivity and understanding on the part of the social worker of his or her own multicultural issues and those of his or her clients. Gender issues also need to be considered in relation to particular ethnic groups, in addition to issues of economics, education, religion, generation, race, and minority/majority status. This is not only critical to the development of a relationship but is also an integral component of the assessment and intervention process.

The communication of empathy, warmth, and positive regard are important with juvenile offenders, who are likely to be resistant to what they may perceive to be intrusion on the part of a social worker. Of equal importance is the social worker's ability to empower the juvenile to believe in his or her ability to change the situation. Usually this antisocial behavior fits the juvenile's social-ecological context. He or she has merely learned to adapt to and survive in this state generated by feelings of confusion, anger, and an overall sense of hopelessness (Robinson, 1994). Parents are at times unable to provide the monitoring and natural consequences commensurate with the adolescent's need to negotiate a change in peer groups, as well as in criminal and substance-abuse activities. Following the establishment of a meaningful, trusted relationship, the well-trained social worker can offer other alternatives to juveniles that can provide them with a sense of control in dealing with the adversities of their situations.

Concurrently, while working with the juvenile, the social worker must also establish a working relationship with the family based on trust, warmth, and genuineness. It is important for the social worker to communicate a level of understanding about the stresses that the parents might be experiencing and empower them to change the situation as well. Initially, however, it is important to determine what the parents want for themselves and if they are invested in changing the situation. Keep in mind that the worker–client relationship is fluid, ever-changing, and dynamic; however, it is first necessary for the parents to perceive that there is a problem and be able to acknowledge the level of pain or discomfort that the problem has created in their life. Once this is accomplished, the social worker can then communicate a desire to help the parents find solutions and regain a reasonable measure of control.

In cases of juvenile delinquency, the parents may view their relationship with the social worker as being limited to providing information on the juvenile's problems. Although affected by the problem, the parents do not often see themselves as having a part in its solution. However, parents usually perceive their role as giving detailed and accurate accounts of patterns of behavior exhibited by their child, historical narratives, speculations about causes, and possible solutions to the problem that someone else might perform (Greenwood, 1994). Because the parents described here may not see themselves as involved in solution finding, the social worker needs to be empathetic and thank the parents for the helpful information they have provided. The social worker needs to acknowledge the parents' suffering and applaud them for "hanging in there" despite the difficulty of the situation.

Highlight 8.1 relates to the case at the beginning of the chapter and indicates how Marvin's mother might conceptualize her difficulty in terms of perceiving herself as having no control over the solution to her son's problems.

Because Mrs. Simpson is not willing to take responsibility for improving communication with Marvin but sees the problem as belonging to someone else, it is premature to begin talking with her about what she needs to change. For now, the most important approach is for the social worker to empathize with her difficulty and to initially agree with the goal of seeking help for her son.

Conversely, the parents might indicate, both verbally and nonverbally, an interest in and commitment to solving their problems and helping the child solve his or her own, regardless of whether or not the parents feel responsible for them. When the parents reach the point of verbalizing that they cannot handle the situation anymore and are in need of assistance, a fairly positive, cooperative working relationship can usually be developed with a social worker. However, even when parents are highly motivated, it is important to assist them in staying focused on the goals of change and provide encouragement when they are faced with difficult encounters.

Highlight 8.1	Social Worker–Parent Dialogue

SW: What do you think will help you get along with your son?

MRS. SIMPSON: It's not me. Marvin will have to get it into his head that he's gonna have to behave or else he's gonna spend the rest of his life in jail!

SW: Sounds like you have a big problem on your hands. So, what would it take for Marvin to start listening to you?

MRS. SIMPSON: That child will have to start listening to me and stop saying things like I beat him. I didn't threaten to kill him! He runs around and tells everybody I mistreat him. He lies and steals. He refuses to go to school, and everybody at that school thinks it's my fault. I didn't do anything wrong.

SW: It's pretty tough raising a teenager alone. So, what do you think it will take for Marvin to start listening to you so that you don't have to get mad at him?

MRS. SIMPSON: He will have to find out how good he has it before he will start to listen to me. I keep telling him what will happen to him if he doesn't listen, that he's going to end up in detention or some correctional home. I think he has to get good and scared before he realizes how good he's got it here.

SW: What do you think Marvin would say would be helpful to him?

MRS. SIMPSON: I don't know; he never talks to me. He has this attitude that he knows everything and that he can do anything he wants to do when he wants to do it. I'm just not going to take it anymore.

Assessment

In working with the juvenile offender, the primary social worker has the responsibility for assessing the child's overall situation from an ecosystemic perspective. The primary objective is to ensure a comprehensive assessment of major areas of the adolescent's functioning through a behavioral analysis of presenting problems, in addition to an analysis of cognitive variables, family variables, peer-relationship variables, and school performance variables. Data is collected from a variety of sources, including the adolescent client, parents, school personnel, and the social worker's own observations of the adolescent interacting with family members.

Adolescent Client   The assessment process is ongoing so that fresh information about the adolescent's overall situation and the consequences of his or her adaptive and maladaptive behaviors in home, peer, and school environments are evaluated repeatedly throughout the social worker's involvement. Initially, however, the focus is on the presenting problem as it is communicated by all of the individuals involved in the client's systems, as well as by the adolescent. Basically, the adolescent is asked to provide information about major complaints and problems. He or she is asked to describe his or her own behavioral interactions with significant others, as well as performance in home, peer, and school environments. Parents are asked to present their views of the adolescent's description of his or her typical daily activities, school behavior, and problem-coping style.

Due to the fact that many juvenile offenders come from impoverished, single-parent families, it is important to extend the assessment to include environmental factors that might be contributing to, or causing, the presenting problems (Hazel, 1982). Appropriate questions pertaining to the environment include: Is the adolescent living in substandard housing? Are physical needs being met and how? What is the socioeconomic level of the parents and how is that affecting the problems? Are there any medical problems not being addressed? What is the level of interest on the part of the parents? Are there factors within the adolescent's neighborhood that might be impacting the situation? What is the level of peer involvement in the problems? These are just a few of the systemic factors that need to be addressed when working with juvenile offenders. Of equal importance is the assessment of ethnic and cultural issues. In the case of Marvin, these issues may play an important role in his jurisdiction as well as the intervention.

Highlight 8.2 is a suggested format for conducting an assessment interview with the adolescent client. The primary purpose of the interview is to gain as much information as possible on the client's perspective of his or her family, peers, school, and behavioral problems. This information is then considered with data obtained from significant others (i.e., parents, peers, teachers, counselors, and other professionals).

Not only is important to determine the adolescent's perceptions of the areas listed in Highlight 8.2, but it is also important to discuss these areas with the primary parent or caretaker. Oftentimes their perceptions are somewhat different, as are their suggestions for problem solving. Therefore, it is the responsibility of the social worker to compare both perspectives in each individual area and negotiate the differences with both the adolescent and parent or caretaker. In order for interventions to be structured for each of the problem areas, there needs to be mutual agreement on the part of the parties involved on what the real problem is and how it should be resolved. In negotiating the definition of the problem to be solved with the client, it is important to stay close to the client's own definition whenever possible, since he or she will have to make the necessary changes. In addition, it is vital to negotiate a problem that can be solved, given the client's current situation and resources.

As discussed in the previous chapter, cognitive distortions are defined as errors in the process of collecting and using information independent of the particular content of that information. Throughout the ongoing assessment process, the social worker will identify both the adolescent's and the parents' cognitive distortions and negative maladaptive cognitions contributing to dysfunctional behavioral and emotional patterns. They will subsequently be made aware of the part played by these cognitions in maintaining unwanted emotional and behavioral responses, and interventions will then focus on altering these identified dysfunctional cognitions. In assessing cognitive distortions, the social worker focuses on the adolescent's self-statements, beliefs, attitudes, attributions, and self-efficacy expectations accompanying stressful situations and conditions. This information is often contained in client reports of emotional responses, evaluations, plans, and personal historical facts. It is suggested that the social worker assess both the functional and dysfunctional cognition and the role both play in the adolescent's maladaptive behavior.

| **Highlight 8.2** | **Assessment Interview with Adolescent Client** |

I. Adolescent's Perception of the Presenting Problem

The social worker should encourage the adolescent to talk freely about the problems he or she is experiencing. A beginning question might be, "What do you see as the major problem?" This part of the interview would then focus on the following areas:

1. Specific examples stated by the client of each of the problems he or she is experiencing
2. Information concerning the frequency, intensity, and duration of each of the problems
3. The client's beliefs or attitudes about what causes the problem, why it occurs, and what he or she is thinking about when it occurs

II. Influence of Significant Others on Adolescent and Problems

In this section, it is important to glean information from the client concerning feelings toward significant others involved in his or her life, in addition to perceptions of their influence over the problem he or she is experiencing. The following questions might be asked by the social worker:

1. How would you describe your mother? Father? Siblings? (Focus on descriptions of personality factors rather than physical appearance.)
2. How do you think this person would describe you?
3. What would you most like to change about this individual and your relationship with him/her?
4. How do you typically deal with upsetting situations involving your mother? Father?
5. Describe the upsetting situation.
6. What was your response?
7. What were the consequences following your response?
8. What were your thoughts at the time? Your feelings?
9. What could you have done differently, and what would the consequences have been then? What

would you imagine your reactions would be? Your feelings?

Other significant information to obtain would include:

1. Information on the reactions of significant others when the problem behavior occurs (e.g., mother, father, peers)
2. The client's feelings about the reactions of significant others
3. Information on the client's pattern of coping when problems arise and whether his or her coping skills are helpful or harmful to the situation
4. Information on how ineffective coping skills contribute to his or her problematic behavior with significant others
5. The client's level of willingness and ability to change problematic behaviors creating conflict in relationships with others
6. The level of commitment on the part of significant others to engage in the change process

III. Adolescent's Perception of School Behavior

In this section, the social worker would try to obtain information on the adolescent's experiences with school. If he or she has dropped out, it would be important to learn about the problems that precipitated dropping out, from the client's perspective. The following questions could be asked to determine how he or she would describe his or her academic performance in school, attendance record, and interpersonal relationships:

1. How are (were) things at school? Describe what school life is (was) like.
2. What subjects do (did) you do the best in? The worst?
3. How do (did) you get along with your classmates? Your teachers?
4. Do (did) you attend school regularly? If not, why?

Studies have suggested that central symptoms of adolescent depression are similar, if not identical, to those of adult depression and that cognitive distortions, automatic thoughts, and schemata of adolescent clients are quite similar to those observed in adult clients (Clark-Lempers, Lempers, &

Netusil, 1990). Distorted thinking often accompanies depression; therefore, it would be important to consider this factor when completing the assessment. Substance abuse in a parent may mask problems with depression, and it is likely that the adolescent will also be experiencing difficulties in this area. Depression in adolescents frequently manifests itself in maladaptive or delinquent behavior (Bunyan, 1987). Depression must be dealt with by the social worker immediately in order for the juvenile to make any substantial change in his or her situation.

When assessing distorted thinking patterns in juvenile offenders, the social worker will evaluate the thinking in terms of its appropriateness in relation to two criteria: (1) how valid it is as a representation of objective reality, and (2) how reasonable it is as a standard or as an explanation for certain events that occur when there are no clear objective criteria available for determining reality. These beliefs tend to be dysfunctional when they are inflexible, unattainable, or so extreme that the individual is unable to meet them and his or her level of functioning is affected. In determining the pattern of distorted thoughts, it would be significant for the social worker to evaluate the frequency with which they occur or the degree to which the validity of the thoughts is tested by the individual.

Generally, several themes characterize self-statements of the depressed client and provide a useful reference for cognitive assessment of adolescent clients: (1) low self-esteem, (2) self-criticism and self-blame, (3) negative expectations for the future, (4) perception of responsibilities as overwhelming, (5) sense of hopelessness, and (6) anger and blame against individual or agency (Beck, Steen, & Kovach, 1985). Keeping in mind that cognitive distortions are normal to a certain degree, the social worker still needs to note negative cognitions that seem to be contributing to dysfunctional behavior.

According to Friesen and Poertner (1995), adolescents that experience maladaptive behavior and become involved in delinquent acts can lack the necessary skills to function effectively in their current environment and in anticipated role relationships and lifecycle stages. They frequently have failed to receive adequate socialization during childhood, thus depriving them of learning certain vital social skills that prevent them from experiencing a variety of personal and interpersonal difficulties. Social dysfunction may be commonly associated with a lack of social skills essential to achieving self-esteem and forming satisfying interpersonal relationships. In turn, these deficits can lead to parent–child problems, family breakdown, and various mental health problems, in addition to other difficulties (Hepworth, Rooney, & Larsen, 1997). Adolescents who are easily provoked to anger and discharge anger in violent, destructive ways usually lack skills in coping with provocation and controlling anger. Therefore, the social worker needs to assess those coping skills commonly utilized by the client when encountering difficult situations in which impulsive, aggressive behavior is exhibited. It would also be significant to evaluate the deficits in social skills that need to be targeted for possible social skills training (SST) during the intervention phase.

Nuclear Family   It is easy to become overwhelmed by the scope of problems of juvenile offenders and their families. At times, these families may lack even simple problem-solving skills, which further contributes to the family's feelings of helplessness. Keep in mind that families can be extremely resourceful and have an enormous degree of strength and resiliency. Their problem-solving methods may be different from those of the mainstream culture, but a solution perspective allows the social worker to see the potential strengths and resources in these unique and diverse situations. Identifying strengths and successes is much more respectful of the client and less exhaustive for the social worker than focusing on weaknesses. For example, in the case of Marvin's mother, who is a single parent, she has had to raise several children while maintaining steady employment. This has required her to solve hundreds of major and minor problems of daily living at a very young age. This perception reframes her as being a competent woman rather than an irresponsible parent.

An excellent tool for assessing family patterns and strengths is the genogram, which has been described earlier in the text. The genogram is an attempt to map out family coalitions, alliances, historically significant events, life-change events, family myths and rules, and other significant issues that may have an impact on the client (Berg, 1994). Detailing such events helps to place the current problems within the context of the family history as well as the social context of the family. In the case of an adolescent, it might be helpful to develop the genogram with him or her and the primary parent. This can reveal a number of dynamics between the two regarding long-standing family issues. It can also help the adolescent develop insight into these issues and how he or she might be exacerbating the problems the family is currently experiencing. Nonetheless, it is important to have some knowledge of the adolescent's developmental level and the parent's ability to see the relevance of the genogram exercise before using this technique. Otherwise, it might be viewed as superfluous and, potentially, could cause the family and/or adolescent to discredit the social worker's professional expertise.

Problems involving substance abuse are often encountered when assessing the juvenile offender and his or her family. The extent of the juvenile's involvement in alcohol or drug abuse needs to be closely monitored in order to determine if residential treatment is needed. Furthermore, the pattern of drug or alcohol use would be important to know in structuring other interventions for the client. This information might be extremely difficult to assess accurately; however, the parents would likely be able to report on the adolescent's pattern of behavioral symptoms indicative of substance abuse.

As noted by Borduin and colleagues (1995), large numbers of juveniles with conduct disorders grow up in families in which alcoholism is a problem on the part of one or both parents. Alcoholism manifests itself in many different ways and has different effects on family members. For the child of an alcoholic parent, it can have traumatic effects and directly contribute to the development of delinquent behavior. Alcoholism plays a central role in the function and dysfunction of the family and of its individual members, particularly the adolescent; therefore, it is imperative for the social worker to learn to recognize substance abuse when it exists in a family and to what degree it is affecting the adolescent. It is also imperative to learn how to work with these families in collaboration with substance-abuse treatment programs.

Extended Family Systems   In assessing alcoholic families, the social worker will often observe unspoken family attitudes and rules that maintain the parent's pattern of drinking. The family will frequently adopt dysfunctional patterns and roles in order to cope with stress caused by the parent's drunkenness (Combrinck-Graham, 1989). As a result, adolescents may begin acting out both in school and at home as a manifestation of their reactions to the stress and gradually become involved in criminal and other forms of maladaptive behavior. The social worker will need to accurately determine to what extent the adolescent's problems are directly linked to, or resulting from, the parent's alcoholism. Although the ongoing goal should be to involve the alcoholic parent in individual and family treatment programs, few alcoholic parents will actually go to treatment, or the parent's recovery comes too late in the adolescent's formative developmental years to prevent maladjustment. As a result, the social worker is often forced to work with the adolescent alone or with family members alone, excluding the alcoholic parent.

Social Systems   Assessment of the concerns of an adolescent and family system requires extensive knowledge about that system, as well as consideration of the diverse systems (e.g., economic, legal, educational, religious, social) that impinge upon the client. When the social worker assesses the various aspects of an adolescent's level of functioning, she or he must also consider the dynamics of the client's interactions with the formal social systems within his or her environment and to what extent these interactions are problematic. Although not all of these systems may play significant roles in the problems of the adolescent, a comprehensive assessment of all areas is critical to the intervention process.

As human service brokers, social workers need to assess the various resources available to meet the needs of the juvenile offender. They must be familiar with the programs offered, the quality of staff, the general eligibility requirements, and the costs of services provided. The social worker must also know the best way to help clients gain access to those resources. The formal systems with which a juvenile offender will typically interact are the juvenile justice system, the court system, the child welfare system, the educational system, social agencies, medical programs, and so forth.

Resource Systems   Most juvenile offenders have experienced difficulty in school and have a history of unsuccessful experiences in educational institutions. As a result of problems associated with being part of a dysfunctional family system, they often have received little encouragement or positive reinforcement for educational achievements (Zigler et al., 1992). Therefore, they frequently are truant from school or do not attend at all. The social worker needs to work with school personnel on determining the adolescent's status in school and whether there are resources within the educational system that might be beneficial. If the adolescent has a remote desire to remain in or return to school, the linking of him or her to these resources would be highly advantageous. Many communities provide alternative schools for juveniles with behavior and/or academic problems in which more intensive services are provided to address not only academic issues but psychosocial issues as well. A comprehensive assessment of these services would include evaluating the quality of staff providing them, the problems they are designed to address, the eligibility requirements, the referral process, and whether or not they address the individual needs of the client.

With regard to employment services, the issue of unemployment of juveniles is a serious one as the problems associated with this promote deviance among unemployed youth (Sullivan & Wilson, 1995). Career-oriented apprentice-training programs and other vocational opportunities should be explored by the social worker based on the adolescent's areas of interest and identified vocational goals. In communities without these types of programs, social workers should help develop ways to obtain these resources to prevent further lack of opportunities for the adolescent.

Programs and Services   For those juveniles whose crimes or records are not serious and whose families are sufficiently supportive that the youths can continue to reside in the home, there are a variety of programs, such as informal or formal probation, intensive supervision, in-home supervision tracked by private agencies, or after-school and all-day programs in which a youth reports to the program site for part of the day and then returns home to sleep at night. For those youths who must be placed out of their homes but do not represent such a risk that they must be removed from the community, some jurisdictions provide or contract for a wide variety of group homes and other community-living situations (Petersilia, 1995). The majority of these programs offer a counseling component and a variety of intervention strategies aimed at reducing recidivism rates.

According to an evaluation of 80 programs by Andrews and colleagues (1996), appropriate correctional services can reduce recidivism by as much as 50 percent. They defined appropriate services as those that target high-risk individuals; address criminogenic needs, such as substance abuse or anger management; and use styles and modes of treatment (e.g., cognitive and behavioral) that are matched with client needs and learning styles. In addition, a meta-analysis of more than 400 juvenile program evaluations by Durlak and Lipsey (1991) found that behavioral, skill-oriented, and multimodal methods produced the greatest effects and that these positive effects were larger in community programs than in institutional settings.

One role of the social worker in locating services for the juvenile offender would be to assess the community-based services that provide intensive counseling for the adolescent by qualified professionals who are receptive to the social worker's involvement. Programs that use cognitive-behavioral and multimodal approaches to address crime-related factors such as anger management, dispute resolution skills, and substance-abuse resistance training are preferable to simple educational, vocational, or undirected counseling approaches that do not focus on criminogenic needs (Robinson, 1994). Furthermore, programs that are permitted to use these approaches in community settings are more effective than those that use them in institutional settings (Corbett & Petersilia, 1994).

Planning and Contracting

Case Review and Coordination Meeting   Throughout the assessment process, the social worker is focusing on the strengths of the various complex and multifaceted systems in the client's environment. As problems and needs are identified, the social worker emphasizes the strengths of the adolescent, the family, or caregiver in developing a plan to deal with these issues. Planning is the process by which youths, their caregivers, and the social worker decide which objectives to work on. With regard to the case of Marvin, the following objectives might be developed by him with the social worker based on a strength's perspective:

- Find five possible part-time jobs in the classified ads.
- Refer to the social worker for alternative ways to handle anger.
- Consult with a vocational counselor concerning entrance into vocational training program.

The involvement of Marvin in this process adds to the possibility of success.

It is important for the social worker to understand the adolescent's resistance to change and deal with it after a positive working relationship has been developed. A positive relationship is critical to the change process, and the social worker must be perceived by the adolescent as having his or her best interests at heart. Although the adolescent might not agree with the social worker's perception of his or her need to change, he or she will likely be able to identify specific areas in life that are causing pain. Helping the adolescent to take responsibility for some of the pain and discomfort in his or her life is a first step toward dealing effectively with the resistance. For example, in dealing with resistance in Marvin, the social worker could assist him in communicating his feelings about experiencing anger from his mother. If Marvin is able to understand and take responsibility for his part in contributing to the anger, then he and the social worker could look at alternative ways of behaving that might not provoke angry reactions from his mother. Of course, it would be equally important for his mother to take part in this process by accepting responsibility for her own negative behavior and agreeing to alternative ways of dealing with Marvin.

When working with resistant or involuntary clients, understanding that these clients may need to develop some voluntary aspect to their contracts will aid the social worker in progressing further. Even adolescents who meet with the social worker because of a court order do not really have to do so; they have the option of taking the consequences for refusing to do so. All adolescents hope to attain some type of goal through their contacts with a social

---

| **Highlight 8.3** | **Questions for Contract Negotiation** |

SW: I know that coming here is not your idea of how to spend an afternoon. Any idea of what you would like to get out of coming here that will make it worthwhile for you?

MARVIN: I really don't need your help. My life is a pretty big mess right now, and I don't know what you can possibly do about that.

SW: You say your life is a pretty big mess. That must feel pretty bad.

MARVIN: Yeah, I just need to get everyone off my back.

SW: Yes, I can understand why you must feel that way. It must be very difficult for you right now.

MARVIN: Yeah, I guess. I just don't want people messing with my life.

SW: You know, Marvin, that's exactly what I want, too. What do you suppose you have to do so that I stay out of your life and leave you alone?

MARVIN: I guess I need to stop getting into trouble.

SW: How do you suppose you can do that?

---

worker, even if it is only to "get social services and my parents off my back." In order to achieve this goal, which is quite reasonable, the adolescent will have to make certain changes, such as getting up in the morning, going to work or school, cleaning the house, and so forth.

Referring to the case of Marvin at the beginning of the chapter, Highlight 8.3 is an example of questions that can be used in the beginning phase of contract negotiation. In this exchange between the social worker and the adolescent, the worker sets a positive tone by assuming that Marvin wants to stay out of trouble and explaining that she wants the same thing. Having put herself on Marvin's side immediately, the social worker proceeds to negotiate what the client wants in order to achieve his goal of staying out of trouble. Expressing empathy with the client's situation does not mean the social worker is condoning his or her behavior; it only means that the worker is being open-minded and attempting to communicate a sense of fairness to the client.

Involve Family in Planning Process   Because social work services target identified adolescent and family problems in the multiple systems within the client's environment, the service or treatment plan and contract are designed in collaboration with family members. Both would emphasize family empowerment and mobilization of indigenous child, family, and community resources. Goals and objectives would be based on the strengths of the involved systems and the "fit" between these systems and the identified problem. For example, Marvin's engagement in multiple thefts and extensive alcohol use during all-night street behavior with friends undoubtedly involves parent, peer, school, and neighborhood systems. The neighborhood may offer few recreational outlets for adolescents and harbor a significant criminal subculture. Likewise, the peer group may be predominately engaged in antisocial behavior. The school, where Marvin experiences significant academic and behavioral difficulties, is also a system that needs intervention.

Contract with Family and Support Services   Although Marvin's mother is socially isolated, lacks some parenting techniques, and feels powerless and overwhelmed; she is a hard worker, is seriously concerned about her son's behavior, and truly wants him to stay out of trouble and complete his education. Because of several barriers that affect her level of functioning as a parent (e.g., lack of knowledge about parenting, fear of son's reprisal, low social support) she is not able to provide the monitoring and natural consequences her son needs to negotiate a change in peer groups and to attenuate criminal and substance-abuse activities.

In view of the fact that the probability of a favorable long-term outcome may be determined by Mrs. Simpson's strength and competence, the case plan would initially focus on eliminating the barriers to effective parenting. Thus, the social worker could provide individualized skills training in parenting, and considerable attention might be devoted to developing a reliable support system in Mrs. Simpson's natural environment (e.g., tribal elders, extended family, neighbors). These goals would be enumerated in the contract, and specific objectives relating to how and what Mrs. Simpson would do to accomplish the goals would be delineated as well. As Marvin's family is Native American, community needs to be addressed in the contract. As noted, Marvin's mother did not choose to utilize this option; however, the resources and supports could be helpful in a variety of other ways.

Implementation of Plan

Interviewing Skills and Practice Techniques   Serious juvenile offenders are, by far, at the greatest risk for committing additional serious crimes. Unfortunately, interventions with serious juvenile offenders historically have had little success. However, Kazdin (1987) has described several empirically driven interventions as "promising" (e.g., behavioral parent training, cognitive-behavioral therapy), and Lipsey (1984) has argued that such structured, skill-oriented interventions have demonstrated the largest effects on juvenile offenders in general. However, in some clinical trials with serious juvenile offenders, such interventions have failed to produce favorable long-term effects (Borduin et al., 1995).

Overwhelming evidence supports a social-ecological view in which antisocial behavior in youths is conceptualized as multidetermined (Henggeler, 1989). Beacuse several sophisticated casual modeling studies have shown that delinquency is linked directly or indirectly with key characteristics of youths and the family, peer, school, and neighborhood systems in which youths are embedded (Borduin et al., 1995), the primary interventions by social workers with juvenile offenders need to focus on the multiple determinants of antisocial behavior and provide services in the youths' natural environments. Using interventions that are present-focused and action-oriented, the social worker can directly address intrapersonal (e.g., cognitive) and systemic (e.g., family, peer, school) factors known to be associated with adolescent antisocial behavior. Because different combinations of these factors are relevant for different adolescents, the interventions are individualized and highly flexible. An over-riding goal is to empower parents with the skills and resources needed to independently address the difficulties that arise in parenting adolescents.

The primary social worker working with the juvenile offender will undoubtedly need to provide individual counseling that focuses on personal, family, and academic issues. The social worker should be prepared to offer support, feedback, and encouragement for behavioral change. Individual theoretical orientations that would be most effective in working with juveniles would be a blend of psychodynamic (e.g., promoting insight and expression of feelings), client-centered (e.g., providing social approval for school attendance and other positive behaviors), and cognitive-behavioral (e.g., understanding how dysfunctional behavior [aggressiveness, etc.] results from distorted cognitive processes). If the primary social worker does not have the knowledge or training to implement interventions based on these theoretical frameworks, it would be necessary to refer the adolescent to a counselor who can provide these services while coordinating and collaborating with the social worker during the execution of the case plan. A social worker who needs to develop these skills should take every opportunity to seek out continuing education.

Continuing Coordination of Services   In addition, it is important to reiterate that all professionals collaborating in a case involving a juvenile should have an understanding of their own multicultural issues and those of the client. With a broad definition of culture, these issues would relate to economics, education, ethnicity, religion, gender, generation, race, and minority/majority status. When developing a network of resources to refer to, the primary social worker needs to determine if the referral source would be able to address these issues with the client in a culturally appropriate manner.

Although the literature reflects a variety of programs and models of practice used in working with juveniles with conduct disorders, only those interventions that have demonstrated a significant degree of success based on empirical findings are described here. Those would include cognitive-behavioral interventions, social skills training, family-based interventions, case management, and multisystemic therapy.

Cognitive-behavioral interventions have been demonstrated to be highly effective in helping adolescents in the areas of assertiveness training, anger management, communication skills training, coping skills training, problem-solving skills training, and relationship-enhancement training (Sundel & Sundel, 1993). As discussed in the previous chapter, cognitive-behavioral interventions would address the adolescent's self-statements, beliefs, attitudes, attributions, and self-efficacy expectations accompanying stressful situations and conditions. Hence, the social worker would look at the client's reports of emotional responses, plans, evaluations, and personal historical facts to assess both functional and dysfunctional cognitions and the role these cognitions play in the adolescent's particular behaviors. The adolescent's automatic thoughts accompanying reports of stressful situations or conditions are an important source of cognitive data. Those thoughts that occur instantaneously or habitually, and are plausible to the individual, will contain data about the adolescent's present perceptions of situations, past memories, affective responses, and deeper beliefs. In addition, automatic thoughts often contain self-evaluations, and elements of this self-evaluation process in turn encompass past memories, present perceptions, and related affect (Zarb, 1992).

Cognitive restructuring is an excellent intervention to use with adolescent offenders. Cognitive self-control techniques are cognitive-restructuring approaches designed to teach clients to give themselves covert instructions for controlling problem behavior, such as angry outbursts, cognitive impulsivity, and anxiety. In addition, cognitive self-training has also been applied to other adolescent acting-out behaviors.

According to Zarb (1992), most cognitive self-control interventions share the same basic format. First, the conceptual framework is explained to the adolescent by the social worker in simple terms. Then the concept of speaking privately to oneself and the effect this has on behavior is introduced to the client. In order to illustrate this point further, the social worker could use the analogy of how athletes talk to themselves and repeat instructions repeatedly while learning a new sport. Information about the adolescent's private discussions with him- or herself, or verbalizations that accompany dysfunctional target behaviors, is then elicited using the following format:

Situation	Maladaptive Verbalization	Behavior	Consequences
Peer threatening	"I have to hit him."	Hit peer	Suspension from school

In the next phase, the self-defeating nature of the adolescent's verbalizations accompanying target behaviors is explored with the client, and more adaptive self-verbalizations are suggested and modeled by the social worker. These may include a statement of contingencies, statements about the demands of the task, or self-reinforcement for success for completion of a difficult task.

Situation	Verbalization	Behavior	Consequences
Peer threatening	"If I hit him, I'll be suspended. It's not worth it."	Walk away calmly	Feel good about myself

The adolescent is then asked to rehearse these adaptive verbalizations and to rephrase them in his or her own language. The adolescent is also instructed to rehearse the new verbalizations while role-playing difficult situations. Later, he or she is asked to independently identify his or her own dysfunctional self-verbalizations and to generate more adaptive statements. In the final phase, the adolescent is asked to apply these cognitive self-instructional skills to daily situations and to discuss their consequences.

Cognitive self-control techniques are helpful when applied to problems of anger and anxiety in adolescents. They can also be applied to the family as well in an effort to promote social competence within the family and child. By doing such as a part of an early intervention effort, it will likely not only result in increased educational achievement, improved behavioral control, and ultimately decreased delinquency for the juvenile but also will promote improved interactions and a higher level of independent functioning for the family unit (Robinson, 1994).

Programs that use cognitive-behavioral and multimodal approaches to address crime-related risk factors (such as anger management, dispute-resolution skills, and substance-abuse resistance training) are preferable to simple educational, vocational, or undirected counseling approaches that do not focus on criminogenic needs.

Social skills training (SST), along with cognitive-behavioral techniques, contributes further to the social competency of the adolescent client and helps to further reduce delinquency. A rationale for using SST in preventive programs is that efforts to prevent social dysfunction by equipping people with coping skills reduces the possibilities of later maladjustment, unhappiness, failure to develop potentials, and loss of productivity. Many research studies document the importance of adequate socialization during childhood and adolescence to facilitate adequate adjustment (Garbarino, 1992a). Children who are deprived of adequate socialization fail to learn vital social skills and are at risk of experiencing a variety of personal and interpersonal difficulties. Social dysfunction is commonly associated with a lack of social skills essential to achieving self-esteem, forming satisfying interpersonal relationships, and performing various social roles effectively.

Adolescents who are easily provoked to anger and discharge anger in violent and destructive ways often lack skills in coping with provocation. SST is also helpful in dealing with parent–child difficulties. The first step in this process would be for the social worker and adolescent to identify a specific skill deficit in the client that he or she might want to address first. Secondly, they would break the skill into its discrete components of the problematic behavior, as certain fears and uncertainties associated with new behavior must be mastered before the client can perform requisite actions. The adolescent could then be encouraged to practice these new skills with his or her parent(s).

Hepworth and colleagues (1997) describe a format for SST that can be conducted in individual sessions with the client or in a group context utilizing the following steps. The word *adolescent* has been integrated into this discussion.

1. *Discuss the rationale and describe the skill.* This step is critical in helping the adolescent client to believe that developing the skill will benefit him or her. This is done by briefly introducing the skill, alluding in general to situations in which it is applicable, and then eliciting from participants specific relevant social situations that have posed difficulties for them and have led to adverse outcomes because of ineffectual coping.
   Example: Learning to say "No!" with firmness and not giving in to pressure from others helps adolescents avoid things they really do not want to do that get them into trouble.

2. *Identify the components of the skill.* Explain that the skill has a number of different components and list them for the client. Also, encourage the adolescent to discuss any difficulties associated with the components.

3. *Model the skill.* The social worker can model the component of the skill or ask a member of the group to volunteer to model it. A discussion by the adolescent can be helpful in highlighting aspects of the component that contribute to effective or ineffective performance.

4. *Role-play use of each component.* The social worker would set the stage by assigning a role to the adolescent. He or she would be asked to practice each component and give feedback to the social worker. The worker would further explain that the most effective way of learning a skill is to practice until one feels confident in applying the skill.

5. *Evaluate the role play.* Adolescents participating in the role play can then be encouraged to evaluate their own performance and share feelings that inhibit them in the role play. This can help to identify specific barriers that prevent them from implementing the skill effectively.

6. *Combine the components in role play.* After the adolescent has role-played and demonstrated adequate mastery of the various components of the skill, the social worker moves on to the next skill, continually giving positive feedback.

7. *Apply the skill to real-life situations.* Helping the adolescent prepare for applying the skill in real-life situations involves reviewing components of the skill and practicing applications of them. Maximum preparation is further enhanced by anticipating difficulties that will likely arise and preparing him or her to surmount them by rehearsing appropriate thoughts and behaviors. A debriefing session should follow the application of the skill to an actual situation in which the adolescent is given the opportunity to discuss and analyze the experience.

In the area of *family-based interventions*, conduct disorders are often conceptualized as strategies of adjustment that the adolescent has learned to his or her own disadvantage (and to the disadvantage of others) in an attempt to cope with the demands of life. Many research studies have indicated that the families of conduct-disordered children are characterized by a high rate of coercive interactions among family members. Children seemingly engage in excessive rates of behaviors aversive to parents (e.g., noncompliance, demands, aggression, and temper tantrums), and parents often retaliate with equally excessive aversive responses (e.g., threatening demands and criticism) designed to "turn off" their children's negative behavior (Bunyan, 1987). Effective assessment and treatment of conduct disorders requires observation and intervention in the natural environment of the juvenile and, in particular, the systematic involvement of parents and the extended family.

Behavioral interventions and techniques are often effective if used consistently by the parents and in a systematic fashion. To reinforce this, it is recommended that the social worker initially provide a high level of input by visiting the home two to three times per week in order to sufficiently advise and support parents in administering a specified behavioral scheme. These visits should decrease rapidly once the scheme is established and is consistently carried out.

Identification of Barriers and Resolution   In structuring a behavioral program with the family, using the case of Marvin as an example, the social worker might assist Mrs. Simpson and Marvin in reducing the frequency of his demanding, defiant, aggressive, and destructive behavior. In doing so, the social worker might engage in behavioral rehearsal with Mrs. Simpson, which is a technique drawn from behavioral therapy that teaches a client how to handle a specific interpersonal exchange for which she or he might be unprepared. As implied by its name, the individual rehearses or practices a specific behavior to be performed in an upcoming situation. It helps to reduce anxiety and builds self-confidence about being able to handle a problematic situation. The social worker might demonstrate or model the behavior so it can be imitated. Again, using the case of Marvin, the following steps would be followed by the social worker and Mrs. Simpson (Sheafor et al., 1998):

1. *The client would identify the problem or concern and then describe or demonstrate how he or she would usually behave in that situation.* For example, Mrs. Simpson tries to enforce curfew with Marvin; however, he fails to abide by it and comes home an hour or two late. Mrs. Simpson becomes extremely angry, demanding to know where he has been, and Marvin responds back by yelling, "Leave me alone, I'm old enough to come home when I want to!"

2. *The social worker makes suggestions on how the situation might be handled more effectively.* The social worker might suggest that Mrs. Simpson try a different approach, rather than responding with anger. The worker would then discuss with her several different responses and suggest that she try the response that would be most appropriate for this particular situation.

3. *The client is given an opportunity to provide additional information about the problem or concern and is able to ask the social worker to further explain the response suggested.* Mrs. Simpson should be encouraged to discuss her reactions to the alternative response and share her concerns about its feasibility. She should have the opportunity to express her feeling about how Marvin is likely to respond to it.

4. *A role play is used to demonstrate the behavioral changes suggested to the client.* Initially, the social worker would play the role of Mrs. Simpson, and Mrs. Simpson would enact the role of Marvin. The social worker would demonstrate the appropriate response while Mrs. Simpson demonstrates how Marvin is likely to respond. Then the roles are reversed, and Mrs. Simpson tries the new behavior if she feels ready and understands the changes being suggested.

5. *After the role play, the social worker first identifies the positive aspects of the performance, then makes additional suggestions for improvement. If*

necessary, the role play is repeated to further illustrate the preferred way of responding. The social worker should encourage Mrs. Simpson to practice the new behavior until she is satisfied with the performance and feels confident that she can follow through with it.

A major limitation of behavioral rehearsal is that the client may successfully learn what to do in the presence of the social worker but may not be able to generalize it to the real world. Sometimes the real situation poses problems that cannot be anticipated during a practice session.

Family-therapy interventions consistent with a cognitive-behavioral approach are considered to be very effective in work with parents and adolescents. These interventions would be directed toward (1) the family's dysfunctional interaction styles and (2) the family skills deficits in the areas of family communication, family problem solving, and parental child-rearing styles. Various family interventions that would follow this approach are behavior analysis skill training, cognitive restructuring in parent and family sessions, communication skills training, conflict negotiation skills training, discipline effectiveness training, problem-solving training, and relationship enhancement training. A few of the interventions mentioned here can be easily incorporated into the social worker's repertoire of skills in order for him or her to be more effective in working with juvenile offenders and their families.

Monitor Services and Intervention Plan   This type of monitoring aids the child welfare social worker in understanding the adolescent's environment and the supports and pressures that he or she experiences. Having a good relationship with members of the adolescent's environment is important in monitoring the services and plan. The monitoring of services in a public place, such as the school, community center, or neighborhood, requires a respect for the adolescent's dignity and confidentiality. While some members of the school staff must be informed of the worker's meetings with the adolescent, particular attention needs to be paid to maintaining confidentiality.

When working with adolescents and their families around issues of delinquency and behavior, it is critical for the social worker to maintain an ongoing relationship with the family and adolescent through a monitoring of services and plan. This monitoring will most likely occur in those environments in which the adolescent finds himself or herself (home, school, neighborhood). This monitoring is done most effectively when the adolescent is part of the monitoring. Allowing her or him to give feedback on services also places the adolescent in a partnership role in her or his treatment.

Evaluate Outcomes and Terminate Services

Evaluating Outcomes   An evaluation of the effectiveness of the interventions employed by the social worker is a necessary component of the casework process. An intervention needs to be effective and efficient in order to achieve its goals and objectives; therefore, the social worker must be able to utilize different methods to assess effectiveness of direct practice activities. The single-subject case design is especially useful when intervention focuses on a discrete behavior that is fairly easy to measure in terms of frequency, intensity, or duration.

When social work activities primarily center on making referrals, brokering, coordinating services, and advocating, the most appropriate methods to use might be goal-achievement scaling and task-achievement scaling. Self-anchored and rating scales are additional ways of individualizing the measurements used in an evaluation of client change. A goal checklist can be used to combine certain case planning and evaluation activities, thus reducing the time needed to complete evaluation-related paperwork. Sometimes the use of a post-intervention survey of client satisfaction is the only feasible way of gathering information about the probable impact of the intervention (Sheafor et al., 1998). Basically, evaluation always involves some type of measurement. Its importance cannot be overemphasized in terms of trying to observe and measure those things that are relevant and central to the provision of services to clients.

Terminating Services   Termination with the juvenile offender and his or her family is likely to occur for one of two reasons: (1) Either the length of time designated for the social worker to be involved in the case has lapsed, or (2) the goal(s) has been accomplished. Regardless, the termination process is one the social worker must plan from the beginning of her or his involvement in the case and must be discussed openly with the client during the contracting phase of the helping process. Ideally, termination is a mutual decision by social worker and client that occurs when the goals and objectives have been achieved; however, many situations are far from ideal, such as those involving juvenile delinquents, and the adolescent occasionally decides to end the relationship before reaching the agreed-upon objectives.

If the social worker has been ordered by the court to work with the juvenile, the client might want to terminate the relationship, but the social worker may believe there is a need to continue. It must first be decided if all the terms of the order have been met before terminating service. If so, the social worker needs to explain to the adolescent her or his reasons for wanting to continue her or his involvement and explain any possible consequences of terminating. If the adolescent still wishes to terminate, this should be discussed with the individual who has the authority to terminate the worker's involvement, in the adolescent's presence, and a mutual decision should be made in this regard.

The social worker must also anticipate how the termination might affect other people in the adolescent's family and social network. In situations where a termination may place the client or others at risk of harm, it is appropriate to notify others of the termination if this process is consistent with the law and ethics concerning confidentiality and the release of client information.

In situations where the social worker has had a positive relationship with the adolescent and has assisted him or her in the accomplishment of objectives, the termination process can be difficult for both the juvenile and the worker. Therefore, as it approaches, it is desirable to gradually decrease the frequency of contact. If the adolescent has become somewhat dependent on the social worker, this weaning process should be accompanied by efforts to connect the client with natural helpers and informal resources within his or her neighborhood or social network. The feelings of loss and anger that often accompany the end of any important relationship should be discussed by the social worker and normalized for the adolescent.

Follow-Up from a Multisystemic Perspective

Family   One of the important factors to consider in follow-up of an adolescent with delinquent or behavioral issues is the need of the family to have a sounding board following termination. One of the most effective resources for families in these situations is the mutual support of other families with similar circumstances. Programs that administer wraparound services and serve as an effective base for the organizing of mutual aid groups for parents in forming neighborhood community groups that can respond together in reaching out to all their children have been found to be a positive resource. Wraparound programs for adolescents in a community have become an exciting type of program that lends itself to preventive techniques in working with adolescents with delinquent or behavioral issues.

Community   Community follow-up in cases of delinquency is important in not only one case but also in preventive services for many different adolescents and their families. One way that follow-up becomes preventive is in the establishment of programs and systems that can offset the development of delinquency problems. Programs that attempt to network community institutions and services into a safety net by which the community working together can identify difficulties early and prevent their development are those that place prevention as a priority.

Programs and Services   If your community is not one with resources and alternatives for families and adolescents with problems, it is important to ensure that these programs are developed for the types of case situations you encounter. As mentioned, programs and services require a preventive focus that can help identify at-risk youths and supply them with resources to offset their behaviors. A study by Quinn, Epstein, and Cumblad (1995) examined a program that attempted to create a public system of comprehensive, community-based care and individualized wraparound services to children and adolescents with emotional and behavioral disorders (EBD). The evaluation of the program demonstrated positive results for families and their children in a majority of the situations.

Policy   Policies that affect delinquent and behavioral problems are often reflective of the general attitude toward criminal behavior, regardless of the age of the offender. It is important to keep policymakers aware of and involved in the needs of parents and adolescents and in the outcomes of specific rehabilitative services through information and education that describe the programs. The methods for improving policies for juveniles will involve social workers educating their community regarding the positive outcomes of programs and policies that help juveniles and provide a sense of safety in the community.

SUMMARY

This chapter has provided an overview of some of the issues associated with social work practice with adolescents experiencing delinquency and behavioral problems. The chapter example describes a Native American family situation that has unique implications related to culturally appropriate practice. Different theoretical views of practice with adolescents have been described along with several practice techniques. The chapter further emphasized the importance of preventive programs and policies that impact the family and child's environment before the onset of delinquent or behavioral difficulties. Involvement in the community in terms of not only developing resources but also as a network of support has been suggested as vital to helping adolescents achieve their goals. Community programs such as mentoring and wraparound can provide such preventive measures.

Questions for Discussion

1. Describe the difference between status offenses and delinquency cases.
2. What special services does the Indian Child Welfare Act provide for Native American children?
3. Discuss the term *wraparound* and how this macro program is utilized for juveniles.
4. Describe two different theoretical interventions to be used with juvenile delinquents.
5. Describe the behavioral rehearsal process and how it can be applied.
6. Describe how you might set up an evaluation tool for Marvin's situation.

Divorce and Loss

Jen Fungh has experienced much change in her nine years of life: Her family immigrated to this country from China when Jen was 5 years old; her mother developed breast cancer approximately one year ago; her father recently moved out of the home and is wanting a divorce; and her maternal grandmother, who lived with the family for several years, died of congestive heart failure three months ago. Jen has two younger siblings, a 7-year-old sister and a 4-year-old brother. Since the father's departure, the family has experienced extreme hardship both emotionally and financially. Jen's mother has applied for AFDC and food stamps. The children have reacted to the dramatic changes that have taken place within the family in a variety of different ways. Jen's younger brother has begun wetting the bed again, her sister cries a great deal and has withdrawn from playing with friends, and Jen is having difficulty in school, both socially and academically. Mrs. Fungh has considered the temporary foster home placement of the children until her husband is ordered to provide child support and until her physical health improves after the chemotherapy is completed. A child welfare worker has been assigned to the case by the Family Court for the purpose of assisting the family and assessing the need for temporary placement of the children.

INTRODUCTION

In the wake of a generation of high rates of divorce and the deprivation of parental support or care due to the absence of a parent from the home, there is an accumulating subgroup of separating and divorced families in our communities that are being designated as "high conflict" by mental health and legal professionals (Johnston & Roseby, 1997). This fast-growing minority group of families poses serious social policy problems (Garbarino, 1992a). They clog the family court systems and require an inordinate amount of time and resources. Many of the children in these families are suffering emotional problems at clinically significant levels and, consequently, consume a disproportionate share of the community's mental health services (Wolchik, Ruehlman, Braver, & Sandler, 1989). Often the plight of these children is thrust into the background as the parents become embroiled in extreme conflict. Of paramount concern to child welfare specialists is the damage being done to the children's capacity to form trusting, authentic, emotionally gratifying relationships as they grow older. Thus, the strategies and policies for prevention or early intervention assumed by child welfare workers may become critical to the ongoing development of the child who has experienced divorce or loss of a parent.

While professionals recognize that divorce is a crucial time for children affected by it, little attention has been given to a model for counseling children who, generally, are not responsible for what has occurred. These children frequently harbor guilt and feelings of responsibility; therefore, it becomes the task of the social worker to be supportive of the child while maintaining a nonjudgmental attitude toward either parent. Although many children differ widely in their reactions to this life transition, some other common themes observed in children of divorce include the following:

- Feelings of unworthiness
- Divided loyalties and feeling "torn"
- Love/hate feelings toward one or both parents
- A perceived lack of control over what is happening in their lives
- Unrealistic feelings about a possible reunification of their parents
- Denial of the reality of the situation, leading to social isolationism

The social worker who forms a close relationship with the child(ren) and family is particularly helpful in cases of divorce. Working with children who have experienced the loss of the family unit that has provided them with a sense of security throughout their lives can be a significant challenge to the child welfare worker, who has limited knowledge of the dynamics of the underlying problems. The issue of trust becomes of paramount concern for these children and must be dealt with immediately by the social worker and other professionals involved in the child's system (Webb, 1993).

Establishing a Relationship

In their study of 104 children of divorce, Wolchik and colleagues (1989) found that the lower the level of support the children received, the stronger the positive relationship between stress and adjustment problems. In addition, they found that children with high support from nonfamily and family adults during periods of high levels of stress reported fewer adjustment problems than did children with low support. The results of the study further indicated that the relationship between support and adjustment among children of divorce is complex and depends on both the level of stress experienced by the child and the source of support. The researchers also suggest that the value of support from nonparental adults can be beneficial in the following ways to the child experiencing divorce:

1. By buffering the negative impact of divorce events
2. By allaying fears of abandonment or who will take care of the child's basic needs
3. By helping children accurately interpret aspects of the divorce, such as who is responsible or why their parents spend less time with them (Wolchik et al., 1989, p. 489)

The supportive relationship of a child welfare worker can help to diminish the loss of self-esteem that children often experience during and after divorce. Just as in cases involving abuse or neglect, a primary task of a social worker is to establish a level of trust and mutual respect with the family that will set the stage for further involvement. This is initially accomplished by explaining to the parent and child the social worker's role as a child welfare worker and the functions of the agency represented. It is also helpful to explain the nature of the helping process and the fact that social workers are involved for the purpose of assisting parents in seeking a solution to their difficulties.

Just as has been reiterated in previous chapters, it is important for the social worker to normalize some of the feelings the parent and child might be experiencing. Because many children experiencing divorce often identify with the feelings and perceptions of the custodial parent, it can be advantageous to the development of a relationship with the child if at first there is a warm, trusting relationship established with the custodial parent. This can be initially accomplished through the use of empathic communication skills in which the social worker reflects sensitively the inner feelings of the client and communicates empathy regarding these feelings on a level that the client will understand. In addition, it would be helpful to discuss with the parent the normal behaviors and feelings typically manifested by children who are experiencing divorce and a sense of loss. This will enable the parent to normalize some of his ir her own feelings of guilt over what he or she might perceive as being his or her role in contributing to the break-up of the family unit.

With regard to the case of Jen, it would be highly important for professionals outside the family unit to have a significant level of knowledge about the social and cultural norms and values shared by the Chinese culture with regard to divorce and the communication of feelings, and so on. Many cultures view the sharing of personal and private information about marital or family issues as prohibited. Therefore, the social worker must communicate to the family a level of knowledge and understanding of these cultural attitudes early in this phase of the working relationship.

In view of the fact that children frequently feel a loss of control over their environment as a result of what is happening in their lives, the social worker can further enhance the relationship by allowing the child to guide the interview process and assume responsibility for making decisions whenever it

| **Highlight 9.1** | **Interview with Child** |

SW: Hello, Jen. My name is Mrs. Trantham, and I am a social worker with the family court. Do you know what a social worker with the family court does?

JEN: No.

SW: Well, we have a lot of parents and children who come to the court to speak to the judge about some problems they are having. The parents of some of these children are going through a divorce, just like your parents, and they need help with a lot of different things. So the judge asks a social worker, like me, to visit the family and provide any help that I can. But before I can help, I need to spend a little time with the family, especially the children, so I can see how they are doing and what type of help they might need. Are you beginning to understand now what a social worker does?

JEN: Sort of, I guess.

SW: I know it probably seems a little confusing now. Would you like me to help you understand a little better?

JEN: [Nods her head]

SW: Well, most children whose parents are going through divorce are feeling a lot of different things that they don't understand. They usually feel very sad and even a little angry about what is happening to them. They feel sometimes that they have done something wrong and that is why Daddy has left. They also might feel angry with Mom for not being able to make things better. These are things that you might feel uncomfortable talking about right now, and you don't have to, but you might want to later on. I've talked with a lot of children who have gone through what your family is going through, and it's very normal for you to feel a lot of different things right now.

might be appropriate to do so. In the case of Jen, the social worker could begin the interview as shown in Highlight 9.1.

While the social worker's task in this case is to establish a working relationship with the child and the family, it is also necessary to normalize the child's feelings and communicate a level of understanding about the fact that she might not feel comfortable talking about these issues so early in the relationship. Furthermore, by allowing the child to make the decision about when an appropriate time might be to communicate on a deeper level, the social worker communicates respect for her feelings as well as her cultural norms. Additionally, it is important to note here that a denial of the reality of the situation frequently occurs with children of divorce, often leading to physical or psychological isolationism. As a result, they internalize such self-statements as "I will build a wall around myself so that I will not be hurt anymore," "No one understands how bad I feel and how ashamed I am to come from a broken home," and so on.

During the relationship development phase, it might be beneficial to administer a brief assessment scale to the child that would measure the level of depression or sadness he or she might be experiencing. Scales from Hudson's Clinical Assessment Package, Reynolds Child Depression Scale, or Burleson's Self-Rating Scale (Corcoran & Fischer, 1987) would be helpful in planning for the intervention phase of work with the family. Not only do measurement instruments validate a social worker's observations of the child but they can also add credibility to professional recommendations to the parent(s) concerning other resources or interventions that might be needed.

Assessment

The Child It is the theory of many clinical practitioners and child welfare specialists that children who experience divorce in the family progress through the same basic stages as individuals experiencing a loss through death (Webb, 1993). The professional literature indicates that the mourning of losses associated with divorce, and the resulting psychological reactions, parallels in many ways that of grief following death (Webb, 1993). For the social worker involved in working with families experiencing divorce, it is recommended that the stages of a standard loss model, such as that of Kubler-Ross (1969), be utilized in assessing the child and family systems. The Kubler-Ross model relates to the varying emotional reactions of children struggling to come to terms with the realities of divorce. Highlight 9.2 is a brief overview of these five stages of loss.

Highlight 9.2 | Kubler-Ross Model

1. *Stage One: Denial* This stage must be overcome by the child before further progress can be made. In an attempt to reject the reality of separation, children often try to eliminate the thought from their minds and show no signs of reacting to the situation. Unfortunately, parents often model this same inappropriate behavior for their children by hiding any indication of a possible separation. In most cases of divorce, the parents wait until the separation is imminent before informing the child of the pending situation. Denial in preadolescents often manifests itself through isolation types of behavior. In order to keep the thought removed, the child will isolate himself from peers, teachers, and his environment. He may then learn withdrawal types of behaviors and exhibit a lack of interpersonal skills. For example, children who normally have not had difficulty interacting with friends may appear "shy," not wishing to play with peers or talk to adults. The normally quiet child may exhibit loud, "tantrum" types of behavior in an effort to keep others away. As a result of this, the child's self concept begins to evolve into that of an "isolate."

2. *Stage Two: Anger* During the anger phase of accepting a loss due to divorce, the child frequently attempts to strike out at those who are involved in the situation. At times the attacks may be directed toward those who take the place of the parents, such as school personnel. The underlying dynamics in this occurrence have to do with the child's feelings of guilt because of the divorce. He may exhibit unusual assertive or aggressive behaviors: refusing to cooperate with school assignments or home chores, sullenness and withdrawal, or overt hostility toward peers. Anger exhibited toward the social worker might also be experienced initially in the relationship and will need to be dealt with appropriately.

   It is extremely important, at this phase of the social worker's involvement, to be in touch with her own feelings about loss and if, whether or not, she might have some unresolved issues in that area due to her own past experiences with death or divorce.

3. *Stage Three: Bargaining* The child frequently attempts to bring the parents back together during this phase of the "loss model." In doing such, he might become caught up in a "gaming" type of behavior, attempting to renegotiate the parents' relationship by means of the child's own behavior. He may be observed as being unable to focus on the academic material presented in school, or he might be perceived as being in "another world." On the other hand, he might attempt to "overplease" one or both parents whenever any specific requests are made of him. If the child feels that the parents did not respond to angry demands or temper tantrums exhibited previously, he may then believe that by

(Continued)

being "very good" the parents will come back together again. Often he will verbalize this in an attempt to "negotiate a deal."

Another area of bargaining that the child might go through has to do with the debate within himself of the choice of rightness or wrongness attributed to one of the parents. The child may reason, "How can my father be made to see how my mother was wrong (or vice versa)?" An attempt may be made to try to decide which parent is actually to blame for the "evil" of the separation.

4. *Stage Four: Depression* As the child comes to realize that a bargain cannot be reached with the parents, a depression will frequently set in. The child may regret past "evil" behaviors directed toward one of the parents or may feel badly about some missed opportunities and experiences that did or did not occur within the family unit. Eventually, however, the child begins to prepare for the impending loss of the parental relationship. A type of "mourning" will usually occur at this time. The child may be observed to withdraw from activities, from academics, or from social experiences. Here he or she may be seeking attention in other ways, such as through temper tantrums or through more passive acting-out behaviors.

5. *Stage Five: Acceptance* The final stage through which a child progresses in experiencing a loss is the acceptance stage. This might be described as neither a happy stage nor an unhappy one. Perhaps the child has come to avoid the feelings. Nevertheless, in a sense it is a victory. The child has now come to realize that, although the original security of her world is presently gone, individual worth is determined intrinsically and not by external forces. During this phase the child comes to a more mature understanding of the love/hate relationship that she holds toward her parents. She also comes to the realization that future reconciliation is not a distinct possibility and begins to accept the probability of interacting with one parent and another adult in an interpersonal relationship. This stage is a most advantageous one for the child, as it is only after going through a difficult "crisis" situation that one is particularly open for growth. The child has then, with the assistance of the social worker, learned to accept the support of external resources. She has developed a new knowledge of herself and, in addition, both self-confidence and self-esteem have begun to expand. (Hozman and Froiland, 1976, pp. 271–276)

A major difference in mourning loss through divorce versus mourning the loss of a parent through death is the intensity of the anger response following divorce, which is often more pronounced because of the conflicts that precipitated the break-up and the underlying sense of blame and guilt about the failed marriage (Webb, 1993). Obviously, through divorce the bereaved must mourn someone who has not died. Children must also mourn the loss of their intact family, and their mourning is especially complicated because of the possible reversibility of the court's decision. In addition, it can be further complicated by the omnipresent wish and fantasy about parental reunion. Intense and prolonged grief should be expected in situations where the parent is considered to be a central person in the child's life.

Not every child will go through every stage of the loss model, nor will all individuals experience the stages in the order indicated. However, generally speaking, most children may go through the majority of these stages in somewhat the same order. It is possible to pick out a given theme, for example, "guilt," and to follow it through the various stages of denial, anger, depression, and so forth. The social worker, by being aware of the model, can then help to facilitate the child's progress directly to culmination of the acceptance stage.

A thorough assessment of the child in terms of his or her particular *developmental level* is of extreme importance when evaluating children involved in divorce, in order for the social worker to adequately address the developmental needs of these children during the intervention phase of the model. Developmental information is also important in order for the social worker to determine if the child is progressing through the phases of the divorce normally, or if he or she might be experiencing some disabling adjustment reactions to the crisis. It would be significant to obtain information from others on how the child has adjusted to various forms of crisis in the past and what, if any, coping skills he or she might have used. If the manner of coping in the past was adequate but those previously learned skills are not working in the current situation, the social worker should identify the malfunctioning skills for use in structuring an intervention consistent with the developmental level of the child.

Black and Cantor (1989) suggest gathering the information in Highlight 9.3 when assessing children experiencing divorce.

| Highlight 9.3 | **Assessment Information** |

1. *General size and appearance:* A child's physical characteristics, gestures, and mannerisms may bear a striking resemblance to those of one of the parents and, as a result, may be favored by the other parent. Likewise, the child favoring a parent could also be a target of hostility or animosity by the other (displacement). As a marital relationship deteriorates, the parents frequently displace their anger toward the other partner onto the children in the family, particularly the child who resembles the other parent.

2. *Hyperactivity or decreased activity:* Either hyperactivity or decreased activity are significant clues to a child's emotional state. Slowed motor movements may indicate depression, which commonly occurs in children whose parents are divorcing. However, the social worker must search further to determine if depression exists for some other reason: rejection by a parent, school failure, medical illness, and so on. Hyperactivity, along with an inability to concentrate and impulsive behavior, is a common characteristic of attention-deficit hyperactivity disorder (ADHD) in children. Although hyperactivity may be psychologically caused, it may also have a neurological source. As a result, one must be careful not to universally ascribe behavioral characteristics to flaws in parenting.

3. *Intellectual function:* The ability to grasp the significance of the family breakdown will depend to an extent on the child's intelligence. Brighter children with a greater capacity for abstract thinking will think through the possible consequences of a divorce on their future, and their ability to recognize parental manipulation could create less ambivalence in dealing with such a parent. Creative talent or some other manifestations of substantial intellectual ability may cause a child to be the object of parental favoritism. On the other hand, the child's intellectual competence may threaten a parent. Mental retardation can also trigger parental rejection or overprotection, either subtle or overt.

4. *Modes of thinking and perception:* Impaired reality testing in the child may suggest the influence of a family member who is similarly handicapped. The capacity to make reality-based differentiations should be appropriate to the child's age. For example, by age 3 or 4, the child should display some ability to discriminate between fact and fantasy. By 6 or 7, most children should possess that skill. The social worker should carefully analyze the children's perceptions to determine their accuracy. Caught up in a flood of emotions for having witnessed scenes involving charges and counter-charges, children of divorce are often taxed by

(Continued)

mixed loyalties, fears of rejection and abandonment, rage, and feelings of protectiveness. One common result is a tendency on the part of very young children to distort events and issues. Their interpretation of an incident may change, consciously or unconsciously, to match the perception of their favored parent. Careful scrutiny on the part of the social worker may be necessary to determine the extent to which, and the means by which, parents reinforce an impaired view of reality.

5. *Emotional reactions:* Children experiencing divorce usually harbor extremely mixed feelings about their parents during, and sometimes long after, the divorce process. While they usually love both of their parents, they might experience disappointment and anger with one or both of them. These emotions often coexist with fear, affection, and love. As a consequence, they are fearful of injuring one or both parents by their actions, their thoughts, and their feelings.

When interviewing the child, it is important for the social worker to be creative in order to get the child to overcome his or her anxiety sufficiently to generate sincere responses and provide useful information. Therefore, the social worker should clearly transmit the message that the interview is being conducted for the purpose of getting to know the child as a person and provide assistance, not simply to extract information.

6. *Attachment and identification factors:* Identifying a preferred attachment figure is important in cases involving infants, toddlers, and very young children. In the presence of the parents, the social worker would observe the child displaying her or his preferential attachment to an attachment figure, often but not necessarily the mother, through attachment behaviors such as smiling, crying, crawling forward, following, and, perhaps more importantly, clinging and sucking. By observing these behaviors, the social worker can get some indication of to whom the child is more tied. For instance, a small child may specifically crawl to one parent, whereas an older child may choose to sit on the preferred parent's lap. This information helps the social worker determine to whom the very young child is most bonded.

A parent with whom a child is positively identified can greatly influence and support the child's attempts to cope with anxiety, meet expectations, risk failure and rejection in the pursuit of success, and negotiate friendships and heterosexual peer attachments. On the other hand, a child may identify with the parent's negative qualities: feelings, attitudes, convictions, or traits. A common means of detecting to what extent a parent is the object of a child's identification is through the use of fantasy. Children may display in their stories a perception of one parent as strong, powerful, or resourceful, thus inspiring them to acquire the same qualities (positive identification). On the other hand, they may identify with negative qualities that may be apparent (e.g., a boy who sees himself as inadequate because his father failed, a girl who feels rejected because her mother was rejected, or a child who feels doomed to an impulse-ridden existence because of the precedent set by an alcoholic parent). It is the responsibility of the social worker to discriminate between healthy and unhealthy identification. (Black & Cantor, 1989, pp. 130–141)

A thorough assessment of the child experiencing divorce and loss is extremely important regardless of the role of the child welfare worker in his or her involvement with the child and family. The impact of unresolved issues of loss, either through divorce or death, may render life-altering consequences for a child. In order to determine how the social worker and the parents can help children cope successfully with these issues, it is essential to understand the major factors influencing the child's reactions and adjustment to the loss.

Nuclear and Extended Family Systems   The social worker involved in cases of divorce might be required for a number of different reasons to assess the family system. Many child welfare workers are called upon by juvenile and family courts to conduct evaluation studies for the court and make recommendations concerning custody disputes. In some cases where children are involved in heavily contested custody challenges, the court may consider an alternative placement for the child, either indefinitely or until the matter is no longer considered to be injurious to his or her well-being. This might involve placement with a close family member deemed by the social worker to be an appropriate option or foster care placement for those situations in which a suitable family member is not willing or able to provide adequate care. Regardless of the role of the social worker, it is important to assess nuclear and extended families as integral components of the client system.

Severe stress and disorganization are frequently experienced by families during the divorce process and in the first post-divorce year (Sandler et al., 1992). Mothers and fathers are often found to possess feelings of inadequacy, loneliness, alienation, and depression. Behaviorally, they may be less likely to make necessary demands on children, to be consistent in discipline, to reason with children, to communicate effectively with them, or to be affectionate with them. From this arises the observation that certain lifestyle changes that impact the emotional status of the custodial parent are manifested behaviorally in the parent–child relationship.

Two elements that might contribute to the satisfactory adjustment of children who have experienced divorce are (1) the ability of the parents to make the transition from a conflictual spousal relationship to a cooperative co-parenting arrangement and (2) the ability of the children to have free access to both parents. Several studies have found a strong correlation between poor adjustment in children and parental conflict, and the results of many studies indicate that the post-divorce relationship between the parents is the most critical factor in the functioning of the family (Peck, 1989). It is important for spouses to be able to separate the parental role from the marital role following divorce, in an effort to restabilize the family system. In a *functional* co-parenting relationship, a combination of positive and negative feelings usually coexist, though neither to an extreme. Most discussions center on issues of parenting, with the major areas of disagreement revolving around finances and child-rearing practices. Some former spouses get together as a family for children's birthdays, school plays, graduations, and other such events. However, the most important characteristic of a successful co-parenting relationship is mutual respect. This seems to ensure the flexibility required for the ongoing negotiation of child-related issues.

With regard to the child's access to both parents, a *joint custody* arrangement can be superior to sole custody, if parents have been sufficiently able to resolve their hostility and support the child in maintaining a qualitative relationship with the other parent. Many children are dissatisfied with traditional every-other-weekend visits and often feel cut off from the noncustodial parent. Yet the success of a joint custody arrangement largely depends on the degree to which the parents are able to maintain positive communication and structure the arrangement based on the best interests of the child. Furthermore, it depends on the age and the developmental needs of the child as well. Physical joint custody may be ideal for adolescents yet be wholly inappropriate for an infant. The social worker needs to consider this information strongly when called upon to make recommendations to the court concerning custody arrangements.

While an assessment of the degree of flexibility on the part of divorced parents in allowing the child free access to the other parent is important, it is equally important for the social worker to assess the degree of structure in the child's environment. All children have a need for structure and feel more secure in a structured environment. However, structure can mean different things at different developmental stages. For example, an adolescent might need to play a more active role in choosing when he or she will visit a noncustodial parent, yet teens need a clear set of limits about parental expectations in each household. With younger children, a set routine of visitation seems to be best and reassures the child that she or he will be loved and cared for.

Each and every member of the child's nuclear and extended family is affected by the divorce in ways that influence the process for everyone, depending in part on the life-cycle phase of the family (Peck, 1989). For example, there is evidence that close grandparent/grandchild contact is of value to all three generations following a divorce. However, there is the tendency for the families of origin to blame the other party and become as embroiled in the dynamics of the divorce as the two parties. Assessment of the *degree of restabilization* the extended family has achieved following the divorce process is important information for the social worker to consider. Many times this is achieved when a new person is brought into the family system (i.e., extended family member, babysitter, lover); however, the restabilization of a family unit depends on many factors, such as the economic and sociocultural factors affecting the entire family or the distress associated with ongoing parental conflict (Peck, 1989).

As discussed previously, a three-generational family genogram is an excellent tool for assessing the nuclear and extended family systems with regard to the issues being discussed here. It creates a graphic record of family membership, ethnic background, gender and occupational roles, significant events, and patterns of closeness and distance. By keeping the entire cast of characters in mind through the genogram, the social worker is able to extend his or her view of the family to those members who may exert considerable influence on the current situation. Nonfamily members, such as a parent's present or former lover or other individuals who play an important role in family functioning, can be added when appropriate. Additionally, the sequence of births, deaths, and other family events and crises occurring before or after the divorce may offer further insight into the family's difficulties. For example, in the case of the Fungh family, the immigration of the family from China, the death of the maternal grandmother, and Mrs. Fungh's development of breast cancer might provide valuable information.

A family's connections with extended family and social networks before the divorce are significant to note. Grandparents, aunts and uncles, and cousins involved with the child prior to the divorce often assume a supportive role and facilitate the adjustment process. Their involvement can provide a sense of continuity and safety during this tumultuous period, as long as the involvement is from a position of neutrality and reflects an attitude of respect for the child's feelings toward both parents. A display of neutrality on the part of extended family members can have a significant impact on the child's emotional recovery from the divorce (Harvey & Fine, 2004).

Ethnic issues surrounding the morality of divorce can play a major role in the adjustment of the child and family members to the divorce itself (Perez & Pasternack, 1991; Schepard, 2004). The ethnic origins of the family often shape patterns of handling a divorce. Different ethnic groups express their grief over the loss of the family unit in different ways. It is of extreme importance for the social worker to have a significant level of knowledge concerning the values of a child's culture and ethnic group in relation to divorce issues during the assessment and intervention phases of casework activities. Knowledge of religious factors associated with divorce would be equally important. For example, if a child has been raised in a religious environment in which divorce has been perceived as "sinful" or unacceptable according to the standards of the religion, then the social worker would need to assess the child's feelings in this area and the degree to which they might be affecting the child's adjustment.

Informal and Formal Social Systems   Divorce can entail major structural realignments in family, household, and kinship systems. With the rise in single-parent families, cohabitation, and homosexual unions, large numbers of the population do not live in traditional family forms. Oftentimes the boundaries of family systems become somewhat "blurred" with the inclusion of other close relationships outside the family unit. These *informal social systems* are critical to the future adjustment of the child experiencing divorce. An assessment of the various informal social systems would be performed by the social worker and would include the following:

1. Stepfamilies, family friends, or neighbors who have maintained a close relationship with the child
2. Peers of the child who have provided, or are able to provide, a supportive relationship
3. Teachers and other professional individuals who have been involved with the child on a close interpersonal level

The emotional needs of a child of divorce are to a large degree determined by the support he or she receives from these various informal social systems. The lower the level of social support, the stronger the positive relation between stress and adjustment problems (Wolchik et al., 1989). The social worker must first determine what support is forthcoming and, if that support is not from a person within the family system, whether it is likely to continue. If support has not been initiated by these significant individuals, then it will be the responsibility of the social worker to set mechanisms in motion to include such people.

The *formal social systems* would include the child's school, church, family court system, public and private agencies, social service agencies, and so on that might provide relevant services to the child or family in relation to the divorce process. A thorough assessment of these systems is needed in terms of the specific individualized services they could provide that would address the particular needs of the client. For example, with increasing frequency, the view is expressed that schools should provide services to the needs of this specialized population of children. More and more school districts are training teachers to deal effectively with the problems of children from divorced or single-parent families (Perez & Pasternack, 1991). Many schools are providing school counseling personnel during the evening hours for parents who work during the day, in addition to after-school activities so that children may avoid going home to an empty house. School-based intervention strategies have become more common, such as divorce groups for children, bereavement groups, individualized counseling by school guidance personnel, and so on. Research has shown that support groups for children of divorce may serve an important function in lessening the negative effects of divorce processes on children (Farmer & Galaris, 1993).

Family court systems in many areas also provide services to children experiencing divorce in an effort to minimize the traumatic experience of the adversarial nature of the court process. Court counselors and those representing the private sector are often utilized to provide mediation services to families embroiled in divorce issues. Guardian ad litem programs are established under the auspices of court systems to represent children involved in heavily disputed child custody cases. Supervised visitation projects are frequently contracted through the courts to provide supervision over noncustodial parents who are involved in heated custody battles, so they can visit their children on a regular basis. It is extremely important for the child welfare worker involved with children of divorce to be familiar with the various court-related services in the community and how they might be able to address the particular needs of the worker's clients.

Interventions

The child welfare worker involved in cases involving divorce and issues of loss will develop a repertoire of skills and intervention strategies primarily aimed at two ultimate goals: (1) stabilizing the environmental influences that might be affecting the child(ren) and (2) enhancing the level of functioning on the part of the child and his or her family system. Utilizing a social work perspective in terms of targeting the interventions to include all the relevant systems in the child's environment is the major focus of the primary social worker.

With regard to the case of Jen Fungh at the beginning of the chapter, the intervention phase begins with the social worker assisting the parents in receding from a position of ongoing conflict and, as a result, focusing on the specific needs of the child. Throughout this process, the social worker will interface with a variety of systems and will utilize a number of techniques aimed at specific goals developed with the involvement of the child and family.

It is the responsibility of the social worker to coordinate interventions to ensure that mutual goals are developed and achieved by involved professionals, thus preventing a fragmentation in services due to competing demands from individuals with different agendas. Of particular importance is the need for professionals who work in private, confidential settings with families of divorce to make sure they are working with the other helping professionals involved by sharing their various perspectives and reaching consensus about goals, prognosis, and intervention strategies.

Interventions Provided by Court Systems Making family separation and divorce less painful for children and parents requires a fundamental redefinition of the role of the court. Furthermore, it requires new multidisciplinary partnerships between the court and attorneys, mediators, and mental health professionals to arrive at viable solutions. The role of the family court should be one of leadership in bringing the issues, the parties, and their helpers to the table to determine the following (Johnston & Roseby, 1997):

1. How fractured families can coordinate their resources and care for their children after the parents' separation
2. How families can be helped to protect, preserve, and reconstitute the positive aspects of the parent–child and other family relationships, wherever possible
3. How parents can resolve their ongoing disputes and deal flexibly with subsequent child-rearing issues in a timely manner during the years that follow the divorce
4. How the community can help these families while they are raising their children

Within a framework of collaboration, social workers and other mental health professionals cannot work effectively with parents and children involved in divorce in isolation from the legal decision-making process. Some triage and coordination with court-related resources and services is imperative and often must be assumed by the primary social worker assigned to the case. The following court-related services should be considered possible resources for families involved in divorce, whether disputed custody is an issue or not:

1. *Parenting education:* Parenting education may be provided within the court by community agencies in a separate setting or by collaborative efforts between the two. Such programs serve as preventive measures and are designed for the broadest population of families involved in conflictual divorce issues primarily centering on child custody matters. Divorcing couples with children are frequently ordered by the court to attend *parent education* classes to learn about the needs of their children, how to minimize the stress of their own divorce transition, how to problem solve and make decisions together, and how to provide a post-divorce family environment that will protect and promote their children's development (Lehner, 1994; Petersen & Steinman, 1994; Shepard, 1992). Some jurisdictions have mandated parent education for all parents filing for divorce; some require it only when parents register a disagreement about the

custody and care of their children at the time of filing. For other jurisdictions, it is still voluntary.

2. *Mediation:* The majority of court jurisdictions now have some provision for mediation of custody disputes by statute, court rule, or judicial referral (Black & Cantor, 1989; Schepard, 2004). Mediation as originally conceived is the use of a neutral, professionally trained third party (i.e., family law attorney, clinical social worker, or other mental health practitioner) in a confidential setting to help disputing parents clearly define the issues, generate options, order priorities, and then negotiate and bargain differences and alternatives about the custody and care of their children after divorce (Johnston & Roseby, 1997). Mediation empowers parents to make their own decisions, which increases satisfaction and compliance with agreements reached. Parents involved in the mediation process are encouraged to contain their emotional distress and focus on the children's issues. It is an effective preventive measure, as well as the intervention of choice for tailoring visitation schedules to fit the needs of the child and family.

3. *Therapeutic mediation:* Impasse-directed mediation is a therapeutic approach to custody disputes involving high-conflict, bitterly litigating families, all of whom are referred by family courts after failing brief issue-focused mediation or following custody evaluations and judicial orders. It is a confidential service provided outside the court in a private setting. It is designed to assist parents in dealing with the underlying emotional factors that have converged to create an impasse between the parents in developing a psychologically sound agreement based on the needs of their children. The goals of impasse-directed mediation are to develop sound child-access plans, to help the family through its divorce transition, and to build a structure that can support the parents' and children's continued growth and development.

4. *Custody evaluation and recommendations:* When attorney negotiations, mediation, and therapeutic interventions cannot resolve disputes over custody and care of children, mental health professionals (frequently social workers) are called upon to offer expert opinions to the court as to how these disputes should be resolved according to the current legal standard, which is "in the best interests of the child." Evaluators should serve as impartial experts appointed by the court or by stipulation of both parties, and are usually provided access to all parties. Basically, the role of the evaluator is to provide an in-depth assessment of the situation by interviewing the parties and other significant individuals, checking appropriate records and documentation, and so on, and then providing a recommendation to the court on custody and other relevant issues. Oftentimes the final court order is in accord with the evaluator's recommendation.

5. *Supervised visitation:* Rapidly growing programs in this area have been developed in response to some types of highly conflictual divorce disputes. The programs are staffed largely by volunteers or social work interns, and they aim to provide a protective setting for visitation to occur between children and the noncustodial parent. In the most extreme cases, the

supervision may be part of a therapeutic intervention into the parent–child relationship and is undertaken by a trained clinical social worker or counselor. When children are at high risk (because of a parent's psychological disturbance, substance abuse problems, history of emotional or physical abuse, molestation, serious domestic violence, or child abduction), visitation may occur only under the continual supervision of a neutral third person in a closed setting. In other situations, it may be performed in a more open setting by family members or friends.

School-Based Interventions   The social worker assigned to a case involving children of divorce should coordinate and collaborate with pertinent school personnel to insure that appropriate school based resources are being utilized to meet the child's needs and that interventions are being carried out with a degree of consistency. After involving the child's teacher in the assessment process, the social worker would also involve him or her in structuring interventions within the school environment that would be consistent with other services being provided through other client systems.

1. *Support group for children of divorce:* Counseling groups within the school setting that focus on assisting children through the divorce process and dealing with bereavement issues that occur can be extremely beneficial. Children may be referred to groups by teachers, guidance counselors, school psychologists, social workers, and so on. In order for the group process to be effective, it should focus on the development of coping skills during the crisis period, stress management skills, facing and dealing with losses, facilitating self-disclosure, and the development of positive communication skills.

2. *Direct services:* Direct services can be provided to children of divorce through individual as well as group counseling. Individual counseling provided by school guidance personnel or school social workers should be child focused and systemically oriented. A mediation approach that focuses on obtaining parental cooperation and involvement is effective; it works to enhance communication between the parents, with the counselor or social worker assuming the role of a "mouthpiece" for the child.

3. *Indirect services:* In addition to more obvious direct services, schools are in a unique position to provide indirect services that may be helpful to children. These would include training programs or the structuring of teacher in-services directed toward increasing the sensitivity of school personnel to the needs of children of divorce. Mental health personnel and other related professionals could be instrumental in teaching guidance counselors to work with children individually and in groups. Necessary skills and knowledge would include the ability to recognize and address typical and atypical effects of divorce on children, associated behavioral manifestations, factors that affect the degree of trauma experienced by the child, and appropriate and useful methods of assessment and psychometric tools.

Restoration of hopefulness and optimism in the client population should be emphasized (Hutchinson & Spangler-Hirsch, 1989).

Modifications in school curriculum could effectively address the issues associated with divorce in an indirect manner as well. Suggested possibilities might include courses at the secondary level in child development and effective parenting or social studies courses that address family dynamics as influenced by societal changes. Such curriculum changes can facilitate the ability of children to understand change in their lives and to develop coping mechanisms that are useful in preparing them for changes in their own lives and in the lives of others.

Interventions Focused on the Individual Child and Family   With regard to the case of Jen Fungh, the social worker assigned to the case would develop interventions derived from the process of assessing the child and her nuclear and extended family systems. The interventions structured in these areas would need to take into consideration the ethnic and cultural values of the Fungh family and reflect a sensitivity to the relevant issues involved. Within this context, it would be important for the social worker to involve the parties as much as possible in the intervention phase by explaining everything that is being suggested and gaining their consent. This will give them the opportunity to fully consider the pros and cons of the tasks involved, regarding the "fit" of these tasks with their individual system of cultural values and norms.

1. *Family therapy and family counseling.* The use of family therapy techniques in cases involving divorce and loss warrants careful consideration by the social worker as a potentially effective intervention and, depending on the assessment and evaluation, in some cases proves to be the intervention of choice. Because of interfering relationship forces within the family system, it is often futile to work with the individual child without initially dealing with the family dynamics that might be taking place. However, the majority of child welfare workers have received minimal training in family therapy, if any. Regardless, they are frequently placed in the role of counseling the family to some degree and should acquire a reasonable level of theoretical knowledge pertaining to social work models of family treatment. The social worker's understanding of family systems from a strategic and structural vantage point is essential in working with families of divorce. When problems are conceptualized systemically, an individual's problems cannot be understood or changed apart from the context in which they occur (Brandell, 1997). Therefore, a firm grounding in a family systems approach to counseling families is worthwhile.

During divorce, disturbed family relationships are often characterized by rigidity and repetitive, circular, predictable transactions that often contain several messages where words say one thing, but behavior and intent say another (Mishne, 1983). Parents commonly turn to children for help in maintaining the family equilibrium, which in most cases places an enormous burden on them. Scapegoating a child may also occur in a family as a way of restoring homeostasis when the previous family balance included a scapegoat. It is often the responsibility of the social worker to assist the parents in understanding how destructive this can be to the child and to help them develop a more constructive approach to dealing with the situation.

The first phase of work with the family involves explaining to the parents the need for them to give consent for disclosure of any confidential information, with the exceptions of any child abuse or threats of violence, for which reporting is mandated. It should be understood that the social worker can exchange information freely between parents in separate interviews; however, the children's confidences will be privileged. The only kind of feedback parents receive about their child should be general clinical impressions, unless the child consents to the release of more specific information. Parents should be told that the child is always the focus of intervention and that they, as adults, are always viewed in their roles as parents.

Second, in utilizing a family systems approach to working with the family, the social worker would focus on attempting to change the patterns of interaction within the family system. This would include the inclusion of an integrative strength-promoting approach that emphasizes each parent's ultimate concern for the welfare of the children. Using the Fungh case as an example, we will discuss an appropriate strategy for counseling the family in this situation, the goals of which are (1) to improve the co-parental relationship between Mr. and Mrs. Fungh through the development of a more positive interaction style and (2) to address the developmental needs of the children involved.

Based on the assessment, the social worker might conclude that the family needs to deal with the issues surrounding the separation more effectively in order to regain a level of homeostasis. In the Fungh family, this might be more effectively accomplished by focusing on changing faulty family interactional patterns, a common characteristic of families experiencing separation and divorce, to more functional ones. These dysfunctional patterns of communicating often create double-bind situations for the children, in which there is a discrepancy between overt actions and words and nonverbal communication on the part of one or both parents. For example, Mr. and Mrs. Fungh would be encouraged to communicate with their children on a feeling level by acknowledging the conflicting feelings they must have surrounding the divorce. It would be helpful to encourage the parents to suspend their own hostility toward each other and talk with the children together. With the assistance of the social worker, they would need to develop a plan in which they would reach consensus about how to communicate to the children the reasons for the divorce on a level that does not place blame on any particular individual. The social worker might encourage them to talk with each child separately to address individual concerns, after having provided the parents with basic educational information on the developmental levels of their children. Many parents are not aware that children normally perceive and respond to troubling situations based on both their developmental level and chronological age.

Third, within the systems framework, the social worker would then assist the parents in developing an awareness of how to deal with the individual needs of the children. The Fungh children are all manifesting distressing symptoms pertaining to their difficulties in adjusting to the pending divorce, and each child's needs should be addressed through both parents. For example, with regard to Jen, the social worker might assist the mother in communicating to her a level of empathy concerning the feelings of loss that she might be experiencing and how these feelings might be affecting her interpersonal relationships. Any efforts to normalize feelings on the part of parents can be of considerable comfort to a child and, with the parent's assistance, help the child to more effectively integrate these feelings into his or her daily repertoire of activities.

It is believed that social workers, in emphasizing the strengths within the family system and within the individual parents themselves, will be able to help them make positive changes in their patterns of interaction (Friesen & Poertner, 1995). The ultimate results will help the children to progress and grow through the adversity of the divorce, thereby developing a sense of mastery and control over what is happening to them in their environment.

2. Child-focused interventions. In addition to working extensively with the family during the intervention phase of the model, the social worker must also direct a great deal of attention toward the children. They frequently are forced to witness emotionally charged confrontations between their parents that can be extremely upsetting and frightening to them. The social worker is often put in the position of needing to process the child's feelings and perceptions concerning such incidents; therefore, a strategy of providing emotional support during this process needs to be utilized. Highlight 9.4 demonstrates a supportive interaction between the social worker and Jen Fungh after she witnessed a violent argument between her parents, during which the police were called to the home.

Highlight 9.4 | **Supportive Interaction**

SW: Jen, you must have been very scared by all of that.

JEN: Yeah, I thought that my daddy was being arrested.

SW: That must have been awful.

JEN: Yes, and I was afraid that Daddy would hurt Mommy.

SW: Were you ever afraid that Daddy would hurt you, too?

JEN: No, I always go to my room.

SW: You go to your room, when?

JEN: When Daddy and Mommy fight.

SW: Do you get afraid when they fight?

JEN: Yes, but I feel safe in my room.

SW: They can't hurt you in your room.

JEN: No, but . . . [She begins to cry]

SW: But what, Jen? [Reaches out for Jen's hand and holds it gently]

JEN: [Continues to cry and mumbles something about Daddy hurting Mommy]

Utilizing the Kubler-Ross model of loss discussed during the assessment phase, the information obtained would form the basis for structuring interventions that focus on each child separately. Children within the same family often progress through the stages of loss at different intervals, depending on their age and developmental level; therefore, the different assessment information obtained on each child will be used to structure individual interventions. The techniques used during each stage of the loss model can be applied to other stages as well and are not limited to one particular stage. It is important to keep this in mind as we discuss various interventions based on the stages of loss listed in Highlight 9.5. Although the stages of loss will be applied in the chapter on permanency planning, it is useful to refer to them here as they relate specifically to divorce.

Highlight 9.5 | **Kubler-Ross Model in Intervention**

1. *Stage One: Denial* During this phase it would be appropriate for the social worker to communicate the ramifications of the child's behavior to the parents so that they might modify their interactions with the child. In working with the child, a direct confrontation of the behavior is suggested. The important concept at this point is to enable the children to legitimize their feelings, whether good or bad, warm or hostile. These feelings must be properly channeled and understood so that the child may come to express them as an acceptable part of his or her personality (Hozman & Froiland, 1976).

Reality techniques may be used to enable the child to begin to accept the presence of many mixed emotions. *Role playing* and other forms of *behavioral rehearsal* are one way for her to begin testing reality. Various play materials can also be used to help her identify various feelings (e.g., dollhouse and a family of dolls, toy animals, puppets, a play telephone, and drawings or paintings). Through the use of these materials, the social worker can encourage the child to express her reality by making up stories using dolls or puppets, having pretend conversations over the toy telephone, or completing scenes or situations initiated by the worker.

The social worker can also use the technique of *modeling* by demonstrating appropriate coping skills or behavior and encouraging the child to try them out on other significant individuals. Modeling can also take place by encouraging the child to observe individuals (peers, relatives, teachers, etc.) who have experienced a divorce and have accepted the reality with appropriate behaviors.

2. *Stage Two: Anger* During this stage, it is important for the social worker to encourage the child to express feelings of anger in a safe, accepting environment. The worker can assist the child in focusing the anger and to understand its origin (Hozman & Froiland, 1976). This can be done through one-on-one counseling in which the child is allowed the realization of the observed anger. During this process, the social worker would provide her with unconditional positive regard, even as the anger is being expressed. The worker would then attempt to channel the anger and make certain distinctions to enable the child to understand the sources of the anger and the limits of expressing it appropriately. Finally, the social worker would assist the child in focusing the anger on a visual object in order to work through the feelings successfully. For example, allowing the child to hit a stuffed animal or a box or blow up a balloon will help legitimize and direct the feelings. Toys such as bop bags, play dough or clay, movable puppets, and paints are used to release angry feelings through aggression.

(Continued)

In addition to play techniques, the social worker can also use *role reversal* with the child. In this situation, the worker would structure a role-playing situation in which he might play the parent. The child would then be encouraged to safely express negative feelings, with the social worker responding to the feelings appropriately. It would be important for the parents to be informed of the technique in advance and advised on how to respond appropriately when negative feelings are expressed to them.

3. *Stage Three: Bargaining* During this phase, the social worker must be aware that the child's self-perception may be that of an arbitrator (Hozman & Froiland, 1976). He should then assist the child in focusing on the lack of personal responsibility for, or control of, the situation. This can be done by initiating interactions where the social worker explains to the child that she is only responsible for her behavior and not that of others, even her parents. At this point, it might be appropriate for the social worker to refer the child to a social-interaction or problem-solving group, either at school or at a local mental health agency. A divorce adjustment group in which problem-solving approaches dealing specifically with divorce issues are discussed might be beneficial.

During the bargaining stage, the social worker might also use toys that could enhance the child's self-concept. It would be important to allow the child to select from a variety of toys that might include Lego blocks, puzzles, erector sets, and so on. These enable children to achieve a sense of mastery and control by allowing them to solve problems on their own. The social worker would then, through verbal responses, help the child to generalize these concrete successes to real-life situations.

4. *Stage Four: Depression* When a child begins to withdraw from things going on around her or exhibits temper tantrums that might be viewed as a means of getting attention, it would be important for the social worker to intervene immediately in order to assist her in progressing to the acceptance stage. Helping the child verbalize feelings through techniques mentioned previously would be extremely beneficial. She should be encouraged to express any emotion that might be observed in the presence of the social worker, followed by statements of empathy and assurance on the part of the worker that normalcy will return to her life. Acknowledging the child's feelings of sadness and pain is important; however, efforts should be made to avoid over-reassuring remarks such as "everything is okay."

During this phase, it would be helpful for the social worker to encourage new relationships and experiences for the child. Planning with the parent(s) a program for initiating new activities and enlisting the assistance of peers could draw the child back into a level of social activity. In particular, peers who have experienced divorce and are now functioning well socially might be utilized to model desired behaviors for the child.

5. *Stage Five: Acceptance* At this stage, the child has come to a more mature understanding of the situation, in particular the realization that her parents are not going to reconcile. A planned process of terminating with the child will be implemented with the involvement of one or both parents. At this point, the child should be aware of not only the present status of her feelings but also of anticipated future occurrences and how to deal with them appropriately.

Evaluate Outcomes and Terminate Services

Evaluating Outcomes To maintain objectivity, an evaluation consists of comparing baseline measures with outcome measures at the time of termination. In order for the social worker to be assured that the interventions utilized have been effective, a baseline measure is obtained at the beginning of the assessment phase through the administration of scales mentioned previously in the chapter. The scales are also administered after each intervention and then are administered again at termination. This not only provides the social worker with a systematic method of determining the effectiveness of the intervention but also allows the worker to chart and view the degree of progress the client might be making in accomplishing targeted goals. Nurius and Hudson (1993) have described the use of a computerized assessment system that interactively enables workers and their clients to assess client problems and monitor progress over time. According to these authors, computers can eliminate much of the time and effort involved in various aspects of the evaluation process.

Another form of evaluation is through the *feedback* elicited from the client by the social worker concerning perceptions of various parts of the helping process that are found to be useful or detrimental. A child above the level of cognitive reasoning or a parent involved in divorce should be able to provide feedback to the social worker on specific techniques that were utilized and that facilitated satisfactory progression through the grief process. In addition, written evaluations in the form of client-satisfaction surveys can also be completed by clients following termination to provide feedback on their perceptions of the quality of services provided.

Terminating Services   Many child welfare workers involved with families of divorce are employed in agencies or organizations whose function involves providing services according to fixed time intervals, thus requiring termination to be planned at the point of initial contact with the client. Under such circumstances, particularly in cases involving divorce, a number of emotional reactions may be experienced by the client, and the social worker as well. With the issue of loss being a predominant one for the child of divorce, the related feelings are commonly exacerbated by early termination with the social worker. This sense of loss can be a deeply moving experience involving a form of "sorrow" generally associated with the task of separating from a person whom the client may have learned to value. During the course of working with a family experiencing divorce, a form of excessive dependency on the social worker may develop, and, as a result, separation may be viewed as the loss of an irreplaceable person and cause negative reactions to termination (Mishne, 1983). Such reactions in children of divorce can include, but not be limited to, the following:

1. *Displays of anger through emotional outbursts, passive-aggressive behavior, or defiance:* The child may experience the termination process as a form of rejection by the social worker and, as a result, may exhibit an intense anger toward her or other significant individuals in the child's system. The anger might come out in a variety of different forms, ranging from emotional outbursts when challenged by authority figures to the display of passive-aggressive or defiant behavior in which he refuses to follow through on required tasks. The social worker should discuss these reactions in relation to the termination by normalizing the child's feelings and providing some reassurance that she is not abandoning the child. Furthermore, it would be important to affirm the fact that the child will receive support through significant others in his life to help him adjust to the losses he has experienced.

2. *The reoccurrence of old problems or the development of new ones:* As the final termination date approaches, children may experience a certain amount of anxiety or fear of separating from the social worker and may create a new problem, or re-experience an old one, to keep the worker involved. The child might also be testing the loyalty of the social worker through this process as well, anticipating that she will not "leave" if she truly cares about him and, therefore, will remain involved through the problem-resolution period. While it is important for the social worker not to minimize the importance of the problem, it is equally important not to delay the termination by assisting the client in solving the problem without first exploring feelings about termination. When placed in appropriate context, new problems that might arise are generally insignificant.

3. *Increasing dependency on the social worker:* Throughout the intervention phase, it is important for the social worker to stress a child's strengths and abilities in dealing effectively with the divorce, thereby enhancing his self-efficacy and ability to function satisfactorily outside the worker/child relationship. A social worker's lack of focus on strengths by reinforcing weaknesses and deficiencies can increase dependency and severely limit the child's opportunities for growth.

Despite persistent efforts by the social worker, termination prior to the attainment of goals specified in the beginning can cause the helping process to end unsuccessfully, thus creating frustration and anger on the part of the social worker as well as the child. In such cases, it is imperative that the social worker refer the child elsewhere for additional services. The social worker should communicate information about unmet goals to the referral source, with the consent of the family, and receive assurance that there will be some consistency in further casework activities. It is also important for the social worker to discuss directly with the child (1) factors that prevented the accomplishment of goals and (2) how the child might feel about seeking additional help in the future. Furthermore, the social worker will be able to gain a better understanding of the child's emotional reactions to termination and be more effective in assisting him through these reactions by considering his reactions to feelings of loss associated with the divorce and his pattern of coping with these feelings. If the child can be made more aware of his previous negative patterns of coping with separation and loss and develop more positive patterns of coping during the intervention phase, this will enhance his ability to successfully work through the termination process.

SUMMARY

For children, a divorce or loss situation usually drives them into the Kubler-Ross stages of loss. Within each of these stages, the social worker has an opportunity to work with the child in resolving difficult issues. A thorough assessment of the child and family situation is needed in order to provide the right intervention for the child. Different kinds of interventions, including school and family based, can all be effective for the child.

Questions for Discussion

1. What are the Kubler-Ross stages of loss?
2. Why is the normalization of feelings important for children in cases of divorce?
3. What might be the advantages to joint custody?

4. Describe the importance of homeostasis in family functioning.
5. Describe the increase of dependency on the social worker during the termination stage.

Adolescent Sexuality and Pregnancy

Maria is a 16-year-old high school junior whose Hispanic American family has lived in Arizona for many generations. Over the past year, she has been experiencing a number of problems typically associated with adolescence. More recently, Maria has been rejecting the control that her parents have maintained over her and is struggling to be more independent. She is constantly arguing with her mother, and her father has assumed a more passive role when conflicts have arisen. She has been spending a great deal of time with her boyfriend of six months, who is also of Hispanic American heritage. Raphael began pressuring Maria to have sex with him approximately three months after they started dating. When she ultimately agreed, the two began to engage in sexual behavior on a regular basis until Maria became pregnant. She then told her parents, and they immediately demanded that Maria and Raphael marry, totally rejecting the idea of abortion due to the fact that they are Catholic. Adoption was not a preferred alternative because they did not have the financial resources to pay for medical care or placement of their daughter in a home for unwed mothers. Therefore, Maria was referred to a social worker with Children's Home Society by her school counselor, after having made the decision to keep the baby and care for it independently if necessary.

INTRODUCTION

Adolescent sexuality and pregnancy are critical issues in the United States. Although the numbers of teenage births have diminished because of abortions and miscarriages, the numbers of pregnancies have not. Recent statistics indicate that in the United States there are approximately 518,000 births and around 1 million pregnancies a year for women under the age of 19 (Sugland, Manlove, & Romano, 1997). Many complex issues surround teenage pregnancy, beginning with the reasons some teenagers are more likely to become pregnant than others; however, the real purpose of child welfare services related to teenage sexuality is the prevention of pregnancy (Sugland et al., 1997). This is not an easy course of action when the majority of teenagers are not using birth control. Additionally, the type of birth control a teenage couple might utilize is generally less reliable than other types that are available. The reasons for this are the lack of supports to obtain reliable birth control and the adolescent belief that "nothing will happen to me" (Strauss & Clarke, 1992).

DEFINING CONCERNS IN TEENAGE PREGNANCY

Teenage pregnancy is defined as the pregnancy of a woman between the ages of 13 and 19, although child welfare is generally only concerned about those under the age of 18. This age group is not the only juvenile group for which pregnancy occurs. Numerous children under the age of 13 become pregnant each year in the United States, and the age at which pregnancy *can* occur has been dropping (Sugland et al., 1997). The focus of concern in all these cases includes not only the young mother and father who become expectant parents but also the child to be born. The role of the child welfare social worker in pregnancy situations for adolescents and children under the age of 18 is often affected by the age of the adolescent, family income, and ethno-racial background. The younger the age of the child, the more likely a child welfare worker will become involved. This is because births in younger girls (ages 14 and under) are more likely to involve physical risk and/or issues surrounding the biological father of the child, such as incest.

The major issues to deal with when working with a pregnant adolescent are (1) aiding her in the decision-making process concerning whether or not to carry the pregnancy to term, (2) the role of the expectant father, and (3) if the mother will carry the baby to term, determining whether she will parent the child or give it up for adoption. Specific issues to be dealt with in each case where the pregnancy is carried to term include the ability of the adolescent to care for the child, the financial resources available, the continued education of the adolescent, counseling issues related to adoption if the child is adopted, and follow-up in helping the adolescent with issues of parenting, relationships, and birth control.

CAUSES OF ADOLESCENT PREGNANCY

One of the most well-received studies on adolescent pregnancy, done by Furstenberg, Brooks-Gunn, and Chase-Lansdale (1989), concluded that the pregnancy of an adolescent was not purposeful but rather due to her lack of attention to the consequences. Additional researchers have found that the vision adolescents may have of their future, based on a negative present situation, can lead to earlier pregnancies (Cervera, 1993). Statistics have also shown that lower-income adolescents tend to have higher rates of births than do upper-income adolescents. Race and ethnicity also play into the factors that predict births to unwed mothers. Statistics indicate that per 1,000 females aged 15–19, 51 Caucasians, 84.4 Native Americans, and 112.4 African Americans gave birth during the years of the studies (Children's Defense Fund, 1994). The differences in these statistics are as likely to be related to income, education, and living conditions as they are to racial characteristics.

What has also changed in the area of adolescent pregnancies is the number of adolescents choosing to keep their children. At this time, only 5 percent of adolescents who give birth put their children up for adoption. These statistics reflect a change in philosophical and ideological views of single parents and their children. There is more acceptance now of this type of family situation, and in certain cultures, keeping the child is seen as the only appropriate way of handling an unmarried mother and her child.

There are many factors involved in the large numbers of teenage pregnancy. The Child Welfare League of America (1996b) notes the following: "[C]hanges in society's reactions to adolescent sexual activity; limited opportunities for young people; shifts in societal mores and standards of behavior; influence of media exploitation of sexual behavior; alteration in family structures; and the results of poverty" (p. 3) have all had an enormous effect on teens becoming more sexually active. The results of this increased sexual activity are growing risks for sexual diseases and the greater numbers of children living in poverty or in homes without the resources needed to achieve their fullest potential.

Adolescents also face many different developmental issues during these teen years. They are expected to behave as adults but are not permitted to do adult activities, such as engaging in sexual behavior or drinking alcohol. Additionally, as our society has changed and family structures have changed, many teenagers come to view pregnancy as a way out of their home and into a more independent and glamorous life. Many preventive programs go beyond the basic sex education courses and look for ways to provide teenagers with hope and a means of obtaining a better life than they had previously experienced in order to encourage them to wait on pregnancy.

POLICIES

There have never been many specific policies designed for adolescent pregnancy. One reason for the lack of policies stems from the societal ideology that adolescents should not become pregnant; therefore, policies and programs for them may promote their sexual activity. Perhaps the most common policies have been those that have affected the child's and family's legal rights. In 1968, the Supreme Court ruled that out-of-wedlock children had the same legal rights as those born within a marital situation. This decision led to progress in support, inheritance, and welfare laws; custody; visitation; and adoption (Downs, Costin, & McFadden, 1996). The focus of these areas was to provide equity to all involved in an out-of-wedlock pregnancy.

Federal funding has been developed in the form of block grants to states for direct services for adolescent pregnancies and births. Medicaid, the Education for all Handicapped Children Act, vocational education funds, the Independent Living Initiative, and the Maternal and Child Health Block Grant have now been incorporated into larger state block grants as part of these services. Despite these efforts, support for adolescent pregnancy services is inadequate and is being affected even more by welfare reform (Child Welfare League of America, 1996b).

PROCESSES AND PROCEDURES

Processes and procedures in working with adolescents involve preventive as well as residual types of intervention. While the focus in the last 20 years has been primarily on the development of sex education to prevent pregnancy; this approach has not brought about the kind of change sought (Chilman, 1991). Programs that have begun to work with young children on self-esteem and positive goals for their futures appear to have more significant outcomes (Ooms & Herendeen, 1990). Programs focused on these issues are often initiated as part of a school curriculum.

The process of intervention with pregnant adolescents begins with the identification of the pregnancy. In the past, an adolescent would have little recourse in identifying herself as pregnant without consulting medical personnel; however, it is now easy to pick up home pregnancy tests that will give the results within a few minutes. The ways in which this type of medical progress has affected adolescent pregnancy have not been examined, but it may be an important factor in adolescents not having the support they need to either make good decisions about their pregnancies or to receive the support and medical care so needed in the stages of early pregnancy. There are many cases where adolescent pregnancies go unidentified for many months, either because the adolescent is attempting to conceal the fact or because she herself is in denial about the pregnancy. This lack of identification of pregnancy can affect the health of the infant and/or the adolescent mother.

The other issue strongly affected by this lack of early identification or acknowledgment is the number of options the adolescent may have in making a decision. While some abortions are performed in later term, many states have policies that make this illegal. The result is the adolescent either makes a decision based on a lack of action or utilizes abortion procedures that are illegal and often dangerous.

Once a determination of the pregnancy has been made, the adolescent needs to make a decision as to the next step to take. At this point, the support of family members is a critical factor that needs emphasis by the child welfare social worker. The importance of support through this process, regardless of what decision is made, will have far-reaching effects on the adolescent's sense of self and subsequent life. The final decision must be made by the adolescent, and she should not be pressured or coerced into a decision (Child Welfare League of America, 1996b). There are basically three decisions the adolescent can make: (1) have an abortion, (2) carry the pregnancy to term and parent the child, and (3) carry the pregnancy to term and allow for adoption. The father in the adolescent pregnancy situation needs to be given every opportunity to take part in this decision, if possible, and his legal rights need to be clearly laid out for him.

Once a decision has been made, there are numerous counseling areas to be covered, depending upon the decision. These may include dealing with feelings about abortion, adoption, or parenting as a young person. Specific details of how the decision will be carried out also need to be worked through with the adolescent, as well as with the support systems she will have in place. Adequate medical care and other pregnancy services need to be arranged immediately to ensure the well-being of both the mother and baby.

SERVICES AND PROGRAMS

Many services and different types of programs can be utilized by the pregnant adolescent. Among these services are family planning, parenting classes, schools with special programs that provide for the continued education of the adolescent and daycare for the infant, homes for pregnant teenagers, nutrition programs, independent living programs, employment programs, and financial assistance. However, if we consider that the main goal of a child welfare social worker is to prevent adolescent pregnancy, it is important to think about preventive types of services and programs that can be implemented in conjunction with other social service agencies.

Preventive programs can take the form of sex education but need to also include programs that aid adolescents in setting goals for themselves, establishing a sense of respect for themselves, and finding ways to achieve their goals. Independent-living programs are one form of service that can be utilized by child welfare social workers to place adolescents out of a difficult home situation and give them new opportunities. These types of programs would not be effective without support. One idea is the use of independent-living communities, much like family foster care communities, where adolescents in independent-living situations are placed near one another in communities where they can receive support from one another and from agencies.

Other programs involve the utilization of the school system to provide access to social workers and resources to aid adolescents in receiving services easier and with less stigma. These in-house programs might concentrate on individual counseling, group or family intervention, career planning, and early training in parenting and life management.

A THEORETICAL APPROACH TO PRACTICE
WITH ADOLESCENTS

A practice model for working with adolescents takes on the phases of most social work approaches, beginning with building of the relationship right
through to termination. This section will follow that process. However, some
knowledge of a cognitive-social learning theory perspective when working
with adolescents can be beneficial in both the assessment and intervention
phases of practice.

In cognitive-behavioral approaches, certain problem behaviors on the part
of the adolescent are targeted, and specific cognitions related to the problematic
behavior are identified because they function as stimuli in controlling the dysfunctional overt behaviors (Sundel & Sundel, 1993). The child welfare social
worker selects appropriate techniques and uses her creativity in devising ways
of teaching the adolescent more adaptive behaviors to be used in daily life.

Essential theoretical constructs of these approaches include the following:
(1) that behavior is controlled by its consequences and antecedent discrimina-
tive stimuli, (2) that complex behavior patterns are learned through imitation
of observed models, and (3) that learning and performance of behaviors are
commonly mediated by cognitive processes (Zarb, 1992). Particular emphasis
is placed on the influence of reinforcement contingencies that occur and shape
different aspects of an adolescent's personality through social conditioning. Social conditioning is influenced by the parents' child-rearing practices, cultural
and social expectations of family and peers, and the adolescent's exposure to
influential models (i.e., parental models initially, then peer models later on)
(Sundel & Sundel, 1993).

The role of families is central in social work with the pregnant teenager
and is consistent with a cognitive social-learning perspective. Parenting practices and parent role models shape the personality development of the adolescent. Additionally, the family provides the conditions that contribute to effective socialization and is the primary system to which the adolescent refers for a
variety of dependency needs. Therefore, a primary focus of the practice process
should be on building family support while empowering the teenager to attain
specific goals and objectives that have been mutually negotiated between the
worker and the adolescent.

Establishing a Relationship

A collaborative and positive working relationship is established between the
child welfare worker, the adolescent, and the family through a high level of
trust and mutual respect. Throughout the relationship, the adolescent is encouraged to try out newly learned behaviors in her day-to-day life with the an-
ticipation that they will have more rewarding consequences. The significance
of the development of new behaviors will be discussed later as a factor in helping the adolescent to refrain from re-experiencing the trauma of an unplanned
pregnancy.

In working with teenage parents, or with teenage pregnancy in general, it is first imperative for the child welfare social worker to have a significant level of knowledge about the various factors (economic, psychological, educational, etc.) involved in the issue of teenage pregnancy. Knowledge of the precipitating reasons for an adolescent becoming pregnant is not necessarily critical to the establishment of a meaningful worker–client relationship, nor is it crucial to the success of the practice process. Most studies show that the majority of teenagers become parents unwittingly, and the reasons they formulate for wanting to have the child do not necessarily explain why the pregnancy initially occurred (Sugland et al., 1997). The fact is that teenagers become pregnant for many different reasons, not least of which is their belief that it will not happen to them.

A nonjudgmental attitude relating to the adolescent's sexual behavior or reasons for not pursuing a particular course of action in relation to the pregnancy is an integral component of the professional relationship. The establishment of trust between the social worker and adolescent can be jeopardized if the adolescent perceives the social worker as being negative or judgmental toward her situation. In the beginning it is advisable to encourage the adolescent to discuss her feelings concerning being pregnant and becoming a mother. As she begins to open up, the communication of empathy and positive regard for her and the feelings she might be expressing would be critical to this process. An adolescent is likely to experience a need to discuss these feelings as she struggles to resolve them in a way that will enhance her ability to make a number of pressing decisions. Most pressing is the need to make plans about the pregnancy. Understanding the adolescent's possible feelings, including guilt, embarrassment, or shame, will affect how the worker aids her in decision making.

During this phase of the model, it is not only important for the adolescent to discuss her feelings about the pregnancy but it is also important that the social worker encourage her to talk about her feelings concerning the father of the child. The communication of acceptance of these feelings through open-ended questions and good attending behaviors (i.e., regular eye contact, appropriate body language, frequent empathic responses) is an integral part of this process, in order to facilitate openness and spontaneity.

The theoretical statement about the associations between adolescent pregnancy and child abuse and neglect is referred to widely in the literature on this subject. Family instability characterized by physical abuse, emotional deprivation, rejection, and a lack of parental control are all common elements of family systems in which teen pregnancy often occurs (Sugland et al., 1997). Therefore, it is important to explore the adolescent's feelings about her family, particularly in relation to their attitudes and feelings surrounding the pregnancy. In many cases, the teenager experiences rejection by the parents immediately after the pregnancy is disclosed, and frequently she is left to resolve the issues surrounding the pregnancy without family support. This can further exacerbate feelings of guilt, inadequacy, and depression regarding her situation.

Utilizing the preceding case scenario, Highlight 10.1 shows the interaction between the child welfare worker and Maria and demonstrates the first phase

---

Highlight 10.1 | **Establishing a Relationship with the Adolescent**

ELLEN: Hello, Maria. My name is Ellen Bowman, and I am a social worker with Children's Home Society. I've been asked by your guidance counselor, Ms. Cook, to come talk with you and see if I might be of some assistance to you. We provide a variety of services to young women who are experiencing an unplanned pregnancy.

MARIA: Yes, she told me you would be coming.

ELLEN: You aren't required to talk with me if you don't want to. Today I thought I would just stop by to introduce myself and tell you a little about our program. I know you've been dealing with a lot lately; Ms. Cook told me you were struggling with a lot of decisions right now. You must be feeling quite confused.

MARIA: Yeah, I guess so. Everyone keeps giving me advice and telling me what I "should" do. I just know that I don't want to have an abortion; I really want to keep the baby. I just don't think I can handle getting married.

ELLEN: I can understand how you must feel about that. It must seem unfair at times that you have to be faced with so many major decisions at such an early stage of your life.

MARIA: Yeah, my parents expect me to know the right thing to do and do it without question.

ELLEN: We are able to provide counseling services, not only for the expectant mother but for the entire family as well to help them be a little more supportive. Perhaps this is something that would benefit your parents. Would you like to tell me a little about them and how they're reacting to the pregnancy?

MARIA: Yes, well, they're not at all happy about it. They really think Raphael and I need to get married as soon as possible, so the baby won't be born illegitimate. But he can't drop out of school right now, and his family isn't able to help us financially. Besides, he really doesn't want to get married anyway, and I'm not sure that I do either.

ELLEN: Marriage can be a scary thing to someone your age. Tell me, how do you feel about the idea of being a mother?

MARIA: I feel kind of scared. I'm not sure I know how to take care of a small baby. [At this point, it would be helpful to encourage the adolescent to expand on this further.]

ELLEN: Do you think it might be helpful if I came back in a few days to talk about this a little more? Perhaps I could help you sort through some of the confusion you're having and make a decision that will include the support of your family. Would you mind if I talk with your parents to hear their side of this situation?

MARIA: Fine, if you think it'll do any good.

ELLEN: We'll see. You seem like such a sensitive, mature young lady. Why don't you call me in a couple of days so that we can schedule another time to meet. Would that be agreeable with you? In the interim, I'll speak to your parents to see how they might need some assistance in helping you.

MARIA: Okay, that sounds fine. I'll call you next week.

---

of the model, in which attempts are made to establish a relationship with the adolescent.

During this initial contact, the focus is on the relationship and the establishment of trust between social worker and adolescent. It is particularly important not to push the teenager into the position of making some sort of preliminary decision about the pregnancy. It is important to simply normalize what she might be experiencing emotionally. It would be appropriate to encourage her to postpone any decision making until the social worker has made an effort to assist in the development of a plan in collaboration with the family and the teenager.

Although certain negative attitudes might exist in relation to the pregnancy, it is important to remember that the family remains a central resource for meeting both material and emotional needs. Many adolescents are living with their families when they become pregnant. Like their counterparts, they often turn to them for support and approval. When this is not possible, the social worker needs to seek out support resources for the adolescent so she does not become completely isolated and disenfranchised.

Satisfactory negotiation around the issues that accompany teen pregnancy may be complicated in instances where families face long-standing difficulties. Rather than work toward a successful resolution, the family may simply use these issues as a new battleground for playing out chronic family conflicts (Kadushin & Martin, 1987). At the time of the initial contact, it would be important to respond to the parents with empathy and positive regard. Regardless of what their attitudes might be with regard to the pregnancy, it is important to communicate a sense of understanding about what they might be going through as well. The pain that they may be experiencing for their daughter is likely to create responses that are largely based on emotion; therefore, a genuine, positive approach would be most beneficial to the relationship.

In the initial contact with an adolescent's family, it is appropriate to begin the meeting with a brief statement about the agency's purpose and the role of a social worker in working with pregnant adolescents. The information should be presented within the multisystemic framework of practice, emphasizing the social work perspective of working with all the appropriate client systems in an effort to empower an individual to improve her level of functioning. In an effort to engage the family and begin the establishment of a positive working relationship, attempts should be made to encourage honest, open communication of their feelings regarding the pregnancy. As this process is taking place, the worker can focus on reinforcing the strengths that are observed. Regardless of the anger or hurt a family may be experiencing, the social worker must remember that the focus of the helping process is on the strengths, abilities, and capacities of each person, rather than on their weaknesses or deficits. Viewing the family and adolescent from a position of admiration and respect helps the worker to validate their feelings and engage them in a collaborative effort in support of the adolescent. In many instances, it becomes highly beneficial for both the teenager and her parents to then become involved in a joint planning process.

Assessment

It is important to emphasize the fact that the reasons for a teenager becoming pregnant are not significant to the assessment or intervention phases of the practice process. Many teenage girls who become pregnant are attempting to fill a sense of emptiness, to resolve a dependency conflict with a parent, to find an excuse to leave home, or to achieve the normal developmental stage of individuation. Nevertheless, it is important to understand that the adolescent's cognitive status influences behavior in that she has greater difficulty than an adult would in delaying gratification and controlling her internal processes. Trad (1994) found that pregnant adolescents have higher ratings of external locus of control than did nonpregnant adolescents.

Adolescent Client   A thorough and accurate assessment of the adolescent and her situation is critical to the development of a contract and intervention plan. The assessment process involves an exploration of problems and barriers, strengths and resources, developmental level and life transitions, and various systems that impinge on her circumstances. Knowledge of the adolescent's physical and emotional developmental levels, and if they are within the normal range, is an integral part of the assessment process. This knowledge helps to form the basis for the interventions that the social worker formulates with the adolescent and is significant in determining whether she might be able to obtain realistic goals and objectives. For a social worker to assist an adolescent in establishing goals that she might not have the physical or emotional capacity to obtain might exacerbate feelings of inadequacy and failure.

"Beginning where the client is" becomes particularly important in relation to the prioritization of problems that need to be addressed. Therefore, it would be helpful to ask the teenager to initially list three problems she feels need to be dealt with immediately and of these three, establish a "presenting problem" that seems to be the most pressing at the time. If she has difficulty focusing on three problem areas, the technique of brainstorming can be used, where the social worker and the adolescent mutually focus efforts on generating a broad range of possible problems created by her pregnancy. This technique is discussed more thoroughly in the intervention phase of the model.

When discussing problems, it is also important to look at the adolescent's pattern of coping and question her about previous methods of coping with problems. The differentiation between dysfunctional coping patterns and those that have been more helpful to the adolescent would be significant information to note during the assessment. Those dysfunctional coping patterns that the adolescent continues to use in her current situation should be targeted for change, and discussing the adaptation of more productive coping methods needs to be part of the goals for intervention.

While adolescents normally understand the relationship between sexual activity without contraception and the risk of pregnancy, their cognitive orientation often prevents them from grasping the full implications of this behavior. Instead, the adolescent's cognitive disposition is geared to exploration and risk. As a result, many pregnant teens engage in problematic behaviors that reoccur throughout adolescence, and sometimes into adulthood. Therefore, assessment should also focus on the pattern of irrational thoughts and feelings that usually contribute to these behaviors. Teenagers can often engage in dysfunctional and self-defeating thoughts and misconceptions that impair personal functioning. In order for constructive change in problematic behavior to take place, it is important for the social worker to assist the adolescent in identifying the pattern of unrealistic thoughts that might have led her to her present situation. Part of the intervention process would focus on assisting her

---

Highlight 10.2 | **Identifying Irrational Beliefs**

Maria has been dating Raphael for six months and firmly believes that they are in love. As they have become increasingly involved in communicating affection toward one another, Raphael has put more pressure on Maria to have sexual intercourse.

Maria has never had sex before and is somewhat fearful and anxious about the possibility. She begins to think that she might lose Raphael if she does not agree to have sex with him. She also is afraid that he might think she does not love him or that she is "odd" and completely out of touch with the times. She is embarrassed to mention the use of a condom and believes that it is his responsibility to do so.

---

in replacing these unrealistic thoughts with beliefs and behaviors that are aligned with reality and lead to enhanced functioning. Furthermore, this assists the adolescent in developing an internal locus of control, which in turn helps her to exert more external control over environmental influences that have previously controlled her.

Highlights 10.2 and 10.3 are examples of how irrational beliefs contributed to problematic behavior in the case of Maria. It is clear that Maria is immobilized by her perceived inability to change the pattern of thinking that contributes to problematic behavior in a number of areas of her life. As a result, she has developed a form of learned helplessness that adolescents often experience when they believe that outcome is independent of their actions. As compared to other teenagers who may be labeled "resilient" due to their ability to maintain an internal locus of control over environmental influences, pregnant teenagers generally believe they have no internal controls. Thus, this attitude of learned helplessness, compounded by rapid developmental change and a sense of hopelessness about the future, creates the manifestation of a number of deficits (Trad, 1994). The perceived lack of control further exacerbates the pattern of irrational thoughts and beliefs that develop and creates a cyclical pattern of problematic behavior. Maria's involvement in planning and making choices will empower her behavior.

The Nuclear Family   The relationship between parent and adolescent can influence whether the teenager will engage in sexual activity. Parents who are rejecting or neglectful may unknowingly influence the teenager to engage in sexual behavior in search of love and nurturance. Later, after becoming pregnant, the adolescent may separate from the family, both physically and

---

Highlight 10.3 | **Irrational Thoughts or Beliefs**

1. She is not capable of maintaining Raphael's interest in her without having sex with him.
2. She must be "odd" if she doesn't have sex, as everyone else is doing it.

3. She is not able to talk with Raphael about the use of condoms as she doesn't know what to say and believes he might think that she is foolish.

emotionally due to the underlying feelings of rejection. Adolescents who become pregnant have also been found to come from homes marked by familial discord more frequently than those who do not become pregnant.

The mother–daughter relationship is particularly significant with regard to the teenager's pregnancy. Adaptive maturation requires the teenager to successfully differentiate from her mother; however, this can be problematic when the relationship with the mother is conflicted. This information needs to be considered while formulating an assessment.

In assessing the nuclear family of the adolescent, the focus of the assessment is initially centered on (1) the material needs of the adolescent combined with the willingness and capacity of the family to assist with these needs, and (2) the emotional needs of the adolescent with regard to the willingness and capacity of the family in helping to provide these needs as well. If the nuclear family is not available to assist in meeting some or all of the needs, the social worker must look to extended family members or other support systems who have been actively involved in parenting the adolescent to serve as a resource. In this case, the worker would follow the same assessment process as she or he would follow in assessing the nuclear family.

In relation to the material needs of a pregnant teenager, these will largely be determined by her decision regarding keeping the baby or placing the baby for adoption. Should she choose to keep and raise the child as a single parent, the level of assistance the family is able or willing to give is of paramount importance. Family members are frequently called upon to provide child care or financial assistance for a daycare program while the young mother works or attends school. Housing and transportation resources may also be needed for mother and child. Assistance with medical care should also be evaluated as a need in view of the extensive amount of medical services young children typically require. Will the child have access to a pediatrician for routine medical follow-up? Are there medical problems that will require treatment from a specialist? Will these medical providers accept the financial plan provided by the adolescent, either through her family or through public assistance? All of these factors are integral components of the assessment process.

In relation to the emotional needs, the overall relationship of the family members to the pregnant teen needs to be evaluated. Adolescents typically refer to family members who have held most of the responsibilities for parenting them to provide emotional support. Therefore, it would be important to determine which family member(s) have assumed primary responsibility for this role. Would it be the mother, father, maternal or paternal grandparent, aunt, or uncle? It would also be important to assess their willingness and capacity for continuing to provide support during this extremely difficult time. While they might have assumed much of the responsibility in raising the adolescent and caring for her emotional needs, they might not be supportive of her under the current circumstances. Other questions to ask in assessing emotional support of family members would include: What are the bonds of affection within the family? How is affection communicated to the adolescent? How is affection communicated to other family members?

Throughout the assessment process, it is important for the social worker to use a strengths approach and identify the strengths within the family system that will need to be considered when setting goals and objectives. While attempting to identify family strengths, it is helpful to follow the following tenets:

1. An active role by the family members is extremely beneficial for enabling the adolescent to live a normal life, with or without her child.
2. Society needs to demonstrate concern for the needs of families who are providing assistance to teenage parents.
3. Families themselves are the best informants regarding the needs of their children.
4. Family members have strengths that can be helpful to the social work process.
5. All human beings possess the inherent capacity to learn, grow, and change.

Extended Family Systems   Several implications for practice with the family follow. These implications serve to guide the child welfare worker throughout the assessment process and beyond.

1. The relationship between the teenager and her family is an important factor in making the helping process work.
2. The family system is used to identify strengths in the adolescent's ability to care for her child, not problems.
3. The family members who want to provide assistance to the teenage parent are able to determine what they need and can communicate these needs to the social worker.
4. Family members providing assistance to a teenage parent should be provided as much information as possible regarding the needs of the adolescent and child.
5. Family and community strengths are used to acquire normal resources to assist in meeting the needs of the adolescent client.

Because the assessment process recognizes that families are systems and, therefore, complex and multifaceted, it is easy to identify strengths in all families. A unique feature of an assessment process from a strengths approach is that *only* strengths are reinforced. Although problems within the client system are acknowledged, they are emphasized in the intervention process. The primary strengths identified are those that will assist the teenage parent in attaining a normal level of independence in caring for her needs and the needs of her child. It is this list of strengths and identified needs that sets the stage for mutual objectives.

In the case of Maria and Raphael, it would be important for the social worker to discuss the situation openly with both families to assess their level of support and identify strengths within both systems. Let's presume that the families are supportive of Maria keeping the child, whether or not she and Raphael marry. The social worker would focus on offering both teenagers emotional support while determining how the couple may be assisted with other physical needs until the baby is born (e.g., financial assistance for medical care, supplies for the baby).

The adolescent father's involvement in the process is an important issue to consider. The father can serve as a resource and support for the pregnant mother. We must also recognize that the pregnancy is a part of the father's life, and his need for support, as well as his feelings about the final decision, must be addressed.

Social Systems   During the 1960s there was a rapid development of comprehensive, multiservice, interdisciplinary programs for single, White women. These programs initially sought to provide health, educational, and social services for pregnant school-aged girls living at home, for the purpose of preventing school dropout. Today these programs are equally concerned about extending services to pregnant girls of any racial or ethnic group who have decided to keep their child. They draw on the resources of many community agencies and focus on assisting the teenager in completing necessary developmental tasks while improving overall parenting abilities.

Resource Systems   It is the role of the social worker to maintain a level of knowledge about community-based programs that provide services to pregnant teens who decide to keep their babies or choose to place them for adoption. As increasing numbers of teenage girls are choosing to raise their children, either independently or with the assistance of others, social workers are typically more involved in providing services for this group following the birth of the child. Their needs primarily center on health issues, housing, and other personal and interpersonal difficulties. In response to these general needs, the social worker will assist the adolescent with primarily supportive and supplemental services. Therefore, community resources should be assessed in terms of their capacity to provide the following services for adolescent mothers:

1. Medical services that provide prenatal, postpartum, and pediatric care
2. Educational or vocational counseling, training, and placement
3. Financial assistance and budget counseling
4. Psychological counseling; group support services
5. Daycare assistance and services
6. Family planning services and counseling
7. Parent training services; child development education and counseling
8. Legal counseling and services
9. Transportation services
10. Housing resources

For the unmarried teenage mother living independently, loneliness and isolation become a significant problem in spite of the fact that she may continue to be involved with friends and family members. Psychological counseling and mutual-aid group support services are particularly important for this group to assist them in dealing with overwhelming feelings of guilt, rejection, and maternal responsibility.

Programs and Services   If a teenager chooses to place her child for adoption or in an alternative living situation, supportive and supplementary services are also needed in addition to community services. The following services constitute community forms of care:

1. Psychological counseling and support services (before and after placement)
2. Family planning services and counseling
3. Adoption placement services and counseling
4. Medical services that provide prenatal and postpartum care
5. Residential services; maternity home care; adult foster or boarding home care
6. Educational or vocational services and counseling
7. Legal services
8. Transportation services

Clearly, these services cannot provide a comprehensive approach to meeting the needs of the pregnant adolescent; however, the family can play a more central role in assisting the teenager by providing more services, such as economic and child care. This need for and use of informal services must be addressed. In the past, the family as a resource has been virtually untapped by programs that focus on assisting pregnant teens. Programs often designed services that either did not take into account the family's assistance to teenagers or worse still, that undermined the network of familial support. Evidence now suggests that more family planning programs have been reaching out to the family system for assistance in providing services (Laird & Hartman, 1985). Therefore, the primary social worker involved in a teen pregnancy case needs to be certain that the programs utilized promote the involvement of both the nuclear and extended family if possible.

In view of the more stringent demands being made by funding sources and administrators for accountability in social work practice, it is becoming increasingly important for child welfare workers to employ evaluation instruments that measure the outcome of their interventions. Therefore, baseline measures that measure the severity of target problems before the change-oriented interventions are implemented need to be taken during the assessment phase. These baseline measures provide a point against which measures of progress and measures at termination can be compared. The data provided help to evaluate the efficacy of the social worker's involvement with the adolescent.

At the beginning of the assessment phase, it is suggested that the social worker have the adolescent complete a self-administered scale that is easy to administer, score, and interpret. Another advantage of these scales is that they are a reliable and valid means of quantifying the measurement of a particular target population. The Walmyr Assessment Scales (Hudson, 1992) are particularly useful for child welfare workers, as they involve many of the issues relevant to social work. The following scales, developed by Walter Hudson and fellow social workers, would be appropriate for assessment of problems typically experienced by pregnant adolescents: Index of Self-Esteem, Index of Peer Relations, Sexual Attitude Scale, Index of Family Relations, Index of Parental Attitudes, Child's

Attitude Toward Mother, Child's Attitude Toward Father, Index of Brother Relations, Index of Sister Relations, and Generalized Contentment Scale.

Planning and Contracting

Case Review and Coordination Meeting   Planning is the process by which the pregnant teenager, the family (if involved), and the child welfare worker decide which goals to work on and the specific objectives needed to accomplish those goals. All goals need to be mutually agreed upon by the adolescent, the social worker, and the family if possible. They should specify what the adolescent wants to accomplish and provide direction, as well as continuity, in the helping process. *Goals* must be explicitly stated; realistic and achievable; stated in specific, positive terms; measurable and observable; focused on resource acquisition or behavioral change; and emphasize and reinforce strengths. *Objectives* are the building blocks set up to accomplish a specific goal. For example, in the case of Maria, a social worker might establish certain goals and objectives with her and the family based on their desired outcomes. Let's assume that in this case Maria would like to keep her baby and would like the support of her family in doing so. The goals and objectives listed in Highlight 10.4 might be stipulated in the form of a written contract as a means of providing structure and direction in the intervention phase.

These are only a few of the goals and objectives that might be negotiated in this case. Others can be added as previously established goals are accomplished, and additional objectives can be substituted to meet corresponding goals as well. The goals mentioned above relate primarily to resource acquisition rather than behavioral change on the part of the adolescent. With regard to the case of Maria, a goal might be to assist her in identifying dysfunctional thought patterns or beliefs that contribute to low self esteem and replacing them with more functional thoughts.

Highlight 10.4	Contract Goals and Objectives

Goals

1. Learn effective parenting skills.

2. Obtain high school diploma.

3. Obtain suitable child care.

Objectives

1.1 Attend parenting class sponsored by community agency.
1.2 Contract with a parent trainer through juvenile family services department.
2.1 Attend teenage-parent program sponsored by local school board.
2.2 Establish a schedule for studying and personal time with the baby.
3.1 Discuss feasibility of family members providing child care.
3.2 Talk with director of teenage-parent classes about child-care program.

Involve Family in Planning Process   It is important to remember that in order for adolescents to be motivated to make a substantive change in their situation, they must believe that the goals selected will improve their lives by resolving or diminishing their problems. For adolescents who are somewhat reluctant to pursue a particular goal that the social worker and family believe to be critical to the change process, it might be necessary to frame the goal in a way that adequately addresses the problem as the adolescent defines it. For example, parents, but not the adolescent, may see continuing education as an important issue. Framing for the pregnant adolescent how continuing education may meet her goals will help her in processing decisions, not simply reacting to them. In negotiating goals and objectives, the social worker needs to be sensitive to the adolescent's level of discomfort in dealing with the problematic situation and her desire to come to some resolution of it; however, it is extremely important for the adolescent to feel that she has established major goals with the assistance of the social worker and family. This process is consistent with the social work value of client self-determination.

Contract with Family and Support Services   Developing a contract or working agreement with the adolescent and other systems is the primary purpose of contract negotiation. The contract defines what will happen between the adolescent, the social worker, and other systems. It is determined by joint agreement and is a major tool in the social worker's contacts with the other systems. It is through these contacts that the other systems are encouraged to become involved in the change effort. It is evident that people are likely to continue in the change process when there is agreement between the social worker and an individual, family, or group on core problems to be worked on, specific goals, and methods to reach these goals.

To effectively utilize formal community-based services, the social worker needs to understand (1) what services are available, (2) the quality of those services, and (3) how important it is to build relationships with individuals who provide these services. This knowledge is imperative in the contract phase of the model and critical to the intervention phase as well.

In the case of Maria, it would be important to involve the family in the contracting process. The social worker might even consider establishing a separate contract for the family in order to establish structure to their involvement, in addition to keeping them on task during the intervention phase. Highlight 10.5 is an example of an appropriate contract that would be negotiated and completed with Maria. The example includes important content areas in which goals are identified and agreed upon by the client and other expectations are clearly delineated.

The completion of a contract signifies the end of this phase of the change process. It must be recognized, however, that even the most carefully developed plan of action may not be sufficient when the implementation is attempted. The social worker and adolescent must always be open to renegotiating the contract in light of the experience of actually working to achieve change.

Highlight 10.5	Example of Contract

Agreement for Services

Name of client:

_____

Address:

_____

Other parties involved:

_____ .

I.   I have established specific goals and tasks to accomplish these goals with _____, which will enable me to improve my current situation.

I realize that the accomplishment of these goals is necessary in order to resolve major problems in my life and enhance my current situation. During the course of working on these goals, I will discuss with _____ any major obstacles or dilemmas I might encounter, in addition to any other information that might be pertinent to the attainment of these goals.

Furthermore, I will agree to working actively in the planning and implementation of the specified tasks for the purpose of achieving these goals, which are as follows:

1. _____

2. _____

3. _____

4. _____

5. _____

II. I agree to meet with my social worker _____ at least (weekly, biweekly) for the duration of this contract. Furthermore, I agree to be on time for those meetings and if, for any reason, I am not able to meet the appointment time, I will notify her/him at least _____ (hours, days) in advance.

III. I agree to participate in the evaluation of my progress by:
a. completing the _____ measurement scale(s) at specific intervals of time designated by the social worker; and
b. discussing the results of the scale(s) with the social worker in addition to any reactions I might have.

IV. I understand that the terms of this agreement can be renegotiated at any time.

V.   I am in agreement with the terms of this agreement and do hereby agree to abide by them.

Client's Signature _____   Date _____

VI. I have read the terms of this agreement and agree with them. I also agree to work collaboratively with _____ and provide my professional assistance to the best of my ability to assist the client in achieving the goals listed and any others that we might subsequently agree upon.

Social Worker's Signature _____   Date _____

Implementation of Plan

Interviewing Skills and Practice Techniques The major task of the primary social worker during this phase of the intervention would be to continue to engage the adolescent and support members while assisting in the provision of required services that help to meet the goals of the contract. The plan designed to change behavior and/or the situation can now be implemented. It is the responsibility of the social worker to carry out his or her part of the plan, help the adolescent perform the agreed-upon tasks, bring necessary resources to bear on the situation, monitor the progress of the change activity, and help to stabilize positive changes that occur.

As in the establishment of the goals of the contract, the interventions used to attain those goals must reflect the desires of the adolescent and make sense to her. They will flow from the assessment process and address each of the problem areas identified by the adolescent. The interventions must also be consistent with the developmental level of the adolescent and must take into account the teenager's level of skill, in addition to the degree of emotional maturity, in accomplishing certain tasks. Knowledge of the adolescent's ethno-cultural group is also critical to the intervention process. It would be important to discuss the adolescent's views of what needs to be done, particularly in relation to the role of the family in the interventions. For example, with Hispanic adolescents, the family can be an enormous source of strength and resources. Strong ties are often maintained with extended family, who usually provide identity and support for the adolescent. The church can also play a vital role in assisting Hispanic adolescents during periods of crisis. All of these factors need to be taken into consideration by the social worker during the intervention phase of the model.

The child welfare worker will structure interventions for the pregnant adolescent that primarily fall into two categories: case management services and interventions that address psychosocial, cognitive, and familial factors. In addition, it is important that the child welfare worker assist in efforts to improve services to adolescents that include community education; interagency training; and networking, case conferences, and coalition building.

Continuing Coordination of Services Case management services typically needed by pregnant teenagers include outreach, education, crisis intervention counseling, drug treatment and mental health referral, assistance in accessing medical care and social services, assistance with financial and housing resources, general physical assessment of mother and baby, individual intervention strategies, and referral to and coordination of other community services (Borgford-Parnell, Hope, & Deisher, 1994).

Support and Empowerment of Child and Family The second category of interventions, those that address psycho-social, cognitive, and familial factors, includes cognitive restructuring, previewing, communication skills training, behavior-analysis skills training, task-centered interventions, problem-solving skills training, parenting skills training, relationship-enhancement training, assertiveness training, crisis intervention, and family interventions.

Using the case example of Maria, we will look at several interventions the social worker might employ. As a matter of informed consent, it is always important to explain to the adolescent in great detail everything that is involved in the intervention plan and to obtain her consent, either written or oral, prior to implementation. It is equally important to explain the expected outcomes of the interventions, both positive and negative, in order for the adolescent to be able to consent after having considered all the relevant information. In this section, we will focus on a few of the interventions previously mentioned.

The primary function of *cognitive restructuring* is to teach adolescents more-adaptive thought patterns by helping them detect their negative and distorted thought patterns, recognize their negative impact, and replace dysfunctional cognitions with more accurate and adaptive thought patterns. Cognitions are deemed dysfunctional when they appear to be unrealistic or inaccurate and when they contribute to unwanted behavioral and emotional responses. Cognitive-restructuring techniques are based on the premise that if adolescents can be taught to recognize and correct their own distortions of reality, they will then be in a better position to alter their related dysfunctional behavioral and emotional responses. It is important for the social worker to keep in mind, however, that these techniques are designed to modify inaccurate cognitions. When adolescents discuss negative cognitions that appear to be accurate, cognitive restructuring techniques are not used.

The social worker, through the use of cognitive restructuring, wants to get across the notion that unwanted feelings and self-defeating behaviors, such as engaging in sexual activity, can be related to negative or distorted automatic thoughts and beliefs. Highlight 10.6 illustrates how the cognitive restructuring process is begun.

In this interaction, the social worker has been able to get the adolescent to (1) identify the distorted belief, (2) identify the unpleasant emotional and behavioral reactions to the distorted belief, and (3) distinguish between the objective observation of the situation and the subjective interpretation of what occurred. Maria was not able to give any evidence that Raphael liked Amy more, only that it was an immediate thought or belief that she had. She was then able to see the irrational nature of her emotional response and the relationship to the dysfunctional behavior. It is important for the social worker to help the adolescent to understand this connection in order to motivate her to alter these beliefs and thus eliminate the dysfunctional behavior.

Previewing is an intervention and early prevention strategy to assist teenagers in predicting or anticipating the outcome of certain behaviors. Thus, before the behavior is enacted, the adolescent becomes aware of its likely consequences. Previewing is an intervention method to deter sexual activity without effective birth control, and it addresses the psychosocial, cognitive, and familial dimensions of adolescence (Trad, 1994).

Many teenagers fail to reflect upon the long-term outcomes of their actions and become pregnant without realizing the ultimate consequences—the

Highlight 10.6	Cognitive Restructuring Process

ELLEN: Maria, I would like you to describe for me a situation involving Raphael that was upsetting to you.

MARIA: Well, there was the time that he was flirting with my best friend, Amy, and I got real angry with him.

ELLEN: I see. So what did he say to Amy that made you think he was flirting?

MARIA: He said, "Amy, that's a really cool sweater you're wearing. I like the way it clings to your body."

ELLEN: And what thoughts immediately entered your mind when he said that to Amy?

MARIA: I thought that he liked the way Amy looked better than he liked me.

ELLEN: How did you reach this conclusion exactly? What evidence did you have that he liked the way Amy looked better than he liked you? Did he ever tell you that, or has anyone else told you?

MARIA: No, it's just a feeling I had.

ELLEN: Okay, let's suppose for a moment that he really did like the way Amy looked better than he liked the way you looked. Does this necessarily mean that he must like Amy better than he likes you?

MARIA: No, I guess not. I don't believe he likes Amy better than he likes me.

ELLEN: True. So there really is no relationship between his remark and how he feels about you, is there?

MARIA: No.

ELLEN: Therefore, this was really a distorted thought that you were having, wasn't it?

MARIA: Yes, I believe so.

ELLEN: So, when you were thinking this about Raphael and Amy, how did it make you feel?

MARIA: Sad, inferior.

ELLEN: Which then caused you to argue with Raphael?

MARIA: Yes. He really couldn't understand what the big deal was.

responsibility for another life. The tendency to ignore the possible outcome and react impulsively is typical of an adolescent's developmental level. Previewing helps the adolescent predict the probable outcomes of her behavior and heightens her sense of mastery in being able to control future events that can have life-altering consequences. Highlight 10.7 offers an example of a previewing exercise.

In the case of Maria, she was too embarrassed to discuss the use of a condom with Raphael and was not willing to consider the possible consequences of such when she decided to have sex with him. She was fully aware of the fact that the failure to do so could, in fact, cause her to become pregnant; however, she chose to ignore this at the time she decided to have sex with him and was unwilling to focus on the effects of having a baby.

In previewing, the teenager is asked to envision a situation in which she has engaged in self-defeating behaviors (e.g., engaging in sexual relations without discussing the use of a condom). Then, she is asked to anticipate how her life would be transformed if she were to have a baby. Because motherhood might be so remote from her experience, supplementary techniques might be used to enhance her previewing skills. For example, she might be shown a videotape of teenage mothers caring for their infants, and then she would be asked to share her opinions. The social worker would then ask her to predict scenarios involving the infant's daily care. Another group of representations

Highlight 10.7 | **Example of Previewing Exercise**

Ask the adolescent to discuss a particular situation that occurs quite often and causes unpleasant emotional responses for her. Ask her to list in a column labeled *Observations* the activating event that occurred. Then, ask her to compare the way she interpreted the same event. Have her look at the negative automatic thoughts and themes that came into her head and write them down in another column labeled *Interpretations*. Ask the adolescent to write down her *Distorted Belief* in another column, then ask her to give evidence for or against her belief in the *Evidence For* or *Evidence Against* columns. In a final column labeled *Functional Beliefs*, assist her in listing more realistic responses to the activating event.

OBSERVATIONS	INTERPRETATIONS	DISTORTED BELIEF
Raphael said he liked Amy's sweater and the way it clung to her body.	Raphael should be saying things like that to me and not to Amy.	Because Raphael told Amy he liked her sweater and how it looks on her body, he must not like me as much as he likes her.

EVIDENCE "FOR" BELIEF	EVIDENCE "AGAINST" BELIEF
No evidence	Raphael often says he cares for me a great deal.
	Although he likes Amy, he has often said that he could not have her for a girlfriend because she gets on his nerves.

could focus on the more long-term variables, such as the effect of early motherhood on her educational opportunities.

The technique of previewing can also be used with pregnant teens who have chosen to keep their babies by helping them to predict the implications of caring for a young infant and the realities of motherhood. Based on the perceptions the mother has described during the pregnancy, she observes the infant's precursory manifestations and predicts which developmental skills are likely to emerge next. As a result, she is able to provide appropriate support and encouragement for the infant. During this key period, when mother and infant are establishing a bond, she is encouraged to observe the infant closely and become sensitive to the developmental phenomena that the infant is experiencing (Trad, 1994).

Identification of Barriers and Resolution   As in all child welfare situations, the identification of barriers and their resolution is an important part of following through with a plan. In a case of teenage pregnancy, it becomes even more important, as the teenager may need direct skills to offset any obstacles. Often, the teenager can feel so overwhelmed that following through with her plan may prove difficult.

Task-Centered Interventions   Task-centered interventions are based on the task-centered approach to attaining goals. The task-centered method of social work practice is characterized by highly specified tasks consisting of discrete actions to be taken by the adolescent in an effort to accomplish a particular goal (Hepworth et al., 1997). The tasks may include dismissing inaccurate cognitions that cause maladaptive behavior or attending a parenting class at a local community agency.

Even goals stipulated in clear, simple terms can be overwhelming to an adolescent and difficult to accomplish. Therefore, it might be necessary to break them down into subgoals that require the accomplishment of specific tasks for each subgoal before the primary goal is achieved. For example, in cases involving teenage parents, the primary goal might be the development of good parenting skills. Subgoals established for this broad primary goal would be (1) attend a parenting class, (2) read material on parenting, and (3) learn about developmental stages of infants and problems normally manifested during these stages. Specific tasks could be identified for the adolescent to complete for each specific goal. In the first goal (attend a parenting class), a task might be to contact a local agency to inquire about parenting classes. Another might be to attend a group with the local teenage parent program in which parenting issues are frequently discussed.

The social worker needs to first ask the adolescent which tasks she would agree to follow up on and in what order. It might be necessary to assist her in developing tasks; however, she must be in complete agreement with them in order for her to be empowered to accomplish goals independently. If the adolescent is unable to come up with specific tasks for each goal or subgoal, the social worker might engage her in the technique of brainstorming. This is a process in which the social worker and adolescent generate a broad range of possible tasks from which the adolescent is able to choose. If she overlooks significant options, the social worker would suggest additional ones to ensure that she has a broad range of possibilities to consider.

After the tasks are developed, the social worker would then help to prepare the adolescent for the implementation of each task. Hepworth and colleagues (1997) describe this systematic approach, termed the task implementation sequence (TIS), as involving a sequence of discrete steps that encompass major ingredients generally associated with successful change efforts. The TIS involves the following steps:

1. Enhance client's commitment to carry out a specific task.
2. Plan the details of carrying out the task.
3. Analyze and resolve obstacles that may be encountered.
4. Have client rehearse or practice the behaviors involved in carrying out the task.
5. Summarize the plan of task implementation and convey both encouragement and an expectation that the client will carry out the task.

It is important in working toward the accomplishment of ongoing goals to plan tasks that involve incremental changes and build on one another. Planning tasks that are graded in difficulty improves the chances that the adolescent will accomplish them successfully; thus, this can increase the adolescent's motivation to exert greater efforts in the change process.

Monitor Services and Plan   The continued monitoring of services and the plan of intervention takes on more relevance when the adolescent is involved in the process. Issues of control are prevalent for adolescents, and their involvement in the monitoring can bring a sense of control to their situation.

Evaluate Outcomes and Terminate Services

Evaluating Outcomes   In evaluating outcomes, the social worker would re-administer to the adolescent the same scales that were administered during the assessment process (posttest) to determine the degree of change that has occurred in problem areas. The scales could also be administered at various points during the intervention process as well. Then during the termination phase, the social worker would design a chart indicating the various scores and the progress made by the adolescent throughout. Noting a positive level of change in the end provides much incentive for the adolescent to continue in her efforts to accomplish ongoing goals by enhancing her self-esteem and degree of efficacy. Qualitative evaluation is equally important in working with an adolescent. As scales may not reflect the full growth or process outcomes in the intervention, the use of descriptive materials can help the worker and the adolescent to understand.

Terminating Services   The task of terminating with an adolescent can present a number of issues for both the social worker and the adolescent; therefore, the termination process should be planned from the beginning of the relationship. It should be handled with extreme skill and sensitivity in order for the outcome to have a positive impact on the adolescent's ongoing progress. In view of the fact that the social worker has maintained a close, consistent relationship with the adolescent for a significant time, it is likely that both will experience a level of grief with the ending of the relationship. The discussion of the feelings commonly associated with grief help to normalize the process for the adolescent, so she does not perceive the termination as a form of abandonment. It would also be helpful to discuss with her a plan for follow-up, which might also include "leaving a crack in the door," whereby the adolescent can feel free to call should the need arise.

Follow-Up from a Multisystemic Perspective

Family   In cases where pregnant teenagers elect to keep their babies and live alone or with their families, a plan for following up with the adolescent is critical to the ongoing process of change and stability. Prior to and during the termination process, the social worker should explain to the adolescent that there will be follow-up contacts on an informal level to determine if the adolescent is in need of any further assistance. This reduces the level of anxiety for the adolescent about ending her involvement with the social worker, and it also provides an opportunity for the social worker to maintain an interest in the adolescent's progress. During a follow-up contact, the social worker is able to assess the ongoing change efforts and provide assistance for further difficulties. It would be particularly important to determine if the child is receiving adequate care and if any new problems might have developed in this area.

Follow-up contact is equally important with the family of the adolescent to "check on" their continued involvement and support of the adolescent, or the lack thereof. Reinforcement should be given to the family who has maintained support and encouragement of the adolescent, and the social worker should assist them in viewing themselves as having played a significant role in the teenager's progress. Further assistance might be needed by the family in allowing the teenager to make ongoing decisions concerning her child, with which they may disagree. Regardless, the family remains a stabilizing force in the lives of the adolescent and her child; therefore, every effort should be made to support their continued involvement.

Community   Community focus in this area is crucial to offset as much as possible the continuation of the increasing numbers of adolescent pregnancies. Additionally, the involvement of teenage mothers in sharing their experiences with other teenagers is likely to have a greater impact than the involvement of adults in lecturing on these issues. Prevention in this area needs to be thought of as not only preventing pregnancies but also preventing child neglect and maltreatment. Programs that focus on care during pregnancy and child care following the birth are important prevention programs for children, as well as for their teenage mothers.

Programs and Services   With regard to programs and services, the child welfare worker should consistently maintain contact with community agencies that provide services to pregnant adolescents. In addition, the social worker has the responsibility of developing a relationship with the individuals in these programs who have direct contact with the adolescents. It is imperative for there to be ongoing communication between professionals who work with pregnant teens in order for the coordination of services to occur in an effective, timely manner. This also facilitates the development of a level of knowledge about the variety of community resources that need to be utilized based on the specific needs of the adolescent.

Policy   As noted, a major role of the child welfare social worker involved in teen pregnancy is the involvement in programs that focus on teen pregnancy prevention efforts. These programs are largely based in educational and health settings that are accessed by teens, and they predominately focus on sex education and contraceptive practice. While a number of states encourage the development of sex education courses in the schools, a large number provide extremely limited education or none at all. Sex education is also provided under nonacademic auspices through social service organizations, religious agencies, and other health-related programs. In large part, the task of the social worker in these situations involves the provision of essential information about contraceptive options, pregnancy, and childbirth. Little discussion of more complex issues occurs in these settings, and there is an enormous need for the further development of the counseling component of the programs. Additional components recommended would include more in-depth counseling to identify problems and assist teens with their concerns about contraception, sexuality, and their lives in general, and to strengthen teenagers' decision-making skills in preventing and resolving their problems.

SUMMARY

This chapter has identified many of the different intervention aspects in situations related to teenage pregnancy. While the chapter notes different causes of teenage pregnancy, perhaps the most important factor to consider is that teen pregnancy is caused by the lack of interest in adolescents in using precautions. The result of this overt decision is children raising children and a new generation of children affected by poverty and immature parenting. Preventive programs that focus on the importance of adolescents rec-

ognizing the reality of possible pregnancy may be the most successful approach. Utilizing all support systems available to the adolescent is a process that will aid the teenager in being comfortable with her decisions. The adolescent father must not be forgotten in this intervention. New programs that utilize family support in both preventive education and residual aid can provide an informal approach to working with adolescent pregnancies.

Questions for Discussion

1. Discuss whether teenage pregnancy is on the rise and the reasons why.
2. What is the major reason why adolescents become pregnant?
3. Discuss the importance of the involvement of the teenage father in the social work intervention.
4. What role do the parents of the pregnant adolescent have in aiding the adolescent with her decision?
5. Give three examples of macro prevention of teenage pregnancy.
6. What are your personal feelings regarding supplying a teenage pregnant women with abortion information?

Permanency Planning and Adoption

CHAPTER **11**

INTRODUCTION

Despite the best efforts of child welfare agencies, community agencies, and individuals, some children are not safe in their homes and must be placed in substitute care settings by child welfare authorities. If the decision is to remove a child, the new environment is most likely to be some type of foster care arrangement or with relatives. Placing a child in foster care is viewed as a temporary solution to an immediate problem, and reunification of the child with his or her family is the preferred permanency option whenever that can be safely achieved. The child welfare system and agencies that serve children must look beyond foster care and plan for permanent placement for all children who have been removed due to abuse or neglect. The goal of permanency planning is to expeditiously secure a safe, permanent placement for all maltreated children, either by making it possible to remain with or return to their own families in safety, or by finding adoptive homes for them. In many situations, however, adoption may not be a realistic or appropriate option. Consequently, more attention is being focused on alternative permanency placements. Unfortunately, these options do not always provide the same level of permanency available through adoption, but they frequently facilitate continuity of family ties, which may be in the child's best interest.

The Adoption and Safe Families Act amended Title IV-E of the Social Security Act in an effort to provide added safety and permanency for children in foster placement. This legislation has served as the impetus to efforts to

247

reform child welfare practices in most states. An emphasis is placed on the health and safety of children, as well as on expediting and improving planning and decision making for the permanent placement of children in the child welfare system (National Clearinghouse on Child Abuse & Neglect, 2004).

Permanency planning in child welfare is a crucial aspect of the role of a social worker involved in the removal and placement of children. The security of being permanently placed within a family promotes a child's healthy physical and emotional development. Conversely, social scientists have documented correlations between child abuse, frequent and numerous foster care placements, and juvenile delinquency (U.S. Department of Justice, 2002). In this chapter we will discuss nonfamily foster care as a temporary alternative for children who must be removed from their homes, in addition to kinship care (family foster care), which has increasingly become a favored alternative for placement of maltreated children. Also discussed will be the role of the social worker in coordinating the various systems involved, such as the court system, the family, other community agencies, and so on. The ultimate goal of the social work process in this regard is the development of a permanent plan, such as reunification, adoption, or independent living, for the child that is in his or her best interest.

THE ROLE OF THE SOCIAL WORKER

The starting point for consideration of placing children into substitute care and in support of the need for permanency planning is two well-established empirical findings. First, consistent evidence shows that the rate of emotional, social, behavioral, and educational problems found in children in such care is substantially higher than in the general population. Second, it has been found that the children placed in substitute care settings usually come from families with parents showing diverse psychopathology and multiple problems in parenting (Rutter, 2000; Wolkind & Rushton, 1994). The implication is that many of these children are likely to have biological backgrounds that include genetic vulnerabilities and also have experienced seriously adverse environments before coming into care (Rutter, 2000). Generally, there is no single reason for a child being placed in substitute care, but rather, there are usually a configuration of serious personal and environmental problems that have developed over a period of time, during which the child has lacked sufficient support in dealing with these problems. Therefore, during the assessment process and in the course of permanency planning, it is necessary for the social worker to thoroughly assess these problems before and after placement in order to have knowledge of whether or not certain problems have derived from risk factors external to the experience of alternative care (e.g., family or environmental problems) or from the care experience itself.

It is important for the social worker to be involved in the placement process immediately following the child's removal, as this is a critical time for the child during which he or she needs to establish a trusting relationship with a professional who will be following the case from beginning to end. Separation and placement can potentially precipitate a clinical crisis for children. Their developmental maturity often influences their understanding of and emotional reaction to the separation process. Therefore, immediate efforts to develop a relationship with the child will be critical to the adjustment process. This will involve spending a considerable amount of one-on-one time with the child until the placement is secure and there has been significant opportunity for the development of a trusting relationship with the primary caregiver. The ability of a child to establish trust with the social worker and primary caregiver is paramount to other issues and must be a major focus of this initial work.

Assessment

From the beginning of the placement, immediate planning by the social worker needs to be directed toward establishing a permanent, stable living environment for the child outside the foster care system. Any plan in this regard will need to involve the biological parents at some level, regardless of their level of resistance and the barriers they might create in the process. It is important to remember that children are closely tied to their parents and often view them in unrealistic ways. Because they often perceive themselves as being an extension of their family of origin, any negativism communicated about the family will usually be internalized by the child. Therefore, the social worker will need to respect this view and refrain from displaying any critical behavior relating to the parents in the presence of the child.

The first step by the social worker in permanency planning generally involves assessing the extended family system and reviewing the options for family foster care placement (kinship care or "relative placement") on an immediate and possible long-term basis, in the event a timely reunification with the biological parents is not feasible. Generally this occurs during or immediately after placement in shelter care, when a protective investigation of the circumstances precipitating the removal occurs and the court makes a temporary or final disposition. Contacting all family members who have been involved in the child's life or who might be interested and suitable for providing a temporary home for the child would be the first step in gaining information that would ultimately be submitted in the form of a report to the court and likely be incorporated into a case plan.

Reliance on kinship care can bring with it significant differences in child welfare practice, in addition to marked advantages for the maltreated child. Research suggests that kin placements are effective in addressing three major goals of the child welfare system: providing protection for children, support for families, and permanent homes. They typically offer children a safe and nurturing environment. In addition, their close ties to the child and his or her birth family inherently support family bonds (Berrick, 1998). Nevertheless, the social worker has the responsibility of ensuring that the child will remain safe in a relative placement and at the same time providing support and services to the family during the course of the placement. Child welfare agencies have specific policies and procedures that are followed when assessing homes for foster care placement, most of which are required by law. In addition, however, the assessment process by the social worker should also include the following information:

1. *Relationship of family member(s) to child:* How close is the child to the family member(s)? How often have they had contact with the child, and under what circumstances? How do they feel about the child, and how are these feelings demonstrated? If there are other children in the home, how do they perceive the child? How does the family member feel about providing a home, either temporary or permanent, for the child?

2. *Relationship to biological parents:* What is the nature of their relationship to the biological parent(s)? How do they feel about the circumstances surrounding the child's removal? How will these feelings impact the family's ability to provide a neutral, supportive environment for the child?

3. *Ability to ensure a safe environment:* Will the family be able to provide a safe environment for the child without risk of further abuse or neglect? How will they handle visitation in the home of the biological parent(s)? How will they manage discipline of the child? Are there any risk factors in the home that need to be addressed?

4. *Parenting skills of foster parent(s):* What is the general view toward discipline, and how do they discipline children in the home? What are the strengths of their parenting? What areas need further development? How do they communicate affection in the home? How effective are their verbal communication skills? What is their general attitude toward parenting? How do they problem solve with the children in the home? With each other?

5. *Physical setting of home:* Is the home able to accommodate another child? Are sleeping arrangements adequate? What are their daily routines with regard to meal times, bedtime, school related responsibilities, and so on? Are there any hazards to children in the neighborhood?

6. *Ability to meet child's physical and mental health care needs:* How will the foster parent(s) respond to the child's health care needs? Are there any health care issues in the family? If so, how are they addressed? What are the general attitude and knowledge regarding the child's mental health needs? How will they be addressed?

Placement of the Child and Implementation of Plan

Whether a child is placed in kinship foster care or a nonrelative placement, the placement process is usually traumatizing for the child and requires much emotional support from all parties involved. A significant amount of preparation should occur in which the social worker continues to use a crisis intervention model to normalize the child's fears and anxieties, in addition to allowing him or her to feel in some degree of control over the situation. Generally it is useful to arrange at least one preplacement visit, if the child is in a temporary shelter arrangement, in which efforts are made to discuss his or her feelings about the move and address uncertainties that might exist. If the child is of an appropriate developmental age, allowing him or her to believe he or she has some choice in the decision-making process will help him or her feel a sense of much-needed control over his or her tumultuous environment. This is crucial to future adjustment to the home and, in addition, may reduce further emotional trauma.

After formulating the assessment and identifying problems that need to be addressed, the social worker will need to prioritize each problem on the basis of need by identifying those that require immediate attention. For example, using the scenario in Highlight 11.1, we will develop a case plan in which problems will be listed and specific goals and objectives will be established.

After placing Margaret with her aunt, it would be important for the social worker to establish a case plan, which would be done jointly with the foster care provider and Margaret. As indicated, the plan would prioritize problems and develop a corresponding goal for each problem identified. The objectives would be action oriented and would reflect measurable means of attaining each goal. Mary should also be made aware of the plan and what her part might be in implementing it. It is important for parents to be involved in the establishment of a permanency plan for their child, as well as a service plan for themselves, if reunification is to occur. An example of a case or service plan is illustrated in Highlight 11.2.

Highlight 11.1 | ## Margaret's Case

Margaret, age 6, was removed from her mother's care due to having been left alone for days at a time without proper supervision or care. Margaret had a number of health-related problems as the result of a blood disorder and had not been receiving regular medical attention. Her mother, Mary, was a prostitute with a seventh-grade education and no employment training. She also had a serious drug problem. When she left Margaret alone, Mary relied on neighbors to "check on" her daughter, who was occasionally left without sufficient food for the duration of her mother's absence. At the time of Margaret's removal by child welfare authorities, a neighbor had reported the situation to law enforcement, as Mary had been gone for three days and there was no food in the home. Margaret was immediately placed in shelter care while child welfare workers searched for family members who might be able to intervene. Her father had not had contact with her since birth, and the only interested relative was a maternal aunt who lived outside the community. The aunt, who was employed at a local supermarket and married with two children, was not aware of the circumstances. She had been estranged from her sister for the past year and was not allowed any contact with Margaret. She expressed a desire to take Margaret as a foster care provider for an indefinite period of time. Margaret was agreeable to the placement; however, she had been accustomed to living in an unstructured environment without rules or regulations and harbored some of her mother's negative feelings about the aunt. Furthermore, she had not been attending school regularly and was behind her peers academically. As a result, she was resistant to returning to school, where she had manifested a number of serious behavioral problems.

| **Highlight 11.2** | **Service or Case Plan for Margaret** |

Problems Identified

1. Blood disorder and other physical problems due to lack of proper medical care
2. Academic delay due to lack of school attendance
3. Negative feelings about aunt
4. Behavioral problems in school
5. Emotional difficulties resulting from separation and placement

Goals Identified

1. Stabilization of blood disorder and other physical problems
2. Improvement in academic performance
3. Development of positive relationship with aunt and other family members
4. Elimination of behavioral problems at school

5. Satisfactory adjustment to new living environment
6. Reunification of child with mother

Objectives (Means of Accomplishing Goals)

1. Schedule appointment with physician and establish regular medical care plan.
2. Consult with teacher; arrange a plan for additional assistance with school work (tutor).
3. Refer for counseling at mental health outpatient clinic.
4. Meet with teacher to develop behavior management plan.
5. Refer for counseling with involvement of aunt and other family members, if indicated.
6. Provide necessary services to mother in order for reunification to occur.

Evaluate Outcomes and Terminate Services

The case plan may change during the course of work with a client, whereby new goals and objectives may be added in order for a successful outcome to occur. If the final goal of reunification is not feasible, the permanency plan may involve working toward the ultimate goal of adoption or long-term foster care in the relative placement. Permanency plans are required in all cases where children are removed due to maltreatment. Federal law requires the court to hold a permanency hearing, which determines the permanent plan for the child, within 12 months after the child enters foster care and every 12 months thereafter. Many courts review each case more frequently to ensure that the agency is actively engaged in permanency planning for the child (National Clearing House on Child Abuse and Neglect, 2004).

ROLE OF THE COURT AND THE CHILD WELFARE AGENCY

All child welfare decisions are made by caseworkers, supervisors, and jurists representing the juvenile or family division of a state court system. These decisions occur when agency guidelines, policies, or laws are applied to the information gathered in a specific case. Although important case decisions are usually made by social workers, they are usually not made unilaterally and may involve input from family members, other staff in the child welfare agency, and professionals within the community who have been working with the child and family. Any decision to seek removal of a child from the family must be taken to the court and affirmed or denied through a legal process (Downs et al., 2004). Child welfare agencies are mandated by legislative and administrative rules to follow certain policies and procedures relating to the removal and placement of children throughout the varied processes that can occur in any case involving child maltreatment.

The flow chart in Highlight 11.3 provides a clear overview of the child welfare system and delineates certain actions taken by the child welfare agency and court system that are generally followed in the disposition of a case involving child abuse or neglect. The shaded boxes indicate the outcome of permanency plans that are generally developed and followed by child welfare agencies and court systems (U.S. DHHS, 2004b).

MENTAL HEALTH ISSUES

Many children residing in foster care and being placed for adoption have significant mental health problems as the result of abuse and/or neglect. These issues require intensive work and support on the part of the child welfare social worker, both with the child and the foster parent. In social work and throughout the child welfare system, we are seeing an increasing number of children with significant mental health disorders, many of whom are placed in foster care. This demonstrates the need for expanded mental health services within the system. Furthermore, it also points to the need for child welfare social workers to be educated on the types of disorders commonly experienced by maltreated children, how these disorders are manifested, and how they can be addressed more effectively.

Dealing with Loss and Grief

Separation from people to whom we are closely attached is always experienced as a loss. Children who are separated from their families and placed into substitute care are typically subjected to high levels of stress. Their cognitive and developmental maturity levels are often impeded by their limited internal coping abilities, and they frequently maintain an inaccurate perception of the circumstances leading to the separation as a result. During separation and placement, these children are extremely prone to crisis due to their poor coping skills and inadequate problem-solving responses. As a result of the loss of their parents, even those who maltreated them, the crisis they experience can often lead to serious mental health ramifications that can last an entire lifetime.

Many underlying mental health disorders in children placed in the child welfare system are the result of their having experienced the crisis of separation and profound feelings of loss, for which there was no substantive professional intervention provided on an ongoing basis. In order to minimize the emotional scarring that can result, it is first important for social workers and substitute

Highlight 11.3 | **Flowchart of Child Welfare System**

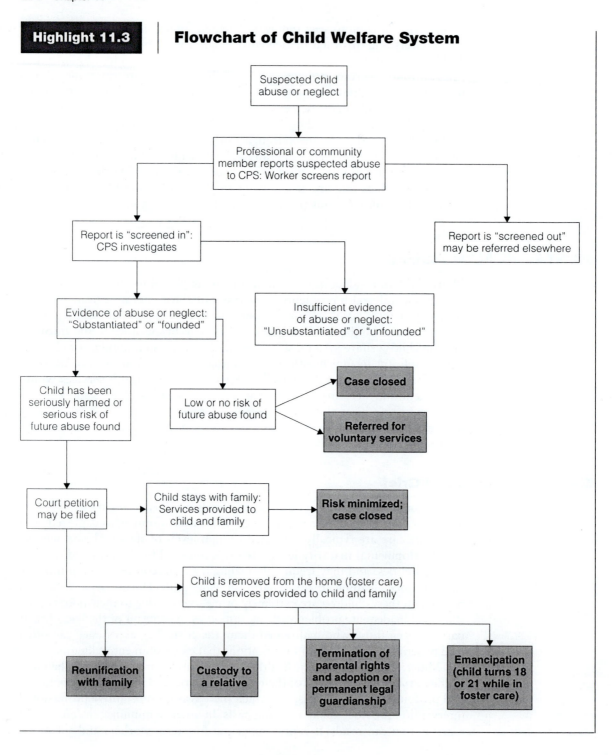

care providers to understand the stages of loss and grief that children typically experience after separation and how the associated feelings are manifested through problematic behaviors that may not be typical of their corresponding developmental level. For the social worker involved in working with these children, it is recommended that the stages of a standard loss and grief model, such as that of Kubler-Ross (1969), be utilized in assessing the child and family systems. Basically, the Kubler-Ross model includes five stages, each of which presents different behavioral responses and varying emotional reactions of children as they struggle to come to terms with the reality of the situation. It is further recommended that child welfare social workers and caregivers become familiar with the stages of grief in children and the typical behaviors that accompany each.

Highlight 11.4 is a brief overview of these five stages as they relate to the separation and placement of maltreated children (Rycas, Hughes, & Garrison, 1989, pp. 89–101). Children who have experienced repeated traumatic separations often become permanently emotionally damaged. To prevent the likelihood of this occurring, it is the responsibility of the social worker to monitor the placement of the child closely to determine how he or she is progressing through the grieving process and whether the behaviors being exhibited are considered "normal" in accordance with the child's developmental level. It is also necessary for the social worker to assist the caregiver in understanding the stages of grief and assist him or her in developing appropriate supportive methods for dealing with the corresponding behaviors. In working with children placed in "temporary" care for a long period of time and who suffer a second, painful separation from their substitute care families when they are returned to their own families or placed in another permanent home, it becomes equally important for the social worker to assist them through the severity of a second loss.

Attachment and Attachment Disorder

One vital role of a family and primary caregiver that influences a child's entire life is to provide an infant with an opportunity to bond. When babies are inconsistently parented within their family of origin or are abused or neglected, they may not develop a healthy attachment to others and, thus, may experience *attachment disorder*. This disorder not only creates an inability to bond with others but also causes self-destructive behaviors, cruelty to others, poor impulse control, habitual lying, and an inability to discern cause from effect (Chicetti & Carlson, 1989). This inability to attach is often replicated in their associations with others as they grow older and attempt to develop new, more intimate relationships.

In the field of child welfare, we have known as early as the late 1960s that the survival of infants is best ensured when proximity to an attachment figure is maintained (Bowlby, 1980; Chicetti & Carlson, 1989). The word *maintained* is an important component of this theory as it is highly destructive to children, for example, to remove them and re-place them in a series of alternative

| Highlight 11.4 | **Kubler-Ross Model and the Placement of Maltreated Children** |

1. *Stage One: Shock/Denial*   This stage must be overcome by the child before further progress can be made. In an attempt to reject the reality of separation, children often try to eliminate the thought from their minds and show no signs of reacting to the situation. Often interpreted as the "honeymoon period," in this stage children may appear extremely compliant and disconnected from the fact that they have been removed from their parent(s). They may deny the event and/or deny the feelings that accompany it. Children in this stage often appear robot-like, stunned, or in a fog. They may go through the motions of daily activity, but there appears to be a lack of commitment to these activities. Essentially, they may seem indifferent in affect and behavior, not showing any emotional reaction to the move to foster care. They may appear to make a good adjustment for a period of time but may actually be emotionally numb and deny the loss.

   One of the most common errors made by social workers, foster parents, and biological parents during this stage is to misinterpret the child's compliant and unemotional behavior as meaning that he or she is making a satisfactory adjustment to the placement. Should this behavior continue for an extended time, it is recommended that the child be evaluated by a child psychiatrist, psychologist, or clinical social worker.

2. *Stage Two: Anger/Protest*   At this stage, the impact of the loss can no longer be denied, and the first emotional response is usually anger. Intense feelings and behaviors associated with anger are commonly experienced by the child during this period, such as guilt, blame, recriminations, and hypersensitivity, as well as persistent protests and oppositional behaviors. In younger children, physical symptoms and emotional outbursts are common. However, in older children, the anger may be directed into destructive behaviors. Confrontations between caregivers and the child are also common and may promote a struggle for control. Therefore, caregivers should provide emotional support and give the child opportuni-

ties for the appropriate expression of feelings while they also set firm limits on the behavior.

3. *Stage Three: Bargaining*   The bargaining stage can also be somewhat misleading and may give caregivers and social workers the impression that the child has sufficiently resolved his or her grief and loss. During this stage, children may exhibit "good-as-gold" behavior in which they will often communicate an intent to change their behavior and undo what they felt they have done to precipitate the placement. Some ritualized behaviors may be observed, which may be the child's attempt to formalize "good behavior" and assure its consistency. A child may also believe that a certain way of thinking will bring about the desired reconciliation; therefore, the behavior exhibited during this stage may appear to be a final attempt to regain control and prevent the finality of the loss. Oftentimes during this stage, a child may try to negotiate agreements with the caregiver or social worker and may offer to do certain things in exchange for a promise to return home.

   A social worker should remember that, while many of the child's behaviors may be inherently desirable, they do not represent a positive change in character or circumstances. Rather, they may represent a desperate attempt to control the environment and to defend against emotional turmoil. It is important for the social worker to work with the caregiver in providing the child with opportunities to feel he or she is regaining some control over the situation by allowing him or her appropriate decision-making authority when opportunities for such arise.

4. *Stage Four: Depression*   This stage is usually characterized by expressions of despair and futility, listlessness, occasional episodes of fear and panic, withdrawal, and a generalized lack of interest in people, surroundings, or activities. The child with depression appears to have lost hope and is experiencing the full emotional impact of the loss. The child may be generally "out of sorts," touchy, and vulnerable to minor stresses,

(Continued)

and he or she may cry easily. Anxiety is often associated with this stage, as the child may be easily frightened, frustrated, and overwhelmed by minor events and stressors. Sporadic play may be evident, but activities are generally mechanical and without investment of interest. The depressed child may also demonstrate an inability to concentrate, in addition to regressive behaviors such as thumb sucking, toilet accidents, or engaging in baby talk. Generalized emotional distress is often seen in younger children (e.g., whimpering, crying, head banging, rocking).

Should the depression be consistently evident for a prolonged time (two weeks or longer), it is recommended that the social worker arrange for the child to be evaluated by a child psychiatrist for appropriate medical and/or psychological follow-up.

5. *Stage Five: Resolution* It is during this stage that the final phase of grieving ends and the child returns to an active life in the present. The child in placement begins to develop stronger attachments in the new home and tries to establish a place in the family structure. A period begins in which he or she starts to invest more emotional energy toward planning the future, and less energy is directed toward ruminating about the past. Depending on the child's developmental level, typical behaviors observed during this stage may include the following:

- Identification as a part of the new family
- Strengthening emotional attachments to new family members
- Decrease in the intensity of emotional distress
- Increase in demonstration of pleasure in normal childhood play and activities
- Recurrence of more goal-directed activities
- Diminished emotional reactions to stressful situations

living situations. Often the result of multiple moves is the development of an inability to bond or attach to a significant other. Therefore, in order for children to be able to formulate secure attachments throughout their childhood, they need to attain and maintain a close proximity to a trusted individual. However, a child's sense of security does not depend so much on the actual presence of the attachment figure as the level of mutual trust and understanding that has developed in the relationship. The fact is that by adolescence, attachments can be maintained without actual physical proximity for long periods of time (Wolfe, 1999).

Attachments to parents must be preserved during placement through frequent and regular visitations. Having foster homes in somewhat close proximity to the natural homes can therefore be an advantage. Even though visitations are not optimal in child welfare agencies (Beyer, 1999), research demonstrates that children who return home have had frequent home visits and shorter placement periods. Home visits can accomplish many things, such as providing opportunities for parents to meet the needs of their children and developing better parental role models. For children, visits provide an opportunity to preserve and build on the attachments to their parents.

Home visitations are usually difficult for everyone involved: the children, the biological parents, and the foster parents. For the children, a myriad of feelings can emerge, including confusion about why they are in care, anger toward their parents for creating the situation requiring placement, shame because children believe they are responsible for the situation, and disloyalty to their parents. These feelings often lead to the children acting out, withdrawing, regressing to previous behavior, or other behaviors. Biological parents often feel guilty about their behavior, resentful toward the agency, competitive toward the foster parents, and confused about why the children cannot be reunited with them. Foster parents bear the brunt of all the children's behavior and have to be committed and diligent in order for the placement to continue and be successful. In spite of the complexities, planned visitation can be useful for all involved. If parents are keenly aware of the reasons for placement, the visitations will allow opportunities to deal with the issues. Parents can learn appropriate behaviors in their responses to their children. The more regular and frequent the visits, the more quickly the parents can deal with their issues. Support for foster parents during the entire placement is also critical, so there is understanding of the children's needs and benefits of the visits.

Social workers who are given the responsibility of permanency planning for maltreated children have a duty to secure placements that will allow children to sufficiently attach to caregivers and, therefore, to make every possible effort to prevent children from having to be moved from a secure home environment to which they have become attached. When moves are imminent and subsequently occur, the social worker should plan to involve the family in programs that focus on parent–child attachment in which there is extensive involvement on the part of the caregiver, in order to help further the child's resiliency. For example, Karol and colleagues (1998) found that fostering mother–infant attachment and developing children's social skills increase the children's success in school. Also, projects that work with neglectful mothers in helping them to give effective physical and emotional care to their children have been successful in producing positive outcomes regarding attachment (Helton & Smith, 2004). A priority should be given to securing resources for foster parents and primary caregivers that will provide education and skill training in the area of parental bonding and attachment.

ADOPTION

According to the Child Welfare League of America (2005), of the 542,000 children in foster care as of March 2003, approximately 126,000 were waiting to be placed for adoption. While adoption is the preferred alternative in permanency planning for children who cannot return to their family, it presents a complex issue. Many adoptive families want healthy infants of any race; however, there are numerous older children awaiting adoption, many of whom have serious physical and emotional problems due to having experienced abuse or neglect. Furthermore, there are numerous sibling groups available for adoption that child welfare agencies are reluctant to separate due to the trauma it will likely cause to the children. These issues present unique challenges, both to the social worker working with the child and the adoptive family, and to the adoptive parents as well.

When placing children for adoption, a number of cultural variables need to be considered. Biological parents of varying cultures or races often stipulate that preference be given to placing the child with a family of the same culture/race, thus limiting the availability of adoptive homes. Today there are numerous children available for adoption, and they represent a variety of cultural or ethnic groups. Whether they are considered "special-needs" children may depend on their geographic area and the demographics of the area, in addition to the types of parents who are seeking to adopt. A recent study conducted by the Dave Thomas Foundation (2002) asked Americans about the types of children they might consider adopting. Of those polled, 78 percent stated they would want a healthy infant of the same race as themselves; 64 percent would consider a sibling group, with the oldest being under 4 years of age; 40 percent would accept a child of another race; 25 percent would adopt a foster child who had been in foster care a number of years; 14 percent would accept a child with medical problems; and 11 percent would adopt a child with behavioral problems.

The statistics cited in the previous paragraph highlight the various categories of children placed for adoption, most of which require a great deal of preadoption planning and preparation on the part of the social worker. If adoption is the ultimate goal of the permanency plan, it will be important for the social worker to work with the child to prepare him or her for placement with a permanent adoptive family, in addition to working with the adoptive family so they will be totally aware of the child's needs. If the goal of the plan is long-term foster care, most judicial jurisdictions will require ongoing supervision of the home by the child welfare agency. This will usually require monthly visits to the home by a social worker, which is consistent with the standards of the Child Welfare League of America. Should problems arise during the supervision period, it will be the responsibility of the social worker to assist the family in addressing them through the formation of another service plan outlining relevant goals and objectives.

Single-parent adoptions are increasing for varying reasons, particularly due to the fact that fewer women feel the need to marry in order to have children. The Child Welfare League of America (2005) reports that the majority of single-parent adoptions are by women, who tend to adopt older, minority, or special-needs children with mental or physical disabilities. Most single, adoptive parents are considered to be more mature with a significant network of support, either friends or relatives, to assist in the care of the children.

The practice involved in the adoption of a child is a sensitive one and one that needs to be handled with care. The role of the social worker in the adoption process is to provide the best family possible to meet the needs of the child. In order to do this, assessments are undertaken to evaluate the adopting family and their strengths as well as the child's needs. Although many children will respond to an adoptive family in a positive way if care is taken in arranging the adoptive process, it is important to recognize that some children will not fare as well despite the strengths of an adoptive family, due to their earlier histories of care and trauma. Social workers doing complete assessments of the child need to recognize the importance of sharing this data with the prospective parents. Ensuring that the family has as much information as possible and is prepared for issues that may arise will offset the possibility of an unsuccessful adoption that does enormous harm to both the child and the family.

Many interventions can be used in aiding a child to transition into an adoptive family. Among these, the use of life books stands out as an innovative method of aiding the child. Life books help adoptive children understand the process their life has undertaken. These books include information about the biological family, adoptive family, and foster families, if applicable. They frame the child's life through pictures, legal documents, letters, and other personal material.

Because there are many more children who are not first choice for adoption, many social service agencies have modified their view of what comprises a perfect adoptive couple. For most of the history of adoption, adoptive couples were seen as needing to be young, financially secure, and within what was considered the traditional family situation; however, child welfare social workers have come to realize more and more the importance of a loving family environment rather than a traditional one. Many more single-parent families, older-parent families, lower-income families, and parental family units reflective of more nontraditional lifestyles are being considered as adoptive family situations today.

Interracial Adoption

An issue that has created increasing conflict is that of interracial adoption. In the child welfare system, there are proportionately more ethnic-minority children available for adoption than White children. In fact, African American children make up close to 39 percent of all children available for adoptions (National Committee for Adoption, 1986). While the Child Welfare League of America supports the placement of a child without prejudice to race of the parents, it also acknowledges the importance of cultural and racial support for children. The League emphasizes, however, that the placement of a child should be for the best interest of the child and not for the adoptive parent. While some studies have indicated that children adopted interracially are well adjusted (Feigelman & Silverman, 1983; Simon & Alstein, 1987), there is still strong belief by many researchers and practitioners on the importance of same-race adoption. The Indian Child Welfare Act of 1978 is one of the most significant pieces of legislation to address the issue of interracial adoption. This act was enacted to offset the numbers of placements of Native American children with families of other backgrounds. Findings during the period preceding this act indicated that Native American children were being placed at alarming numbers in White homes and being removed from their Native American communities. The act provided a procedure that must be taken for the placement of any Native American child. The procedure includes preference being given first to the extended family, second to other families in the child's tribe, and third to families of other Native American tribes.

Those professionals who protest interracial adoption have also begun to promote the placement of children within their own ethnic-racial group by reaching more into specific ethnic-racial communities to seek out placement for more children. An example of one such program is the Illinois Program entitled One Church/One Child. This program, begun by Father Clements in 1979 in Chicago, promoted the adoption of one African American child in each African American church in the Chicago area. This outreach program resulted in the adoption of 37 African American children within a few years. This program has now been adopted throughout the United States (Veronico, 1983).

Special-Needs Adoption

Children with special needs who are in need of adoptive services make up large numbers of older children without families. The issues surrounding these factors were addressed in the 1980 Adoption Assistance and Child Welfare Act. This act enabled the offering of subsidies to families to encourage the adoption of special-needs children. These subsidies were to serve as a means for a family to obtain resources for the child with special needs. Although there was a fear that families would be adopting as a means of obtaining a subsidy, this has not appeared to be the case (Cole, 1987).

Adoption Process

The process involved in adoption requires the child welfare social worker to be open and sensitive in his or her understanding and assessment of potential parents. Once a referral is made to a child welfare agency of the availability of a child for adoption through legal termination of parental rights, voluntary termination of parental rights, or abandonment, the social worker will examine those families who have applied for adoption and attempt to match the families with those children who are available. The difficulty in this process is that many children in need of adoption will be older or of an ethnic-racial background for whom there are fewer family opportunities (McKenzie, 1993).

McKenzie (1993) has also observed the system barriers in the adoption process, including the reunification phase, preparation for adoption planning (including termination of parental rights), and adoption planning. These planning stages before adoption often cause delays in the process. These delays are difficult on both the child and adoptive family. Although they are an important and required piece of the process, special attention to the needs of the parent and child during these periods is critical.

The process of adoption also requires an extensive home study of the potential adoptive parents. These home studies are utilized to provide the social worker with an understanding of the situation in which a child is to be placed and an opportunity to aid the family in preparation for the child. While a home study needs to identify issues that may be harmful to a child (a criminal abuse record, a history of child maltreatment, etc.), most of these home visits should focus on aiding the potential parents in their prospective parenting role. In the past, home visits were utilized more as a moral analysis of the parents.

Although an infant may be placed immediately in a home, an older child might visit the home for limited periods before an adoption takes place. This is due in part to the fact that the majority of adoptions that disrupt are with older children (Rosenthal, 1993). Very often, adoptions occur with the foster parents who have been caring for a child. Although controversial studies exist, foster care adoptions are less likely to disrupt, according to several child welfare experts (Downs et al., 1996; Gil & Amadio, 1983). This fact has led more and more agencies to seek out foster parent situations in which an adoption is a high priority.

In certain situations, the safeguards surrounding the adoption process have been reduced. Open adoption occurs when birth parents meet adoptive parents and biological parents may participate in a child's adoptive life to some extent. The relinquishment of parental rights is complete, but some contact is continued. The amount of contact varies with each individual situation.

Openness in adoption has been examined by Henry, McRay, Ayers-Lopez, and Grotevant (2003). Openness can be defined along a continuum. On one end are closed adoptions where minimal information is shared with the adoptive parents by the agency. The information is sufficient and covers medical and other features, but there is no contact between the birth and adoptive parents. The other end of the continuum involves full disclosure wherein birth parents and adoptive parents participate fully in the process. This contact may continue throughout the life of the child. The midpoint is where more information is shared, sometimes through the agency or through the birth parent. Generally the birth and adoptive parents do not physically meet, but letters and pictures may be shared. A variety of events may be part of open adoptions. Birth parents may write letters to their children, which are shared with them by the adoptive parents. Adoptive parents may share child information with the birth parents. Broader openness may be shared among all parties involved.

A longitudinal study by Henry and colleagues (2003) was conducted over a 12-year period, with about 30 private child-placement agencies responding to inquiries at three different times during the 12-year period. The study results indicate movement toward openness in adoptions throughout the years. In the initial 1987 contacts, most adoptions offered some openness; only a small number of adoptions were closed. At the end of the study in 1999, over three-fourths of the agencies offered full disclosure, and very few offered closed-adoption placements. The biggest influence on the change toward openness was found to be that of the birth parents. Agency staff have also achieved a high comfort level with open adoption, describing the change as beneficial for all involved. In particular, child contact with birth parents appears to minimize the child's feelings of abandonment.

Black-market adoption is a term used to refer to the "selling" of children for profit. In these situations, a third party is generally involved in finding infants and young children for adoption and setting up deals with their parents (generally a young, single mother) in exchange for financial gain. Although many independent adoptions occur, the financial support is generally limited to the medical care and minor support of the parent during the pregnancy.

INDEPENDENT LIVING

An eventual transition to self-sufficient adulthood is an ultimate goal for all children in foster care, whether they will return to a family, be adopted, or live independently. Many of the children residing in foster care are older and for varying reasons have not been placed with relatives or in adoptive homes. Research demonstrates that when these children emancipate from the foster care system, they experience great risk in terms of economic, physical, and emotional safety. Inevitably they are required to leave the foster care system by age 18, oftentimes with little preparation for living independently and few resources. A number of them return to the care of the state, either through the welfare or criminal justice systems, or they end up as part of the homeless population. Public agencies are now recognizing the need to make fundamental changes in their programs and services for these older children, particularly in the areas of education, employment, life skills, and decision making. Through amended changes to the Federal Independent Living Program in 1990, funds may be used by states to provide counseling, educational assistance, life skills training, and vocational support to children in care (Child Welfare League of America, 2005).

Social workers assigned to work with older children in foster care have a responsibility to advocate for the provision of these services prior to the statutory age of release and throughout the duration of their time in foster care. A well-developed plan immediately after foster care placement would involve the provision of counseling services that would sufficiently prepare the child for independent living, perhaps without the support of family or close friends. At the very least, this plan should also include a thorough assessment of the child's needs for independent living; provision of life-skills activities; referral to relevant training programs, support, and case management services that would prepare him or her for independent living; and referral to independent-living coordinators at the local or county level. For most of these adolescents, the family support becomes the community child welfare agencies that must act in the role of parents by assuming responsibility for ensuring that their needs are being met after leaving care. To strengthen the system of support that contributes to permanence for young people emancipating from the foster care system, it is suggested that child welfare agencies and social workers do the following:

- Provide more information about permanency options and support in making decisions related to permanency to young people, families, foster/kinship caregivers, prospective adoptive parents, and service providers.
- Encourage discussions of permanence both inside and outside of the legal context so that child welfare staff can help emancipating youths build the networks of support they need to make successful transitions.

- Ensure early and continuing access to supportive adults, including biological family members, identified family/kin, mentors, former service providers, and other community members who can be part of a long-term network of support.
- Provide a continuum of support and preparation for adulthood that begins when a child or youth enters foster care and continues through the post-emancipation period.
- Stabilize foster care placements to ensure educational continuity and achievement.
- Increase youth involvement in the planning and delivery of services to transitioning youths at the local, state, and national levels.

SUMMARY

The importance of permanency planning cannot be overlooked when examining the child welfare system. Permanency planning must begin with the first contact on the part of the social worker after a child has been removed from a home. In the social worker role, you must be ready to make decisions regarding the child that will disrupt their life as little as possible in this transition. In order to do this it is often important to think of kinship placements first. Children often go through the stages of grief and loss when they are removed from their families and social workers need to be sensitive to these issues. If permancy planning does not end up with the child returning home, then careful steps must be taken to move the child into an adoptive or independent living situation.

Questions for Discussion

1. What is kinship care and in what ways does it work and not work?
2. What are your views about a permanency plan?
3. What is the difference between substantiated and unsubstantiated abuse?
4. Describe the stages of loss.
5. What is your view of open adoption?

Alternatives and Early Intervention

INTRODUCTION

This chapter begins with a description of prevention, early intervention, and intervention, followed by a brief summary related to the need to develop alternatives to better serve the vulnerable children and families in this country. The chapter continues with summaries of prevention and early intervention programs that research evaluation studies have proven to be effective. Programs that offer serious potential are also presented. Because prevention and early intervention programs are the first line of defense for vulnerable children and families, these programs are presented as alternatives and supplements to the current programs in child welfare systems. The chapter concludes with a discussion and recommendations for collaboration among child welfare and other public and private service providers so that a more seamless system of services can be available to the field. Special attention is provided to collaborations that address poverty. The chapter concludes with more radical alternatives to the current child welfare system, such as privatization; examples of privatization initiatives are included.

PREVENTION AND EARLY INTERVENTION STRATEGIES

Prevention programs serve to inoculate families due to the fact that the programs offer services to support well-being outcomes. Early intervention programs target services to children and families at some low risk in order to stabilize family functioning and deal with issues before they reach crisis levels. Intervention programs are organized around families in crisis, where the safety of children is compromised and out-of-home placement may be needed on a temporary or permanent basis.

Many of the federal and state programs are aimed at families in crises and are intervention oriented. Therefore, not much of the available funding is used for prevention efforts. However, prevention and early intervention policies have recently been incorporated into many federal programs, including the Departments of Health and Human Services, Justice, Education, and others. National advocacy organizations have long-standing standards and guidelines supporting prevention and early intervention programs. In collaboration with advocacy groups, many states and local jurisdictions have also funded prevention and early intervention programs.

It is critical that programs, policies, and funding be updated and provide more support for prevention and early intervention programs. It is also critical that policies at federal, state, and local levels mandate collaboration and integration of services so that vulnerable families can be served in a more comprehensive way and services can be individualized to meet family needs.

Child welfare agencies serve hundreds and thousands of vulnerable families and children. However, there are crises in child welfare systems, and changes are needed to ameliorate these crises. Fragmentation, duplication, and staffing problems have been problematic. In addition, agencies do not have sufficient resources, and technologies now used are not keeping pace with the complex needs of the populations. Even though there have been many improvements due to passage and implementation of laws and innovations, the child welfare systems cannot and should not be responsible for the needs of all vulnerable children and families. Child welfare agencies must partner with other agencies in order to meet the needs of children and families.

Innovations in child protection, such as multiple tracks that offer flexibility in responses to maltreatment reports and early service interventions, have been effective. The use of multidisciplinary teams, implementation of family-centered approaches, better data systems, and other factors have also been helpful. However, many CPS systems continue to be problematic. Many families have been reported for maltreatment a number of times before they receive adequate services. These situations in which children are exposed to continued maltreatment of various types produce cumulative negative effects on children, who often experience developmental delays in many domains, including physical, intellectual, emotional, and social. Changes are therefore needed to better protect children.

Children have generally entered foster care placement because of parental maltreatment. Concern about long stays in foster care brought about passage of the Adoption and Safe Families Act (ASFA) that included adoption subsidies and streamlined the permanency planning process, and permanency for thousands of children has been assured through adoptive placements. Efforts on behalf of both public and private organizations have been very successful in the recruitment of adoptive homes for children with special needs. However, there are many more children for whom parental rights have been terminated than there are available adoptive homes.

On average, 60 percent of all substantiated maltreatment reports involve neglect; 40 percent involve physical, emotional, and sexual maltreatment. Even though the majority of children entering foster care are from impoverished families, data on all foster care children document that they have substantial developmental delays. Child welfare agencies are not able to attend to the myriad problems children have when they enter the foster care system. These problems are often compounded when children experience multiple changes in placements, often requiring changes in schools. Substantial numbers of children exit foster care without having achieved adequate educational levels, cannot find employment, and are often homeless. The overall outlook for their future is dim.

Even though there has been a reduction in the number of teenage pregnancies, the data suggest that many teens experience second and third unplanned pregnancies, do not finish high school, seek assistance from welfare, and face rather bleak futures. Unless widespread programs are developed to offer quality child care, parent education, educational and vocational training, family planning, and other needed medical or mental health resources, these intergenerational problems will continue.

Following are studies of home visitation and parent education programs that have proven to be effective and offer tremendous resources to child welfare agencies. These programs should be considered as some of the key ingredients to improving service delivery to teenage mothers, to caregivers involved in maltreatment situations, and to parents whose children are in danger of being removed and/or are preparing for reunification. These programs are effective prevention and early intervention programs; the outcome studies are compelling.

Home Visitation Programs

The numbers of participants in home visitation are increasing; in 1993 there were 200,000 and by 1997 the numbers had increased to 500,000. Home visitation programs generally conduct assessments of all participants, provide services, and evaluate the effectiveness of their programs. The assessments often include participant health and mental health status, knowledge of infant and child development, social support systems, educational backgrounds, environmental risks, safety of the participant's home, and propensity toward child maltreatment.

Home Visitation with Teen Parents   Home visitation programs usually begin offering services to teenage mothers prior to the birth of their children and continue for specified periods of time. In response to the high out-of-wedlock births to teenagers, South Carolina provided a low-intensity program (one visit) to all mothers and their infants who were Medicaid eligible. One portion of the study was to determine the cost effectiveness of the program.

The nurses who provided the visits participated in focus groups and reported that the programs had positive impacts on the parents and infants who were served (Wager, Lee, Bradford, Jones, & Kilpatrick, 2004). The study found that providing these services to teen mothers was important because teenagers often did not have prenatal care, did not complete high school, were more likely to have repeat pregnancies during their adolescence, and were recipients of welfare (Maynard & Rangarajan, 1994). In another study of first-time mothers, researchers found that participants in a home visitation program for Hispanic adolescents in Texas experienced better health results than a control group, as both mothers and babies in the treatment group had more positive birth outcomes (Nguyen, Carson, Parris, & Place, 2003).

In Oklahoma, a home-visitation educational program provided a high-intensity program to adolescents and nonadolescents. The educational materials included information about parenting skills and infant and child development; the sessions were presented by paraprofessionals who had been trained and closely supervised. These sessions began prior to and continued after the births. The program participants were tested prior to the program and six months after the home visitations had begun. The results indicated that both the adolescents and nonadolescents had improved their knowledge of infant development, empathic responsiveness to children, the roles of children and parents in families, and knowledge about safety in homes. At the end of the study, participants were more aware and participated in more community resources (Culp, Culp, Blankmeyer, & Passmark, 1998).

This study is relevant for a number of reasons. Mothers who have knowledge of infant development are more likely to have appropriate expectations of infant responses and therefore are less likely to be stressed about normal infant responses. Additionally, being able to show empathic responses to babies is a critical factor in the development of healthy parent–child attachments.

A qualitative study in Alaska examined participant responses to a public health–sponsored home-visitation program in which nurses visited first-time mothers. A content analysis was conducted of essays that participants wrote about involvement in the program. The participants regarded their experiences very highly and reported learning a great deal about their pregnancies, child care, infant development, and understanding infant needs. The information helped participants become more confident and allayed much of their fear about parenthood (DeMay, 2003).

Kitzman and colleagues (2000) conducted home visitations with primarily African American women in urban Tennessee. Participants were randomly as-signed to a home-visited treatment group or a control group. The intent of the study was to determine the results of home visiting on African American women in an urban area. Home visitations took place prior to the children's births and through their second birthday. The study examined the children three years after the final home visitations. The home-visited women had fewer subsequent pregnancies and lower rates of welfare, and they were more likely to be married and have employed partners.

Home Visitation and Child Maltreatment Home visitation programs have also been effective in the reduction of child abuse and neglect. David Olds has done extensive and rigorous research of home visitation programs. In a randomized study, 400 women participated in a nurse home visitation program. The nurses visited prior to birth and through the second birthday of the children. The objective of the study was to determine if rates of maltreatment continued to be reduced during the third and fourth years of the children's lives.

The study indicated that the rates of child abuse and neglect were reduced during the time of the home visitations, but there were no maltreatment differences in the third and fourth years of the children's lives. Other factors measured showed positive outcomes, including the safety in the households and reduced numbers of emergency room usage (Olds, Henderson, Kitzman, & Cole, 1995).

In a follow-up study of 400 pregnant women who had received home visitations before and two years after birth, researchers studied the results when the children had reached 15 years of age (Olds et al., 1997). Consistent with the previous study, the home visited groups were compared to the control group. The results indicated that after 15 years, home visited families had lower substantiated maltreatment rates, lower subsequent birth rates, lower rates of welfare usage, lower rates of alcohol and drug issues, and lower arrest rates. The conclusions of the researchers were that home visiting can reduce future pregnancies and reduce maltreatment. The authors did not provide information about the sustained positive outcomes in this study compared to the previous study in which positive outcomes were not sustained.

Parent Education Programs

Parent education programs have been effective for enhancing physical development, child health status, and the educational achievement of children. Using an experimental research design, the Abecedarian Project was a long-term program in the Research Triangle in North Carolina that offered educational and other services to a treatment group and other services to a control group (Ramey & Ramey, 2000). The program was designed for high-risk children and their mothers with the intent of providing broad education, health care, and support. In the treatment group, three randomized interventions were provided to the treatment group; for one group, preschool education for the first five years of life was provided along with kindergarten and educational support through the second grade; for the second group, only preschool was provided; and for the third group, only educational support was provided. The control group received family support, free health care, and nutritional supplements; no educational supports were provided to the control group.

The child participants in the program were mostly African American and lived with single parents. At the end of the first segment, the officials decided to provide educational supports for children as they entered school. The treatment group therefore received educational support in school and at home for three additional years; summer camp experiences were also provided. Professional educators visited the homes of the children and worked with the parents and with the teachers. Assessments were conducted at the end of the second three-year period, when the children were 12 years of age, and when they were 15.

Those children participating in the Abecedarian Project with preschool scored higher than the control group on all measures: IQ scores were higher; the number of repeated grades was lower; mathematics and reading scores were higher. The mothers of participating children also made significant progress in their own educational and employment goals due in part to having free, quality child care. While this program was costly and not likely to be replicated on a large scale, it serves to demonstrate that a comprehensive approach can have life-changing effects on high-risk parents and children.

Parent Education for Teen Parents   Parent education programs are also a crucial resource for teenage parents. In a parent education program established specifically for unmarried teen parents whose children were at risk of maltreatment, the evaluation showed positive results for the children as well as the parents (Clewell, Brooks-Gunn, & Benasich, 1989). The program, studied over a three-year period, offered 12 sessions in which topics included bonding, child development, discipline, communication, and other topics of the participants' choosing. The study showed that of over 300 teen mothers who had completed the training, only 7 percent had been reported for maltreatment of their children. There was also a trend toward delayed pregnancies and increased commitment to educational pursuits.

It is particularly important to provide services to low-income, high-risk parents. One year-long program targeted African American women who had little or no prenatal care (El-Mohandis, Katz, El-Khorazaty, McNeely-Johnson, & Shops, 2003). The behaviors that the parent education program wanted to influence were health care usage measured by routine and regular health care visits, and immunization schedules. Participants were randomly assigned to treatment and control groups. The intervention involved home visits with parents and infants assigned to developmental playgroups, hospital-based group sessions, and social services. The intervention results for mothers and infants were measured at the completion of the intervention and one year after. The outcomes indicated that treatment group had more well-child visits, and immunization schedules were timely and appropriate. This study therefore shows that parent education can influence health care behaviors.

Survival Training for Parents (STP) is a parent education program developed for parents of adolescents (Huhn & Zimpfer, 1989). This is a particularly meaningful program because so few programs target adolescent issues related to drug usage, sexual activity, and other developmental challenges faced by adolescents. This program offered parenting principles based on the Adlerian parenting model; there were six sessions, each of which lasted two-and-a-half hours. The participants included parents with their young adolescents. Three of the sessions focused on adolescent development, and three focused on the role of parents and parenting skills needed in adolescence. The intended outcomes were improved communication between parents and their children, increased self-esteem of the youths, and improved relationships through better communication. Parents became more confident in their parenting skills, and self-esteem of the adolescents increased.

Parent Education and Child Maltreatment   Since the 1960s, parent education has been a commonly used intervention for parents and caretakers in situations where maltreatment of children has been substantiated. Many of these programs were developed after states passed mandatory reporting laws. Parent education became a part of most case plans, many of which were court ordered. However, practitioners often did not connect the programs to the specific risks that needed to be addressed, such as disciplinary practices, budgeting, child development, and others. Unfortunately, parent education had been viewed as a generic approach to treatment of child abuse and neglect instead of a remedy for particular needs of parents. Specific parental issues or challenges must be identified and the selection of the parent education program based on that need. The rationale for using parent education must be clearly understood.

Some high-intensity parent education programs are expensive. One parent-education program developed as a brief and less-costly program was offered from health-based clinics to parents considered high risk who had children aged from birth to age three (Huebner, 2002). Three groups of parent education classes made up of weekly, two-hour classes were held over a total of eight weeks. The evaluation took place over a period of four years, where teaching groups were conducted in pediatric clinics. The curriculum was based on the Systematic Training for Effective Parenting (STEP) program and sought to provide parents skills in dealing with anger management, problem solving, and relationships; information about community resources was also provided.

The evaluation had a quasiexperimental design. Pre- and post-data were collected using a number of well-known scales, including the Parenting Stress Index, the Home Observation for Measurement of the Environment, and the Nursing Child Assessment Teaching Scale. Most parents had been maltreated as children, poorly educated, and in the lower socioeconomic level. The results of the measures used indicated significant improvement in all areas. The results were magnified for parents who attended more classes and therefore had a higher dosage of parent education.

Another program found effective in reducing child abuse and neglect was adapted for Asian and Pacific Islanders (Cheng, 2004). Approximately 300 participants were randomly assigned to treatment and control groups; the treatment groups were provided an adapted version of Dare to Be You (DTBY). The sessions were held during the evenings with dinner provided; children were also involved in the training in separate group sessions. There were pretests, posttests immediately after the training, and posttests one year after training. The measurements showed significant reductions in the use of corporal punishment and improvements in stress management and parental satisfaction. This study is particularly useful because it demonstrated the effectiveness of the program for an ethnically diverse population; it also demonstrated that children and parents can be trained at the same time in different groups and that the curriculum was appropriate for the age and developmental level of children.

Prevention Programs Identified by the Children's Bureau

In an effort to identify effective prevention programs, the Children's Bureau established the Emerging Practices in the Prevention of Child Abuse and Neglect. The following are summaries of the programs selected as exemplars. These programs are aimed at reducing child abuse and neglect, enhancing child development through parent education, and offering family support to build family resiliency.

The University of Maryland was home to Family Connections, a community-based program targeting families with a school-aged child at risk of neglect and/or abuse. The program identified needed services, then developed and implemented service plans. Collaborating with community agencies, Family Connections reduced caregivers' and children's physical and mental health problems; promoted positive relationships between the parents and children, thereby reducing maltreatment; and helped to reduce economic problems. Using an experimental, random, pre/posttest design with a control group, the evaluation used validated, well-known instruments to collect data at baseline, three months, and nine months after services were provided. Findings from the evaluation concluded that risk factors were reduced, protective factors increased, the maltreatment incidents decreased, and there was positive impact on the well-being of children.

The Circle of Security was a parent education and psychotherapeutic group process located in Spokane, Washington. The intent of the program was to deal with children with attachment issues, provide parent/caregivers with empathic skills and the capacity to develop positive attachments with children, and provide the community with information about high-risk families. The evaluation design was quasiexperimental with pre- and posttests. There was no randomization nor was there a control group. Data were collected at baseline and one year after the program's completion. The findings indicated that parental attachments with children were improved and caretakers provided more positive responses to children.

The Families and Centers Empowered Together (FACET) program was a family support and empowerment program in Delaware. Offering services and training opportunities, the program used parent councils as a major part of the operation. The parent councils selected the training materials. As a resource center, FACET sought to reduce family isolation, build family resiliency, and assist parents in advocating for the educational needs of improved family coping and communication. Initial data was positive, but more rigorous evaluations are needed to determine the true potential for replication.

EFFECTIVE INTERVENTION STRATEGIES

This country needs to provide more prevention and early intervention activities to deal with vulnerable children and families. At the same time, we need to expand those intervention services we know work and stop providing those with no evidence base.

Child welfare agencies have challenges in recruiting and retaining foster parents. It is common for 50 percent of the foster parents to stop providing care to children within one year for a number of reasons. In a recent Utah study (Harris & Middleton, 2002), a similar percentage of foster parents terminated care after one year because of dissatisfaction with the agency and caseworkers, because of the complex needs of the children, or for their own reasons.

Programs such as Family-to-Family, originally developed by the Annie Casey Foundation, have been scrutinized and found to work well in providing a comprehensive response to issues involved with foster care and adoption. Family-to-Family brings a neighborhood-based response that is also family centered in its response to the dilemmas in foster care. Operating under a set of principles, those involved in establishing Family-to-Family in communities bring all of the stakeholders and major players together in a team. This team is composed of biological parents, other relatives if appropriate, foster parents, children, and community agencies. Instead of caseworker/agency decision making, there is a switch to group decision making in which all team members participate. They participate in program orientation and training, in assessment of the situation, in group decision making, and in a continuous communication process.

According to Omang and Bonk (1999), the activities in Family-to-Family are sequenced, beginning with positive change in the placement system, developing and implementing the team for decision making, training all stakeholders in safety issues, and providing feedback regularly. Biological families have a significant role to play, which is a departure from routine foster care services.

The findings are that foster parent retention has greatly improved and placement disruption has decreased, thus providing much more stability for the children. Strong partnerships have been created throughout the neighborhoods, which can only lead to community ownership for the care and protection of foster children. Individualized plans are made for each child, and case plans are implemented accordingly. This program is one that could be adapted in all states to produce more stability for children in foster care by creating neighborhood-based support for families in need.

Shared Family Care

Shared family care is a program with application in a number of areas. Domestic violence shelters provide shared family care to mothers and children seeking safety. Some substance abuse programs provide residential care for children and mothers during the time mothers are in treatment. The program is also appropriate for parents who are leaving drug and alcohol treatment and need a transitional home for themselves and their children. There are also some residential treatment centers for children whose parents sleep over in the facilities. In addition to other advantages, these programs enhance parenting capacity and are therefore valuable resources to child welfare agencies.

Shared family care can also be a resource for families in times of crises and prevent out-of-home placements of children. The hosting foster family provides mentoring, support, and other services to families for whom their best interest is in leaving high-risk environments. Because the payment rate is comparable to treatment foster care, this kind of placement offers many advantages over out-of-home placements for children (Barth, 1994). It provides an opportunity for families to be kept intact and for parents to acquire new parenting skills.

Collaboration

Child welfare agencies have examined the vast numbers of families and children in the child welfare system who are also consumers of other programs, such as mental health, substance abuse, domestic violence, welfare, and others. Some child welfare agencies have found ways to coordinate and collaborate so that there is less duplication and all resources are maximized to the fullest extent. A number of collaborations can pave the way to more integration of services.

Collaboration with Schools   Certainly collaboration between school officials and child welfare staff could benefit foster children in schools. Focus groups were conducted with foster children, teachers, and child welfare workers to identify the perceptions that they all had about each other and how they felt about issues related to foster children in school systems (Altshuler, 2000). The perceptions provided information about what each group thought of the other and pointed to the need for changes.

Information from the focus groups indicated a high degree of distrust among the groups; neither teachers nor foster students felt child welfare staff really cared about the youths. School officials believed child welfare workers intentionally withheld information from them, but child welfare workers felt constrained by confidentiality rules not to release certain information. The information revealed definite challenges for foster children in school. Teachers and other school officials treat them differently because they are foster children, and deferential treatment usually causes more problems for the students.

The results of the focus groups provided an impetus for the child welfare agencies and schools to work together. Commitments were made to keep children in the same schools, even if alternative foster placements were necessary. Schools agreed to find mentor teachers for the students to provide extra assistance when needed. Agreement was reached about the delivery of cross-training so both child welfare staff and school officials were aware of the foster children's needs, school administration rules, and policies under which child welfare agencies operate. Some states have amended confidentiality laws to permit information-sharing with interdisciplinary teams. Other jurisdictions have specific protocols outlining what information can be shared and under what circumstances.

Multiple-Agency Collaboration   Luongo (2002) suggested that a critical need exists to develop collaborations among child welfare, juvenile justice, substance abuse, mental health agencies, and schools. The need for attending to these issues is supported by data indicating that children in foster care have emotional and physical problems; their parents often have alcohol, drug, and mental health issues. Many youths in the juvenile justice system have problems with drugs and alcohol and have been diagnosed with mental health illness.

There are currently three models for dealing with these co-occurring problems. The first model deals with each problem separately and sequentially; the second deals with the issues simultaneously or in a parallel model; the third model is the integrative model. The integrative model is when the issues are dealt with concurrently. This requires cross-training of all staff.

Currently, professionals in child welfare, juvenile probation, mental health, substance abuse treatment, and school programs have all been trained and educated with specific theoretical models unique to each discipline. When each professional intervenes with children and families, the interventions are based on his or her specific discipline; the professionals generally are unaware of other issues. Many child welfare workers, for example, are unfamiliar with addictions. The integrative model involves cross-training all staff so that they become familiar with all other treatment interventions. The professionals become a team and respond as a whole to the needs of the children and families. There is shared decision making, policies are updated, and outcome statements are expanded to accommodate the integration of services.

One collaborative program involved substance-addicted women with mental health issues and a background of trauma. A Massachusetts grant-funded program sought ways to coordinate services to women with these three issues. Initially, all agencies had separate funding streams, separate policies, and separate skill sets and knowledge and belief systems. Each agency conducted its own assessment and created its own service plan for each woman. This created duplication and fragmentation of services.

The grantees used a relational system change, which is a model based on relationships. Over a long period, state and local agency staff in mental health, addictions, and trauma were cross-trained so that participants could understand each other's policies, funding streams, theoretical bases for services, and other factors. The results of efforts to develop collaboration produced positive results for these women with co-occurring needs. Policies were changed to support collaboration and service integration; integrated supervision was established, and clients received all needed services (Markoff, Finkelstein, Kammerer, Kreiner, & Prost, 2005).

Neighborhood Approach to Child Welfare

The New York City Administration for Children's Services developed a neighborhood-based system of care model that can be replicated in many cities in the country (Chahine, Straaten, & Williams-Isom, 2005). The administration realigned the core services of foster care, preventive, and protective services so these services could be provided within the district geographic boundaries. The administration used the data from their child welfare information management system to develop neighborhood networks of services that could be responsive to the identified needs in each district. There are 59 districts in all five boroughs in the city. Of the 59 districts, the administration identified 18 in which most foster placements were made. These districts were identified as having the highest levels of substance abuse, health problems, lack of affordable housing, and other problems.

There were several objectives for the development of neighborhood-based programs. In those areas heavily impacted with environmental risks, services were available in the communities where the families lived; when out-of-home placements became necessary, children were placed in the same neighborhood, close to their families. Visitation with family members was managed more easily. All decisions about children and families were made by all those involved.

All of the neighborhood stakeholders participated in regularly scheduled meetings. Family needs, identified through assessments, were discussed at the meetings, and decisions were made about which agency resources were most appropriate. Originators of the neighborhood strategies identified the pieces necessary for the neighborhood networks to be successful. By building partnerships among public and private entities, churches, and other faith-based organizations, the communities have begun to view the challenges of vulnerable families as the communities' challenges.

Child Welfare and Welfare Agencies

When poverty is added to the challenges of vulnerable families, their capacity to function is greatly diminished. The effects of poverty have been documented in many studies. Children born into poverty are more likely to have significant health issues, including low birth weight, susceptibility to illnesses, poor cognitive functioning, and other factors that provide enormous challenges in surviving their childhood intact and becoming self-sufficient, well-functioning adults. A higher percentage of these children become teenage parents, do poorly in school, and become involved in the child welfare and juvenile justice systems.

Families in poverty generally have several environmental risks. For example, Taylor, Derr, and Abu-Bader (1998) found that 50 percent of child welfare families have domestic violence as a co-occurring risk factor. The Annie E. Casey Foundation established that four co-occurring issues are key factors that impede the ability of impoverished families to move out of poverty, secure, and retain employment: substance abuse, domestic violence, prior incarceration, and depression (Annie E. Casey Foundation, 2005). These factors create huge challenges for poor families in their efforts to become self-sufficient. There are other related issues. Maltreatment has been more evident in low-income families. In addition, adults who have been part of the justice system because of drugs or alcohol are often not offered employment in certain areas because they had been arrested and have criminal records. Behaviors of partners in domestic violence situations impact the employability of some women. Abusive male partners influence their women in the workplace because they do not want them working, often contacting them in their workplace and causing problems so the women are either fired or have to quit. For women receiving welfare, the rate of backgrounds with sexual abuse and other trauma is about 40 percent higher than the general population.

Depression has also been a problem for women who are in poverty; their rates of depression are much higher than in the general population. A number of states that have conducted research and evaluation of welfare programs found high depression rates among the recipients of cash assistance. The data revealed that about 20 percent fewer depressed women, compared to women who were not depressed, are likely to work more than 20 hours a week. Furthermore, incomes are lower for depressed women than women who are not depressed (Michalopoulos, Schwartz, & Adams-Cardullo, 2000). Even though depression is an illness easily treated by medication and psychotherapy, low-income individuals, particularly women, are less likely to seek out and benefit from these services. Their lack of familiarity and distrust of mental health agencies result in lack of treatment. One successful program used pediatricians to identify maternal depression when the mothers would bring their children in for medical treatment. The pediatricians, who had received training on diagnosing depression, were able to screen and refer mothers to appropriate treatment.

There is a natural collaboration between child welfare and welfare agencies. These agencies generally share the same populations. When child welfare staff locate relatives to find alternatives to stranger placements, TANF child-only payments are provided to relatives who cannot meet licensing requirements. Some TANF agencies provide supplemental payments and services to children in relative care. In Alabama, TANF agencies offer counseling, child care, food assistance, respite care, and emergency intervention services. Some states contract with community programs to offer services to families who are close to reaching time limits and leaving cash assistance (Andrews, Bess, Jantz, & Russell, 2002). The TANF legislation provides states with the option of modifying requirements for victims of domestic violence.

Alabama provides financial assistance and other services to domestic violence victims, and the assistance does not count against the total time an individual is able to receive benefits in the TANF programs. Some states allow participation in domestic violence programs to serve as the mandatory work activities. Other states have developed cross-training models so that welfare, domestic violence, and other agencies are aware of available services and how best to facilitate employment activities.

A work program in New Jersey was designed and implemented to deal with individuals seeking employment who had addiction problems. Case managers help to deal with the problems that have devastated employment opportunities by assisting the participants in locating child care, transportation, and housing. The case managers also access other resources as necessary to help participants maintain their sobriety (Dion, 1999). The program's evaluation showed positive results.

A jointly funded project operating in New York City and other cities provides families receiving cash assistance with other needed programs, such as drug treatment, parenting skills, literacy training, and health care (National Center on Addiction and Substance Abuse at Columbia University, 2001).

Evaluations showed increased rates of abstinence (60 percent) and decreased rates of marijuana and cocaine use.

Time Dollars

Time dollars is an alternative method of using currency to provide services. Created by Edgar Cahn (Cahn & Rowe, 1992), it can be described as a new enterprise that has been used in different ways in several jurisdictions throughout the country. Time is considered currency, and an individual can volunteer his or her time to provide a service and then be reimbursed in time dollars that can be exchanged for a needed service in return.

Time-dollar initiatives hold promise because it is highly unlikely that Congress and state legislatures will ever appropriate sufficient funds for vulnerable families, children, the elderly, and other oppressed populations. In previous years, laws have been passed and programs have been funded with promises for increased funding to keep pace with standard-of-living costs. Due to many factors, priorities have changed, budget crises have arisen, and funding for many programs has been reduced.

Boyle (2004) explains that time dollars is related to the principle of coproduction. Coproduction considers individuals being served or assisted as coworkers and coproducers. The term *client* is not used because the individuals are not passive recipients. The roles of professionals are also changed because they become more like team members than benefactors.

There are four basic values in time dollar initiatives: (1) People are considered assets, and every person can make a contribution; (2) work is redefined to include whatever is needed to build healthy neighborhoods, protect children, and keep families intact; (3) reciprocity is the idea of give and take and the connection to each other; and (4) social networks are the infrastructure within which the initiatives work, citizens interact, and individuals commit to provide services that generate capital and reciprocity (Boyle, 2004, p. 9).

The possibilities for implementing time dollars are endless. In one situation, impoverished pregnant mothers were provided with time dollars they used to reduce the costs of their medical care. The time dollars provided to them were raised when community people held baby showers and gave time dollars to them as gifts. In other situations, individuals with automobiles provided transportation to individuals to doctors, supermarkets, and other places and received time dollars for their efforts.

Time dollars can be used in crime prevention. Citizens can participate by serving on citizen patrols and alerting police to possible crimes and then be compensated by time dollars they can exchange for needed services. Homeless people can use time dollars, received for helping others in the community, for entry into shelters.

Creating time dollar initiatives requires adherence to the principles and resourcefulness, along with openness and flexibility. In some cases, legislative changes may be needed; legislation related to time dollars has been introduced and successfully passed in a few states.

PRIVATIZING CHILD WELFARE AS AN ALTERNATIVE

Many state legislatures and governors have overhauled their child welfare systems in response to specific high-profile cases involving children who were injured or killed. In some situations, the responses to individual cases have been "knee-jerk" reactions in which laws were passed mandating excessive monitoring that further burden child welfare staff. Because the responsibilities of child welfare agencies are so broad and encompassing, it is difficult to produce positive results for the children and families in the systems. Indeed, many legislators, advocates, and child welfare administrators have called for change; many of these changes have resulted in privatization of child welfare services.

In her report about child welfare reform through privatization, Snell (2001) made a number of allegations about the current child welfare systems. Some of her criticisms include the following:

- Child welfare advocates are focused on preserving the family and reunifying children with abusive families.
- Between 1989 and 1991, 39 percent of children who were killed as a result of neglect or abuse were children known to child welfare agencies.
- The best safety interests of the children through adoption were not met.
- The foster-care system provides financial incentives to keep children in foster care.
- There is no accountability for child welfare services to place children in adoptive homes.
- Children remain in foster care too long and are moved between multiple foster homes.
- Termination of parental rights has burdensome administrative costs due to the requirements of proof that the state made "reasonable efforts" to reunify the child with his/her biological family.

Through these statements, Snell indicted the current child welfare systems; in addition, her report provided accurate numbers reflecting the growth in maltreatment reports, foster care, and adoptive placements. Additionally, stories of individual children who had sustained life-threatening abuse and death during involvement with child welfare systems were presented to illustrate the need to privatize child welfare services. Snell promoted moving services from poorly run bureaucracies that represented government interference to privatization similar to efforts in Kansas and California. Several states have, in fact, begun to privatize their child welfare systems.

The Florida legislature decided to privatize foster care on a statewide basis in 1998 (American Federation of State County Municipal Employees [AFSCME], 2004). Prior to the legislation, Florida had piloted privatization in five areas. Four of the five pilots failed; the successful one was in Sarasota County. Sarasota, an affluent community, had spent more money than the Department of Child and Families (DCF) had on personnel in order to reduce caseloads. According to AFSCME, the governor mandated the privatization effort in spite of the failed pilots. The legislation mandated that the outcomes of privatization also be evaluated. In order to evaluate the efforts, it was necessary to have information from the automated information system. Funding for HomeSafenet, Florida's information system, began in 1993 but was not completely operational at the time of writing this text. It was therefore not possible to obtain baseline data with which to compare progress or lack thereof with the transitions to privatization. AFSCME maintained that "after eight years, millions of dollars and numerous studies, there was no evidence that privatized child welfare made life any better for Florida's most vulnerable citizens or for the taxpayers" (AFSCME, 2004, p. 14).

A crisis in Wisconsin prompted a study in Milwaukee, the most populated city in the state. The state was considering the transfer of all child welfare from a county-administered program to a centralized state-administered system. The Institute for Wisconsin's Future (Emspak, Zullo, & Rose, 1995) conducted a study of the child welfare program in Milwaukee. Similar to other jurisdictions in Wisconsin and across the country, Milwaukee had an increase in maltreatment reports and, as a consequence, a substantial increase in foster care placements from 1986 through 1993. The high caseloads created a high practitioner turnover rate. The researchers conducted the study for the legislature prior to decisions about privatization. They focused on the 10 percent of children who were in foster care under the auspices of private agencies; 90 percent of the children were the responsibility of the public agency. The costs of care and quality of all foster care services were evaluated. The results indicated that the private agencies had a higher cost in provision of foster care services. In addition, the public agency staff achieved permanency planning for the children at a faster rate than the private agencies. The study concluded that the crisis in Milwaukee was due to inadequate funding for the child welfare programs and that privatization would exacerbate the problems, not solve them.

Privatization of adoption in Michigan, however, produced favorable results for children. In 1987, the state agency began to rely on private agencies for adoptive placements and began offering incentives to the agencies. These private adoption agencies were successful because of four activities: having time limits to move children into adoption, narrowly defining *abandonment,* providing incentives to agencies, and having available information on children available for adoption (Craig, Kulik, James, Nielsen, & Orr, 1998).

In 1996, Michigan increased the percentage of adoptive placements by 19 percent. The population of children was considered to have special needs because many of them were older and had behavioral, emotional, and physical problems. Even before ASFA was passed, Michigan had timelines in which permanency decisions had to be made about children in foster care. Michigan also had an adoption exchange where information about available children is shared on a broad basis.

One of the most innovative steps that Michigan took was to provide financial incentives to the adoption agencies. The highest rate was paid when children were placed within five months of the termination date; the next highest was for children placed within seven months. Enhanced preplacement rates were also available. The outcomes studies on this privatization effort were positive: children were placed on a timely basis, agencies received incentives, and the state child welfare staff attended to other responsibilities.

Texas also had a positive experience in privatizing the development and implementation of the child welfare management information system (MIS). The need for a management information system was evidenced in 1989 when almost 8,000 children were in foster care. At that time, the state had nine computer systems and file cards that only managed the foster care data. There was no capacity to share information with other counties and the data for CPS and other services were maintained in different ways. The department struggled with the development of an MIS for several years until the department was reorganized and all child welfare programs and adult protective services were moved into one department. The changes brought about by the automated system obviously have benefited the staff, who are now able to offer better services.

State child welfare agencies that have privatized services have generally retained CPS under their purview. Even though Arkansas did not privatize services, the state moved a portion of child protection out of CPS in an attempt to improve services. Arkansas was the first state to transfer child protection activities to law enforcement (Snell, 2000). In 1997, Arkansas law enforcement became responsible for child abuse reports, and the CPS agency retained responsibility for neglect cases. The legislature appropriated $8 million for start-up costs, and funds were transferred from the CPS agency to law enforcement. Even though the data indicates the investigations were initiated within 24 hours in over three-fourths of the cases, the Center for the Study of Social Policy (CSSP) evaluated the effort and reported concerns. The transfer has not resulted in close working relationships between all law enforcement personnel and the CPS staff. As would be expected, the focus of law enforcement officials was on collecting evidence and not on assisting families, one of the core goals of CPS agencies. Many law enforcement officers accustomed to dealing with what they consider more serious criminal issues were not pleased to have the responsibility of investigating child maltreatment. Law enforcement officers were also reported as screening out calls that should have been investigated.

Arizona had a partnership with Family Builders, which essentially provided flexibility in response to maltreatment reports. This activity was consistent with national CPS guidelines supporting flexibility in response to child abuse and neglect calls. In Arizona, situations initially assessed as being low risk but where families needed services were referred to Family Builders. The results of the pilot in two counties were positive. Because the service was voluntary, families had a choice about whether to accept services or not. For those families who became involved with the program, the recidivism rates were much lower than for families who did not take part in the program.

Kansas privatized all child welfare services, with the exception of child protective services. At the time the decision was made to privatize, Kansas had been part of a class-action lawsuit brought by the American Civil Liberties Union for a number of years. This fact alone was not unusual, as other states have been part of a class-action lawsuit or a settlement agreement. However, in response to class-action lawsuits, many state child welfare agencies have pursued the specific issue of the lawsuit, whether it involves foster care or another program. Kansas decided to overhaul their system instead of tinkering with one or two programs. In 1995, the Kansas legislature directed the department to privatize child welfare.

With thoughtful consideration, Kansas established four basic principles under which they began the process. Kansas Social and Rehabilitation Services (SRS) established accountability statements in their goal statements. SRS also decided that effectiveness and quality could be achieved through competition among private vendors. Of particular importance was the decision that one case manager, not several staff, would deal with the families and their children. SRS also decided that services would be available on a statewide basis (Craig et al., 1998, p. 11).

There were a number of obstacles to overcome before making the transition a success. Kansas did not have a management information system at the time, and there were potential problems with maintaining eligibility for several federal funding sources. In addition, privatization has sometimes jeopardized job retention, and there is usually staff resistance to privatization.

Resembling a managed care initiative, Kansas designed the privatization system to be outcome based, to combine funding sources promoting a seamless delivery approach and capitation or set rates per child and family. Through an open competition, SRS selected nonprofit agencies with which they had relationships. A single agency was awarded the contract for all adoptions; foster care and group care were awarded to three agencies; and family preservation was awarded to five private agencies. Even though oversight of several agencies may have required awesome oversight, the private agencies each had expertise and experience with the programs they were awarded.

The foster care providers were provided a flat rate per child over a year, different from previous practice when providers were paid a daily rate for every day the child was in care. This provided the agency with flexibility, and agencies could work toward permanency for the child without fear of losing revenues. Family preservation contracts and adoptive placements were based on an average cost per family.

The Kansas privatization initiative has been considered a success. The foster care outcomes were reached during the first six months, and data showed the children were kept safe, placement disruptions were minimized, and the children were generally placed in close proximity to their biological parents. Lutheran Social Services, the adoption agency, increased adoptive placements by 44 percent with low numbers of disruptions. Likewise, the data on family preservation services were also positive as agencies averted the expected number of placements.

Even though the data has generally shown success, the initiative has not always been popular. AFSCME suggested that some private providers had terminated relationships with SRS because of poor reimbursement rates and poor treatment by privatization agencies. They also suggested that the amount available for mental health was inadequate; CPS workers had confusion about what their roles were; multiple placements of children were occurring; and staffing the private agencies was problematic.

SRS did concede that the transfer of large numbers of foster children to private agencies did not provide sufficient time for adequate planning. Foster parents were confused, as were judges. In hindsight, SRS suggested to other states that more time be allocated for the transfer of foster children in privatization plans. After SRS privatized, more comprehensive maltreatment assessments led to higher placement rates, and this produced a financial hardship on the agencies that had a fixed contract amount.

Because the thorough evaluations of privatization in Kansas are generally positive, many states are debating the issue. Undoubtedly, many child welfare agencies will privatize at least one or two services.

THE PRIVATIZATION DEBATE

Child welfare agencies have been struggling to produce positive outcomes mandated by the passage of ASFA. Even though the law intended to reduce the numbers of children in out-of-home placement, the 1999 numbers indicate a substantial increase. Additionally, the law intended to reduce the time that children spent in foster care, but in 1999, 4 percent more children had been in foster care for three years and an additional 5 percent had been in foster care at least or more than 5 years. The number of children available for adoption has substantially increased with a corresponding challenge to locate adoptive placements for them.

These data are disturbing because entry into foster care is generally through CPS. However, the numbers of maltreatment reports that are founded or substantiated have been decreasing for several years. Therefore, foster care placement rates do not appear to be strongly connected to maltreatment rates. There may be a number of reasons for this phenomenon, including families encountering more environmental risks that seriously threaten the safety of children, the inclination to place children to assure their safety, and others. There are no studies that account for the differences.

The controversy about how well child welfare agencies achieve outcomes continues. In many states, legislatures and policy makers have not considered that the solutions to the problems may be outside the realm of child welfare agencies. The span of responsibility for child welfare agencies is broad. It includes child protection, in-home services, foster care, group care, residential care, services to unmarried parents, adoption, and others. Conducting comprehensive and accurate assessments of the children and families and then providing effective intervention strategies are awesome and challenging tasks. The responsibilities must be shared with other stakeholders. Privatization should be considered. Decisions and activities must be thoughtful and involve all of the stakeholders, including the families. Not finding alternatives to the present conditions is unacceptable.

SUMMARY

This chapter presented alternatives to the current way of doing business. Prevention and early intervention activities were discussed as alternatives. Moving to prevention is critical because the dilemmas that vulnerable families and children face cannot be overcome if we continue to focus on the intervention strategies.

The chapter provided a number of programs that studies show are effective. These programs, while found to be quite effective with outcomes sustained over time, are not used by all child welfare agencies. Home visiting has been studied over long periods and found to be quite effective in a number of situations. Parent education has also been found to be effective for different populations; different education programs are needed depending upon the populations and the issues involved. Even though child welfare agencies frequently refer parents and caregivers to parent education classes, perhaps appropriate matches between needs and programs are not being made and outcomes may be questionable.

The Department of Health and Human Services and other federal agencies have been moving toward prevention in funding and in spreading the word through their resource centers. The Children's Bureau has sought out exemplars, and some are presented in the chapter. A meta-analysis indicated that gains from family

support are relatively small. States and localities need to be cognizant of the research and make more appropriate decisions about funding programs, given the resource base.

The chapter continued with information about coordination, collaboration, and services integration. Child welfare agencies cannot and should not be expected to achieve outcomes single-handedly. They need to partner with public and private agencies in order to achieve positive outcomes for families and children. Examples of successful collaborations are presented. Because poverty is such a powerful negative force to be reckoned with, programs that deal with poverty and other issues are presented.

Finally, the chapter discussed alternatives to the present structures. There have been efforts to privatize certain aspects of child welfare services in a number of jurisdictions and states. Some privatization efforts have been well-planned and implemented; positive outcomes have been achieved. Michigan in particular has done well with privatization of adoption. Kansas implemented a much bigger effort by privatizing all but child protective services, and the outcomes have also been positive. Undoubtedly, many other states and local jurisdictions will privatize most or some of their child welfare responsibilities.

Questions for Discussion

1. Why should this country invest in prevention and early intervention?
2. Given the current level of spending, how can we shift to prevention when there are so many families in crisis?
3. Discuss collaboration and service integration. Why are they important?

4. Should all child welfare services be privatized? What agencies should be involved in the effort?
5. Discuss the role of families in developing collaboratives and in privatizing services.

Leadership and Change

CHAPTER **13**

Adrian B. Popa

INTRODUCTION

The focus of this book has been to expose you to a child welfare practice and to empower you as a social work professional to lend the leadership needed in the child welfare practice arena and to implement different models. Your role in thinking about alternative strategies and taking steps toward a more macro focus of equality for children and families will lead to better prevention as well as intervention. The practice and outcomes from different unifying models will in many ways depend upon the leadership available in the field of child welfare, as well as in society. As a professionally trained social worker, you will have the opportunity and responsibility not only to participate in advocating for the field and the values it represents but also to seek leadership roles that allow you to impact social and civic change through professional core values of service, social justice, dignity, human relationships, integrity, and competence. This chapter will introduce you to leadership theory from a structural functionalist perspective and deconstruct leadership as it applies to social work. The chapter will also describe the field of child welfare in the larger context of a political system. Leadership in the field of child welfare will also be described on the organizational level, as well as the role of leadership in developing and influencing organizational culture. The chapter will conclude with the role of child welfare leadership in impacting and mediating change.

LEADERSHIP

Distinctive leaders such as Jane Adams, Florence Kelley, Mary Ellen Richmond, Mary Parker Follett, and many others contributed to the development and distinction of the social work profession. Their role of providing leadership, aid, advocacy, activism, community, and social program development to the malnourished, homeless, disenfranchised, and neglected citizens of our society mobilized a volunteer-driven practice into becoming a well-recognized profession.

Conceptualizing and understanding the role of leadership in the social work profession is increasingly important to a changing profession influenced by social, cultural, economic, political, and demographic factors that impact human service delivery systems (Rank & Hutchison, 2000). Societal changes and conditions of ambiguity introduce a paradox with evolving definitions of effectiveness that place a strain on the profession to evolve while maintaining its original leadership role and professional identification. Social work authors, researchers, and educators (Brillian, 1986; Glisson, 1989; Austin, 1988; Rank & Hutchison, 2000) have witnessed an ongoing cycle in the focus placed on leadership in the field of social work. Social workers were visible community activists in the pre-industrial and industrial eras and introduced human relationships and participative leadership in organizations during a time of mechanization, assembly lines, and male-dominated workforce (Follet, 1926). The visibility and emphasis of social work leadership has also been dormant as the construct receives limited emphasis in social work education and training.

Trends in Leadership Theories

The history of leadership has been studied and interpreted by varying disciplines, each utilizing theoretical frameworks representative of their professional foundation. Many books have implemented a structural functionalist framework rooted in industrial psychology and management sciences to describe leadership theories and their historical development (Crow & Grogan, 2005). Although a functionalist approach is limited in its utility, it offers a relatively clear description of evolving leadership theories. In their reviews of leadership theory, Stogdill (1948, 1974) and Ghiselli (1959) described distinct periods of leadership study and exploration. Each theory introduced a unique way to examine and interpret leadership, complementing and expanding the knowledge base gained from earlier approaches. Early leadership thought is embedded within trait approaches, followed by behavioral approaches explored throughout the industrial era. Situational approaches to leadership developed thereafter to address gaps in behavioral theory and application across varying settings and situations. Transactional and transformational approaches were most recently developed to expand situational approaches and address current complexities of external and internal organizational climates.

Trait Theory   Trait theory was one of the earliest lenses to emerge in exploring, debating, and understanding leadership. The assertion of this early thought is simply that certain individuals may have a genetic predisposition and possess qualities distinct from individuals who do not emerge as leaders. Early theories attribute leadership success to extraordinary abilities, such as high energy, uncanny intuition and foresight, and persuasive powers, and additional hereditary features of height, weight, and physique. These studies explored and identified physical characteristics (e.g., height, appearance), personality (e.g., self-esteem, dominance, emotional stability), and aptitude (e.g., general intelligence, verbal fluency, creativity) (Yukl, 2002). A review several decades later between 1949 and 1979 of 163 trait studies included managerial studies that explored a wider selection of traits and skills with an increased variety of measurement techniques (Stogdill, 1974). Similar traits were found related to leadership effectiveness, with some additional emerging relevant traits and skills (Yukl, 2002) (see Highlight 13.1).

Yukl (1989) categorizes trait theory and research contributions into three stages. The initial stage of trait exploration was strongly influenced by "great man" theories, philosophical and religious writings. Studies used observations and interviews that led to rudimentary descriptions of leaders, conceptualization, and construction of inventories. Traits related most consistently to managerial effectiveness were those of high self-confidence, energy, initiative, emotional maturity, stress tolerance, and belief in internal locus of control.

Highlight 13.1	Traits and Skills Differentiating Leaders from Nonleaders

Traits	Skills
Adaptable to situations	Clever (intelligence)
Alert to social environment	Conceptually skilled
Ambitious, achievement-oriented	Creative
Assertive	Diplomatic, tactful
Cooperative	Fluent in speaking
Decisive	Knowledgeable about the work
Dependable	Organized (administrative ability)
Dominant (power motivation)	Persuasive
Energetic (high activity level)	Socially skilled
Persistent	
Self-confident	
Tolerant of stress	
Willing to assume responsibility	

Motivational traits (McClelland & Boyatzis, 1982) of successful leaders reflect a self-actualizing interest in building up organizations and empowering others rather than in self-aggrandizement or domination of others (Yukl, 1989).

The second stage of trait theory represents an exploration of skills related to leader effectiveness (Yukl, 1989). Technical, conceptual, and interpersonal skills vary greatly from situation to situation and from one organization to another. The third stage of trait theory exploration continues to the present in studying trait interaction with leader effectiveness. It is within this development that the trait approach has introduced an idea of balance, in tempering one trait with another. Balance is achieved not only between or within traits but also between competing values (Quinn & Rohrbaugh, 1983), the task and concern for people (Blake & Mouton, 1982), and the concern for a leader's needs balanced against the concern of peers, superiors, and clients (cited in Yukl, 1989).

Behavioral Theory   Scrutiny of trait approaches led to expansion of approaches that measured the complexity of leadership. The process of addressing trait theory limitations and attempts to identify and predict leadership potential gave birth to emerging behavioral research. Prior to the 1950s, leadership was conceptualized as a construct encompassing a set of personality traits or typology that provided a map for interpreting leadership. Leadership research slowly progressed from observation, identification, and description of skills, personality, and features to a methodology that explored the activity and behavior of leaders. The strong emergence of behavioral studies began before World War II and continued to develop pre- and postwar resolution. Two of the most influential research programs that contributed to establishment of behavioral leadership research in the late 1940s were the beginning of behavioral investigation by Rensis Likert (1967) at the University of Michigan and the series of studies at Ohio State University (Fleishman, 1953; Fleishman, Harris, & Burtt, 1955; Shartle, 1956; Stogdill & Shartle, 1948).

Behavioral leadership studies shifted research inquiry from a single dimension to a multidimensional behavioral approach. Schriesheim and Bird (1979) recognized the contributions of the Ohio State studies on conceptual, methodological, and organizational levels. Early behavioral research played an important role in reconceptualizing leadership research from a trait to behavioral approach. This multidimensional perspective led to situational theories. This multidimensional perspective also served as a methodological model for situational approaches explored with individuals, groups, and organizations (Stogdill, 1959, 1967), in addition to informing instrument development and measurement strategies.

Situational Theory   Situational leadership approaches began where trait and behavioral approaches concluded and addressed ongoing gaps in leadership theory. Situational approaches investigated situational variables representing follower characteristics, leadership behavior, and internal and external elements within the organizational environment. A primary theme of contingency and situational leadership theory is that the relationship between leadership style and performance is unpredictable, inconsistent, and highly variable (Kanji & Moura E Sa, 2001). Mello (2003) described situational or contingency approaches as focused on the moderating effect that certain situational variables have on the relationship between leader traits and behaviors and outcomes (cited in Kanji & Moura E Sa, 2001, p. 702). Situational theory proposes that leadership effectiveness is a function or outcome of multiple facets of a leadership situation.

A leadership situation includes the ability and competency to diagnose, adapt, and communicate in the organizational setting (Hersey, Blanchard, & Johnson, 2001). The approach suggests that a successful leader has the ability to diagnose and understand the situation, alter behavior and resources to meet contingencies of the situation, and communicate effectively with others. Hersey and colleagues based their theory on early work by Schein (1965), who explored organizational culture and leadership.

A successful manager must be a good diagnostician and must value a spirit of inquiry. The abilities and motives of the people under the manager vary; therefore, managers must have the sensitivity and diagnostic ability to be able to sense and appreciate the differences (cited in Hersey et al., 2001, p. 171).

Situational theory contributed to deconstructing an abstract view of leadership to a tangible and applicable diagnostic tool widely implemented by practitioners in training and development that continues to receive notoriety across varying disciplines. Foremost, situational leadership practice is based on a leader's diagnoses of employees' ability and willingness to adapt leadership behavior that best influence specific employee tasks throughout varying situations.

Transactional and Transformational Leadership Theory

In his review and analysis of leadership theory, James McCregor Burns (1978) integrated multiple leadership perspectives to develop a theoretical approach that would address increasing complexities and diversification of organizational cultures. In addition, Burns expanded upon the transactional framework developed within sociological leadership research explored by Max Weber (1947) and described the development of transactional leadership as the outcome from the exchange relationship between leader and follower. The transaction between leader and follower involves an exchange of costs and benefits. Transactional approaches rooted in Weber's description of bureaucracy are based on the premise that relationships between leader and follower are based on an exchange or bargaining process where leader and follower can address mutual needs and deficiencies of the other through an exchange of services or behaviors.

Burns (1978) explored the transactional exchange process to emphasize the relationship that is initiated in the transactional process. This relationship leads to a transformational leadership approach that is no longer strictly independent but united to develop mutual support for a common purpose. Burns borrowed and elevated transforming leadership principles from theoretical constructs found in humanistic psychology and the work of Carl Rogers (1942) and Abraham Maslow (1954). The unique power of transforming leadership is manifested through the ability to mobilize others to achieve higher-order needs through movement from one stage of development to a higher level of functioning. The overall outcome and transformation experienced in elevating the level of human conduct and ethical aspiration in both leader and follower are distinct elements that distinguish transforming leadership from other closely related approaches.

Bernard Bass (1985) expanded transforming leadership into what is now referred to as transformational leadership. A central premise of transformational leadership is developing, intellectually stimulating, and inspiring followers who are eager to collectively participate within a unit or team structure toward a cooperative purpose. Rather than using *transforming leadership* as an adjective form of a verb suggesting leadership as a process, Bass modifies *leadership* to suggest a condition or a state as an adjective form of a noun (Wren, 1995). An additional distinction is that the direction of influence within transformational leadership is unidirectional and not a mutually interactive growth process.

Bass (1985) describes the transformational leadership process as encompassing factors of (1) charisma, (2) intellectual stimulation, (3) individual consideration, and (4) inspirational motivation. These leadership behaviors have been associated with influencing intrinsic motivators that heighten follower performance beyond expected and routine levels. Although Bass (1996, 1999) considers transformational leadership to be influential across any situation or culture, the theory is limited in identifying conditions or situations under which this leadership style is inappropriate or possibly lacks effectiveness or fit within the environment (Yukl, 2002).

Highlight 13.2 summarizes these leadership theories.

Highlight 13.2 | Summary of Leadership Theories

Theory	Trait	Behavioral	Situational/ Contingency	Transactional/ Transformational
Theoretical Framework	Traits are inherited	Effective leadership is found in behavior	Influences of situation on leadership	Exchange process based on contingent rewards
Focus	Physical characteristics, personality, aptitude, motives, skills, energy, temperament	Group production and production, morale, turnover, absenteeism, grievance, costs, motivation, decentralization	Situational variables, adaptation of leadership to subordinates and situation, relations, structure, power	Transactions, interactive growth process, individual consideration, inspirational motivation, collective participation

Leadership in Social Work

The distinction and complexity of leadership in nonprofit and governmental human service organizations has been consistently reviewed, described, and analyzed by Austin (1983, 1988). The emerging characteristics of the nonprofit leader are shaped and reflective of not only the organizational characteristics shared among multiple types of formal organizations but also by the distinct elements that compose the attributes of human service organizations. The parallel resemblance between the human service executive and the public administrator is found in the implementation of policy, organizational continuity, and a bottom-line performance of "breaking even." The public administrator or the human service leader does not have a personal monetary investment in the financial performance of the organization. The key element Austin found that distinguishes the human service executive from the corporate executive or the public administrator is "that the most important yardstick for judging executive performance in a human service organization is the quality of the services actually produced by the organization" (Patti, 1987, p. 23). The distinction is further expanded by the human service executive duties of balancing two widely diverse social structures that provide service and the overall organization of human service production.

Throughout his search and analysis of the human service executive, Austin (1989) found leadership to be influenced by the interactive and adaptive process between the individual and structural context. Different environments within similar organizations also impacted and shaped the executive position, requiring a strategic blend of approaches that would fit the organization, situation, and circumstance. His findings led him to believe that the executive role or definition is not universal and that one executive style does not produce similar performance across multiple settings and situations.

The human service executive position involves an inclusive but wide-ranging responsibility for leading multiple systems involving management as it relates to personnel motivation, production and productivity, resource mobilization, planning and organizational development, and multiple facets that are led and influenced by the human service organizational culture. In an attempt to explore leadership influence on the creation of organizational culture and performance, Glisson (1989) examined leadership among 47 workgroups of 319 individuals in 22 different human service organizations. The intent of the study was to identify leadership dimensions that affect worker attitudes linked to promoting successful human service organizational efforts. The relationship of three leadership dimensions with job satisfaction and organizational commitment of workers in human service organizations was investigated through varying questionnaires measuring leadership and worker attitudes of organizational commitment, job satisfaction, role conflict, and ambiguity, and additional scales to measure skill variety, task significance, and task identity. A strong relationship was discovered between commitment and leader power and maturity. Significant relationships were also found between each of the three leadership dimensions and job satisfaction. After controlling for organization and job and worker characteristics, only the relationship with leader maturity remained significant. A major conclusion from this study in conceptualizing leadership ability as linked to a collection of traits is that a leader is able to impact follower belief and identification with organizational goals and values, influence followers to implement extensive effort for the organization, and engage followers with methods that enhance commitment to the organization.

Several authors (Austin, 1989; Cooke, Reid, & Edwards, 1997; Ginsberg, 1995; Stoesz, 1997) have increased interest in leadership roles in human service organizations. In a further attempt to explore social, cultural, economic, political, and demographic transformations occurring on both state and national levels, researchers and direct practitioners have begun to investigate how these factors are changing the complexity of human service delivery systems and organizations. Cooke, Reid, and Edwards (1997) describe several key leadership skills expected of social work managers as they lead agencies into the complexities of the near future. Although Cooke and colleagues primarily explored early leadership indicators of traits, skills, and abilities, future developments and direction within the field of social work will require leadership with the ability to effectively manage and maintain the image and direction of agencies and the skills to network and collaborate, build coalitions, and work with multiple stakeholders while balancing hostile and unpredictable environments (cited in Rank & Hutchison, 2000).

To better understand the development of leadership expectations within the field of social work, Rank and Hutchison (2000) examined perceived leadership behavior and philosophy of social workers through the lenses of those who lead the profession. The main intent of their exploratory study was to investigate how social work leaders within the Council on Social Work Education and the National Association of Social Workers perceived social work leadership. A random sample of 75 deans from several hundred social work programs and 75 executive directors and presidents was selected to participate in an open-ended questionnaire.

Qualitative findings from interview responses direct attention to five emerging common elements that define the concept of leadership within the profession of social work. The five elements of social work leadership encompass (1) proaction, (2) values and ethics, (3) empowerment, (4) vision, and (5) communication. The second question probing the perceived leadership differences across disciplines revealed that 77 percent of the respondents perceived social work leadership as distinct and specific to the profession. Rank and Hutchison (2000) found that emerging themes of (1) commitment to the NASW Code of Ethics, (2) a systemic perspective, (3) a participatory leadership style, (4) altruism, and (5) concern about the public image of the profession distinguished the social work profession from other disciplines.

Rank and Hutchison (2000) concluded their findings by clearly indicating that leadership development is a key component to the growth of the profession. Respondents expressed the importance of infusing leadership development content within social work curriculum and the responsibilities of the

| Highlight 13.3 | **Personal Reflection: Your 15 Minutes of Leadership** |

A critical leadership lesson is that everyone learns about leadership from past experiences. With reflection and ongoing refinement, we can all improve our leadership practices. Everyone has enjoyed a moment of leadership excellence at some point in life; whether in high school or college, on the athletic field, in the family setting, in a community or church group, or at work, we have all made things happen through other people that otherwise would not have occurred. We all have led and impacted the course of a certain outcome. Reflect back on a moment in your life when you were most proud of your leadership practice and the outcome. Write down the information related to the incident to capture the details of that moment.

1. What leadership approach(es) would best explain your leadership practice?
2. Did any of your leadership practices reflect your personal moral standards and/or social work values/ethics? How? Why?
3. What did your leadership practice(s) impact and/or influence?
4. Can you duplicate the practice(s) in other settings and situations?

Source: Adapted from N. M. Tichy & E. Cohen. (1995). *The leader's companion.* New York: Free Press.

professional representing bodies of CSWE and NASW to pursue leadership development initiatives. A general recurring and concluding theme was that leadership is a neglected area of emphasis within the profession and that further investigation is needed to explore outcomes of social work leaders and how leadership styles relate to developing positive organizational cultures and positive organizational performance. Highlight 13.3 provides a personal reflection exercise to help you refine your leadership practices.

Leadership Challenge in the Child Welfare System

Child welfare organizations are complex bureaucratic entities that encounter accumulating challenges as a result of competing and overlapping systems. Organizational output is reflected through outcomes from direct services that are mediated by administrative regulations, legislative representation, varying partnerships with private and not-for-profit community organizations, and class-action lawsuits. Child welfare organizations compete with other divisions within the Department for Health and Human Services and state agencies for diminishing resources with increasing expectations prompted by federal regulations (Adoption and Safe Families Act, 1997) and current class-action lawsuits (*Angela v. Clinton*; *David C. v. Leavitt*) that inform and drive concurring expectations to refine and improve performance, outcomes, and efficiency of service delivery.

Direction in the field of child welfare is mediated by policy, regulations, and administrative goals that develop through formal practices of lobbying, testifying, and researching and informal practices of bargaining and negotiating. Conflict within the child welfare system is often unavoidable as divergent interests compete for few resources within a large political arena. This bureaucratic ecosystem is rooted and functions primarily within a political framework (see Highlight 13.4) (Bolman & Deal, 1997).

Highlight 13.4 | **Overview of the Four-Frame Model**

	Frame			
	Structural	**Human Resource**	**Political**	**Symbolic**
Metaphor for organization	Factory or machine	Family	Jungle	Carnival, temple, theater
Central concepts	Rules, roles, goals, policies, technology, environment	Needs, skills, relationships	Power, conflict, competition, organizational politics	Culture, meaning, metaphor, ritual, ceremony, stories, heroes
Image of leadership	Social architecture	Empowerment	Advocacy	Inspiration
Basic leadership challenge	Attune structure to task, technology, environment	Align organizational and human needs	Develop agenda and power base	Create faith, beauty, meaning

Source: Adapted from L. G. Bolman & T. E. Deal. (1997). *Reframing organizations.* San Francisco: Jossey-Bass.

Bolman and Deal (1997) developed four frames to bring the organizational world into focus. The frames were developed as tools to allow order and create an image to gather information, analyze, and decide how to best approach situations. The frames initiate a mental model in order to organize facts and emerging information. Bolman and Deal relate the story of how a critic once noted to Cezanne that one of his paintings looked nothing like a sunset. Cezanne responded, "Then you don't see sunsets the way I do." Like artists, social work leaders need to find varying lenses to interpret and articulate meaning. They must be able to clarify and express their vision in order to empower others to also consider varying perspectives.

Although the field of child welfare may resemble varying features across all frames, the political frame most closely resembles the systemic and organizational culture of child welfare organizations. The political frame portrays organizations as lively "political arenas that host a complex web of individual and group interests" (Bolman & Deal, 1997, p. 163). The field of child welfare is represented by coalitions of various individuals and interest groups. Coalitions include children, families, and the general public; political interest groups; foundations and associations; federal, state, and local agencies; and other sources that represent the legislative, judicial, and executive branches of government. Goals in child welfare agencies are typically developed by the legislative and executive bodies to whom the agency is accountable. This development process is complex, as individual and group objectives and available resources interplay within a political bargaining arena to influence objectives and decisions. Because members of coalitions naturally encounter differences

| **Example of the Four-Frame Model**

In the field of child welfare, Congress and the federal Department of Health and Human Services (DHHS) function as authorities, and child welfare social workers function as partisans. Congress and DHHS make binding decisions about policies, regulations, reviews, audits, and fiscal allocation. The federal agency initiates political control, and state agencies are the recipients of federal decisions. State agencies, foundations that study child welfare issues, academic institutions, and special interest groups in turn try to influence decision makers. The leadership challenge on a systemic level is in presenting rigorous and applicable research findings, best-practice models, testi-monies, and benchmarks in order to influence and inform current policy direction or to point out negative social, economic, and political outcomes of current policies. Partisans may use varying tactics of splitting authorities by lobbying to Congress and proposing strategic bills and reputable testimonies reflective of current child welfare practices. Partisans may also form coalitions and partner with specialists in the field (American Public Human Service Association, National Child Welfare League of America, National Association of Public Child Welfare Administrators, National Clearinghouse on Child Abuse, etc.) in attempts to strengthen their bargaining position.

in values, ideology, information, interests, power, and scarce resources, conflict is typically inevitable.

Scarce resources or limited power often force trade-offs for parties lacking influence. The political frame describes authority as one of many forms of power. Although the political frame recognizes the importance of individual and group needs, it emphasizes that conflict develops as a result of scarce resources and incompatible preferences. Bolman and Deal (1997) refer to Gamson's (1968) description of two major players within a political system: authorities and partisans. Authorities have the power to make decisions binding on partisans. The relationships between these two players are described in the following way: "[A]uthorities are the recipients or targets of influence, and the agents or initiators of social control. Potential partisans have the opposite roles, as the agent or initiator of influence, and targets or recipients of social control" (cited in Bolman & Deal, 1997, p. 168) (see Highlight 13.5).

Leadership Challenge in Child Welfare Organizations

On an organizational scale, the field of child welfare is represented in varying organizational settings typically constructed within DHHS state-level divisions, not-for-profit organizations, and community partners. DHHS state agencies are divided by services, and divisions are bound and held accountable to federal mandates and regulations. Despite federal regulations governing a wide spectrum of health and human services, individual states have sovereignty to develop programs and allocate funds and services to specific needs of the state. State legislatures and DHHS govern child welfare services administered by the Division of Child and Family Services (DCFS).

Child welfare programs encounter organizational dynamics fraught with a multitude of challenges. Excessive workloads (Guterman & Jayaratne, 1994) accompanied by low wages, poor working conditions within a diminished sense of accomplishment (Vinokur-Kaplan, 1991), and ongoing exposure of personal risk to assault (Regehr, Chau, Leslie, & Howe, 2002) are varying stressors encountered by child welfare workers. Even the most productive and effective child welfare leaders face tremendous challenges in the systems they direct. Leadership and administrative bodies encounter a series of organizational limitations, including low employee salaries, unpredictable risk of violence to employees, staff shortages, high caseloads, administrative burdens, inadequate supervision and training, limited opportunities for professional development, and additional struggles that impact and contribute to the lack of organizational performance (McGowan & Meezan, 1983). Studies have found that organizational struggles may contribute to unintended outcomes of low employee morale and job satisfaction, frequent employee turnover, poor consumer satisfaction and service outcomes, and impact on overall service delivery (Glisson and Hemmelgarn, 1998; Jimmieson & Griffin, 1998; Johnson & McIntye, 1998; Nunno, 1997; Parkin & Green, 1997; Schmit & Allschied, 1995; Silver & Manning, 1997; Wagar, 1997).

Federal agencies, associations, and philanthropies have joined to explore and address the plight of child welfare organizations and services. Despite the bleak outlook in the field of child welfare, advances and successes have been achieved in several large states plagued with horrific bureaucratic struggles. Systemic reforms in the Illinois's and New York City's Health and Human Services led to victories over a stale service delivery system known for bureaucratic gridlock and highly questionable practices. The Illinois child welfare system introduced performance contracting in order to identify organizational gaps of leadership, worker victimization, strategic planning, and partnerships. The commitment was to change the climate and address systemic weaknesses through numerous performance initiatives. Reform efforts involved employee participation and accountability to impact service delivery on all levels. New York's commissioner focused primarily on leadership reform across frontline supervision and casework staff. Creating a culture that focused on leadership development on all agency levels, providing staff with resources necessary to do their jobs, and supporting staff in professional development revived a system entrenched in national news headlines. Both the Illinois and New York City reforms recognized and validated the importance of leadership practices and the role of leadership in developing organizational culture.

Organizational Culture

The sheer size of the federal or state Department of Health and Human Services and Division of Child and Family Services introduces complexities for leaders interested in vitality and ongoing renewal. Large-scale organizations typically reflect numerous layers of authority with elaborate organizational charts and overlapping lines of communication. The impersonality and dehumanization often experienced in large organizations leave employees feeling anonymous, powerless, and without a sense of empowerment in impacting the navigation and vision of the agency. Effective leaders minimize organizational conditions

| Highlight 13.6 | Three Layers of Culture |

1. *Artifacts and creations:* Visible structures and process. Quarterly and annual reports, policies and procedures, newsletters, memoranda, wall dividers, furnishings, office location and size, technology, visible and audible behavior patterns. Easy to observe but difficult to decipher.
2. *Espoused values:* Stated strategies, goals, and philosophies.

3. *Basic underlying assumptions that guide behavior:* Assumptions (about reality, time and space, human nature, human relations, and human activity) that guide individual perception, thinking, and feeling about work, performance goals, human relationships, and performance of colleagues.

that create individuality or indifference and create cultures that encourage employee communication, participation, and commitment (Wren, 1995).

Edgar Schein (1992) first explored and studied organizational culture across multiple organizational settings. He defined the culture of an organization as a "pattern of shared basic assumptions that the group learned as it solved its problems of external adaptation and internal integration, that has worked well enough to be considered valid and, therefore, to be taught to new members as the correct way to perceive, think, and feel in relation to those problems" (p. 12).

This definition of culture isolates assumptions, adaptations, perceptions, and learning as key facets that workers experience within organizations. Understanding organizational culture is a key role of leadership. Social work leaders need to develop the ability to diagnose and perceive limitations, strengths, and opportunities within an organization and help the culture adapt to attitudes and behaviors of caseworkers, supervisors, regional administrators, and many other professionals within the agency. Understanding culture will allow leaders to craft organizations on multiple layers. Schein described artifacts and creations, values, and basic assumptions as cultural layers (see Highlight 13.6).

The Role of Leadership in Developing Culture

Shared expectations, values, and attitudes that influence individual, team, and organizational practices develop or emerge in small or large organizations. The emerging culture will reflect the leader's assumptions and also the internal interactions created by subordinates. Leaders in the field of child welfare have opportunities to develop and transmit organizational culture. Schneider (1990) developed several in-depth culture-embedding mechanisms (see Highlight 13.7).

Primary Embedding Mechanisms   Primary embedding mechanisms create organizational culture. One of the most powerful embedding mechanisms available to child welfare agency leaders is expressing what they believe in or care about. These values are typically conveyed through formal or informal

Highlight 13.7	Culture-Embedding Mechanisms

Primary Embedding Mechanisms

- What leaders pay attention to, measure, and control on a regular basis
- How leaders react to critical incidents and organizational crises
- Observed criteria by which leaders allocate scarce resources
- Deliberate role modeling, teaching, and coaching
- Observed criteria by which leaders allocate rewards and status
- Observed criteria by which leaders recruit, select, promote, retire, and excommunicate organizational members

Secondary Articulation and Reinforcement Mechanisms

- Organization design and structure
- Organizational systems and procedures
- Organizational rites and rituals
- Design of physical space, facades, and buildings
- Stories, legends, and myths about people and events
- Formal statements of organizational philosophy, values, and creed

conversations, measures, controls, rewards, and other systematic methods they implement to deal with agency operations. Leaders aware of this process can relay powerful messages that are often consistent with their own behaviors. Ineffective leaders will be inconsistent in what they say or pay attention to and create organizations with subordinates investing time, energy, and additional resources in trying to decode leadership behaviors, objectives, and motives.

Child welfare agencies may experience success and victories but will also encounter routine crises. The manner in which agency leaders react and address crises creates norms, values, and working procedures for the organizational culture. Trials and tribulations often allow underlying assumptions to surface in unanticipated ways. Crises often produce emotional involvement, anxiety, and other survival responses that, when mobilized, can provide periods of intense learning. Child welfare leaders face yearly assaults on agency operations, policies, and procedures introduced by federal or state legislature. Their knowledge and ability to deal with such crises will reveal some of their assumptions about the importance of subordinates and vision of the agency. Leaders subjectively define crises, and subordinates will look to the leaders for interpretation and assumptions.

Budget development and resource allocation are two more areas that reveal leader assumptions and beliefs. Resource allocation influences agency goals, programs, services, the means to accomplish them, and the leadership process to be used. Federal regulations, bills, and initiatives are additional constraints on decision making, as they limit the perception and consideration of alternatives. The mechanism and process through which an agency leader communicates, allocates, delivers, and balances a budget reveals assumptions, beliefs, and values to agency subordinates.

Visible agency leadership behavior has key value for communicating assumptions and values to current employees and especially to newcomers. A vast difference also lies in the formal versus the informal delivery process. Caseworkers and supervisors develop more-lasting impressions of leadership when agency leaders are observed informally. Informal settings translate formal messages delivered through memoranda and meetings into observable and modeled actions that clearly convey assumptions and values.

Employees of child welfare agencies also learn and develop an understanding of the organization from their own experience through promotions, performance appraisals, and discussions about what the organization values and what it punishes. The nature of the rewarded and punished behavior conveys an underlying organizational message. Successful child welfare leaders will ensure that their values and assumptions are learned by subordinates and directly linked to a reward, promotion, and status system consistently reflective of those assumptions. The success of the leader will also depend on his or her ability to consistently and creatively allocate varying rewards for daily behaviors over the long term.

A subtle yet potent mechanism that conveys and contributes to embedding cultural assumptions is the process of selecting new agency employees. Recruitment and hiring may reflect an intended and conscious plan to accrue and coalesce a group of employees that most closely resemble agency cultural assumptions and values. Success of the culture often lies in the subtlety of recruitment that contributes to confirming or disregarding the assumptions of the organizations. Assumptions and values are further reinforced through promotion criteria or the process of termination. Both of these mechanisms communicate the foundation and current climate of the organization.

Secondary Articulation and Reinforcement Mechanisms   Schneider (1990) observed and developed secondary mechanisms that work only if they are consistent with the primary mechanisms (see Highlight 13.7). If consistent, these mechanisms contribute to organizational ideologies and formalize content learned at the beginning stages of culture development instilled by primary mechanisms. Their inconsistency, however, will either be ignored or will develop as a source of internal conflict. These mechanisms are essentially the visible cultural artifacts that may be difficult to interpret without cultural knowledge obtained from leaders or current employees.

Design and structure of organizations take numerous forms and may reflect traditional hierarchical and bureaucratic functions focused on division of labor, functional responsibility, and mechanization grounded in organizational design structured around the skill sets of individual leaders, employees, and internal relationships. The design or periodic restructuring of organizations provides opportunities for leaders to embed their assumptions about tasks, the means to accomplish those requirements, and the appropriate relationships to foster among subordinates. The structure and design can be used to reinforce the identity of the organization and leadership assumptions, but rarely does structure embed assumptions because employees interpret them in different ways.

A visible and routine part of organizational life is found in the daily meetings, monthly or quarterly reports, memoranda, procedures, documentation reports, forms, and other ritual tasks. Despite complaints of large bureaucracies, recurrent processes clarify operations and communication. Agency leaders have opportunities to reinforce certain assumptions by developing systems and routines that allow them to flourish. On the polar end of bureaucracies, agency systems and procedures can formalize the process of participative leadership or decentralized leadership and thus reinforce the message that child welfare agencies care about elements of collaboration and cooperation.

Rites and rituals created by the assumptions of leadership resemble a similar mechanism to systems and procedures but are even less decipherable to new employees who lack the knowledge of leadership assumptions. Although rites and rituals are often found within organizational meetings, office sporting events, office competitions, and other activities, they reveal only a limited perspective in a wider range of assumptions found within the organizational culture. One can decipher a limited piece of culture but will be unable to generalize it to larger and more global assumptions.

Physical designs depict the visible features of organizations, not only to employees but also to clients, families, new employees, consultants, and visitors. The message gained from the structural design of the workplace has the potential to convey or reinforce the leadership values and assumptions. Leaders who have an outward ideology often embody and visibly manifest their character and leadership styles. Child welfare organizations with clear assumptions and convictions around communication will likely develop an open-office layout in order to confirm emphasis on equality, ease of communication and collaboration, and importance of relationships. Organizations structurally divided into offices, cubicles, and partitions naturally convey a different set of assumptions and values to the visitor, outsider, or new employee.

Schneider (1990) asserts that leaders play a key role in embedding the assumptions that they hold or represent and therefore create organizational culture. Primary embedding mechanisms communicate culture content to new employees. Due to the fact that leaders do not have a choice about whether or not to communicate culture, they are left with deciding how much to manage what they communicate. The key is to realize that primary mechanisms must be used and that they must be consistent with each other. The exercise in Highlight 13.8 will help improve your understanding of organizational culture.

| **Highlight 13.8** | **Organizational Culture Class Exercise** |

Individually consider the following: Organizational culture is often manifested through rituals, stories, symbols, language, gestures, norms, shared values, and assumptions.

1. In an organization that you are familiar with (through current or past experience), how was the culture (unwritten rules, norms, values, etc.) communicated to you and how was it reinforced?
2. How did this influence your behavior within that organization? Use Schein's "layers" or Schneider's "mechanisms" to help guide your thinking.
3. What was the role of leadership in communicating/enforcing the culture?
4. How did the organization's culture impact behavior of others in the organization?
5. How would you diagnose the culture of an organization?

Source: Adapted from S. J. Parkes. (2002). *Organizational behavior.* Lecture Series: University of Utah.

CHANGE

Leading Change in Child Welfare Organizations

Leaders in the field of child welfare have multiple roles. Leaders inform and develop social policy, collaborate with federal and state entities to implement policies and regulations, negotiate and allocate resources for programs, and direct and guide child welfare organizations. In addition to some of these direct roles, leaders are also increasingly expected to anticipate crucial changes in their field and in their organization, implement changes, and support employees in adapting to changes. The role of child welfare leaders is also centered on managing change dictated or informed by federal or state initiatives, organizational policies and procedures, organizational restructuring, fiscal reallocation or cutbacks, local and community agency collaboration, media representation, and unanticipated class-action lawsuits.

Howell and Costley (2006) describe two different patterns of change. *Episodic change* occurs infrequently and often resembles a misalignment between the operations of an organization and the environmental demands. Howell and Costley describe it as dramatic, often accumulating inertia as a result of an organization's inability to rapidly adapt to the change in its environment. In child welfare, changing rules often amounts to the inability or delay of agencies to adapt and reflect the new or changing federal regulations. Inertia is rooted in organizational routines, outdated organizational structure, leadership with long tenure, worker complacency, and worker turnover. The costs of episodic change may resemble serious misalignments with federal policy, poor organizational performance, and service delivery. As leaders create and introduce change, it is their responsibility to clarify to the organization what needs to be done. This type of leadership may implement situational leadership approaches and, especially, transformational leadership practices.

Continuous or incremental change accumulates over time. Howell and Costley (2006) describe continuous change as a process involving ongoing modification in the work processes. It is typically initiated by the reaction of organizational instability and may include improvisation and learning of new methods throughout the agency. Child welfare agencies may introduce various practice models to address the fidelity of services. Through institution of new practice models that resemble marginal changes, small and incremental changes will accumulate to create a substantial organizational change. Continuous change that impacts the caseworker or supervisory skill set requires training and strengthening of new skills. Continuous change requires agency leadership to model behavior, identify weaknesses in practice, coach individual members in practice and implementation, and encourage ongoing learning behaviors in organizational members (Howell & Costley, 2006).

Several theorists have described and proposed varying patterns of change in organizations. The following principles describe a synthesis of current thinking on best practices in implementing major change in organizations (Kotter, 1996; Lewin, 1951; Tichy & Cohen, 1997; Yukl, 2006) and are framed within

Lewin's classic model for implementing change. Lewin's model describes change as a process resembling metaphorical elements of unfreezing, changing, and refreezing.

Unfreezing   The initial stage of unfreezing involves developing a motivation to change. Leaders in the field of child welfare must understand the political process and distribution of power, and identify the stakeholders whose support is necessary if change is to be introduced. Regardless of the change magnitude, Yukl (2006, p. 302) describes the need to identify likely supporters and opponents in order to explore:

> Which key people will determine whether a proposal will be successfully implemented? Who is likely to support the proposal? How much resistance is likely and from whom? What would be necessary to overcome the resistance? How could skeptics be converted into supporters? How long will it take to get approval from all of the key parties?

Leaders and members involved in the change process must have or develop the skills to strategically highlight the threats to the organization and the opportunities that are not apparent to the whole group. Creating a sense of urgency can only be accomplished if organizational members understand the risk of inaction, complacency, or stagnation. The urgency message needs to be clear so that members understand the consequences and cost of inaction. Child welfare leaders on all levels need to share case outcomes, family and child complaints, child development and fiscal consequences of delayed or multiple placements, child development implication of transitional care, and other indicators that may develop clarity in the need for change. Agency leaders may even arrange meetings between children, families, and individuals delivering services; develop and implement policy; or analyze services. Successful benchmarks may also be presented as a means to offer successful models that have implemented change in service delivery, agency culture, and operations. Edgar Schein (1992) offered three procedures that contribute to unfreezing people from established ways (cited in Howell & Costley, 2006, p. 370):

1. There must be enough disconfirming data to cause serious discomfort that established patterns of working are no longer appropriate.
2. The disconfirming data should be directly relevant to desired goals or values.
3. Organization members must perceive the possibility of resolving the problem of disconfirming data while maintaining their organization's integrity.

Organizational members should also be prepared to adjust to change (Yukl, 2006), and leaders should provide a sense of psychological safety while stretching for a new ideological vision (Lewin, 1951). Yukl (2006) suggests that coping with threatening aspects of change relies heavily on awareness and clarity of expectations. Rather than introducing change on an abstract level, leaders need to deconstruct and present practical aspects of change and clarify what will be required of varying members. A realistic preview of anticipated struggles and brainstorming sessions on strategy will equip members with immediate tools and increasing confidence. Training should also be offered if the change process requires specialization. The information age has also offered opportunities to electronically communicate, learn, and train across disciplines and also to develop emotional support networks.

Changing   The changing process will require leaders to guide and establish new ways of behaving, perceiving, and thinking. The changing phase is heavily reliant on building broad and immediate coalitions in order to enlist support of a guiding team of individuals. Yukl (2006) describes the role of task forces in the process of changing as critically important when it involves modification of the formal structure and relationships among subunits. Task forces in child welfare agencies can focus on developing action plans for implanting a new strategy, designing procedures for renewed activities, studying how the flow of communication will be impacted by change, or developing methods to analyze implementation, progression, and impact of change on services and the agency. For example, a task force to improve service delivery to single teen mothers should include people from all service delivery systems, varying disciplines, organizations, or local agencies that effect the quality of service. Lastly, the task force should also meet with the population it serves to increase representation and further validate information. Task force membership in the process of adapting and implementing change will develop cooperation, support, and ownership from immediate or ancillary stakeholders.

Lewin (1951) describes the changing process as highly reliant on the leader's ability to develop and deliver a vision for change. The vision should include the goals of the change and clearly describe the future as a significant improvement over the current situation with active endorsement and commitment of the leader's guiding coalition (Howell & Costley, 2006, p. 371). The change process will require that leaders and guiding coalitions develop and articulate clear direction for the change and monitor the progress of change. Yukl (2006) describes the need for feedback when venturing through uncharted waters. Feedback on the effects of change should be accumulated and analyzed to evaluate progress and inform further refinement of the change process. Leadership will need to track the effects of change on member performance and evaluate the efficacy of change.

A successful change effort is also highly reliant on the support offered to employees throughout the change process (Lewin, 1951). Although overcoming resistance to change is the primary goal, developing cooperation and commitment to executing the needed changes is the sustainable and long-term goal. Child welfare leaders on all levels must enable and empower service providers (i.e., caseworkers, supervisors, regional directors) by providing needed resources, training, and information to develop confidence and the discretion to implement the needed changes. Supportive leadership behavior also takes the form of removing or minimizing bureaucratic restraints and other existing barriers that hamper the change effort (Howell & Costley, 2006).

Both Lewin (1951) and Yukl (2006) emphasize the need to develop opportunities for early successes. Yukl found that individual or team confidence increases as members experience successful progress in early phases of a new project. He also observed that early skeptics become supporters as they observed evidence of progress initiated by efforts to do things a new way. Members are naturally more willing to undertake a new venture if they perceive that their efforts lead to success and the costs of failure are minimal. It is during these small wins that Lewin suggests implementing contingent reward behavior by offering visible recognition and celebrating successful implementation. Celebrating and rewarding small wins visibly validates employee effort and confirms successful progress that potentially triggers additional commitment to the change process.

Refreezing   Lewin (1951) describes the stage of refreezing as a process of reinforcing the changed behaviors, processes, structures, technology, or whatever has been changed (cited in Howell & Costley, 1996). This final stage requires gathering data that confirms the fidelity of the changes and removes the sense of urgency that precipitated the change efforts. Leaders in child welfare agencies can gather data from process evaluations and outcome studies evaluating behavioral change, operations, and immediate outcomes. Information can also be gathered from stakeholders, children and families receiving services from child welfare agencies, or internal sources like service providers, supervisors, and directors. Once this data becomes distributed, the changes are institutionalized, incorporated into operations, and reflected in the fabric of the organizational culture.

Lewin's (1951) model describes the changes experienced on the individual, group, or organizational level (Schein, 1992). The model describes the conditions, the process, and the role of leadership as a change agent. All three phases naturally overlap but need to be addressed in the change process. Unfreezing is needed to address the natural hesitancy to change; without refreezing, the organization stands to regress to its previous conditions (Howell & Costley, 1996). Leaders in the field of child welfare will experience, initiate, or mediate change. In order to be effective in leading organizational change, leaders need to rely on a best-practice framework that will navigate their excursion in developing and changing an organization.

Energizing Individuals

As a leader working with and developing others, you need to think about how the combination of the five factors in Highlight 13.9 affects people. Each individual deals with change and emotions differently. The goal is to use whatever combination of these factors each person needs to help him or her work through transition.

| **Highlight 13.9** | **Class Exercise: Energizing Organizations through Change** |

Take a few minutes and consider how you would use each of the following five elements to energize people within an organization about change.

1. *Urgency:* How will you give people a sense of urgency? Think of emerging threats and opportunities. Think of drawing the dire consequences of inaction in a verbal picture people will immediately understand.
2. *Mission:* How will you craft an inspiring mission? How will you connect your mission to people on a level that is important to them individually without being so vague that it loses meaning?
3. *Stretch:* What goals and objectives will you set? How will you make your stretch goals seem worthy of striving for?
4. *Teamwork:* How will you instill a sense that you are all (including yourself) preparing for change?
5. *Confidence:* How will you give people the confidence that can help them overcome their fears?

Think about each individual on your team. Record what you will do with that person individually in order to energize him or her.

Team Member	Urgency	Mission	Stretch Goals	Teamwork	Confidence

Source: Adapted from N. M. Tichy & E. Cohen. (1995). *The leader's companion.* New York: Free Press.

SUMMARY

Leadership theory has a long history with an expansive set of progressive approaches. Many of the approaches resemble the historical times of humanity and industry. The earliest approach focused on leadership traits explored through philosophical dialogue, skills related to leader effectiveness, and trait interaction with leader effectiveness. Behavioral leadership approaches shift inquiry from a single dimension to a multidimensional behavioral approach. Situational leadership approaches explore the unpredictability, inconsistency, and highly variable behavior of leadership. Transactional approaches emphasize the relationship that develops from an exchange or bargaining process. Lastly, transformational leadership uses charisma, intellectual stimulation, individual consideration, and inspirational motivation to influence intrinsic motivators that heighten follower performance beyond expected routine.

Leadership in the field of social work was vibrant in the early days of activism and community organization but has since received inconsistent attention. Recent social work authors are increasing attention to the leadership role in the profession of social work. Some adamantly relate fidelity of leadership to outcomes of services, and national social work leaders describe the role of social work leadership as transformational in nature.

Leaders in the field of child welfare experience numerous struggles and victories that require an understanding of systems and functions within a political frame. Developing a political interpretive lens will allow leaders on all levels to gather information, analyze, and decide how to best approach situations. Social work leaders also need to develop the ability to diagnose and anticipate limitations, strengths, and opportunities on organizational levels. Leaders are required to develop and adapt organizational culture to attitudes and behaviors and further craft agencies on multiple layers.

One of the most important and difficult leadership responsibilities is to navigate and mediate the process of change in organizations. Change may be episodic or incremental. Resistance to change is expected and should be viewed as a natural defensive response, not as a dysfunctional character limitation. Leaders need to become comfortable with change and be prepared to implement best-practice principles proven to address procedures and implications of change.

Questions for Discussion

1. What makes a good manager?
2. Explain the transactional exchange process.
3. What are the responsibilities of the human service executive?
4. Discuss the five elements of social work leadership.
5. What are the challenges of managers in a child welfare organization?
6. Explain a few strategies to lead change in child welfare organizations.

Bibliography

Aaronson, M. (1989). The case manager home visitor. *Child Welfare, 68*(3), 339–346.

ABT Associates. (2001). *National evaluation of family support programs.* Washington, DC: U.S. Department of Health and Human Services, Administration on Children, Youth, and Families.

Acevedo, G., & Morales, J. (2001). Assessment with Latino/Hispanic communities and organizations. In R. Fong & S. Furuto (eds.), *Culturally competent practice.* Boston: Allyn & Bacon.

Adams, J. A. (1993). Quality assurance in sexual abuse evaluation: An idea whose time has come. *Journal of Child Sexual Abuse, 2*(3), 103–106.

Addams, J. (1918). The subjective necessity for social settlements. *Hull House.* Chicago: University of Illinois.

Adoption and Safe Families Act of 1997, Public Law 105-89.

Albers, E., Reilly, T., & Rittner, B. (1993). Children in foster care: Possible factors affecting permanency planning. *Child and Adolescent Social Work Journal, 10*(4), 329–341.

Allen, R., & Petr, C. (1998). Rethinking family-centered practice. *American Journal of Orthopsychiatry, 68*(1), 4–16.

Altshuler, S. (2000). From barriers to successful collaboration: Public schools and child welfare working together. *National Association of Social Workers, 48*(1).

Alwon, F., & Reitz, A. (2000). *The workforce crisis in child welfare.* Washington, DC: Child Welfare League of America.

Amato, P. R. (1993). Urban-rural differences in helping friends and family members. *Social Psychology Quarterly, 56*(4), 249–262.

Amer-Hirsch, W. (1989, September/October). Educating youth about AIDS: A model program. *Children Today,* 16–19.

American Civil Liberties Union. (2005). *Caught in the Net: The Impact of Drug Policies on Women and Families. American Civil Liberties Union: Break the Chains: Communities of Color and the War on Drugs.* New York: Brennan Center for Justice, New York University.

American Humane Association. (1986). *Standards for child protective services.* Denver, CO: Author.

American Psychiatric Association. (1994). *DSM IV.* Washington, DC: Author.

American Public Human Services Association (APHSA). (1990). *The National Commission on Child Welfare and Family Preservation: Factbook on public child welfare services and staff.* Washington, DC: Author.

American Public Welfare Association (APWA). (1987). *Guidelines for a model system of protective services for abused and neglected children and their families.* Washington, DC: Author.

APWA. (1995). *Guidelines for a model system of protective services for abused and neglected children and their families.* Washington, DC: Author.

Anderson, J. D. (1992). Family-centered practice in the 1990s: A multicultural perspective. *Journal* of *Multicultural Social Work*, 1(4), 17–29.

Andrews, D. Z., Zinger, I., Hoge, R. D., Bonta, J., Gendreau, P., & Cullen, F. T. (1996). Does correctional treatment work? A clinically relevant and psychologically informed meta-analysis. In D. I. Greenberg (ed.), *Criminal careers*, Vol. 2. Aldershot, England: Dartmouth.

Angela R. v. Clinton, No. LRC-91-415 1991 U.S. Dist. E.D. Ark. July 8, 1991).

Annie E. Casey Foundation. (1999). *Advocasey, (1)*3.

Annie E. Casey Foundation. (2005). *KidsCount: An essay*. Baltimore, MD: Annie E Casey Foundation.

Ansell, D., & Kessler, M. (2003). Rethinking the role of independent living in permanency planning. *Child Law Practice*, 22(4), 66–68.

Antle, B. J., Wells, L. M., Salter-Goldie, R., DeMatteo, D., & King, S. M. (1997). *The challenges of parenting for families living with HIV/AIDS*. Unpublished manuscript.

Archacki-Stone, C. (1995). *Family-based mental health services: Children in families at risk*. Combrinck, NY: Guilford.

Ashby, L. (1997). *Endangered children: Dependency, neglect, and abuse in American history*. New York: Twayne.

Attias, R., & Goodwin, J. (1985). Knowledge and management strategies in incest cases: A survey of physicians, psychologists and family counselors. *Child Abuse and Neglect*, 9, 527–533.

Austin, D. M. (1983). Administrative practice in human services: Future directions for curriculum development. *Journal of Applied Behavior Science*, 19(2), 141–151.

Austin, D. M. (1988). *The political economy of human service programs*. Greenwich, CT: JAI.

Axin, J., & Stern, M. J. (2001). *Social welfare: A history of the American response to need* (5th ed.). Boston: Allyn & Bacon.

Baily, T., & Baily, W. (1986). *Operational definitions of child emotional maltreatment: Final report*.

Augusta, ME: National Center for Child Abuse and Neglect.

Baker, A., & Dale, N. (2002). Psychiatric crises in child welfare residential treatment. *Children's Services*, 6(3), 213–230.

Baker, A., Wulczyn, F., & Dale, N. (2005). Covariates of length of stay in residential treatment. *Child Welfare*, 89(3), 184–194.

Baladerian, N. J. (1994). Intervention and treatment of children with severe disabilities who become victims of abuse. *Developmental Disabilities Bulletin*, 22(2), 93–99.

Balgopal, P. R., Patchner, M., & Henderson, C. H. (1988). Home visits: An effective strategy for engaging the involuntary client. *Child and Youth Services*, 11(1), 65–76.

Balswick, J., & Balswick, J. (1995). Gender relations and marital power. In B. B. Ingoldsby & S. Smith (eds.), *Families in multicultural perspective* (pp. 297–315). New York: Guilford.

Barbell, K., & Freundlich, M. (2001). *Foster care today*. Washington, DC: Casey Family Programs.

Barbell, K., & Wright, L. (1999). Foster family care in the next century. *Child Welfare Journal of Policy, Practice and Program*. Washington, DC: Child Welfare League of America.

Barone, C., Weissberg, R. P., Kasprow, W. J., Voyce, C. K., Arthur, M. W., & Shriver, T. P. (1995, Spring). Involvement in multiple problem behaviors of young urban adolescents. *The Journal of Primary Prevention*, 15(3), 261–283.

Barth, R. (1994). Shared family care: Child protection and family preservation. *National Association of Social Workers*, 39(5), 515–524.

Barth, R., Gibbs, P., & Siebenaler, K. (2001). *Assessing the field of post-adoption service: Family needs, program models, and evaluation issues* (Contract No. 100-99-006). Washington, DC: U.S. Department of Health and Human Services.

Barton, W., & Butts, J. A. (1990, April). Viable options: Intensive supervision programs for juvenile

delinquents. *Crime and Delinquency*, 36(2), 238–256.

Bass, B. M. (1985). *Leadership and performance beyond expectations*. New York: Free Press.

Bass, B. M. (1996). *A new paradigm of leadership: An inquiry into transformational leadership*. Alexandria, VA: U.S. Army Research Institute for the Behavioral and Social Sciences.

Bass, B. M. (1999). Two decades of research and development in transformational research. *European Journal of Work and Organizational Psychology*, 8(1), 9–33.

Bazemore, G. (1992). On mission statements and reform in juvenile justice: The case of the "balanced approach." *Federal Probation*, 56(3), 64–70.

Beck, A. T., Steen, R. A., & Kovach, M. (1985). Hopelessness and eventual suicide: A 10-year prospective study of patients hospitalized with suicidal ideation. *New York Academy of Science*, 142(5), 559–563.

Bell, W. (1983). *Contemporary social welfare*. New York: MacMillan.

Belsky, J. (1993). Etiology of child maltreatment: A developmental-ecological analysis. *Psychological Bulletin*, 114(3), 413–434.

Berg, I. K. (1994). *Family-based services: A solution-focused approach*. New York: W. W. Norton & Co.

Berliner, L., & Elliott, D. M. (1996). Sexual abuse of children. In J. Briere, L. Berliner, J. A. Bulkley, C. Jenny, & T. Reid (eds.), *The APSAC handbook on child maltreatment* (pp. 51–71). Thousand Oaks, CA: Sage.

Berrick, J., Barth, R., & Needel, B. (1993). A comparison of kinship foster homes and family foster homes. In R. P. Barth, J. D. Berrick, & N. Gilbert (eds.), *Child welfare research review*. New York: Columbia University.

Berrick, J. D. (1991). Sexual abuse prevention training for preschoolers: Implications for moral development. *Children and Youth Services Review*, 13, 61–75.

Berrick, J. D. (1997). Assessing quality of care in kinship and foster care. *Family Relations*, 46, 273–280.

Berrick, J. D. (1998). When children cannot remain home: Foster family care and kinship care. *Protecting Children from Abuse and Neglect*, 8(1), 72–87.

Berry, M., & Barth, R. (1988). A study of disrupted placements of adolescents. *Child Welfare* 69(3), 213–214.

Besharov, D. (1988). *Protecting children from abuse and neglect. Policy and practice*. Springfield, IL: Charles C. Thomas.

Beyer, M. (1999). Parent-child visits as an opportunity for change. In *The prevention report*. Washington, DC: The National Resource Center for Family Centered Practice.

Bicknell-Hentges, L. (1995). The stages of reunification process and the tasks of the therapist. In L. Combrick-Graham (ed.), *Children in families at risk: Maintaining the connections* (pp. 326–349). New York: Guilford.

Birmingham, B. M., & Bussey, M. (1996). Certification for child protective services staff members: The Texas initiative. *Child Welfare*, 75(6), 727–740.

Black, D., Wolkin, S., & Hendriks, J. H. (1989). *Child psychiatry and the law*. London: Gaskell.

Black, H. C. (1992). *Black's law dictionary* (8th ed.). St. Paul, MN: West.

Black, J. C., & Cantor, D. J. (1993). *Child custody*. New York: Columbia University.

Black, M. M., & Dubowitz, H. (1999). Child neglect: Research recommendations and decisions. In H. Dubowitz (ed.), *Neglected children* (pp. 261–277). Thousand Oaks, CA: Sage.

Blake, R. R., & Mouton, J. S. (1982). Management by grid principles or situationalism: Which? *Group and Organizational Studies*, 7, 207–210.

Blitsch, T., Mears, S., & Sharma, S. (1995). Child welfare in America through the family preservation movement. *Guru Nanak Journal of Sociology*, 16(1), 31–48.

Bolman, L. G., & Deal, T. E. (1997). *Reframing organizations*. San Francisco: Jossey-Bass.

Booz-Allen/Hamilton. (1987). *The Maryland Social Services Job Analysis and Personnel Qualification Study, Executive Summary*. Baltimore: Maryland Department of Human Resources.

Borduin, C., & Henggeler, S. (1987, July–Sept.). Post-divorce mother–son relations of delinquent and well-adjusted adolescents. *Journal of Applied Developmental Psychology*, 8(3), 203–288.

Borduin, C. M., Cone, L. T., Mann, B. J., Henggeler, S. W., Fucci, B. R., Blaske, D. M., & Williams, R. A. (1995). Multisystemic treatment of serious juvenile offenders: Long-term prevention of criminality and violence. *Journal of Consulting and Clinical Psychology*, 63(4), 569–578.

Borgford-Parnell, D., Hope, K. R., & Deisher, R. W. (1994). A homeless teen pregnancy project: An intensive team case management model. *American Journal of Public Health*, 84(6), 1029–1030.

Bowlby, J. (1969). *Attachment and loss, Volumes 1 & 2*. New York: Basic Books.

Bowlby, J. (1980). *Loss: Sadness and depression (Volume 3: Attachment and loss)*. New York: Basic Books.

Boyle, D. (2004). *The co-production principle and time dollars: A report printed for the privatization of child welfare*. Los Angeles: Reason Public Policy Institute.

Brandell, J. R. (1997). *Theory and practice in clinical social work*. New York: Free Press.

Brezina, T. (1998). Adolescent maltreatment and delinquency: The question of intervening processes. *Journal of Research in Crime and Delinquency*, 35(1), 71–99.

Briere, J. (1992). *Child abuse trauma: Theory and treatment of the lasting effects*. Newbury Park, CA: Sage.

Brillian, E. (1986). Social work leadership: A missing ingredient? *Social Work*, 31(5), 325–331.

Brown, E. F., Limb, G. E., Munoz, R., & Clifford, C. A. (2001). *Title IV-B child and family services plans: An evaluation of specific measures taken by states to comply with the Indian Child Welfare Act*. Seattle, WA: Casey Family Programs.

Brown, S. E., Whitehead, K. R., & Braswell, M. C. (1981). Child maltreatment. An empirical examination of selected conventional hypotheses. *Youth and Society*, 13, 77–90.

Browne, C. (1995). Empowerment in social work practice with older women. *Social Work*, 40, 358–364.

Browne, C., & Mills, C. (2001). Theoretical framework: Ecological model, strengths perspective, and empowerment theory. In R. Fong & S. Furuto (eds.), *Culturally competent practice* (pp. 10–32). Boston: Allyn & Bacon.

Bunyan, A. (1987). "Help, I can't cope with my child": A behavioral approach to the treatment of a conduct-disordered child within the natural home setting. *British Journal of Social Work*, 17, 237–256.

Burford, G., & Hudson, J. (2000). *Family group conferencing: New directions in community-centered child and family practice*. New York: Aldine de Gruyter.

Burndoroff, S., & Scherer, D. (1994, June). Wilderness family therapy: An innovative treatment approach for problem youth. *Journal of Child and Family Studies*, 3(2), 175–191.

Burns, J. M. (1978). *Leadership*. New York: Harper & Row.

Byington, D. B., & McCammon, S. (1988, Spring). Networking as an approach to advocacy: A campus sexual assault awareness program. *Response to the Victimization of Women & Children*, 11(1), 11–13.

Cahn, E., & Rowe, J. (1992). *Time dollars: The new currency that enables Americans to turn their hidden resource-time into personal security and community renewal*. New York: Rodale.

Cameron, G. (1990). The potential of informal social support strategies in child welfare. In M. Rothery & G. Cameron (eds.), *Child maltreatment: Expanding our concept of helping* (pp. 145–168). New York: Lawrence Erlbaum.

Cameron, G., Vanderwoerd, J., & Peirson, L. (1997). *Protecting children and supporting families*. New York: Aldine de Gruyter.

Cantos, A. L., Gries, L. T., & Slis, V. (1997). Behavioral correlates of parental visiting during family foster care. *Child Welfare League of America, 126*(2), 309–327.

Carlo, P. (1991). Why a parental involvement program leads to family reunification: A dialogue with childcare workers. *Residential Treatment for Children and Youth, 9*(2), 37–48.

Centers for Disease Control and Prevention. (1993). *HIV/AIDS surveillance report: Year-end 1993, 5*(4).

Centers for Disease Control and Prevention. (1995). *HIV/AIDS surveillance report: Year-end 1995, 7*(4).

Centers for Disease Control and Prevention. (1997). *National HIV prevalence surveys 1997 summary*. Atlanta: Author.

Cervera, N. J. (1993). Decision making for pregnant adolescents: Applying reasoned action theory to research and treatment. *Families in Society: The Journal of Contemporary Human Services, 74*(6), 355–365.

Chahine, Z., Straaten, J., & Williams-Isom, M. (2005). The New York City neighborhood-based services strategy. *Child Welfare, 84*(2).

Chapman, J. R., & Smith, B. (1987). Response of social service and criminal justice agencies to child sexual abuse complaints. *Response, 10*(3), 7–13.

Chasnoff, I. J. (1988). Drug use in pregnancy. *Pediatric Clinics of North America, 35*(6), 1403–1412.

Cheng, S. (2004). *Factors that influence the effectiveness of a parenting program for Asians and Pacific Islanders*. Unpublished dissertation, College of Social Work, University of Utah, Salt Lake City.

Children's Defense Fund. (1988). *Teenage pregnancy: An advocate's guide to the numbers*. Washington, DC: Author.

Children's Defense Fund. (1994). Births to teens. *CDF Reports, 16*(8).

Child Welfare League of America (CWLA). (1986, 1988, 1989, 1990). *Standards for in-home services for children and families; standards for pregnant adolescents and young parents; standards for adoption services; standards for foster care; standards for abused or neglected children and their families*. Washington, DC: Author.

CWLA. (1988). *Standards for health care services for children in out-of-home care*. Washington, DC: Author.

CWLA. (1990a). *Staffing study of health and rehabilitation services in Florida*. Washington, DC: Author.

CWLA. (1990b). *Standards for adoption*. Washington, DC: Author.

CWLA. (1990c). *Standards for child welfare services*. Washington, DC: Author.

CWLA. (1991). *Core training for child welfare caseworkers curriculum*. Washington, DC: Author.

CWLA. (1995). *Standards for child welfare services*. Washington, DC: Author.

CWLA. (1996a). *Standards for child protective services*. Washington, DC: Author.

CWLA. (1996b). *Standards for child welfare services*. Washington, DC: Author.

CWLA. (2003). *The child welfare workforce challenge: Results from a preliminary study*. Washington, DC: Author.

CWLA. (2004). *CWLA statement: Children of color in the child welfare system*. Washington, DC: Author.

Children's Defense Fund. (1988). *Teenage pregnancy: An advocate's guide to the numbers*. Washington, DC: Author.

Chilman, C. S. (1991, April). Working poor families: Trends, causes, effects and suggested policies. *Family Relations, 40*, 191–198.

Chung, D. (1992). Asian cultural commonalities: A comparison with mainstream American culture. In S. Furuto, R. Biswas, D. Chung, K. Murase, & F. Ross-Sheriff (eds.), *Social work practice with Asian Americans*. Newbury Park, CA: Sage.

Cicchetti, D., & Carlson, V. (Eds.). (1989). *Child maltreatment: Theory and research on the causes and consequences of child abuse and neglect*. New York: Cambridge University.

Clark-Lempers, D. S., Lempers, J. D., & Netusil, A. (1990, February). Family financial stress, parental support and young adolescent academic achievement and depressive symptoms. *Journal of Early Adolescence, 10*(1), 21–36.

Clewell, B., Brookes-Gunn, J., & Benasich, A. (1989). Evaluating child-related outcomes of teenage parenting programs. *Family Relations, 38*, 201–209.

Close, M. (1980). Child welfare and people of color: Denial of equal access. *Social Work Research and Abstracts, 19*, 12–29.

Cohen, N. A. (Ed.). (1992). *Child welfare: A multicultural focus*. Boston, MA: Allyn & Bacon.

Cohen, N. A. (Ed.). (2000). *Child welfare: A multicultural focus*. Boston: Allyn & Bacon.

Cohn, A. (1979). Essential elements of successful child abuse and neglect treatment. *Child Abuse and Neglect 3*, 491–496.

Cohn, A., & Daro, A. (1987). Is treatment too late? What ten years of evaluative research tells us. *Child Abuse and Neglect, 11*, 433–442.

Colapinto, J. A. (1995). Dilution of family process in social services: Implications for treatment of neglectful families. *Family Process, 34*(1), 59–74.

Cole, E. S. (1987). Adoption. In A. Minahan (ed.), *Encyclopedia of social work: Vol. 1* (18th ed., pp. 64–75). Silver Springs, MD: National Association of Social Workers.

Combrinck-Graham, L. (1989). *Children in family contexts: Perspectives on treatment*. New York: Guilford.

Compton, B. R., & Galaway, B. (1994). *Social work processes* (5th ed.). Pacific Grove, CA: Brooks/Cole.

Conte, J. R., Fogarty, L., & Collins, M. E. (1991). National survey of professional practice in child sexual abuse. *Journal of Family Violence, 6*(2), 149–166.

Cook, K. (1998). *Working in child welfare*. Unpublished manuscript. Wilfrid Laurier University, Ontario, Canada.

Cooke, G. (1992). Legal regulation of child sexual abuse evaluation and testimony. *American Journal of Forensic Psychology, 10*(4), 15–20.

Cooke, P. W., Reid, P. N., & Edwards, R. L. (1997). Management: New developments and directions. In R. L. Edwards (ed.), *Encyclopedia of social work* (19th ed., Supplement, pp. 229–242). Washington, DC: National Association of Social Workers.

Corbett, J., & Petersilia, J. (1994). Up to speed. *Federal Probation, 58*(3), 51–57.

Corcoran, K., & Fischer, J. (1987). *Measures for clinical practice: A sourcebook.* New York: Free Press.

Corey, M. S., & Corey, G. (1997). *Groups: Process and practice* (5th ed.). Pacific Grove, CA: Brooks/Cole.

Costin, L., Karger, H. J., & Stoze, D. (1996). *The politics of child abuse in America.* New York: Oxford University.

Cowan, A. (2004). New strategies to promote the adoption of older children out of foster care. *Children and Youth Services Review, 26,* 1007–1020.

Cowger, C. D. (1994, May). Assessing client strengths: Clinical assessment for client empowerment. *Social Work, 39*(3), 262–267.

Cox, E., & Longres, J. (1981). *Critical practice-curriculum implications.* Paper presented at the Annual Meeting of the Council on Social Work Education, Louisville, KY.

Craig, C., Kulik, T., James, T., Nielsen, S., & Orr, S. (1998). *Blueprint for the privatization of child welfare.* Chicago: Reason Public Policy Institute.

Crewdson, J. (1988). *By silence betrayed: Sexual abuse of children in America.* Boston: Little, Brown.

Cross, T., Bazron, B., Dennis, C., & Isaacs, M. (1989). *Towards a culturally competent system of care: A monograph on effective services for minority children who are severely emotionally disturbed.* Washington, DC: CASSP Technical Assistance Center.

Crosson-Tower, C. (2002). *Understanding child abuse and neglect.* Boston: Allyn & Bacon.

Crosson-Tower, C. (2004). *Exploring child welfare: A practice perspective.* Boston: Allyn & Bacon.

Crow, G. M., & Grogan, M. (2005). The development of leadership thought and practice in the United States. In F. English (Gen. Ed.), *Sage handbook of educational leadership: Advances in theory, research, and practice* (pp. 334–361). Thousand Oaks, CA: Sage.

Culp, A., Culp, R., Blankmeyers, M., & Passmark, L. (1998). Parent education home visitation program: Adolescent and nonadolescent mothers comparison after six months of intervention. *Infant Mental Health Journal, 19*(3), 111–123.

Curry, J. (1991). Outcome research on residential treatment: Implications and suggested directions. *American Journal of Orthopsychiatry, 61,* 348–358.

Curtis, P., Alexander, G., & Lunghofer, L. (2001). A literature review comparing the outcomes of residential group care and therapeutic foster care. *Child and Adolescent Social Work Journal, 18*(5), 377–391.

Cyphers, G. (2001). *Report from the child welfare workforce survey: State and county data findings.* Washington, DC: American Public Human Services Association.

Dave Thomas Foundation for Adoption and Evan B. Donaldson Institute. (2002). Experiences of African-American adolescent fathers. *National Adoption Attitudes Survey.* Retrieved from http://www.davethomasfoundationforadoption.org

David C. v. Leavitt, No. 93-C-206W (Feb. 25, 1993).

Delgado, R. (1992). Generalist child welfare and Hispanic families. In N. A. Cohen (ed.), *Child welfare: A multicultural focus* (pp. 130–156). Boston: Allyn & Bacon.

Demay, D. (2003). The experience of being a client in an Alaska public health nursing home visitation program. *Public Health Nursing, 20*(3), 228–236.

DePanfilis, D., & Zuravin, S. J. (1998). *Child maltreatment recurrences among families serviced by child protective services, final report.* Washington, DC: National Center for Child Abuse and Neglect.

Devore, W., & Schlesinger, E. G. (1987). *Ethnic-sensitive social work practice.* Columbus, OH: Merrill.

Dhooper, S. S., Royse, D. D., & Wolfe, L. C. (1990). Does social work education make a difference? *Social Work, 35,* 57–61.

Dion, M. (1999). *Reaching all job seekers, employment programs for hard-to-employ populations.* Washington, DC: Mathematica Policy Research Inc.

Dore, M. M., Doris, J. M., & Wright, P. (1995). Identifying substance abuse in maltreating families: A child welfare challenge. *Child Abuse and Neglect, 19*(5), 531–543.

Downs, S., Costin, L. B., & McFadden, E. J. (1996). *Child welfare and family services: Policies and practice* (5th ed.). New York: Longman.

Downs, S. W., Moore, E., McFadden, E. J., Michaud, S. M., & Costin, L. B. (2004). *Child welfare and family services: Policies and practice* (7th ed.). Boston: Allyn & Bacon.

Drake, B. (1994, September). Relationship competencies in child welfare service. *Social Work, 39*(5), 595–602.

Dubowitz, H., Feigelman, S., & Zuravin, S. (1993). *A profile of kinship care.* Washington, DC: Child Welfare League of America.

Durlak, J., & Lipsey, M. (1991, June). A practitioner's guide to meta-analysis. *American Journal of Community Psychology, 19,* 291–332.

Edelstein, S., Kropenske, V., & Howard, J. (1990). Project training, education and management skills: Meeting the needs of infants prenatally exposed to drugs (T.E.A.M.S.). *Social Work, 35*(4), 313–318.

Egami, Y., Ford, D. E., Greenfield, S. F., & Crum, R. M. (1996).

Psychiatric profile and sociodemographic characteristics of adults who report physically abusing or neglecting children. *American Journal of Psychiatry, 153*(7), 921–928.

Egan, G. (1975). *The skilled helper.* Monterey, CA: Brooks/Cole.

El-Mohandes, A., Katz, K., El-Khorazaty, M., McNeely-Johnson, D., & Shops, P. (2003). *The effects of a parenting education program on the use of preventive pediatric health care services among low-income, minority mothers: A randomized controlled study.* American Academy of Pediatrics.

Emspak, F., Zullor, R., & Rose, S. (1996). *Privatizing foster care services in Milwaukee County: An analysis and comparison of public and private service delivery systems.* Milwaukee, WI: The Institute for Wisconsin's Future.

English, P. C. (1978). Failure to thrive without organic reason. *Pediatric Annals, 7*(11), 774–781.

Evans, S., Reinhart, J., & Succop, R. (1983). Failure to thrive: A study of 45 children and their families. *Journal of American Academy of Child Psychiatry, 11,* 440.

Everson, M., & Boat, B. (2000). Sexualized doll play among children: Implications for the use of anatomical dolls in sexual abuse evaluations. *Journal of the American Academy of Child and Adolescent Psychiatry, 29,* 736.

Fahlberg, V. (1991). *A child's journey through placement.* Indianapolis, IN: Perspectives Press.

Falicov, C. (1983). *Cultural perspectives in family therapy.* Rockville, MD: Aspen Press.

Faller, K. C. (1988). Criteria for judging the credibility of children's statements about their sexual abuse. *Child Welfare, 67*(5), 389–401.

Faller, K. C. (1991). What happens to sexually abused children identified by child protective services? *Children and Youth Services Review, 13,* 101–111.

Fanshal, D. (1982). *On the road to permanency: An expanded database for service to children in foster care.* New York: Child Welfare League of America, Columbia University School of Social Work.

Fanshal, D., & Shinn, E. (1978). *Children in foster care.* New York: Columbia University.

Farmer, S., & Galaris, D. (1993). Support groups for children of divorce. *The American Journal of Family Therapy, 21*(1), 40–50.

Feigelman, W., & Silverman, A. R. (1983). *Chosen children: New patterns of adoptive relationships.* New York: Praeger.

Filip, J., McDaniel, N. S., & Schene, P. (Eds.). (1992). *Helping in child protective services: A casework handbook.* Englewood, CA: The American Humane Association.

Finkelhor, D. (1979). *Sexually victimized children.* New York: Free Press.

Finkelhor, D. (1984). *Child sexual abuse: New theory and research.* New York: Free Press.

Finkelhor, D. (1993). Epidemiological factors in the clinical identification of child sexual abuse. *Child Abuse & Neglect, 26,* 509–524.

Finkelhor, D., Hotaling, G., Lewis, I. A., & Smith, C. (1990). Sexual abuse in a national survey of adult men and women: Prevalence, characteristics, and risk factors. *Child Abuse & Neglect, 14*(1), 19–28.

Fleishman, E. A. (1953, June). The measurement of leadership attitudes in industry. *Journal of Applied Psychology,* 153–158.

Fleishman, E. A., Harris, E. F., & Burtt, H. E. (1955). *Leadership and supervision in industry.* Columbus: Bureau of Educational Research, Ohio State University.

Fleming, J., Mullen, P., & Bammer, G. (1997). A study of potential risk factors for sexual abuse in childhood. *Child Abuse & Neglect, 21,* 49–58.

Florida Department of Juvenile Justice. (2006). *Department of Juvenile Justice main services.* Retrieved from http://www. djj.state.fl.us/

Follet, M. P. (1926). The giving of orders. In H. C. Metcalf (ed.), *Scientific foundations of business administration.* Baltimore, MD: Williams & Wilkins Co.

Fong, R., Boyd, T., & Browne, C. (1999). The Gandhi technique: A bicultural approach for empowering Asian and Pacific Islander families. *Journal of Multicultural Social Work, 7,* 95–110.

Fong, R., & Furuto, S. (2001). *Culturally competent practice.* Boston: Allyn & Bacon.

Fosberg, S. (1981). Family day care in the United States: Summary of findings. *Final Report of the National Day Care Home Study, Vol 1.* (DHHS Publication No. [OHDS]80-30282). Washington, DC: U.S. Department of Health & Human Services, Administration for Children, Youth and Families.

Fox, K., & Gilbert, B. (1994). The interpersonal and psychological function of women who experienced childhood physical abuse, incest and parental alcoholism. *Child Abuse and Neglect, 18,* 849–858.

Fraser, M. W., Richman, J. M., & Galinsky, M. J. (1999). Risk, protection, and resilience: Toward a conceptual framework for social work practice. *Social Work Research, 23*(2), 131–143.

Freundlich, M., & Avery, R. (2005). Planning for permanency for youth in congregate care. *Children and Youth Services Review, 27,* 115–134.

Friesen, B. J., & Poertner, J. (Eds.). (1995). *From case management to service coordination for children with emotional, behavioral, or mental disorders.* Baltimore, MD: Brookes.

Furman, R., & Jackson, R. (2002). Wrap-around services: An analysis of community-based mental health services for children. *Journal of Child and Adolescent Psychiatric Nursing, 15*(3), 124–131.

Furstenberg, F. F. (1994). History and current status of divorce in the United States. *Future of Children, 4*(1), 29–43.

Furstenberg, F. F., Brooks-Gunn, J., & Chase-Lansdale, L. (1989). Teenaged pregnancy and childbearing. *American Psychologist, 44,* 313–320.

Gamson, W. A. (1968). *Power and discontent.* Florence, KY: Dorsey.

Garbarino, J. (1980). Preventing child maltreatment. In R. H. Price, R. F. Ketterer, B. C. Bader, & J. Monahan (eds.), *Prevention in mental health: Research, policy, and practice* (pp. 63–80). Beverly Hills, CA: Sage.

Garbarino, J. (1992a). *Children and families in the social environment*. New York: Walter de Gruyter.

Garbarino, J. (1992b). *Toward a sustainable society: An economic, social and environmental agenda for our children's future*. Chicago: Noble Press.

Garbarino, J., Gutterman, E., & Seeley, J. W. (1986). *The psychologically battered child*. San Francisco: Jossey-Bass.

Gaudin, J. (1993). *Child neglect: A guide for intervention (The User Manual Series)*. Washington, DC: U.S. Department of Health and Human Services.

Gaudin, J. M. (1999). Child neglect: Short-term and long-term outcomes. In H. Dubowitz (ed.), *Neglected children: Research, practice and policy* (pp. 89–108). Thousand Oaks, CA: Sage.

Geertz, C. (1983). *Local knowledge*. New York: Basic Books.

Gelles, R. (1996). *The book of David: How preserving families can cost children's lives*. New York: Basic Books.

General Accounting Office. (2003). *GAO studies child welfare recruitment and retention*. Washington, DC: Author.

Germaine, C., & Gitterman, A. (1980). *The life model of social work practice*. New York: Columbia University.

Gershenson, C. P. (1990). *Preparing for the future backwards: Characteristics of the ecology for children and youth in long-term out-of-home care*. Unpublished manuscript, prepared for the Casey Family Program Symposium on Long-Term Care, Seattle, WA.

Ghiselli, E. E. (1959). Traits differentiating management personnel. *Personnel Psychology, 12*, 535–544.

Gil, D. G. (1971). Sociocultural perspective on physical child abuse. *Child Welfare, 50*(7), 389–395.

Gil, D. G. (1981). The United States versus child abuse. In L. Pelton (ed.), *The social context of child abuse and neglect* (pp. 281–324). New York: Human Services Press.

Gill, M. M., & Amadio, C. M. (1983). Social work and law in a foster care/adoption program. *Child Welfare, 62*(5), 455–467.

Ginsberg, L. (1995). Concepts of new management. In L. Ginsberg & P. R. Keys (eds.), *New management in human services* (2nd ed.). Silver Spring, MD: NASW.

Giovannoni, J.-M. (1991). Substantiated and unsubstantiated reports of child maltreatment. *Children and Youth Services Review, 11*(4), 299–318.

Glisson, C. (1989). The effect of leadership on workers in human service organizations. *Administration in Social Work, 13*(3/4), 99–116.

Glisson, C., & Hemmelgarn, A. (1998). The effect of organizational climate and interorganizational coordination on the quality and outcomes of children's service systems. *Child Abuse & Neglect, 22*(5), 401–421.

Glover, N. (1995). The incidence of incest histories among clients receiving substance abuse treatment. *Journal of Counseling and Development, 73*, 475–480.

Godman, R. (1998). *Child welfare*. Unpublished manuscript. Wilfrid Laurier University, Ontario, Canada.

Goldstein, A., McGowan, S., Antle, B. J., Brownstone, D., Donoghue, S., James, M., et al. (1996). Leading the way: Innovating support for children, youth, parents and guardians affected by HIV and AIDS. *The Social Worker, 64*, 67–73.

Graef, M., & Hill, E. (2000, September/October). Costing of child protective services staff turnover. *Child Welfare, 79*(5), 186–199.

Gray, E. (1986). *Child abuse: Prelude to delinquency*. Findings of research conference conducted by the National Committee for Prevention of Child Abuse. Washington, DC: U.S. Department of Justice.

Green, J. (1999). *Cultural awareness in the human services*. Boston: Allyn & Bacon.

Green, R. (2003). *Who will adopt the children left behind?* The Urban Institute. Caring for Children. Brief No. 2.

Greenwood, P. W. (1994). What works with juvenile offenders: A synthesis of the literature and experience. In R. P. Corbett & J. Petersilia (eds.), *Up to speed: A review of research for practitioners*. In *Federal Probation, 58*(4), 63–67.

Grigsby, K. (1994). Maintaining attachment relationships among children in foster care. *Families in Society, 75*(5), 269–276.

Gustavsson, N. S. (1992). Drug-exposed infants and their mothers: Facts, myths, and needs. *Social Work in Health Care, 16*(4), 87–100.

Guterman, N., & Jayaratne, S. (1994). Responsibility at-risk: Perceptions of stress, control and professional effectiveness in child welfare direct practitioners. *Journal of Social Service Research, 20*(1/2), 99–120.

Gutierrez, L., Parsons, R., & Cox, E. (1998). *Empowerment in social work practice*. Pacific Grove, CA: Brooks/Cole.

Gutiérrez, L. M. (1990). Working with women of color: An empowerment perspective. *Social Work, 35*, 149–153.

Haapala, D. A., & Kinney, J. M. (1988). Avoiding out-of-home placement of high-risk status offenders through the use of intensive home-based family preservation services. *Criminal Justice and Behavior, 15*(3), 334–348.

Hammond-Ratzlaff, A., & Fulton, A. (2001). Knowledge gained by mothers enrolled in a home visitation program. *Adolescence, 36*(143).

Harris, N. (1988). Child Protective Services risk assessment. In: *Guidelines for a model system of protective services for children and their families*. Washington, DC: American Public Welfare Association.

Harris, N., Kirk, R., & Besharov, D. (1992). *Child welfare staffing patterns*. Alexandria, VA: National Child Welfare Leadership Center.

Harris, N., & Middleton, S. (1992). *Retention of foster homes in Utah.* Salt Lake City: Social Research Institute, University of Utah.

Harris, N., & Middleton, S. (2000). *Turnover in the Division of Child and Family Services.* Salt Lake City: Social Research Institute, College of Social Work, University of Utah.

Hartman, A., & Laird, J. (1983). *Family-centered social work practice.* New York: Free Press.

Harvey, J. H., & Fine, M. (2004). *Children of divorce: Stories of loss and growth.* Mahwah, NJ: Lawrence Erlbaum.

Harvey, V. S. (1995). Interagency collaboration: Providing a system of care for students. *Special Services in the Schools, 10*(1), 165–181.

Hawkins, J. D., Jenkins, J. M., Catalano, R. F., & Lishner, D. M. (1988). Delinquency and drug abuse: Implications for social services. *Social Service Review, 62*(2), 258–284.

Hayes, C. D., Palmer, J. L., Zaslow, M., & National Research Council Panel on Child Care Policy. (1990). *Who cares for America's children? Child care policy for the 1990s.* Washington, DC: National Academy of Sciences.

Hazel, K. N. (1982). New hope for the teenage outcast: The family placement of disturbed and delinquent adolescents. *International Journal of Offender Therapy and Comparative Criminology, 26*(1), 62–71.

Helton, L. R., & Smith, M. K. (2004). *Mental health practice with children and youth: A strengths and well-being model.* New York: Hayworth.

Henggeler, S. W. (1989). *Delinquency in adolescence.* Newbury Park, CA: Sage.

Henggeler, S. W., Schoenwald, S. K., & Pickrel, S. G. (1995). Multisystemic therapy: Bridging the gap between university and community-based treatment. *Journal of Consulting and Clinical Psychology, 63*(5), 709–717.

Henry, S., McRay, R., Ayers-Lopez, S., & Grotevant, H. (2003). The impact of openness on adoption agency practices: A longitudinal

perspective. *Adoption Quarterly, 6*(3), 31–57.

Hepworth, D. H., & Larsen, J. (1993). *Direct social work practice: Theory and skills* (4th ed.). Pacific Grove, CA: Brooks/Cole.

Hepworth, D. H., Rooney, R. H., & Larsen, J. A. (1997). *Direct social work practice: Theory and skills* (5th ed.). Pacific Grove, CA: Brooks/Cole.

Hepworth, D. H., Rooney, R. H., & Larsen, J. A. (2002). *Direct social work practice: Theory and skills* (6th ed.). Pacific Grove, CA: Brooks/Cole.

Hersey, P., Blanchard, K., & Johnson, D. E. (2001). *Management of organizational behavior: Leading human resources.* Upper Saddle River, NJ: Prentice Hall.

Hertz, D. (1977). Psychological implications of adolescent pregnancy patterns of family interaction in adolescent mothers-to-be. *Psychosomatics, 18*(1), 13–16.

Hibbard, R. A., & Zollinger, T. W. (1990). Patterns of child sexual abuse knowledge among professionals. *Child Abuse and Neglect, 14*, 347–355.

Hill, B. K., Hayden, M., Lakin, K., Mendke, J., & Amado, A. (1990). State-by-state data on children with handicaps in foster care. *Child Welfare, 69*, 447–462.

Hill, R. (1972). *The strengths of black families.* New York: Emerson Hall.

Ho, M. K. (1987). *Family therapy with ethnic minorities.* Newbury Park, CA: Sage.

Holder, W. M., & Corey, M. (1986). *Child protective services in risk management: A decision-making handbook.* Charlotte, NC: Action for Child Protection.

Hooper-Briar, K. (1994). *Framework for action.* Oxford, OH: Institute for Educational Renewal.

Howell, J. P., & Costley, D. L. (2006). *Understanding behaviors for effective leadership.* Upper Saddle River, NJ: Prentice Hall.

Hozman, T. L., & Froiland, D. J. (1976). Families in divorce: A proposed model for counseling the children. *The Family Coordinator, 25*(3), 271–276.

Hudson, J., & Galaway, B. (Eds.). (1995). *Child welfare in Canada:*

Research and policy implications. Toronto: Thompson Educational.

Hudson, W. (1982). *The clinical measurement package: A field manual.* Homewood, IL: Dorsey.

Hudson, W. (1992). *Walmyr assessment scales.* Tempe, AZ: Walmyr.

Huebner, C. (2002). Evaluation of a clinic-based parent education program to reduce the risk of infant and toddler maltreatment. *Public Health Nursing, 19*(5), 377–389.

Huhn, R., & Zimpfer, D. (1989). Effects of a parent education program on parents and their preadolescent children. *Journal of Community Psychology*, 311–319.

Humphreys, I., & Rappaport, J. (1994). Researching self-help mutual aid groups and organizations: Many roads, one journey. *Applied and Preventive Psychology, 3*, 217–231.

Humphreys, K., Mairs, B. E., & Stoffelnayr, B. (1994). Are twelve-step programs appropriate for disenfranchised groups? Evidence from a study of post-treatment mutual help involvement. *Prevention in Human Services, 11*, 165–179.

Hutchinson, R. L., & Spangler-Hirsch, S. L. (1989). Children of divorce and single-parent lifestyles. In C. Everett (ed.), *Children of divorce: Developmental and clinical issues* (pp. 5–23). New York: Haworth.

Indylr, B., Belville, R., Luchapelle, S., Gordon, G., & Dewart, T. (1993). A community-based approach to HIV case management: Systematizing the unmanageable. *Journal of Social Work, 38*, 380–387.

Inkelas, M., & Halfron, N. (1997). Recidivism in child protection services. *Children and Youth Services Review, 19*, 139–161.

Institute of Applied Research. (2000). *Child protective services multiple response demonstration impact evaluation.* St. Louis, MO: Author.

Ivanoff, A. M., Blythe, B. J., & Tripodi, T. (1994). *Involuntary clients in social work practice: A research-based approach.* New York: Aldine de Gruyter.

Jan, S. J., & Smith, C. (1998). A test of reciprocal causal relationships among parental supervision, affective ties and delinquency. *Journal of Research in Crime and Delinquency, 34*, 307–336.

Jenkins, S., & Norman, F. (1972). *Filial deprivation and foster care.* New York: Columbia University.

Jenny, C., & Roesler, T. A. (1993). Quality assurance: A response to "the backlash" against child sexual abuse diagnosis and treatment. *Journal of Child Sexual Abuse, 2*(3), 89–97.

Jimmieson, N., & Griffin, M. (1998). Linking client and employee perceptions of the organization: A study of client satisfaction with health care services. *Journal of Occupational & Organizational Psychology, 71*(1), 13–27.

Johnson, J., & McIntye, C. (1998). Organizational culture and climate correlates of job satisfaction. *Psychological Reports, (82),* 843–850.

Johnson, K. (1991, Fall). Review essay—Black Africans and Native Americans: Color, race and caste in the evolution of red and black peoples (Review of Forbes, Jack D.). *The Journal of Ethnic Studies, 19*(3), 135–142.

Johnston, J. R., & Roseby, V. (1997). *In the name of the child: A developmental approach to understanding and helping children of conflicted and violent divorce.* New York: Free Press.

Jones, D. P. H. (1991). Ritualism and child sexual abuse. *Child Abuse and Neglect, 15,* 163–170.

Kadushin, A. (1984). *Child welfare services* (4th ed.). New York: Macmillan.

Kadushin, A. (1987). Child welfare services. In A. Minahan (ed.), *Encyclopedia of social work* (18th ed., pp. 265–275). Washington, DC: National Association of Social Workers.

Kadushin, A., & Martin, J. A. (1987). *Child welfare services* (4th ed.). New York: Macmillan.

Kaleidoscope Inc. (1999). *Changing patterns in childcare.* Author.

Kamerman, S. (1983, January/February). The new mixed economy of welfare: Public and private. *Social Work,* 5–10.

Kamerman, S., & Kahn, A. (1989). *Social services for children and families in the United States.* New York: Columbia University School of Social Work, Annie E. Casey Foundation.

Kamerman, S. B., & Kahn, A. J. (1990). Social services for children, youth, and families in the United States. *Children and Youth Services Review, 12*(1–2), i–184.

Kanji, G. K., & Moura E Sa, P. (2001). Measuring leadership excellence. *Total Quality Management, 12*(6), 701–718.

Kaplan-Sanoff, M. (1996). The impact of maternal substance abuse in young children. In E. J. Erwin (ed.), *Putting children first: Visions for a brighter future for young children and their families.* Baltimore, MD: Paul H. Brooks.

Karol, A. A., Greenwood, P. W., Everingham, S. S., Hoube, J., Kilburn, M. R., Rydell, C. P., et al. (1998). *Investing in our children: What we know and don't know about the cost and benefits of early childhood interventions.* Santa Monica, CA: Rand.

Kassebaum, G., & Chandler, D. B. (1992). In the shadow of best interest: Negotiating the facts, interests, and interventions in child abuse cases. *Sociological Practice, 10,* 49–66.

Katz-Leavy, J. W., Lourie, I. S., Stroul, B. A., & Ziegler-Dendy, C. (1992). *Individualized services in the system of care.* Washington, DC: CASSP Technical Assistance Center, Georgetown University Child Development Center.

Kazdin, A. (1987, September). Treatment of antisocial behavior in children: Current status and future directions. *Psychological Bulletin, 102,* 187–203.

Keefe, S. E., Padilla, A., & Carlos, M. L. (1978). The Mexican-American extended family as an emotional support system. In M. J. Casas & S. E. Keefe (eds.), *Family and mental health in the Mexican-American community* (pp. 49–68). Los Angeles: Spanish Speaking Mental Health Research Center, University of California at Los Angeles, Monograph No. 7.

Keller, T. E., Wetherbee, K., LeProhn, N. S., Payne, V., Sim, K., & Lamont, E. R. (2002). Competencies and problem behaviors in children in family foster care. Variations by kinship placement, status and race. *Children and Youth Services Review, 23*(12), 914–940.

Kelly, S., & Blythe, B. (2000). Family preservation: A potential not yet realized. *Child Welfare, 79,* 29–43.

Kempe, C. H., Silverman, F., Steele, B., Droegmueller, W., & Silver, H. (1962). The battered child syndrome. *Journal of the American Medical Association, 181,* 17–24.

Kendall, P. (1991). *Child and adolescent therapy: Cognitive-behavioral procedures.* New York: Guilford.

Kessler, R. C., Gillis-Light, J., Magee, W. J., Kendler, K. S., & Eaves, L. J. (1997). Childhood adversity and adult psychopathology. In I. H. Gotlib & B. Wheaton (eds.), *Stress and adversity over the life course: Trajectories and turning points* (pp. 29–49). Cambridge, UK: Cambridge University.

Kirk, R. (2001). *A critique of the evaluation of family preservation and reunification programs: Interim report.* National Family Preservation Network.

Kirk, R., Reed-Ashcroft, K., & Pecora, P. (2002). Implementing intensive family preservation services: A case of infidelity. *Family Preservation Journal 6*(2), 59–82.

Kirst-Ashman, K. K., & Hull, G. H., Jr. (1993). *Understanding generalist practice.* Chicago: Nelson-Hall.

Kitzman, H., Olds, D., Sidora, K., Henderson, C., Hanks, C., Cole, R., et al. (2000). Enduring effects of nurse home visitation on maternal life course: A 3-year follow-up of a randomized trial. *JAMA, 283*(3).

Knitzer, J. (1982). *Unclaimed children: The failure of public responsibility to children and adolescents in need of mental health services.* Washington, DC: Children's Defense Fund.

Knudsen, D. D., & Miller, J. L. (Eds.). (1991). *Abused and battered: Social and legal responses to family violence.* Hawthorne, NY: Walter de Gruyter.

Konker, C. (1992). Rethinking child sexual abuse: An anthropological perspective. *American Journal of Orthopsychiatry*, 62(1), 147–153.

Korbin, J. (1982). The cultural context of child abuse and neglect. *Child Abuse and Neglect*, 6, 3–11.

Kotter, J. P. (1996). *Leading change*. Boston: Harvard Business School.

Kramer, L., & Houston, D. (1998). Supporting families as they adopt children with special needs. *Family Relations*, 47, 423–432.

Kubler-Ross, E. (1969). *On death and dying*. New York: Macmillan.

Laird, J., & Hartman, A. (Eds.). (1985). *A handbook of child welfare: Context, knowledge, and practice*. New York: Free Press.

Larzelere, R., Dinges, K., Schmidt, M., Spellman, D., Criste, T., & Connell, P. (2001). Outcomes of residential treatment: A study of the adolescent clients of Girls and Boys Town. *Child and Youth Forum*, 30(3), 175–186.

Leathers, S. J. (2002). Foster children's behavioral disturbance and detachment from caregivers and community institutions. *Children and Youth Services Review*, 24(4), 239–268.

Leeman, L. W., Gibbs, J. C., & Fuller, D. (1993). Evaluation of a multicomponent group treatment program for juvenile delinquents. *Aggressive Behavior*, 19(4), 281–292.

Lehner, L. (1994). Education for parents divorcing in California. *Family & Conciliation Courts Review*, 32(1), 50–54.

Leigh, J. (1984). *Empowerment strategies for work with multiethnic populations*. Paper presented at the Council on Social Work Education, Annual Program Meeting, Detroit, MI.

Leslie, L. K. (2000). Children in foster care: Factors influencing outpatient mental health service use. *Child Abuse and Neglect*, 24(4), 465–476.

Leung, P., Cheung, K. F., & Stevenson, K. (1994). A strengths approach to ethnically sensitive practice for child protective services workers. *Child Welfare*, 73(6), 707–721.

LeVine, E. S., & Sallee, A. L. (1999). *Child welfare: Clinical theory and practice*. Dubuque, IA: Eddie Bowers.

Lewin, K. (1951). *Field theory in social science*. New York: Harper & Row.

Libby, A., Coen, A., Price, D., Silverman, K., & Orton, H. (2005). Inside the black box: What constitutes a day in a residential treatment centre. *International Journal of Social Welfare*, 14, 176–183.

Lightburn, A., & Pine, B. A. (1996). Supporting and enhancing the adoption of children with developmental disabilities. *Children and Youth Services Review*, 18(1/2), 139–162.

Likert, R. (1967). *Human organizations*. New York: McGraw-Hill/Irwin.

Lindholm, K. J. (1983). *Child abuse and ethnicity: Patterns of similarities and differences*. Los Angeles: Spanish Speaking Mental Health Research Center.

Lindholm, K. J. (1986). Child sexual abuse within the family: CIBA foundation report. *Journal of Interpersonal Violence*, 1(2), 240–242.

Lindsey, D. (1988). *National study of public child welfare salaries*. Portland, ME: National Resource Center for Child Welfare Management and Administration.

Lindsey, D. (1994). *The welfare of children*. New York: Oxford Press.

Lindsey, D. (2004). *The welfare of children* (2nd ed.). New York: Oxford Press.

Lipsey, M. (1984, November). Is delinquency prevention a cost-effective strategy? *Journal of Research in Crime and Delinquency*, 21, 279–302.

Litrownik, A., Newton, R., Mitchell, B., & Richardson, K. (2003). Long-term follow-up of young children placed in foster care: Subsequent placements and exposure to family violence. *Journal of Family Violence*, 18, 1–19.

Litzelfelner, P., & Petr, C. G. (1997). Case advocacy in child welfare. *Social Work*, 42(4), 392–402.

Lockhart, L. L., & Wodarski, J. S. (1989). Facing the unknown: Children and adolescents with AIDS. *Social Work*, 34(3), 215–221.

Loeber, R., & Farrington, D. P. (2001). Child delinquents: Development, intervention, and service needs. Thousand Oaks, CA: Sage.

Logan, S., Freeman, E., & McRoy, R. (1990). *Social work practice with black families*. New York: Longman.

Lukes, S. (1976). *Power: A radical view*. London: Macmillan.

Lum, D. (1992). *Social work practice with people of color: A process stage approach* (2nd ed.). Monterey, CA: Brooks/Cole.

Lum, D. (1996). *Social work practice with people of color* (3rd ed.). Monterey, CA: Brooks/Cole.

Lum, D. (1999). *Social work practice and people of color: A process-stage approach* (4th ed.). Belmont, CA: Wadsworth.

Lum, D. (2000). *Social work practice and people of color*. Pacific Grove, CA: Brooks/Cole.

Lum, D. (2003). *Culturally competent practice*. Pacific Grove, CA: Brooks/Cole.

Luongo, P. (2002). Partnering child welfare, juvenile justice and behavioral health with schools. *Professional School Counseling*, 3(5).

Macaskill, A., & Ashworth, P. (1995, October). Parental participation in child protection case conferences: The social workers view. *The British Journal of Social Work*, 25(5), 581–597.

Magazino, C. J. (1983). Services to children and families at risk of separation. In B. G. McGowan & W. Meezan (eds.), *Child welfare: Current dilemmas, future directions* (pp. 211–254). Itasca, IL: F. E. Peacock.

Mak, A. S. (1990). Testing a psychosocial control theory of delinquency. *Criminal Justice and Behavior*, 17(2), 215–230.

Maluccio, A. N. (1990). Family preservation services and the social work practice sequence. In J. K. Whittaker, J. Kinney, E. M. Tracy, & C. Booth (eds.), *Reaching high-risk families: Intensive family preservation in human services* (pp. 113–126). Hawthorne, NY: Aldine de Gruyter.

Maluccio, A. N., Fein, E., & Olmstead, K. A. (1986). *Permanency planning for children:*

Concepts and methods. New York: Routledge.

Marin, G., & Marin, B. V. (1991). *Research with Hispanic populations*. Newbury Park, CA: Sage.

Markoff, L., Finelstein, N., Kemmerer, N., Kreiner, P., & Prost, C. (2005). Relational systems change: Implementing a model of change in integrating services for women with substance abuse and mental health disorders and histories of trauma. *Journal of Behavioral Health Services and Research*, 32(2), 227–240.

Maslow, A. H. (1954). *Motivation and personality*. New York: Harper & Row.

Mather, J. (1999). *Training outcomes in Ontario, Draft Report*. Ontario, Canada: Ontario Association of Children's Aid Societies.

Mauer, M. (1990). *Young black men and the criminal justice system: A growing national problem*. Washington, DC: The Sentencing Project.

Maynard, R., & Rangarajan, A. (1994). Teen parents and the reauthorization of welfare. *TANF Reauthorization Resource*, 3(1). Washington, DC: Welfare Information Network.

McCallum, S. (1995). *Safe families: A model of child protection intervention*. Unpublished doctoral dissertation. Wilfrid Laurier University, Ontario, Canada.

McCarthy, M. (1999). Perinatal AIDS decreasing rapidly in USA. *Lancet*, 354, 573.

McClelland, D. C., & Boyatzis, R. E. (1982). Leadership motive pattern and long-term success in management. *Journal of Applied Psychology*, 67(6), 737–743.

McGoldrick, M. (1996). Ethnicity and family therapy: An overview. In M. McGoldrick, J. K. Pearce, & J. Giordano (Eds.), *Ethnicity and family therapy* (pp. 3–30). New York: Guilford.

McIsaac, H. (1994). Editor's notes. *Family and Conciliation Courts Review*, 32(4), 420–431.

McKay, J., Alberman, A., McClellan, A., & Snider, E. (1994). Treatment goals, continuity of care and outcomes in a day hospital substance abuse rehabilitation program. *American Journal of Psychiatry*, 151, 254–259.

McKenzie, J. K. (1993). Adoption of children with special needs. *The Future of Children*, 3(1), 62–76.

McMillen, J., Zima, B., Scott, D., Auslander, W., & Munson, M. (2005). Prevalence of psychiatric disorders among older youths in the foster care system. *Journal of the American Academy of Child and Adolescent Psychiatry*, 44(1), 88–95.

McPhatter, A. (1997). Cultural competence in child welfare: What is it? How do we achieve it? What happens without it? *Child Welfare*, 76, 1–12.

McPhee, B. (1997). *Child welfare: Out-of-the-box services*. Unpublished doctoral dissertation. University of Toronto.

Meezan, W. (1983). Child welfare— An overview of the issues. In B. G. McGowan & W. Meezan (eds.), *Child welfare: Current dilemmas, future directions*. Itasca, IL: F. E. Peacock.

Mello, J. A. (2003). Profiles in leadership: Enhancing learning through model and theory building. *Journal of Management Education*, 27(3), 344.

Merkel-Holquin, L. (2000). Practice diversions and philosophical departures in the implementation of family group conferencing. In G. Buford & J. Hudson (eds.), *Family group conferencing: Perspectives on policy, practice and research* (pp. 224–231). Hawthorne, NY: Aldine de Gruyter.

Meyers, M. (1995, November/December). Child day care in welfare reform: Are we targeting too narrowly? *Child Welfare*, 74, 1071–1090.

Middleman, R. R., & Goldberg, G. (1974). *Social service delivery: A structural approach to social work practice*. New York: Columbia University.

Miller, L. B., & Fisher, T. (1992). Some obstacles to the effective investigation and registration of children-at-risk issues gleaned from a worker's perspective. *Journal of Social Work Practice*, 6(2), 129–140.

Mills, C., & Usher, D. (1996, September–October). A kinship care case management approach. *Child Welfare*, 75(5), 600–618.

Mills, R., Dunham, R., & Alpert, G. (1988). Working with high-risk youth in prevention and early intervention programs: Toward a comprehensive wellness model. *Adolescence*, 23(88), 643–660.

Minty, B., & Pattinson, G. (1994, December). The nature of child neglect. *The British Journal of Social Work*, 24(6), 733–797.

Mishne, J. (1983). *Clinical work with children*. New York: Free Press.

Mitchell, L. B., & Savage, C. (1991). *The relationship between substance abuse* (working paper #854), p. 1. Chicago: The National Committee for the Preventing of Child Abuse.

Moroney, R. (1986). *Shared responsibility*. New York: Aldine de Gruyter.

Morris, J. (1997). Gone missing? Disabled children living away from their families. *Disability & Society*, 12(2), 241–258.

Moss, H., & Engles, R., Jr. (1959). *Children in need of parents*. New York: Columbia University.

Mulak, G., Cohen, S. T., & Teets-Grimm, K. (1992). Hospitals and school districts: Creating a partnership for child protection services. *Social Work in Health Care*, 17(1), 39–51.

Mundal, L. D., VanDer Weele, T., Berger, C., & Fitsimmons, J. (1991). Maternal infant separation at birth among substance using pregnant women: Implications for attachment. *Social Work in Health Care*, 16(1), 133–143.

Napoli, M., & Gonzales-Santin, E. (2001). Intensive home-based and wellness services to Native American families living on reservations: A model. *Families in Society: The Journal of Contemporary Human Services*, 82(3), 315–324.

National Adoption Information Clearinghouse (NAIC). (2004). *Adoption disruption and dissolution: Numbers and trends*. Washington, DC: U.S. Department of Health and Human Services.

National Association of Social Workers (NASW). (1982). *New Standards for classification of social work practice*. Silver Spring, MD: Author.

NASW. (1996). *Personal responsibility and work opportunity reconciliation act of 1996, Public law 104–193: Summary of provisions*. Washington, DC: Author.

National Clearinghouse on Child Abuse and Neglect. (2004). *Decision making for the permanent placement of children*. Washington, DC: U.S. Department of Health and Human Services.

National Commission on AIDS. (1991). *America living with AIDS: Report of the National Committee on Acquired Immune Deficiency Syndrome*. Washington, DC: Author.

National Committee for Adoption. (1986). *Encyclopedia of adoption*. Washington, DC: Author.

National Household Survey on Drug Abuse Reports. (2003). *Children living with substance dependent parents*. Washington, DC: The National Household Survey on Drug Abuse Reports, Substance Abuse Mental Health Services Administration.

Navaie-Waliser, M., Martin, S., Campell, M., Tessaro, I., Kotelchuck, M., & Cross, A. (2000a). Factors predicting completion of a home visitation program by high-risk pregnant women: The North Carolina maternal outreach workers program. *American Journal of Public Health, 90*(1).

Navaie-Waliser, M., Martin, S., Campell, M., Tessaro, I., Kotelchuck, M., & Cross, A. (2000b). Social support and psychological functioning among high-risk mothers: The impact of the Baby Love Maternal Outreach Worker Program. *Public Health Nursing, 17*(4), 280–291.

Nelson, B. (1995). *Making an issue of child abuse: Political agenda setting for social problems*. Chicago: University of Chicago.

Nelson, B. J., & Frantz, T. T. (1997). Family interactions of suicide survivors and survivors of non-suicidal death. *Omega, 33*(2), 131–146.

Nelson, B. S., & Harrison, M. (1997). Bridging the politics of identity in a multicultural classroom. *Theory into Practice, 35*(4), 256–263.

Nelson-Gardell, D., & Harris, D. (2003, January/February). Childhood abuse history, secondary traumatic stress and child welfare workers. *Child Welfare, 82*(1), 5–27.

Netting, E., Kettner, P., & McMurty, S. (1993). *Social work macro practice*. White Plains, NY: Longman.

Netting, F. E. (1986, Fall). The religiously affiliated agency: Implications for social work administration. *Social Work and Christianity, 13*, 50.

New York State Department of Social Services. (1992). *Comprehensive risk assessment—Adapted from the New York State risk assessment and service planning model*. Albany, NY: Division of Administration and Office of Human Resource Development.

Nguyen, J., Carson, M., Parris, K., & Place, P. (2003). A comparison pilot study of public health field nursing home visitation program interventions for pregnant Hispanic adolescents. *Public Health Nursing, 20*(5), 412–418.

Nugent, W. (1992). The affective impact of a clinical social worker's interviewing style: A single-case experiment. *Research on Social Work Practice, 2*(1), 6–27.

Nunno, M. (1997). Institutional abuse: The role of leadership, authority, and the environment in the social sciences literature. *Early Child Development and Care, 133*, 21–40.

Nurius, P. S., & Hudson, W. (1993). *Computer assisted practice: Theory, methods, and software*. Belmont, CA: Wadsworth.

O'Connor, L., Morgenstern, J., Givson, F., & Nakashian, M. (2005). Nothing about me without me: Leading the way to collaborative relationships with families. *Child Welfare, 84*(2), 153–171.

Office of Child Abuse and Neglect. (2003). *Child abuse and neglect research*. Washington, DC: U.S. Children's Bureau, Administration of Children and Families, Department of Health and Human Services.

Office of Juvenile Justice and Delinquency Prevention. (2002). *Permanency planning for abused and neglected children*. Washington, DC: U.S. Department of Justice.

Okamura, A., & Jones, L. (2000). Re-professionalizing child welfare services: An early evaluation of Title IV-E training program. *Research in Social Work Practice, 10*, 607–621.

Okayama, C., Furuto, S., & Edmondson, J. (2001). Components of cultural competence: Attitudes, knowledge, and skills. In R. Fong & S. Furuto (eds.), *Culturally competent practice*. Boston, MA: Allyn & Bacon.

Okazawa-Rey, M. (1998). Empowering poor communities of color: A self-help model. In L. Gutierrez, R. Parsons, & E. Cox (eds.), *Empowerment in social work practice* (pp. 52–64). Pacific Grove, CA: Brooks/Cole.

O'Keefe, M. (1995). Predictors of child abuse in maritally violent families. *Journal of Interpersonal Violence, 10*(1), 3–25.

Olds, D., Eckenrode, J., Henderson, C., Kitzman, H., Powers, J., Cole, R., et al. (1997). Long-term effects of home visitation on maternal life course and child abuse and neglect. *JAMA, 278*, 637–643.

Olds, D., Henderson, C., & Kitzman, H. (1994). Does prenatal and infancy nurse home visitation have enduring effects on qualities of parental caregiving and child health at 25 to 50 months of life? *Pediatrics, 93*(1).

Olds, D., Henderson, C., Kitzman, H., & Cole, R. (1995). Effects of prenatal and infancy nurse home visitation on surveillance of child maltreatment. *Pediatrics, 95*(3).

Omang, J., & Bonk, K. (1999). *Family to family: Building bridges for child welfare with families, neighborhoods and communities: Policy and practice*. Baltimore, MD: Annie E. Casey Foundation.

Ontario Children's Aid Society. (1998). *Inquest finding and recommendations*. Ontario, Canada.

Ooms, T., & Herendeen, L. (1990). *Teenage pregnancy programs: What have we learned?* Background briefing report and meeting highlights, Family Impact seminar, May 29, 1989. Washington, DC: American Association for Marriage and Family Therapy.

Ozawa, M. N., & Lum, Y. (1996). How safe is the safety net for poor children? *Social Work Research, 20*(4), 238–254.

Pallone, S. R., & Malkemes, L. C. (1984). *Helping parents who abuse their children: A comprehensive approach for intervention.* Springfield, IL: Charles C. Thomas.

Parkes, S. J. (2002). Organizational behavior. Lecture Series: University of Utah.

Parkin, W., & Green, L. (1997). Cultures of abuse within residential child care. *Early Child Development and Care, 133,* 73–86.

Patti, R. J. (1987). Managing for service effectiveness in social welfare: Toward a performance model. *Administration in Social Work, 11*(3), 7–22.

Pearson, M. A. (1994). Therapy with felony-convicted male juvenile offenders. *Issues in Mental Health Nursing, 15,* 49–57.

Peck, J. S. (1989). The impact of divorce on children at various stages of the family lifecycle. In *Children of divorce: Developmental and clinical issues* (pp. 81–106). New York: Haworth.

Pecora, P., & Austin, D. (1983, November/December). Declassification of social services jobs: Issues and strategies. *Social Work, 28*(6), 421–426.

Pecora, P., Briar, K., & Zlotnik, J. (1989). *Addressing the program and personnel crisis in child welfare: Technical assistance report, Commission on Family and Primary Associations.* Silver Springs, MD: National Association of Social Workers.

Pecora, P., Fraser, M., & Haapala, D. (1990). Intensive home-based family treatment: Client outcomes and issues for program design. In K. Wells & D. Biegel (eds.), *Family preservation services: Research and evaluation* (pp. 3–32). Newbury Park, CA: Sage.

Pecora, P., Whittaker, J., Maluccio, A., Barth, R., & Plotnick, R. (1992). *The child welfare challenge: Policy, practice and research*

(2nd ed.). New York: Walter de Gruyter.

Pecora, P., Williams, J., Kessler, R., Downs, C., O'Brien K., Hiripi, E., & Morrello, S. (2003). *The foster care alumni studies assessing the effects of foster care: Early results from the Casey National Alumni Study.* Casey Family Programs.

Pecora, P., Williams, J., Kessler, R., Downs, C., O'Brien, K., Hiripi, E., & Morrello, S. (2005). *The foster care alumni studies: Improving family foster care. Findings from the Northwest Foster Care Alumni Study.* Casey Family Programs.

Pecora, P. J., Fraser, M., Haapala, D., & Bartholomew, G. (1987). *Defining family preservation services: Three intensive home-based treatment programs* (Research Rep. No. 1). Salt Lake City: University of Utah, Social Research Institute.

Pelton, L. H. (1989). *For reasons of poverty: A critical analysis of the public child welfare system in the United States.* New York: Praeger.

Pelton, L. H. (1991). Child welfare system. *Social Work, 36*(4), 337–343.

Pennell, J., & Buford, G. (2000). Family group decision making: Protecting children and women. *Child Welfare, 79*(2), 131–159.

Perez, Y., & Pasternack, R. (1991). To what extent can the school reduce the gaps between children raised by divorced and intact families? *Journal of Divorce and Remarriage, 15*(3/4), 143–157.

Petersen, V., & Steinman, S. B. (1994). Helping children succeed after divorce. *Family and Conciliation Courts Review, 32*(1), 27–39.

Petersilia, J. (1995, Summer). A crime control rationale for reinvesting in community corrections. *Spectrum, 68,* 16–27.

Petr, C. G., & Barney, D. D. (1993). Reasonable efforts for children with disabilities: The parents' perspective. *Social Work, 38*(3), 247–254.

Petras, D., Derezotes, D., & Wills, S. (1999). *Dialogues on child welfare issues report: Parent-child bonding and attachment:*

Research implications for child welfare practice. Chicago: University of Illinois at Chicago, Jane Addams College of Social Work.

Phillips, E., Phillips, E. A., Fixen, D., & Wolf, M. (1973). Achievement place: Behavior-shaping works for delinquents. *Psychology Today, 7,* 75–79.

Phillips, M. H., DeChillo, N., Kronenfeld, D., & Middleton-Jeter, V. (1988). Homeless families: Services make a difference. *Social Casework, 69,* 48–53.

Pinderhughes, E. (1983). Empowerment for our clients and for ourselves. *Social Casework, 64,* 331–338.

Plasse, B. (1995). Parenting group for recovering addicts in a day treatment center. *Social Work 4*(1), 65–73.

Polansky, N. A., Chalmers, M. A., Buttenwieser, E., & Williams, D. P. (1981). *Damaged parents: An anatomy of child neglect.* Chicago: University of Chicago.

Popple, P. R., & Leighninger, L. (1996). *Social work, social welfare and American society* (3rd ed.). Boston: Allyn & Bacon.

Powell, M. B. (1991). Investigating and reporting child sexual abuse: Review and recommendations for clinical practice. *Australian Psychologist, 26*(2), 77–83.

Powers, J. L., Mooney, A., & Nunno, M. (1990). Institutional abuse: A review of the literature. *Journal of Child and Youth Care, 4*(6), 81–95.

Prevent Child Abuse America. (2001). *Total estimated cost of child abuse and neglect in the United States: Statistical evidence.* Chicago: Author.

Pruitt, J. A., & Kappius, R. E. (1992). Routine inquiry into sexual victimization: A survey of therapists' practices. *Professional Psychology: Research and Practice, 23*(6), 474–479.

Quinn, K. P., Epstein, M. H., & Cumblad, C. L. (1995). Developing comprehensive, individualized community-based services for children and youth with emotional and behavior disorders: Direct service providers' perspectives. *Journal of Child and Family Studies, 4*(1), 19–42.

Quinn, R. E., & Rohrbaugh, J. (1983). A spatial model of effectiveness criteria: Towards competing values approach to organizational analysis. *Management Science, 29,* 363–377.

Rafael, T., & Pion-Berlin, L. (1999). *Parents Anonymous: Strengthening families.* Washington, DC: Department of Justice.

Ramey, C., & Ramey, S. (2000). Persistent effects of early childhood education on high-risk children and their mothers. *Applied Developmental Science, 4*(1), 2–14.

Rank, M., & Hutchison, W. S. (2000). An analysis of leadership within the social work profession. *Journal of Social Work Education, 36*(3), 487–502.

Rapping, E. (1997). There's self-help and then there's self-help: Women and the recovery movement. *Social Policy, 27,* 240–262.

Red Horse, J. G., Martinez, C., & Day, P. (2001). *Family preservation: A case study of Indian tribal policy.* Seattle, WA: Casey Family Programs.

Re-Entry Policy Council. (1995). *Report on the re-entry policy: Charting the safe and successful return of program to communities.* New York: Re-Entry Policy Council.

Regehr, C., Chau, S., Leslie, B., & Howe, P. (2002). An exploration of supervisor's and manager's responses to child welfare reform. *Administration in Social Work, 26*(3), 17–36.

Reid, W. J., & Epstein, L. (1977). *Task-centered practice.* New York: Columbia University.

Reilly, T. (2003). *Transition from care: Status and outcomes of youth who age out of foster care.* Washington, DC: Child Welfare League of America.

Reilly, T., & Platz, L. (2004). Post-adoption service needs of families with special needs children: Use, helpfulness, and unmet needs. *Journal of Social Services Research, 30*(4), 51–67.

Reissman, F., & Carroll, D. (1995). *Redefining self-help: Policy and practice.* San Francisco: Jossey-Bass.

Report by Select Committee on Children, Youth, and Families.

(1990). *Discarded children: No place to call home.* Washington, DC: U.S. Government Printing Office.

Roberts, A. R. (2004). *Juvenile justice sourcebook: Past, present, and future.* New York: Oxford University.

Robinson, S. (1994). *Implementation of the cognitive model of offender rehabilitation and delinquency prevention.* Unpublished doctoral dissertation, University of Utah, Salt Lake City.

Rogers, C. R. (1942). *Counseling and psychotherapy.* New York: Houghton Mifflin.

Rose, S., & Meezan, W. (1993, June). Defining child neglect: Evolution, influences and issues. *The Social Service Review, 67*(2), 279–293.

Rosenthal, J. A. (1993). Outcomes of adoption of children with special needs. *The Future of Children, 3*(1), 77–88.

Ross-Sheriff, F., & Husain, A. (2001). Values and ethics in social work practice with Asian Americans: A South Asian Muslim case example. In R. Fong & S. Furuto (eds.), *Culturally competent practice.* Boston: Allyn & Bacon.

Russell, D. (1986). *Secret trauma: Incest in the lives of girls and women.* New York: Basic Books.

Russell, D. E. (1984). *Sexual exploitation: Rape, child sexual abuse, and workplace harassment.* Beverly Hills, CA: Sage.

Russell, M. (1987a). *National study of public child welfare job requirements.* Portland: University of Southern Maine National Center for Management and Administration.

Russell, M. (1987b). *Public child welfare job requirements.* Portland, ME: National Child Welfare Resource Center for Management and Administration.

Rutter, M. (2000). Children in substitute care: Some conceptual considerations and research implications. *Children and Youth Services Review, 22*(9), 685–703.

Ryan, K. (1996). The chronically traumatized child. *Child and Adolescent Social Work Journal, 13,* 287–310.

Rycus, J., & Hughes, R. (1998a). *Child welfare field guides, Vol. 2.*

Columbus, OH: Institute for Human Services.

Rycus, J. S., & Hughes, R. (1998b). *Field guide to child welfare,* Vols. I–IV. Washington, DC: Institute for Human Services, Child Welfare League of America.

Rycus, J. S., Hughes, R. C., & Garrison, J. K. (1989). *Child protective services: A training curriculum.* Washington, DC: Child Welfare League of America.

Rzepnicki, T. L., Sherman, J. R., & Littell, J. H. (1991). Issues in evaluating intensive family preservation services. In E. M. Tracy, D. A. Haapala, J. M. Kinney, & P. Pecora (eds.), *Intensive family preservation services: An instructional sourcebook.* Columbus, OH: Case Western Reserve University.

Saleebey, D. (1992). *The strengths perspective in social work practice.* New York: Addison-Wesley.

Sallee, A. L., & Lloyd, J. C. (Eds.). (1991). *Family-based services.* Riverdale, IL: National Association for Family-Based Services.

Salter, A. C. (1992). Response to the "abuse of the child sexual abuse accommodation syndrome." *Journal of Child Sexual Abuse, 1*(4), 173–176.

Samantrai, K. (1992a). Factors in the decision to leave: Retaining social workers with MSWs in public child welfare. *Social Work, 37,* 454–458.

Samantrai, K. (1992b). To prevent unnecessary separation of children and families: Public law 96–272, policy and practice. *Social Work, 37*(4), 295–302.

Samantrai, K. (2004). *Culturally competent public child welfare practice.* Pacific Grove, CA: Brooks/Cole.

Sandler, I. N., West, S. G., Baca, L., Pillow, D. R., Gersten, J. C., Rogosch, F., et al. (1992). Linking empirically based theory and evaluation: The family bereavement program. *American Journal of Community Psychology, 20*(4), 491–520.

Schacter, R. (1978). Kinetic psychotherapy. *Family Coordinator, 27*(3), 283–288.

Schein, E. (1992). *Organizational culture and leadership.* San Francisco: Jossey-Bass.

Schein, E. H. (1965). *Organizational psychology*. Upper Saddle River, NJ: Prentice Hall.

Schene, P. (1998). *Implementing concurrent planning: A handbook for child welfare administrators*. Portland, ME: National Child Welfare Resource Center for Organizational Improvement.

Schene, P. (2001). *Implementing concurrent planning: A handbook for child welfare administrators*. Portland: National Resource Center for Organizational Improvement, University of Southern Maine.

Schepard, A. (2004). *Children, courts, and custody: Interdisciplinary models for divorcing families*. New York: Cambridge University.

Scherer, D. G., & Brondino, M. J. (1994). Multisystemic family preservation therapy: Preliminary findings from a study of rural and minority serious adolescent offenders. *Journal of Emotional and Behavioral Disorders, 2*(4), 198–206.

Schmidt, M., & Allschield, S. (1995). Employee attitudes and customer satisfaction: Making theoretical and empirical connection. *Personnel Psychology, 48*, 521–536.

Schneider, B. (1990). *Organizational climate and culture*. San Francisco: Jossey-Bass.

Schriesheim, C. A., & Bird, B. J. (1979). Contributions of the Ohio State studies to the field of leadership. *Journal of Management, 5*(2), 135–145.

Select Committee on Children, Youth, and Families. (1990). *Discarded children: No place to call home*. Washington, DC: U.S. Government Printing Office.

Sells, J. (2001). *Child welfare privatization reform efforts in the states*. Washington, DC: American Health Care Association.

Shartle, C. L. (1956). *Executive performance and leadership*. Englewood Cliffs, NJ: Prentice Hall.

Sheafor, B. W., Horejsi, C. R., & Horejsi, G. A. (1995). *Techniques and guidelines for social work practice*. Boston: Allyn & Bacon.

Sheafor, B. W., Horejsi, C. R., & Horejsi, G. A. (1998). *Techniques and guidelines for social work practice*. Boston: Allyn & Bacon.

Shepard, M. (1992). Child-visiting and domestic abuse. *Child Welfare, 71*(4), 357–367.

Shulman, L. (1984). *The skills of helping individuals and groups* (2nd ed.). Itasca, IL: Peacock.

Shulman, L. (1992). *The skills of helping: Individuals, families, and groups*. Chicago: Peacock.

Sicklund, M. (1992, February). Offenders in juvenile court. *1988 OJJDP Update on Statistics*, pp. 1–11.

Sieppert, J., Hudson, J., & Unrau, Y. (2000). Family group conferencing in child welfare: Lessons from a demonstration project. *Families in Society: The Journal of Contemporary Human Services, 81*(4), 382–391.

Silver, P., Poulin, J., & Manning, R. (1997). Surviving the bureaucracy: The predictors of job satisfaction for the public agency supervisor. *The Clinical Supervisor, 15*(1), 1–20.

Simon, B. (1990). Rethinking empowerment. *Journal of Progressive Human Services, 1*(1), 27–40.

Simon, B. L. (1994). *The empowerment tradition in American social work: A history*. New York: Columbia University.

Simon, R. J., & Alstein, H. (1987). *Transracial adoptees and their families: A study of identity and commitment*. New York: Praeger.

Smith, C., & Stem, S. (1997). Delinquency and antisocial behavior: A review of family processes and intervention research. *Social Services Review, 71*, 382–420.

Snell, L. (2000). *Child welfare reform and the role of privatization*. Chicago: Reason Public Policy Institute.

Snyder, H. N. (2000). *Counting America's youth: Easy access to population data*. Washington, DC: U.S. Department of Justice, Office of Justice Programs, Office of Juvenile Justice and Delinquency Prevention.

Staff, I., & Fein, E. (1992). Together or separate: A study of siblings in foster care. *Child Welfare, 71*(3), 257–270.

Stehno, S. (1986, May/June). Family-centered child welfare services: New life for a historic idea. *Child Welfare, 65*(1), 231–240.

Stevenson, K. M., Cheung, K. M., & Leung, P. (1992). A new approach to training child protective services workers for ethnically sensitive practice. *Child Welfare, 71*(4), 1–305.

Stoesz, D. (1997). *The end of social work*. In M. Reisch & E. Gambrill (eds.), *Social work in the 21st century*. London: Pine Forge.

Stogdill, R. M. (1948). Personal factors associated with leadership: A survey of the literature. *Journal of Psychology, 25*, 35–71.

Stogdill, R. M. (1959). *Individual behavior and group achievement*. New York: Oxford University.

Stogdill, R. M. (1967). Basic concepts for a theory of organization. *Management Science, 13*, 666–676.

Stogdill, R. M. (1974). *Handbook of leadership: A survey of the literature*. New York: Free Press.

Stogdill, R. M., & Shartle, C. L. (1948). Methods for determining patterns of leadership behavior in relation to organization structure and objectives. *Journal of Applied Psychology, 32*, 286–291.

Strauss, S. S., & Clarke, B. A. (1992). Decision-making patterns in adolescent mothers. *Image: Journal of Nursing Scholarship, 24*(1), 69–74.

Struck, C. (1995, Autumn). Prediction and prevention of child and adolescent antisocial behavior: Special sectia. *Journal of Consulting and Clinical Psychology, 63*, 515–584.

Struck, S. D. (1994). Early intervention programs: An encouraging past and promising future. *Contemporary Education, 65*(3), 137–141.

Sue, D. W., & Sue, D. (1995). Asian American. In N. Vacc, S. B. DeVaney, & J. Wittmer (eds.), *Experiencing and counseling multicultural and diverse populations* (pp. 63–89). Bristol, PA: Accelerated Development.

Sugland, B., Manlove, J., & Romano, A. (1997). *Perceptions of opportunity and adolescent fertility operationalizing across race/ethnicity and social class*. Washington, DC: Child Trends.

Sullivan, R., & Wilson, M. F. (1995). New directions for research in prevention and treatment of delinquency: A review and proposal. *Adolescence, 30*(117), 1–17.

Sundel, S. S., & Sundel, M. (1993). *Behavior modification in the human services: A systematic introduction to concepts and applications* (3rd ed.). Newbury Park, CA: Sage.

Tatara, T. (1992). *Characteristics of children in substitute and adoptive care: A statistical summary of VCIS national child welfare data*. Washington, DC: American Public Welfare Association.

Taylor, M. J., Derr, M., & Abu-Bader, S. (1998). *Understanding families with multiple barriers to self-sufficiency*. Salt Lake City, UT: Social Research Institute.

Teare, R. J., & Sheafor, B. W. (1995). *Practice-sensitive social work education: An empirical analysis of social work practice and practitioners*. Alexandria, VA: Council on Social Work Education.

Teram, E. (1988). From self-managed hearts to collective action: Dealing with incompatible demands in the child welfare system. *Children and Youth Services Review, 10*, 305–315.

Terpstra, J. (1992). Foreward. In K. H. Briar, V. H. Hanse, & N. Harris (eds.), *New partnerships: Proceeding from the National Public Child Welfare Training Symposium, 1991*. Miami, Florida.

Teyber, E. (1992). *Helping children cope with divorce*. New York: Lexington Books.

The Source. (1998). *Sexual abuse and chemical dependency*. Berkeley: National Abandoned Infants Assistance Resource Center, University of California.

The National Center on Addiction and Substance Abuse at Columbia University. (2001). CASAWORKS for families: A promising approach to welfare reform and substance abusing women. New York: Author.

Tichy, N. M., & Cohen, E. (1997). *The leadership engine*. New York: Harper Collins.

Trad, P. V. (1993). Adolescent pregnancy: An intervention challenge. *Child Psychiatry and Human Development, 24*(2), 99–113.

Trad, P. V. (1994). Teenage pregnancy: Seeking patterns that promote family harmony. *The American Journal of Family Therapy, 22*(1), 42–56.

Trasler, G. (1960). *In place of parents*. London: Routledge & Kegan Paul.

Trattner, W. (1994). *From poor law to welfare state: A history of social welfare in America*. New York: Free Press.

U.S. Bureau of the Census. (1998). *Money income and poverty status in the U.S., 1997*. Washington, DC: Department of Commerce.

U.S. Department of Health and Human Services (U.S. DHHS), Administration for Children and Families, Office of Public Affairs. (1997). *Change in welfare caseloads since enactment of the new welfare law*. Washington, DC: Author.

U.S. DHHS. (2003). *National study of child protective services systems and reform efforts: Review of state CPS policy; Findings on local CPS practices: Literature review*. Washington, DC: Office of the Assistant Secretary for Planning and Evaluation, Department of Health and Human Services.

U.S. DHHS. (2004a). *Child health USA*. Washington, DC: U.S. Department of Health and Human Services, Health Resource and Services Administration, Maternal and Child Health Bureau.

U.S. DHHS. (2004b). *Child maltreatment: 2002*. Washington, DC: Administration for Children, Youth and Families. Department of Health and Human Services.

U.S. DHHS. (2004c). *Emerging practices in the prevention of child abuse and neglect*. Washington, DC: Office on Child Abuse and Neglect. Department of Health and Human Services.

U.S. DHHS. (2005). *General findings from the federal child and family services review*. Retrieved from http://www.dhhs.gov

U.S. Department of Justice. (1992). *U.S. Department of Justice Statistics*. Washington, DC: Office of Juvenile Justice and Delinquency Prevention.

U.S. Department of Justice. (2001). *Fact sheet: Drug offenses, juvenile court, 1989–1998*. Washington, DC: Author.

Vann, B. H., & Rofuth, T. W. (1993). Child care needs of welfare recipients in Maryland's welfare reform program. *Journal of Sociology and Social Welfare, 20*(2), 69–88.

Veronico, A. (1983). One church, one child: Placing children with special needs. *Children Today, 12*, 6–10.

Vinokur-Kaplan, D. (1991). Job satisfaction among social workers in public and voluntary child welfare agencies. *Child Welfare, 70*, 81–91.

Voluntary Cooperative Information System (VCIS). (1988). *Characteristics of children in substitute and adoptive care*. Washington, DC: American Public Welfare Association.

Vosler, N. R. (1996). *New approaches to family practice: Confronting economic stress*. Thousand Oaks, CA: Sage.

Vourlekis, B. S., & Greene, R. R. (1992). *Social work case management*. New York: Aldine de Gruyter.

Wagar, T. (1997). Is labor-management climate important? Some Canadian evidence. *Journal of Labor Research, 18*(1), 101–112.

Wager, K., Wickham, F., Bradford, W., Jones, W., & Kilpatrick, A. (2004). Qualitative evaluation of South Carolina's postpartum/infant home visitation program. *Public Health Nursing, 21*(6), 541–546.

Wagner, R., van Reyk, P., & Spence, N. (2001). Improving the working environment for workers in children's welfare agencies. *Child and Family Social Work, 6*(2), 161–179.

Waldfogel, J. (1998, January/February). Reforming child protective services. *Child Welfare, 79*(1), 43–58.

Walter, U. M., & Petr, C. G. (2004). A template for family-centered interagency collaboration. *Families in Society, 81*(5), 494–503.

Weaver, H., & White, B. (1997). The Native American family circle: Roots of resiliency. *Journal of Family Social Work, 2*(1), 67–79.

Webb, N. B. (1993). *Helping bereaved children: A handbook for practitioners*. New York: Guilford.

Weber, M. (1947). *The theory of social and economic organization* (A. N. Henderson & T. Parsons, Eds. & Trans.). Glencoe, IL: Free Press.

Weber, M. (1998). How we can better protect children from abuse and neglect. *Protecting Children from Abuse and Neglect: The Future of Children, 8*(1), 129–132.

Weil & Finegold. (2002). *Welfare reform: The new act*. Washington, DC: The Urban Institute.

Weinbach, R. W. (1998). *The social worker as manager: A practical guide to success* (3rd ed.). Boston: Allyn & Bacon.

Weitzman, L. (1987). *The divorce revolution*. New York: Free Press.

Wells, K., & Tracy, E. (1996). Reorienting intensive family preservation services in relation to public child welfare practice. *Child Welfare, 75*(6), 667–692.

Wells, S. J., Stein, T. J., Fluke, J., & Downing, J. (1989). Screening in child protective services. *Social Work, 34*(1), 45–48.

Weston, D., Klee, L., & Halfon, N. (1989). Mental health. In M. W. Kirst (ed.), *Conditions of children in California* (pp. 205–224, 359–363). Berkeley: University of California.

White, B., & Madara, E. (1995). *The self-help sourcebook* (5th ed.). Denville, NJ: American Self-Help Clearinghouse.

Whittaker, J., & Maluccio, A. (1989). Changing paradigms in residential services for disturbed/disturbing children: Retrospect and prospect. In R. P. Hawkins & J. Breiling (eds.), *Therapeutic foster care: Critical issues* (pp. 81–102). Washington, DC: Child Welfare League of America.

Whittaker, J. K. (1988). *Family support and group child care*. Washington, DC: Child Welfare League of America.

Widom, C. (1991). Childhood victimization: Risk factors for delinquency. In M. E. Colten & S. Gore (eds.), *Adolescent stress: Causes and consequences* (pp. 201–219). New York: Aldine de Gruyter.

Willis, W. (1998). Families with African-American roots. In E. W. Lynch & M. J. Hanson (eds.), *Developing cross-cultural competence: A guide for working with children and their families* (pp. 165–207). Baltimore, MD: Charles H. Brooks.

Windle, M., Windle, R., & Scheidt, D. (1995, September). Physical and sexual abuse and associated mental disorders among alcoholic inpatients. *The American Journal of Psychiatry, 152*, 1322–1328.

Winefield, H. R., & Barlow, J. A. (1995). Client and worker satisfaction in a child protection agency. *Child Abuse and Neglect, 19*(8), 897–905.

Wing, L. (1993). The definition and prevalence of autism: A review. *European Child Adolescent Psychiatry, 2*, 61–74.

Winters, K., Slenchfield, R., & Fulkerson, J. (1993, Winter). Patterns and characteristics of adolescent gambling. *Journal of Gambling Studies, 9*(4), 371–386.

Wolchik, S. A., Ruehlman, L. S., Braver, S. L., & Sandler, I. N. (1989). Social support of children of divorce: Direct and stress buffering effects. *American Journal of Community Psychology, 17*(4), 485–499.

Wolfe, D. A. (1991). Child care use among welfare mothers—A dynamic analysis. *Journal of Family Issues, 12*(4), 519–536.

Wolfe, D. A. (1999). *Child abuse: Implications for child development and psychopathology*. Thousand Oaks, CA: Sage.

Wolock, I., Sherman, P., Feldman, L., & Metzer, B. (2001). Child abuse and neglect referral patterns. *Child and Youth Services Review, 23*(1), 21–47.

Wood, L., Herring, A. E., & Hunt, R. (1989). *On their own: The needs of youth in transition*. Elizabeth, NJ: Association for the Advance-

ment of the Mentally Handicapped.

Wren, J. T. (1995). *The leader's companion*. New York: Free Press.

Yankey, J. (1987). Public social services. In *Encyclopedia of Social Edition* (18th ed., pp. 417–425). Silver Springs, MD: National Association of Social Workers.

Yoshikami, R. (1983). *Placement of foster children in group care facilities: An analysis of a decision-making system*. Unpublished dissertation, University of California, Berkeley.

Young, N. (2003). *Permanency options for children affected by substance abuse*. Washington, DC: National Center on Substance Abuse and Child Welfare, Children's Bureau.

Yuriko, E., Ford, D., Greenfield, S., & Crum, R. (1996). Psychiatric profile and socioedemographic characteristics of adults who report physical abusing or neglecting children. *American Journal of Psychiatry, 153*, 921–928.

Yukl, G. (1989). Managerial leadership: A review of theory and research. *Journal of Management, 15*(2), 251–289.

Yukl, G. (2002). *Leadership in organizations* (4th ed.). Upper Saddle River, NJ: Prentice Hall.

Yukl, G. (2006). *Leadership in organizations* (5th ed.). Upper Saddle River, NJ: Prentice Hall.

Yuriko, E., Ford, D., Greenfield, S., & Crum, R. (1996). Psychiatric profile and sociodemographic characteristics of adults who report physically abusing or neglecting children. *American Journal of Psychiatry, 153*, 921–928.

Zarb, J. M. (1992). *Cognitive-behavioral assessment and therapy with adolescents*. New York: Brunner/Mazel.

Zetlin, A., Weinberg, L., & Kimm, C. (2003). Are the educational needs of children in foster care being addressed? *National Association of Social Workers, 25*(1532), 105–119.

Zigler, E., & Styfco, S. J. (1994). Head Start: Criticisms in a constructive context. *American Psychologist, 49*(2), 127–132.

Zigler, E., Taussig, C., & Black, K. (1992). Early childhood intervention: A promising preventative for juvenile delinquency. *American Psychologist, 47,* 997–1004.

Zill, N., & Coiro, M. J. (1992). Assessing the condition of children.

Children and Youth Services Review, 14(5), 119–136.

Zlotnick, C., Ryan, C. E., Miller, I. W., & Keitner, G. I. (1995). Childhood abuse and recovery from major depression. *Child Abuse and Neglect, 19*(12), 1513–1516.

Zuckerman, E. (1983). *Child welfare.* New York: Collier Macmillan.

Zuravin, S. J., & DePanfilis, D. (1997). Factors affecting foster care placement of children receiving child protective services. *Social Work Research, 21*(1), 34–42.

Index

CPSIA information can be obtained
at www.ICGtesting.com
Printed in the USA
FFOW03n0850161214